The 70-293 Cram Sheet

This Cram Sheet contains the distilled, key facts about the Planning and Maintaining a Microsoft Windows Server 2003 Network Infrastructure exam. Review this information as the last thing you do before you enter the testing center, paying special attention to those areas where you think you need the most review.

After you have set a completion date for your studies and completed all your review, look over the information here to verify that you know most of it, until you're confident you'll be able to successfully recall the information during the actual exam. Good luck!

NETWORK INFRASTRUCTURE DESIGN

1. Explain the main components of a network design process, such as prioritizing design goals; defining requirements for the conceptual, logical, and physical design views; and assessing any risks during the design phase.

2. The physical network design diagram often includes such items as the physical communication structure of your environment and the total server layout on that network.

3. The physical network design diagram can be defined further with the location and placement of network connectivity equipment, such as bridges, hubs, switches, modems, routers, and other network devices.

4. When creating a network configuration diagram, you should document all name resolution services in use, including whether broadcast resolutions are intentionally used, on top of any WINS or DNS implementations; you should also outline IP addressing methods in use and their configuration as well as any remote access connections into the network, whether dial-up or VPN.

IP ADDRESSING

5. The current default IP addressing scheme is IP version 4 (IPv4), which uses a 32-bit address field and a 32-bit mask field.

6. IPv4 addressing can be classful, which uses a specific class (A, B, C) of IP address and an associated default subnet mask. It can also use the class addressing scheme with variable length subnet masks (VLSM). IP addressing can also be configured to use Classless Inter-Domain Routing (CIDR) with a specified prefix length.

7. The D class of IPv4 addressing is set up for multicast use and uses the 224.0.0.0 to 239.255.255.255 range of addresses. It's normally configured without using a subnet mask.

8. The E class of IPv4 addressing is set up for experimental use and uses the 240.0.0.0 to 255.255.255.255 range of addresses. It'snormally configured without using a subnet mask.

9. Automatic Private IP Addressing (APIPA) allows a DHCP client to self-configure an IP address and subnet mask when a DHCP server isn't available. APIPA selects an IPv4 address from 169.254.0.1 through 169.254.255.254, with a subnet mask of 255.255.0.0. APIPA addressing is not routable, and client communications are limited to the local subnet.

10. Hosts that are connected directly to the Internet and do not use NAT or a proxy server require a unique public IP address.

11. Hosts that are connected indirectly to the Internet, such as those that use NAT or a proxy server, can be configured to use IP addressing from the Address Allocation for Private Internets ranges or other private IP addressing schemes.

12. When designing and planning the number of hosts per subnet, you need to plan for optimization of both the number of subnets and the number of hosts per subnet.

13. The four main types of IP addressing are manual, DHCP dynamic, DHCP reservation, and APIPA.

14. DHCP reservations are used when the DHCP service doles out IP addresses to host systems that require the same IP address at all times.

15. DHCP dynamic addressing is the "standard" type of IP addressing in use; host systems receive a random IP address from the scope of available IP addresses for their subnet.

16. APIPA addressing is used when a small, nonrouted network needs a simple IP addressing solution or when a DHCP server is suddenly unavailable.

81. DNS stub zones are read-only copies of the DNS zone that contains a subset of the records associated with that zone. They also host information about the DNS servers that are authoritative for that domain.

82. Standard DNS zones cannot use a zone replication method based on Active Directory replication. Secure dynamic updates cannot be performed, either.

83. You can configure your DHCP servers to dynamically update DNS when the DHCP server configures a DHCP client with an IP address.

84. DNS clients running Windows 2000, Windows XP, and Windows Server 2003 can update DNS directly.

85. WINS forward-lookup resource records use a name query to WINS servers to provide name resolution of DNS queries for hostnames not found in a DNS zone.

86. WINS-R resource records in a reverse lookup zone provide name resolution for reverse queries not found in the DNS zone.

87. You should disable recursion on Internet-facing DNS servers that are authoritative for one or more internal DNS zones.

88. HOSTS files on systems have traditionally been used to resolve a fully qualified domain name (FQDN) to an IP address. These files are read from the top down, ignoring duplicate entries lower in the name list (because resolution stops after a match is made). To remain valid, they need to be manually updated on all systems.

89. LMHOST files on systems have traditionally been used to resolve NetBIOS names to an IP address. To remain valid, they need to be manually updated on all systems for consistency.

90. A single WINS server can service up to 10,000 clients for NetBIOS name resolution requests on most small to mid-sized networks.

91. Convergence time is the time it takes for a new entry in a WINS database to be replicated from the WINS server where changes were made to all other partner WINS servers.

92. WINS push partners replicate their changes with their push partners when a predefined change or update threshold has been reached on the originating WINS server.

93. WINS pull partners replicate their changes with their pull partners when a predefined time interval has lapsed on the WINS server, regardless of the number of changes made to the records database.

94. The four types of WINS traffic are Registration, Renewal, Query, and Release.

95. WINS burst mode handling is used to issue shortened temporary name registrations to clients when the WINS server is started with a clean database or during high traffic times.

96. WINS servers store a maximum of 25,000 name registrations by default and refresh queries in their queues before dropping additional queries.

97. DHCP servers must be authorized in Active Directory before they can assign IP addresses to clients.

SECURITY AND AUTHENTICATION

98. Be familiar with the three default IPSec policies defined: Client (Respond Only), Server (Request Security), and Server (Require Security).

99. IPSec policies can be deployed via Group Policies in Active Directory and via Local policy deployments.

100. IPSec provides security at the Network and Transport layers and is transparent to all layers above them.

101. Kerberos version 5 is the default authentication method used with IPSec policies in an Active Directory domain.

102. Public key certificates are used for external systems, such as those that access the environment via the Internet, and by internal systems that cannot run Kerberos version 5.

103. Preshared keys can be used between systems and require that both parties manually configure IPSec.

104. IPSec Monitor can be used for advanced IPSec troubleshooting to view the details of an active IPSec policy applied locally or to a domain.

105. The IP Security Policy MMC can be used to create, delete, and modify IPSec policies.

106. The RSoP tool can be used to determine the IPSec policies that are assigned but not being applied to IPSec clients. The tool shows the filter rules, filter actions, authentication methods, tunnel endpoints, and connection type for the policy being applied.

107. You can use Event Viewer to view IPSec Policy Agent events in the audit log, IPSec driver events in the system log, IKE events in the audit log, and IPSec policy change events in the audit log.

108. Extensible Authentication Protocol (EAP) is a PPP–based authentication protocol used to support authentication for generic tokens, one-time password schemes, MD5 challenges, and Transport Layer Security (TLS) for smart cards and certificate support.

109. Legacy systems in which one or both computers are running Microsoft Windows NT 4.0 use NTLM version 1 (NTLM v1) and/or NTLM version 2 (NTLM v2) as the authentication protocol.

110. NTLM v2 is the authentication protocol for non-domain systems, such as standalone servers and systems installed in workgroups.

49. When you use IPSec in Transport mode, IPSec encrypts only the payload.

50. Use the 80/20 or 50/50 rules for the fault-tolerant distribution of IP addresses from one scope so that more than one DHCP server can be used to service the same scope.

51. Windows Server 2003 DHCP Server service is a cluster-aware application.

52. In a centralized DHCP infrastructure, all DHCP functionality is managed on a few centrally located servers.

53. DHCP client reservations ensure that the DHCP server always assigns the same IP address to a host that uses the given scope.

54. The DHCP Routers option enables you to set the default gateway for all DHCP clients on a subnet.

55. You can manage DHCP client options by assigning different levels for each managed DHCP server. To do this, you can set options globally, at the scope level, and at the class level.

56. The DHCP service on each server must be authorized in Active Directory.

57. When a DHCP client wants to request an IP address from a DHCP server, it sends out a DHCPDISCOVER request.

58. When a DHCP server receives a DHCP client request (DHCPDISCOVER), it responds by sending a DHCPOFFER response.

59. When a DHCP client receives a response (DHCPOFFER) from the DHCP server(s), it sends back a DHCPREQUEST message to the DHCP server.

60. The DHCP server responds to DHCPREQUEST messages from DHCP clients with an DHCPACK message, acknowledging that it received the reply and acceptance of the IP address.

61. When the DHCP service is running, each DHCP server requests access to the authorized server list when it first starts up; after that, access requests are sent every 60 minutes for authorized servers and every 10 minutes for unauthorized servers.

62. The DHCP Audit log can be used to review critical events and errors.

NETWORK NAMING

63. The DHCP DNS option enables you to set the preferred primary and secondary DNS server for DHCP clients.

64. The DHCP WINS option enables you to set the preferred primary and secondary WINS server for DHCP clients.

65. The DHCP WINS node type option enables you to set the preferred NetBIOS name resolution method for DHCP clients.

66. The B-node (BROADCAST) WINS node type option (0x1) uses broadcasts only to resolve NetBIOS names.

67. The P-node (PEER-TO-PEER) WINS node type option (0x2) uses a NetBIOS name server/WINS server only to resolve NetBIOS names.

68. The M-node (MIXED) WINS node type option (0x4) uses broadcasts first; if the broadcast was unsuccessful, it then uses a WINS server to resolve NetBIOS names.

69. The H-node (HYBRID) WINS node type option (0x8) uses a WINS server first; if the WINS server was unsuccessful, it then uses broadcasts to resolve NetBIOS names.

70. Approximately 4MB of RAM is used when the DNS server is started without any zones. The DNS server consumes additional server memory for each zone or resource record added to the server.

71. Approximately 100 bytes of server memory are used for every resource record added to a server zone.

72. Caching-only DNS servers perform name resolution on behalf of clients and then cache the results; they are not configured to be authoritative for any DNS zones and, therefore, generate no DNS zone traffic.

73. Nonrecursive DNS servers that have had recursion disabled prevent the DNS server from using recursion to resolve names on behalf of clients. The server does not forward requests.

74. Forwarding-only DNS servers build up a name resolution cache relating names to IP addresses. This cache is used to resolve hostnames in an effort to manage DNS traffic between your network and the Internet.

75. Conditional forwarder DNS servers forward DNS queries according to the DNS domain name in the query.

76. Domain naming conventions for DNS names are outlined in RFC 1123. The allowed characters are all uppercase letters (A–Z), lowercase letters (a–z), numbers (0–9), and the hyphen (-).

77. Standard DNS zone files, also known as traditional DNS zone files, are zone files stored as text files on the server's hard drive.

78. Active Directory–integrated DNS zones store DNS zone information in Active Directory. The zones are in multimaster formatting, meaning they can be updated on any server hosting the information.

79. Standard Primary DNS zones are read/write copies of the DNS zone. They can be directly updated only on the server storing this copy of the zone.

80. Standard Secondary DNS zones are read-only copies of the DNS zone and are updated only when zone transfers occur.

NETWORKING CONCEPTS

17. Maximum throughput of an ethernet network depends mainly on the number of users on the network, the capabilities of the network hardware, and the frame size.

18. Standard considerations for utilization levels on an ethernet network are as follows: Light use is anything from 0% to 50% utilization; moderate to heavy use is anything from 50% to 80% utilization, and saturation occurs at 80% or higher consistent use.

19. In a shared ethernet system, all hosts are connected to the segment and compete with one another for bandwidth.

20. A switched ethernet system has one or more direct point-to-point connections between hosts or segments. Because of these direct connections, the hosts connected to the switched ethernet segment via a switch do not compete with each other for the available bandwidth.

21. On ethernet networks, limit your shared ethernets to no more than 50% average utilization and 80% peak utilization. You should remain under 200 hosts per shared LAN segment.

22. Hubs operate at the Physical layer of the OSI model (Layer 1). They are simple devices (no logic control) that join network segments and are invisible to all hosts on the network.

23. Most switches operate at the Data Link layer of the OSI model (Layer 2). Layer 2 switches form a border for your collision domains.

24. Some switches operate at the Network layer of the OSI model (Layer 3). Layer 3 switches form a border for your broadcast domains.

25. Routers operate at the Network layer of the OSI model (Layer 3), moving IP or IPX packets to their destination addresses. Routers are also used to connect dissimilar physical networks, to connect WANs, and to segment LANs. Routers form a border for your broadcast domains.

26. Full-duplex network communications effectively double the available bandwidth because the network traffic can be simultaneously transmitted and received at full wire speed on each transmit and receive path.

27. Half-duplex network communications can transmit and receive only at separate times.

28. Packet filtering checks all packets on the selected interface and can drop all packets not explicitly allowed.

29. Packet filter allow and deny settings are called filter actions.

30. Circuit-level filtering inspects all sessions on a particular interface.

31. Protocol filtering checks the protocols in use on the selected interface and can drop any protocols that are not explicitly allowed.

32. Demand-dial connections are point-to-point connections that generally are not active unless intentionally enabled, which makes them less susceptible to packet snooping.

33. One-way initiated demand connections are normally configured so that one router is always the answering router and the other router is always the calling router.

34. VPNs are network connections that are formed when a tunneling protocol is used to tunnel data over an existing network, such as the Internet or an intranet.

35. Dial-up connections are network connections that are formed when a specifically enabled network device, such as a modem or an ISDN device, connects two devices over a Public Switched Telephone Network (PSTN).

36. The Protected Extensible Authentication Protocol (PEAP) is available as an authentication method for 802.11 wireless clients, but it is not supported for VPN clients or other remote access clients. It can be used as an authentication method only when the Internet Authentication Service (IAS) is used.

NETWORK PROTOCOLS

37. The Routing and Remote Access Service (RRAS) supports RIP versions 1 and 2 as well as OSPF.

38. RIP routers maintain their routing tables by sending announcements to other RIP routers about the networks it can and cannot reach.

39. RIPv1 uses IP broadcast packets for its announcements.

40. RIPv2 uses IP multicast packets for its announcements.

41. RIP is typically used in networks with up to 50 routers, where no destination is farther than 14 hops away.

42. OSPF is a link-state protocol based on an algorithm that computes the shortest path between one host and other hosts.

43. OSPF is typically used in networks with more than 50 routers and with multiple redundant paths, where destinations might be farther than 14 hops away.

44. VPN supports Point-to-Point Tunneling Protocol (PPTP) and Layer Two Tunneling Protocol (L2TP) (with IPSec) for securing traffic.

45. PPTP tunnels use Microsoft Point-to-Point Encryption (MPPE) for encrypting traffic.

46. MPPE levels are 40-bit, 56-bit, or 128-bit encryption.

47. When you use IPSec in Tunnel mode, IPSec encrypts both the IP header and the payload.

48. IPSec in Tunnel mode protects the entire IP packet by treating it as an Authentication Header (AH) or Encapsulating Security Payload (ESP) payload.

EXAM CRAM™ 2

MCSE Windows Server 2003 Network Infrastructure

Jason Zandri

que®

CERTIFICATION

MCSE Windows Server 2003 Network Infrastructure (Exam 70-293)

International Standard Book Number: 0-7897-3012-x

Library of Congress Catalog Card Number: 2003103923

Printed in the United States of America

First Printing: December 2003

06 05 04 03   4 3 2 1

Trademarks

Warning and Disclaimer

Bulk Sales

Que Publishing offers excellent discounts on this book when ordered in quantity for bulk purchases or special sales. For more information, please contact

U.S. Corporate and Government Sales

1-800-382-3419

corpsales@pearsontechgroup.com

For sales outside of the U.S., please contact

International Sales

1-317-428-3341

international@pearsontechgroup.com

Publisher
Paul Boger

Executive Editor
Jeff Riley

Development Editor
Susan Brown Zahn

Managing Editor
Charlotte Clapp

Project Editor
Elizabeth Finney

Copy Editor
Lisa M. Lord

Indexer
John Sleeva

Proofreader
Leslie Joseph

Technical Editors
Will Willis
Richard Coile

Team Coordinator
Pamalee Nelson

Multimedia Developer
Dan Scherf

Interior Designer
Gary Adair

Cover Designer
Anne Jones

Page Layout
Michelle Mitchell

QUE®
CERTIFICATION

Que Certification • 800 East 96th Street • Indianapolis, Indiana 46240

A Note from Series Editor Ed Tittel

You know better than to trust your certification preparation to just anybody. That's why you, and more than two million others, have purchased an Exam Cram book. As Series Editor for the new and improved Exam Cram 2 series, I have worked with the staff at Que Certification to ensure you won't be disappointed. That's why we've taken the world's best-selling certification product—a finalist for "Best Study Guide" in a CertCities reader poll in 2002—and made it even better.

As a "Favorite Study Guide Author" finalist in a 2002 poll of CertCities readers, I know the value of good books. You'll be impressed with Que Certification's stringent review process, which ensures the books are high-quality, relevant, and technically accurate. Rest assured that at least a dozen industry experts—including the panel of certification experts at CramSession—have reviewed this material, helping us deliver an excellent solution to your exam preparation needs.

Best Study Guides

We've also added a preview edition of PrepLogic's powerful, full-featured test engine, which is trusted by certification students throughout the world.

As a 20-year-plus veteran of the computing industry and the original creator and editor of the Exam Cram series, I've brought my IT experience to bear on these books. During my tenure at Novell from 1989 to 1994, I worked with and around its excellent education and certification department. This experience helped push my writing and teaching activities heavily in the certification direction. Since then, I've worked on more than 70 certification-related books, and I write about certification topics for numerous Web sites and for *Certification* magazine.

In 1996, while studying for various MCP exams, I became frustrated with the huge, unwieldy study guides that were the only preparation tools available. As an experienced IT professional and former instructor, I wanted "nothing but the facts" necessary to prepare for the exams. From this impetus, Exam Cram emerged in 1997. It quickly became the best-selling computer book series since "...*For Dummies*," and the best-selling certification book series ever. By maintaining an intense focus on subject matter, tracking errata and updates quickly, and following the certification market closely, Exam Cram was able to establish the dominant position in cert prep books.

You will not be disappointed in your decision to purchase this book. If you are, please contact me at etittel@jump.net. All suggestions, ideas, input, or constructive criticism are welcome!

Ed Tittel

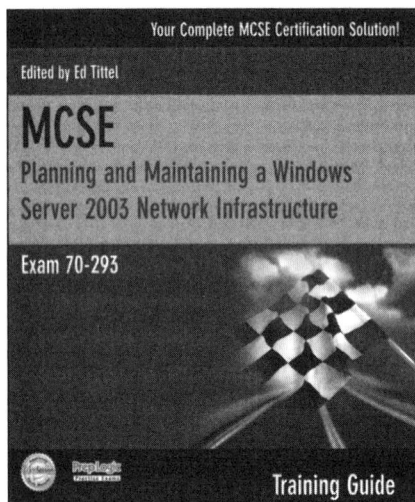

Contents at a Glance

Table of Contents

About the Author

. . . .

Jason Zandri currently holds the position of Technical Account Manager at Microsoft Corporation and has worked as a technical trainer and consultant for a variety of corporate clients in Connecticut over the past six years. He has also written a number of CompTIA and Microsoft prep tests for Boson Software as well as a number of published articles for 2000trainers.com, MCMCSE.com, Serverwatch.com, and *Certification Magazine*.

His professional CompTIA certifications include A+ Certified Technician, I-Net+ Certified Technician, Server+ Certified Technician, Network+ Certified Technician, and Security+ Certified Professional.

His professional Microsoft certifications include Microsoft Certified Trainer (MCT), Microsoft Certified Professional—NT4/W2K (MCP), Microsoft Certified Systems Administrator—W2K (MCSA), Microsoft Certified Systems Administrator: Security—W2K (MCSA: Security), Microsoft Certified Systems Engineer—NT4/W2K (MCSE), and Microsoft Certified Professional + Internet—NT4 (MCP+I). Other accredited certifications include Certified Information Systems Security Professional (CISSP) from ISC^2.

When not parked in front of his computers, you can find Jason and his wife, Renia, sifting through their movie collection looking for the "right" movie for that particular evening.

Please feel free to email Jason with your comments at Jason@Zandri.net. Please be sure to put "70-293" (or something similar) in the subject line.

Best of luck in your studies!

About the Technical Editors

Will Willis, MCSE, A+ Certified Technician, Network+, B.A., is a Senior Network Administrator for an international software development company in the Dallas, Texas, area. He is responsible for the network and server infrastructure, documentation, disaster recovery preparedness, antivirus strategies, firewalls/network security, infrastructure (servers, routers, switches, hubs, and so on) maintenance and upgrades, and the reliability and availability of network resources.

Will started out as a help desk tech, providing technical support over the phone for PC hardware and software and later moved up to a desktop/LAN support specialist position working on a team of eight to support a 3,000+-user multiple-site network. From that position, Will moved into a job as a network manager, where he administered multiple Active Directory domains and servers running BackOffice applications Exchange Server, IIS, Site Server, SQL Server, and SMS. He can be reached at WWillis@Inside-Corner.com and enjoys spending time with his family and writing and recording original music when not busy being a techie. Will has co-authored eight books and scores of technical articles to date. He has also written practice exams and tech-edited many titles. His first album of guitar-based instrumental music, *Darkness into Light*, was released in late 2002. Will is also a seminary student, pursuing a Master of Arts in Theology. More information on Will can be found at http://www.willwillis.us.

Richard D. Coile works for New Horizons Training Center of Tampa Bay as the lead Microsoft Certified Trainer and senior network administrator. His certifications include MCSE+ I, MCSE: Security, MCSE (W2K and NT4), MCT, CompTIA's A+, iNet+, Security+, and Network+ and Prosoft's CIW–CI. He has a masters degree in education technology from the University of Central Florida. He has been working with computers since 1986. While in college, he worked for Tandy Computers as a computer sales specialist and provided computer support for his customers. You can reach him at coilerd@richlantech.com or richard.coile@newhorizons.com.

Acknowledgments

· ·

I'd like to think that putting a book together is a simple task of transferring knowledge I have to paper, but it is anything but that, and it is never a one-person effort. I knew it would be a load of work, but I didn't have a proper perspective on just how much until I was in the thick of it, especially at night and on the weekends around a day job. When you wonder who dreams up those little sayings like "When you're knee deep in alligators, it is difficult to remember that the original objective was to drain the swamp," I think it's a safe bet to guess it was a writer, publisher, or perhaps both.

Was it really this much time and effort? Yes. Was it worth it? I would still have to say yes. I remember being the person on the other side of the book, studying for my exams and saying, "Gee, did the author mean this or that?" or "How come they glossed over this, I thought there was a need for much more material," and so on. This writing opportunity has given me the chance to get all those questions answered first hand, with much more clarity in understanding than any conversations over a Sam Adams with a writer or publisher could have ever hoped to offer. I mean, what is a more vivid memory from when you were a kid—when your Mom told you to not touch the stove because it was hot or after you got burned by touching it?

That said, I owe a debt of gratitude to Dawn Rader, Lisa Lord, Susan Brown Zahn, Richard Coile, Will Willis, and countless others I never had the chance to say "thank you" to for providing me with the additional required knowledge and wisdom needed to complete this task.

Last and certainly not least, I really do need to say an extra special "thank you" to my wife, Renia, who offered me her tempered, no-nonsense support to this project; she complained very little about the time it took away from the two of us and reminded me when it was just too late to work on it anymore and told me to go to bed.

Thank you, everyone.

We Want to Hear from You!

As the reader of this book, *you* are our most important critic and commentator. We value your opinion and want to know what we're doing right, what we could do better, what areas you'd like to see us publish in, and any other words of wisdom you're willing to pass our way.

As an executive editor for Que Certification, I welcome your comments. You can email or write me directly to let me know what you did or didn't like about this book—as well as what we can do to make our books better.

Please note that I cannot help you with technical problems related to the topic of this book. We do have a User Services group, however, where I will forward specific technical questions related to the book.

When you write, please be sure to include this book's title and author as well as your name, email address, and phone number. I will carefully review your comments and share them with the author and editors who worked on the book.

Email: feedback@quepublishing.com

Mail: Jeff Riley
           Executive Editor
           Que Publishing
           800 East 96th Street
           Indianapolis, IN 46240 USA

For more information about this book or another Que Certification title, visit our Web site at www.examcram2.com. Type the ISBN (excluding hyphens) or the title of a book in the Search field to find the page you're looking for.

Introduction

. . . .

Welcome to Que's *70-293 Exam Cram 2*! Whether this is your first or your fifteenth *Exam Cram 2* series book, you'll find information here that will help ensure your success as you pursue knowledge, experience, and certification. This introduction explains Microsoft certification programs in general and talks about how the *Exam Cram 2* series can help you prepare for the Microsoft Certified Systems Engineer exams. Chapter 1, "Microsoft Certification Exams," discusses the basics of Microsoft certification exams, including a description of the testing environment and a discussion of test-taking strategies. Chapters 2, "Server Roles and Security," through 7, "Planning, Implementing, and Maintaining Security Infrastructure," are designed to remind you of everything you'll need to know to take—and pass—the 70-293 MCSE certification exam. The two practice exams at the end of the book should give you a reasonably accurate assessment of your knowledge—and, yes, I've provided the answers and their explanations to the tests. Read the book and understand the material, and you'll stand a very good chance of passing the test.

Exam Cram 2 books help you understand and appreciate the subjects and materials you need to pass Microsoft certification exams. *Exam Cram 2* books are aimed strictly at test preparation and review. They do not teach you everything you need to know about a topic. Instead, I'll present and dissect the questions and problems I've found that you're likely to encounter on a test. I've worked to bring together as much information as possible about Microsoft certification exams.

Nevertheless, to prepare yourself completely for any Microsoft test, I recommend that you begin by taking the Self-Assessment included in this book, immediately following this introduction. The Self-Assessment tool helps you evaluate your knowledge base against the requirements for a Microsoft Certified Systems Engineer (MCSE).

Based on what you learn from the Self-Assessment, you might decide to begin your studies with some classroom training, some practice with Windows Server 2003, or some background reading. On the other hand, you might decide to pick up and read one of the many study guides available from

Microsoft or third-party vendors on certain topics, including the award-winning *MCSE Training Guide* series from Que Publishing. I also recommend that you supplement your study program with visits to `http://www.examcram2.com` to find additional practice questions, get advice, and track the MCSE program.

I also strongly recommend that you install, configure, and play around with the software you'll be tested on because nothing beats hands-on experience and familiarity when it comes to understanding the questions you're likely to encounter on a certification test. Book learning is essential, but without a doubt, hands-on experience is the best teacher of all! The CD in this book contains the PrepLogic Practice Exams, Preview Edition exam simulation software. The Preview Edition exhibits the full functionality of the Premium Edition, but offers questions sufficient for only one practice exam. To get the complete set of practice questions and exam functionality, visit `http://www.preplogic.com`.

The Microsoft Certified Professional Program

The Microsoft Certified Professional (MCP) program currently includes the following certification titles, each boasting its own special abbreviation (as a certification candidate and computer professional, you need to have a high tolerance for acronyms):

➤ *MCP (Microsoft Certified Professional)*—This is the entry-level certification title from Microsoft. Passing any one of the current Microsoft certification exams qualifies you for the MCP credential. You can demonstrate proficiency with other Microsoft products by passing additional certification exams.

➤ *MCSA (Microsoft Certified Systems Administrator)*—This certification is for anyone who has a high level of networking expertise with Microsoft operating systems and software products. This credential is designed to prepare you to manage, maintain, and support information systems, networks, and internetworks built around the Microsoft Windows Server system and Windows XP and Windows 2000 desktop computers. New MCSA candidates must pass four exams to become certified. Microsoft currently offers two tracks for the MCSA credential—MCSA on Windows 2000 and MCSA on Windows Server 2003. There is also a new specialization in the area of security called MCSA: Security on Microsoft

Windows 2000. The exam requirements for attaining each MCSA credential are detailed in Tables I.1 and I.2. The security specialization requirements are also discussed following the tables.

NOTE

Required core exams that are also available as elective exams can be counted only once toward a candidate's certification. An exam can count as fulfilling a core requirement or it can count as an elective, but the same exam cannot count as both a core exam and an elective exam.

Table I.1	**MCSA on Windows 2000 Exam Requirements**
Client Operating System Exams	
Candidates Must Pass One of the Following Exams	
Exam Number	**Exam Title**
70-210	Installing, Configuring, and Administering Microsoft Windows 2000 Professional
	OR
70-270	Installing, Configuring, and Administering Microsoft Windows XP Professional
Networking System Exams	
Candidates Must Pass Two of the Following Exams	
70-215	Installing, Configuring, and Administering Microsoft Windows 2000 Server
70-218	Managing a Microsoft Windows 2000 Network Environment
Elective Exams	
Candidates Must Pass One of the Following Elective Exams (or Two of the Following CompTIA Exams)	
70-028	Administering Microsoft SQL Server 7.0
70-081	Implementing and Supporting Microsoft Exchange Server 5.5
70-086	Implementing and Supporting Microsoft Systems Management Server 2.0
70-088	Implementing and Supporting Microsoft Proxy Server 2.0
70-214	Implementing and Administering Security in a Microsoft Windows 2000 Network
70-216	Implementing and Administering a Microsoft Windows 2000 Network Infrastructure
70-224	Installing, Configuring, and Administering Microsoft Exchange 2000 Server
70-227	Installing, Configuring, and Administering Microsoft Internet Security and Acceleration (ISA) Server 2000, Enterprise Edition

(continued)

Table I.1   MCSA on Windows 2000 Exam Requirements *(continued)*

Elective Exams

Candidates Must Pass One of the Following Elective Exams (or Two of the Following CompTIA Exams)

Exam Number	Exam Title
70-228	Installing, Configuring, and Administering Microsoft SQL Server 2000 Enterprise Edition
70-244	Supporting and Maintaining a Microsoft Windows NT Server 4.0 Network
CompTIA A+ Exam and CompTIA Network+ Exam	Passing both of these exams qualifies as having passed one Microsoft elective exam.
CompTIA A+ Exam and CompTIA Server+ Exam	Passing both of these exams qualifies as having passed one Microsoft elective exam.
CompTIA Security+	Passing this exam qualifies as having passed one Microsoft elective exam. It also serves as MCSA: Security specialization requirement.

Table I.2   MCSA on Windows Server 2003 Exam Requirements

Client Operating System Exams

Candidates Must Pass One of the Following Exams

Exam Number	Exam Title
70-210	Installing, Configuring, and Administering Microsoft Windows 2000 Professional
OR	
70-270	Installing, Configuring, and Administering Microsoft Windows XP Professional
Networking System Exams	
Candidates Must Pass Two of the Following Exams	
70-290	Managing and Maintaining a Microsoft Windows Server 2003 Environment
70-291	Implementing, Managing, and Maintaining a Microsoft Windows Server 2003 Network Infrastructure

(continued)

Table I.2 MCSA on Windows Server 2003 Exam Requirements (continued)

Elective Exams

Candidates Must Pass One of the Following Elective Exams (or Two of the Following CompTIA Exams)

Exam Number	Exam Title
70-086	Implementing and Supporting Microsoft Systems Management Server 2.0
70-227	Installing, Configuring, and Administering Microsoft Internet Security and Acceleration (ISA) Server 2000, Enterprise Edition
70-228	Installing, Configuring, and Administering Microsoft SQL Server 2000 Enterprise Edition
CompTIA A+ Exam and CompTIA Network+ Exam	Passing both of these exams qualifies as having passed one Microsoft elective exam.
CompTIA A+ Exam and CompTIA Server+ Exam	Passing both of these exams qualifies as having passed one Microsoft elective exam.
CompTIA Security+	Passing this exam qualifies as having passed one Microsoft elective exam. It also serves as the MCSA: Security specialization requirement.

To obtain the MCSA: Security specialization, you must pass the MCSA 2000 core exams and then pass Exam 70-214, Implementing and Administering Security in a Microsoft Windows 2000 Network. You must then pass either Exam 70-227, Installing, Configuring, and Administering Microsoft Internet Security and Acceleration (ISA) Server 2000, Enterprise Edition *or* the CompTIA Security+ exam.

> If you are already certified as an MCSA on Windows 2000, you can expedite the certification process for becoming an MCSA on Windows Server 2003. Just pass a single upgrade exam—70-292, Managing and Maintaining a Microsoft Windows Server 2003 Environment for an MCSA Certified on Windows 2000. After you've passed this one upgrade exam, you're certified as an MCSA on Windows Server 2003.

➤ *MCSE (Microsoft Certified Systems Engineer)*—Anyone with a current MCSE is recognized as having a high level of networking expertise with Microsoft operating systems and products. This credential is designed to recognize people who have the skills to plan, design, implement, maintain, and support information systems, networks, and internetworks built around Microsoft Windows Server 2003, Windows XP, Windows 2000, Windows NT 4.0, Windows 9x, and the Windows Server system family of products. The road to becoming an MCSE can start by attaining MCSA credentials. New MCSE candidates must pass seven exams to become certified. Microsoft currently offers two tracks for the MCSE credential—MCSE on Windows 2000 and MCSE on Windows Server 2003. There is also a new specialization in the area of security called MCSE: Security on Microsoft Windows 2000.

New MCSE candidates who are not already certified as MCSEs or MCSAs on Windows 2000 must pass seven tests to meet the MCSE requirements. It's not uncommon for the entire process to take a year or so, and many people find that they must take a test more than once to pass. The primary goal of the *Exam Cram 2* test preparation guides is to make it possible, given proper study and preparation, to pass all Microsoft certification tests on the first try. The exam requirements for attaining each MCSE status are detailed in Tables I.3 and I.4. The security specialization requirements are also discussed following the tables.

Table I.3 MCSE on Windows 2000 Exam Requirements	
Client Operating System Exams	
Candidates Must Pass One of the Following Exams	
Exam Number	**Exam Title**
70-210	Installing, Configuring, and Administering Microsoft Windows 2000 Professional
	OR
70-270	Installing, Configuring, and Administering Microsoft Windows XP Professional
Networking System Exams	
Candidates Must Pass the Following Three Exams	
70-215	Installing, Configuring, and Administering Microsoft Windows 2000 Server
70-216	Implementing and Administering a Microsoft Windows 2000 Network Infrastructure
70-217	Implementing and Administering a Microsoft Windows 2000 Directory Services Infrastructure
Networking Design Exams	
Candidates Must Pass One of the Following Exams	
70-219	Designing a Microsoft Windows 2000 Directory Services Infrastructure
70-220	Designing Security for a Microsoft Windows 2000 Network
70-221	Designing a Microsoft Windows 2000 Network Infrastructure

(continued)

Table I.3 **MCSE on Windows 2000 Exam Requirements** *(continued)*	
Networking Design Exams	
Candidates Must Pass One of the Following Exams	
Exam Number	**Exam Title**
70-226	Designing Highly Available Web Solutions with Microsoft Windows 2000 Server Technologies
70-297	Designing a Microsoft Windows Server 2003 Active Directory and Network Infrastructure
Elective Exams	
Candidates Must Pass Two of the Following Elective Exams	
70-019	Designing and Implementing Data Warehouses with Microsoft SQL Server 7.0
70-028	Administering Microsoft SQL Server 7.0
70-029	Designing and Implementing Databases with Microsoft SQL Server 7.0
70-056	Implementing and Supporting Web Sites Using Microsoft Site Server 3.0
70-080	Implementing and Supporting Microsoft Internet Explorer 5.0 by Using the Microsoft Internet Explorer Administration Kit
70-081	Implementing and Supporting Microsoft Exchange Server 5.5
70-085	Implementing and Supporting Microsoft SNA Server 4.0
70-086	Implementing and Supporting Microsoft Systems Management Server 2.0
70-088	Implementing and Supporting Microsoft Proxy Server 2.0
70-214	Implementing and Administering Security in a Microsoft Windows 2000 Network
70-218	Managing a Microsoft Windows 2000 Network Environment
70-219	Designing a Microsoft Windows 2000 Directory Services Infrastructure
70-220	Designing Security for a Microsoft Windows 2000 Network
70-221	Designing a Microsoft Windows 2000 Network Infrastructure
70-222	Migrating from Microsoft Windows NT 4.0 to Microsoft Windows 2000
70-223	Installing, Configuring, and Administering Microsoft Clustering Services by Using Microsoft Windows 2000 Advanced Server
70-224	Installing, Configuring, and Administering Microsoft Exchange 2000 Server

(continued)

Table I.3 MCSE on Windows 2000 Exam Requirements *(continued)*

Elective Exams

Candidates Must Pass Two of the Following Elective Exams

Exam Number	Exam Title
70-225	Designing and Deploying a Messaging Infrastructure with Microsoft Exchange 2000 Server
70-226	Designing Highly Available Web Solutions with Microsoft Windows 2000 Server Technologies
70-227	Installing, Configuring, and Administering Microsoft Internet Security and Acceleration (ISA) Server 2000 Enterprise Edition
70-228	Installing, Configuring, and Administering Microsoft SQL Server 2000 Enterprise Edition
70-229	Designing and Implementing Databases with Microsoft SQL Server 2000 Enterprise Edition
70-230	Designing and Implementing Solutions with Microsoft BizTalk Server 2000 Enterprise Edition
70-232	Implementing and Maintaining Highly Available Web Solutions with Microsoft Windows 2000 Server Technologies and Microsoft Application Center 2000
70-234	Designing and Implementing Solutions with Microsoft Commerce Server 2000
70-244	Supporting and Maintaining a Microsoft Windows NT Server 4.0 Network
CompTIA Security+	Passing this exam qualifies as having passed one Microsoft elective exam. It also serves as the MCSE: Security specialization requirement.

If you are already certified as an MCSE on Windows NT 4.0, you do not need to pass an elective exam to attain the MCSE on Windows Server 2003 credential. You need to pass only six exams, instead of seven. The core exam requirements are the same for MCSEs on Windows NT 4.0 who want to become certified as MCSEs on Windows Server 2003 as for new candidates; the MCSE on Windows NT 4.0 credential qualifies as an elective exam.

Table I.4 MCSE on Windows Server 2003 Exam Requirements

Client Operating System Exams

Candidates Must Pass One of the Following Two Exams

Exam Number	Exam Title
70-210	Installing, Configuring, and Administering Microsoft Windows 2000 Professional
OR	
70-270	Installing, Configuring, and Administering Microsoft Windows XP Professional

Networking System Exams

Candidates Must Pass the Following Four Exams

70-290	Managing and Maintaining a Microsoft Windows Server 2003 Environment
70-291	Implementing, Managing, and Maintaining a Microsoft Windows Server 2003 Network Infrastructure
70-293	Planning and Maintaining a Microsoft Windows Server 2003 Network Infrastructure
70-294	Planning, Implementing, and Maintaining a Microsoft Windows Server 2003 Active Directory Infrastructure

Networking Design Exams

Candidates Must Pass One of the Following Exams

70-297	Designing a Microsoft Windows Server 2003 Active Directory and Network Infrastructure
70-298	Designing Security for a Microsoft Windows Server 2003 Network

Elective Exams

Candidates Must Pass One of the Following Elective Exams

70-086	Implementing and Supporting Microsoft Systems Management Server 2.0
70-227	Installing, Configuring, and Administering Microsoft Internet Security and Acceleration (ISA) Server 2000, Enterprise Edition
70-228	Installing, Configuring, and Administering Microsoft SQL Server 2000 Enterprise Edition
70-229	Installing, Configuring, and Administering Microsoft SQL Server 2000 Enterprise Edition
70-232	Implementing and Maintaining Highly Available Web Solutions with Microsoft Windows 2000 Server Technologies and Microsoft Application Center 2000

(continued)

Table I.4 **MCSE on Windows Server 2003 Exam Requirements** *(continued)*

Elective Exams

Candidates Must Pass One of the Following Elective Exams

Exam Number	Exam Title
70-297	Designing a Microsoft Windows Server 2003 Active Directory and Network Infrastructure
70-298	Designing Security for a Microsoft Windows Server 2003 Network
CompTIA Security+	Passing this exam qualifies as having passed one Microsoft elective exam. It also serves as the MCSE: Security specialization requirement.

To obtain the MCSE: Security specialization, you must pass the MCSE 2000 core exams and then pass Exam 70-220, Designing Security for a Microsoft Windows 2000 Network and Exam 70-214, Implementing and Administering Security in a Microsoft Windows 2000 Network. You must also pass either Exam 70-227, Installing, Configuring, and Administering Microsoft Internet Security and Acceleration (ISA) Server 2000, Enterprise Edition *or* the CompTIA Security+ exam.

> **TIP**
>
> If you are already certified as an MCSE on Windows 2000, you can expedite the certification process for becoming an MCSE on Windows Server 2003. Just pass two exams—70-292, Managing and Maintaining a Microsoft Windows Server 2003 Environment for an MCSA Certified on Windows 2000, and 70-296, Planning, Implementing, and Maintaining a Microsoft Windows Server 2003 Environment for an MCSE Certified on Windows 2000. After you've passed these two upgrade exams, you're certified as an MCSE on Windows Server 2003.

> **NOTE**
>
> After you become an MCSA on Windows Server 2003, you can upgrade your status to the MCSE on Windows Server 2003 credential by passing the remaining exams required for MCSEs. You can take a Windows Server 2003 networking design exam *or* a Windows 2000 networking design exam to satisfy the MCSE on Windows Server 2003 design skills requirement.

➤ *MCSD (Microsoft Certified Solution Developer)*—The MCSD for Microsoft .NET credential reflects the skills required to create multitier, distributed, and Component Object Model (COM)–based solutions, in addition to desktop and Internet applications, using new technologies. To obtain MCSD certification, you must demonstrate the ability to analyze and interpret user requirements; select and integrate products, platforms, tools, and technologies; design and implement code; customize applications; and perform necessary software tests and quality assurance operations.

To obtain the MCSD for Microsoft .NET credential, you must pass a total of five exams: four core exams and one elective exam. The requirements for obtaining the MCSD for Microsoft .NET credential are summarized in Table I.5.

Table I.5 **MCSD for Microsoft .NET Exam Requirements**	
Core Exam: Solution Architecture	
Candidates Must Pass the Following Exam	
Exam Number	**Exam Title**
70-300	Analyzing Requirements and Defining Microsoft .NET Solution Architectures
Core Exams: Web Application Development	
Candidates Must Pass One of the Following Two Exams	
Exam Number	**Exam Title**
70-305	Developing and Implementing Web Applications with Microsoft Visual Basic .NET and Microsoft Visual Studio .NET
70-315	Developing and Implementing Web Applications with Microsoft Visual C# .NET and Microsoft Visual Studio .NET
Core Exams: Windows Application Development	
Candidates Must Pass One of the Following Two Exams	
70-306	Developing and Implementing Windows-based Applications with Microsoft Visual Basic .NET and Microsoft Visual Studio .NET
70-316	Developing and Implementing Windows-based Applications with Microsoft Visual C# .NET and Microsoft Visual Studio .NET
Core Exams: XML Web Services and Server Components Development	
Candidates Must Pass One of the Following Two Exams	
70-310	Developing XML Web Services and Server Components with Microsoft Visual Basic .NET and the Microsoft .NET Framework
70-320	Developing XML Web Services and Server Components with Microsoft Visual C# and the Microsoft .NET Framework
Elective Exams	
Candidates Must Pass One of the Following Elective Exams	
70-229	Designing and Implementing Databases with Microsoft SQL Server 2000 Enterprise Edition
70-230	Designing and Implementing Solutions with Microsoft BizTalk Server 2000 Enterprise Edition
70-234	Designing and Implementing Solutions with Microsoft Commerce Server 2000

➤ *MCAD (Microsoft Certified Application Developer) for Microsoft .NET*—The MCAD credential provides industry recognition for professional developers who build powerful applications using Microsoft Visual Studio .NET and Web services. MCAD candidates are required to pass two core exams and one elective exam in an area of specialization. Table I.6 details the exam requirements for earning the MCAD credential.

Table I.6 **MCAD for Microsoft .NET Exam Requirements**	
Core Exams: Web or Windows Application Development	
Candidates Must Pass One of the Following Four Exams	
Exam Number	**Exam Title**
70-305	Developing and Implementing Web Applications with Microsoft Visual Basic .NET and Microsoft Visual Studio .NET
70-315	Developing and Implementing Web Applications with Microsoft Visual C# .NET and Microsoft Visual Studio .NET
70-306	Developing and Implementing Windows-based Applications with Microsoft Visual Basic .NET and Microsoft Visual Studio .NET
70-316	Developing and Implementing Windows-based Applications with Microsoft Visual C# .NET and Microsoft Visual Studio .NET
Core Exams: XML Web Services and Server Components Development	
Candidates Must Pass One of the Following Two Exams	
70-310	Developing XML Web Services and Server Components with Microsoft Visual Basic .NET and the Microsoft .NET Framework
70-320	Developing XML Web Services and Server Components with Microsoft Visual C# and the Microsoft .NET Framework
Elective Exams	
Candidates Must Pass One of the Following Elective Exams	
70-229	Designing and Implementing Databases with Microsoft SQL Server 2000 Enterprise Edition
70-230	Designing and Implementing Solutions with Microsoft BizTalk Server 2000 Enterprise Edition
70-234	Designing and Implementing Solutions with Microsoft Commerce Server 2000
70-305*	Developing and Implementing Web Applications with Microsoft Visual Basic .NET and Microsoft Visual Studio .NET
70-306*	Developing and Implementing Windows-based Applications with Microsoft Visual Basic .NET and Microsoft Visual Studio .NET

(continued)

Table I.6 MCAD for Microsoft .NET Exam Requirements (continued)

Elective Exams

Candidates Must Pass One of the Following Elective Exams

Exam Number	Exam Title
70-315*	Developing and Implementing Web Applications with Microsoft Visual C# .NET and Microsoft Visual Studio .NET
70-316*	Developing and Implementing Windows-based Applications with Microsoft Visual C# .NET and Microsoft Visual Studio .NET

*Note: Exams 70-305, 70-306, 70-315, and 70-316 can be used as valid elective exams only if they are not used to satisfy the core exam requirement.

➤ *MCDBA (Microsoft Certified Database Administrator)*—The MCDBA on Microsoft SQL Server 2000 credential reflects the skills required to implement and administer Microsoft SQL Server databases. To obtain MCDBA certification, you must demonstrate the ability to derive physical database designs, develop logical data models, create physical databases, create data services by using Transact-SQL, manage and maintain databases, configure and manage security, monitor and optimize databases, and install and configure Microsoft SQL Server. To become an MCDBA on Microsoft SQL Server 2000, you must pass a total of three core exams and one elective exam. Table I.7 outlines the exam requirements for becoming an MCDBA.

Table I.7 MCDBA on Microsoft SQL Server 2000 Exam Requirements

Core Exams: SQL Server Administration

Candidates Must Pass One of the Following Two Exams

Exam Number	Exam Title
70-228	Installing, Configuring, and Administering Microsoft SQL Server 2000, Enterprise Edition
70-028	Administering Microsoft SQL Server 7.0

Core Exams: SQL Server Design

Candidates Must Pass One of the Following Two Exams

70-229	Designing and Implementing Databases with Microsoft SQL Server 2000, Enterprise Edition
70-029	Designing and Implementing Databases with Microsoft SQL Server 7.0

(continued)

Table I.7 MCDBA on Microsoft SQL Server 2000 Exam Requirements *(continued)*	
Core Exams: Networking Systems	
Candidates Must Pass One of the Following Three Exams	
Exam Number	**Exam Title**
70-290	Managing and Maintaining a Microsoft Windows Server 2003 Environment
70-291	Implementing, Managing, and Maintaining a Microsoft Windows Server 2003 Network Infrastructure
70-215	Installing, Configuring, and Administering Microsoft Windows 2000 Server
Elective Exams	
Candidates Must Pass One of the Following Elective Exams	
70-216	Implementing and Administering a Microsoft Windows 2000 Network Infrastructure
70-293	Planning and Maintaining a Microsoft Windows Server 2003 Network Infrastructure
70-305	Developing and Implementing Web Applications with Microsoft Visual Basic .NET and Microsoft Visual Studio .NET
70-306	Developing and Implementing Windows-based Applications with Microsoft Visual Basic .NET and Microsoft Visual Studio .NET
70-310	Developing XML Web Services and Server Components with Microsoft Visual Basic .NET and the Microsoft .NET Framework
70-315	Developing and Implementing Web Applications with Microsoft Visual C# .NET and Microsoft Visual Studio .NET
70-316	Developing and Implementing Windows-based Applications with Microsoft Visual C# .NET and Microsoft Visual Studio .NET
70-320	Developing XML Web Services and Server Components with Microsoft Visual C# and the Microsoft .NET Framework
70-015*	Designing and Implementing Distributed Applications with Microsoft Visual C++ 6.0
70-019*	Designing and Implementing Data Warehouses with Microsoft SQL Server 7.0
70-155*	Designing and Implementing Distributed Applications with Microsoft Visual FoxPro 6.0
70-175*	Designing and Implementing Distributed Applications with Microsoft Visual Basic 6.0

*Note: Exams 70-015, 70-019, 70-155, and 70-175 are scheduled to be discontinued after June 30, 2004.

Taking a Certification Exam

After you've prepared for your exam, you need to register with a testing center. Each computer-based MCP exam costs $125, and if you don't pass, you can retest for an additional $125 for each try. In the United States and Canada, tests are administered by VUE and Prometric. Here's how you can contact them:

➤ **VUE**—You can sign up for a test or get the phone numbers for local testing centers through the Web at `http://www.vue.com/ms`.

➤ **Prometric**—You can sign up for a test through the company's Web site at `http://www.2test.com`. Within the United States and Canada, you can register by phone at 800-755-3926. If you live outside this region, you should check the Prometric Web site for the correct phone number.

To sign up for a test, you must have a valid credit card or contact VUE or Prometric for mailing instructions to send a check (in the United States). Only when payment is verified or your check has cleared can you actually register for the test.

To schedule an exam, you need to call the number or visit the Web page for VUE or Prometric at least one day in advance. To cancel or reschedule an exam, you must call before 7 p.m. Pacific standard time the day before the scheduled test time (or you might be charged, even if you don't show up to take the test). When you want to schedule a test, you should have the following information ready:

➤ Your name, organization, and mailing address.

➤ Your Microsoft test ID. (Inside the United States, this usually means your Social Security number; citizens of other nations should call ahead to find out what type of identification number is required to register for a test.)

➤ The name and number of the exam you want to take.

➤ A method of payment. (As mentioned previously, a credit card is the most convenient method, but alternative means can be arranged in advance, if necessary.)

After you sign up for a test, you are told when and where the test is scheduled. You should try to arrive at least 15 minutes early. You must supply two forms of identification—one of which must be a photo ID—and sign a nondisclosure agreement to be admitted into the testing room.

All Microsoft exams are completely closed book. In fact, you are not permitted to take anything with you into the testing area, but you are given a blank sheet of paper and a pen (or in some cases an erasable plastic sheet and an erasable pen). I suggest that you immediately write down on that sheet of paper all the information you've memorized for the test. In *Exam Cram 2* books, this information appears on a tear-out sheet inside the front cover. You are given some time to compose yourself, record this information, and take a sample orientation exam before you begin the real thing. I suggest that you take the orientation test before taking your first exam, but because all the certification exams are more or less identical in layout, behavior, and controls, you probably don't need to do this more than once.

When you complete a Microsoft certification exam, the software tells you immediately whether you've passed or failed. If you need to retake an exam, you have to schedule a new test with VUE or Prometric and pay another $125.

> **NOTE**
>
> The first time you fail a test, you can retake the test as soon as the next day. However, if you fail a second time, you must wait 14 days before retaking that test. The 14-day waiting period remains in effect for all retakes after the second failure.

Tracking MCP Status

As soon as you pass any Microsoft exam, you attain MCP status. Microsoft generates transcripts that indicate which exams you have passed. You can view a copy of your transcript at any time by going to the MCP secured site and selecting Transcript Tool. This tool enables you to print a copy of your current transcript and confirm your certification status.

After you pass the necessary set of exams, you are certified. Official certification is normally granted after three to six weeks, so you shouldn't expect to get your credentials overnight. The package for official certification that arrives includes a Welcome Kit containing a number of elements (see Microsoft's Web site for other benefits of specific certifications):

➤ A certificate suitable for framing, along with a wallet card and lapel pin.

➤ A license to use the applicable logo, which means you can use the logo on advertisements, promotions, documents, letterhead, business cards, and so on. Along with the license comes a logo sheet, which includes camera-ready artwork. (Note that before you use any of the artwork, you must sign and return a licensing agreement that indicates you'll abide by its terms and conditions.)

➤ A subscription to *Microsoft Certified Professional Magazine*, which provides ongoing data about testing and certification activities, requirements, and changes to the program.

Many people believe that the benefits of MCP certification go well beyond the perks that Microsoft offers to newly anointed members of this elite group. I'm starting to see more job listings that request or require applicants to have MCP, MCAD, and other certifications, and many people who complete Microsoft certification programs can qualify for increases in pay and responsibility. As an official recognition of hard work and broad knowledge, one of the MCP credentials is a badge of honor in many IT organizations.

How to Prepare for an Exam

Preparing for any MCSE-related test (including Exam 70-293) requires that you obtain and study materials designed to provide comprehensive information about the product and its capabilities that will appear on the specific exam for which you are preparing. The following list of materials can help you study and prepare:

➤ The exam preparation materials, practice tests, and self-assessment exams on the Microsoft Training & Services page at http://www.microsoft.com/traincert. The Exam Resources link offers examples of the new question types on the MCAD and MCSD exams. You should find the materials, download them, and use them!

➤ The exam-preparation advice, practice tests, questions of the day, and discussion groups on the http://www.examcram2.com e-learning and certification destination Web site.

In addition, you might find the following materials useful in your quest for Windows Server 2003 expertise:

➤ *Microsoft training kits*—Microsoft Press offers a training kit that specifically targets Exam 70-293. For more information, visit http://www.microsoft.com/mspress/certification/mcse.asp. This training kit contains information that's useful in preparing for the test.

➤ *Study guides*—Several publishers, including Que Publishing, offer certification titles. Que Publishing offers the following:

   ➤ *The* Exam Cram 2 *series*—These books give you information about the material you need to know to pass the tests.

➤ *The* MCSE Training Guide *series*—These books offer more detail than the *Exam Cram 2* books and are designed to teach you everything you need to know about the subject an exam covers. Each book comes with a CD-ROM containing interactive practice exams in a variety of testing formats.

Together, these two series make a perfect pair.

➤ *Classroom training*—CTECs, online partners, and third-party training companies (such as New Horizons, Wave Technologies, Learning Tree, and Data-Tech) all offer classroom training on Windows Server 2003. These companies aim to help you prepare to pass Exam 70-293 (or other exams). Although training runs upward of $350 per day in class, most people lucky enough to partake find this training to be quite worthwhile.

➤ *Other publications*—There's no shortage of materials available about Windows Server 2003. The "Need to Know More?" resource sections at the end of each chapter in this book give you an idea of where to look for more information.

This set of required and recommended materials represents an unparalleled collection of sources and resources for Windows Server 2003 and related topics. I hope you'll find that this book belongs in this company.

What This Book Is Designed To Do

This book is designed to be read as a pointer to the areas of knowledge you will be tested on. In other words, you might want to read the book one time, just to get an insight into how comprehensive your knowledge of computers is. The book is also designed to be read shortly before you go for the actual test and to give you a distillation of the entire field of Windows application development in as few pages as possible. You can use this book to get a sense of the underlying context of any topic in the chapters—or to skim-read for Exam Alerts, bulleted points, summaries, and topic headings.

I've drawn on material from Microsoft's own listing of knowledge requirements, from other preparation guides, and from the exams themselves. I've also drawn from a battery of third-party test-preparation tools and technical Web sites and my own experience with application development and the exam. My aim is to walk you through the knowledge you will need—looking over your shoulder, so to speak—and point out what's important for the exam (through Exam Alerts, practice questions, and so on).

The 70-293 exam makes a basic assumption that you already have a strong background of experience with the Windows platform and its terminology. On the other hand, because the Windows 2003 Server environment is so new, no one can be a complete expert. I've tried to demystify the jargon, acronyms, terms, and concepts. Also, wherever I think you're likely to blur past an important concept, I've defined the assumptions and premises behind that concept.

What This Book Will Not Do

This book will *not* teach you everything you need to know about computers, or even about a given topic. Nor is this book an introduction to computer technology. If you're new to network administration and looking for an initial preparation guide, check out http://www.quepublishing.com, where you can find a whole section dedicated to the MCSA/MCSE certifications. This book reviews what you need to know before you take the test, with the fundamental purpose of reviewing the information needed for the Microsoft 70-293 certification exam.

This book uses a variety of teaching and memorization techniques to analyze exam-related topics and to recommend ways to input, index, and retrieve everything you need to know to pass the test. Again, it is *not* an introduction to managing a Windows 2003 network.

About This Book

If you're preparing for the 70-293 certification exam for the first time, I've structured the topics in this book to build on one another. Therefore, the topics covered in later chapters might refer to previous discussions in earlier chapters.

I suggest you read this book from front to back. You won't be wasting your time because nothing I've written is a guess about an unknown exam. I've had to explain certain underlying information on such a regular basis that I've included those explanations here.

After you've read the book, you can brush up on a subject area by using the Index or the Table of Contents to go straight to the topics and questions you want to reexamine. I've used the headings and subheadings to provide outline information about each topic.

Chapter Formats

Each *Exam Cram 2* chapter follows a regular structure and includes graphical cues about especially important or useful material. The structure of a typical chapter is as follows:

➤ *Opening hotlists*—Each chapter begins with lists of the terms you'll need to understand and the concepts you'll need to master before you can be fully conversant with the chapter's subject matter. I follow the hotlists with a few introductory paragraphs, setting the stage for the rest of the chapter.

➤ *Topical coverage*—After the opening hotlists, a series of sections covers the topics related to the chapter's subject.

➤ *Alerts*—Throughout the topical coverage, I highlight material most likely to appear on the exam by using a special Exam Alert layout that looks like this:

> This is what an Exam Alert looks like. An Exam Alert stresses concepts, terms, software, or activities that will most likely appear in one or more certification exam questions. For that reason, any information offset in Exam Alert format is worthy of extra attentiveness on your part.

Even if material isn't flagged as an Exam Alert, *all* the content in this book is associated in some way with test-related material. What appears in the chapter content is critical knowledge.

➤ *Notes*—This book is an overall examination of computers. As such, I'll dip into many aspects of Windows 2003 Server. When a body of knowledge is deeper than the scope of the book, I use notes to indicate areas of concern or specialty training.

> **NOTE** Cramming for an exam will get you through a test, but it won't make you a competent IT professional. Although you can memorize just the facts you need to become certified, your daily work in the field will rapidly put you in water over your head if you don't know the underlying principles of application development.

➤ *Tips*—I supply tips that help you to build a better foundation of knowledge or to focus your attention on an important concept that reappears later in the book. Tips provide a helpful way to remind you of the context surrounding a topic under discussion.

> You should also read Chapter 1, "Microsoft Certification Exams," for helpful strategies used in taking a test and for additional tips on how to figure out the correct response to a question and what to do if you draw a complete blank.

➤ *Exam Prep Questions*—This section presents a short list of test questions related to the specific chapter topic. Each question is followed by an explanation of both correct and incorrect answers. The practice questions highlight the areas found to be most important on the exam.

➤ *Need To Know More?*—Every chapter ends with a section titled "Need To Know More?" This section provides pointers to resources that I found helpful in offering further details on the chapter's subject matter. If you find a resource you like in this collection, use it, but don't feel compelled to use all these resources. I use this section to recommend resources that I have used on a regular basis, so none of the recommendations will be a waste of your time or money. These resources might go out of print or be taken down (in the case of Web sites), so I've tried to reference widely accepted resources.

The bulk of the book follows this chapter structure, but there are a few other elements that I would like to point out:

➤ *Practice Exams*—The practice exams, which appear in Chapters 8 and 10 (with answer keys in Chapters 9 and 11), are close approximations of the types of questions you are likely to see on the current 70-293 exam.

➤ *Answer keys*—These keys supply the answers to the sample tests, complete with explanations of both correct and incorrect responses.

➤ *Glossary*—This extensive glossary defines important terms used in this book.

➤ *The Cram Sheet*—This tear-out sheet inside the front cover is a valuable tool that represents a collection of the most difficult-to-remember facts and numbers I think you should memorize before taking the test. Remember, you can dump this information out of your head onto a piece of paper as soon as you enter the testing room. This information is usually facts that I've found require brute-force memorization. You need to remember this information only long enough to write it down when you walk into the test room. Be advised that you will be asked to surrender all personal belongings before you enter the exam room.

You might want to look at the Cram Sheet in your car or in the lobby of the testing center just before you walk into the testing center. The Cram Sheet information is divided under headings, so you can review the relevant parts just before the test.

➤ *The CD*—The CD contains the PrepLogic Practice Tests, Preview Edition exam simulation software. The Preview Edition exhibits the full functionality of the Premium Edition, but offers questions sufficient for only one practice exam. To get the complete set of practice questions and exam functionality, visit http://www.preplogic.com.

Contacting the Author

If you have any questions, comments, or even constructive criticism, please feel free to drop me a note. I have done my best to write this book following the Microsoft objectives and having the bulk of the text reflect a last-pass review for the reader, and I am interested in any feedback that is appropriate. I want to write solid technical articles and books that appeal to a large range of readers and skill levels, and I can be sure of my success at that only through your feedback.

Please feel free to email me with your comments at Jason@Zandri.net. Be sure to put "70-293" in the subject line (or something similar), as I filter much of my email because of an oppressive amount of unwanted "junk" mail.

Thanks for choosing me as your personal trainer, and enjoy the book. I would wish you luck on the exam, but I know that if you read through all the chapters and work with the product, you won't need luck—you'll pass the test on the strength of real knowledge!

Self-Assessment

A Self-Assessment is included in this *Exam Cram 2* book to help you evaluate your readiness to tackle Microsoft certifications. It should also help you understand what you need to know to master the topic of this book—namely, Exam 70-293 Planning and Maintaining a Microsoft Windows Server 2003 Network Infrastructure. Before you tackle this Self-Assessment, however, continue reading about concerns you might face when pursuing the Microsoft Certified Systems Engineer (MCSE) on Windows Server 2003 credential.

MCSEs in the Real World

The next section describes an ideal MCSE candidate, even though only a few candidates meet this ideal. In fact, this description of that ideal candidate might seem downright scary, especially with the changes made to the program to support the new Windows Server 2003 platform, which is being touted as Windows Server System. But take heart: Although the requirements to obtain an MCSE might seem formidable, they are by no means impossible to meet. However, be keenly aware that it does take time, involves some expense, and requires real effort to get through the process.

Increasing numbers of people are attaining Microsoft certifications, so the goal is within reach. You can get all the real-world motivation you need from knowing that many others have gone before, so you will be able to follow in their footsteps. If you're willing to tackle the process seriously and do what it takes to obtain the necessary experience and knowledge, you can take—and pass—all the certification tests needed for the MCSA or MCSE.

Besides MCSE, other Microsoft certifications include those described in the next section.

Current Microsoft Certification Tracks

The current makeup of the Microsoft certification tracks is explained in the following sections.

Microsoft Certified Professional (MCP)

To become a Microsoft Certified Professional (MCP), you need to sign up for and pass one of the available exams, which includes just about any of the current or recently retired exams. Some exams are currently retired and others are slated for retirement. A retired exam is no longer offered at testing centers, but usually it does not mean that candidates need to retake new exams to retain their certification. For example, if you have taken and passed Exam 70-086: Implementing and Supporting Microsoft Systems Management Server 2.0 and used it as an elective for your MCSE on W2K certification, you do not need to take another exam to replace it now that it is retired; you would still be an MCSE on W2K.

The Microsoft certification program has been making an ongoing effort to remain current with technology advancements, which obviously means that exams are retired on a regular basis. In most cases, there is no impact on candidates' requirements to retain their certification, but it is always best to take a look at the Exams Scheduled for Discontinuation table at http://www.microsoft.com/traincert/mcpexams/status/examstoretire.asp to see whether any of the discontinuations affect your certification status.

You can find information on retired exams at the Microsoft Web sitehttp://www.microsoft.com/traincert/mcpexams/status/examsretired.asp. For information about discontinuing exams, visit the Microsoft Web site at http://www.microsoft.com/traincert/mcpexams/status/retired.asp.

Quite a few certification exams are currently slated for retirement on June 30, 2004, according to information on the Microsoft Web site (http://www.microsoft.com/traincert/mcpexams/status/examstoretire.asp).

Microsoft Certified Systems Administrator (MCSA) on Windows 2000

To become a Microsoft Certified Systems Administrator (MCSA) on Windows 2000, you need to sign up for and pass three core exams (one client operating system and two networking) and one elective exam, for a total of four exams.

For the core exams/client operating system requirement of one required exam, you need to pass one of these two exams:

➤ Exam 70–210: Installing, Configuring, and Administering Microsoft Windows 2000 Professional

➤ Exam 70–270: Installing, Configuring, and Administering Microsoft Windows XP Professional

For the core exams/networking system requirement of two required exams, you need to pass both of these exams:

➤ Exam 70–215: Installing, Configuring, and Administering Microsoft Windows 2000 Server

➤ Exam 70–218: Managing a Microsoft Windows 2000 Network Environment

For the one elective exam requirement, you need to take and pass one of the exams in the following list:

➤ Exam 70–028: Administering Microsoft SQL Server 7.0

➤ Exam 70–081: Implementing and Supporting Microsoft Exchange Server 5.5

➤ Exam 70–086: Implementing and Supporting Microsoft Systems Management Server 2.0

➤ Exam 70–088: Implementing and Supporting Microsoft Proxy Server 2.0

➤ Exam 70–214: Implementing and Administering Security in a Microsoft Windows 2000 Network

➤ Exam 70–216: Implementing and Administering a Microsoft Windows 2000 Network Infrastructure

➤ Exam 70–224: Installing, Configuring, and Administering Microsoft Exchange 2000 Server

➤ Exam 70–227: Installing, Configuring, and Administering Microsoft Internet Security and Acceleration (ISA) Server 2000, Enterprise Edition

➤ Exam 70–228: Installing, Configuring, and Administering Microsoft SQL Server 2000 Enterprise Edition

➤ Exam 70–244: Supporting and Maintaining a Microsoft Windows NT Server 4.0 Network

Also, in place of these electives, you can substitute any of the following third-party certifications or certification combinations:

➤ CompTIA Security+ (This single certification can be substituted for any of the listed electives.)

➤ CompTIA A+ and CompTIA Network+ (Both certifications are required as a substitution for any of the listed electives.)

➤ CompTIA A+ and CompTIA Server+ (Both certifications are required as a substitution for any of the listed electives.)

Microsoft Certified Systems Administrator: Security (MCSA: Security) on Windows 2000

To become a Microsoft Certified Systems Administrator: Security (MCSA: Security) on Windows 2000, you need to sign up for and pass three core exams and two security specialization exams, for a total of five exams.

For the core exams/client operating system requirement of one required exam, you need to pass one of these two exams:

➤ Exam 70–210: Installing, Configuring, and Administering Microsoft Windows 2000 Professional

➤ Exam 70–270: Installing, Configuring, and Administering Microsoft Windows XP Professional

For the core exams/networking system requirement of two required exams, you need to pass *both* of these two exams:

➤ Exam 70–215: Installing, Configuring, and Administering Microsoft Windows 2000 Server

➤ Exam 70–218: Managing a Microsoft Windows 2000 Network Environment

For the two security specialization exams requirement, you need to take and pass this exam:

➤ Exam 70-214: Implementing and Administering Security in a Microsoft Windows 2000 Network

Also, you need to take and pass one of the following two exams (passing both is *not* required):

➤ Exam 70-227: Installing, Configuring, and Administering Microsoft Internet Security and Acceleration (ISA) Server 2000, Enterprise Edition

➤ Exam SY0-101: CompTIA Security+

Microsoft Certified Systems Administrator (MCSA) on Windows 2003

To become a Microsoft Certified Systems Administrator (MCSA) on Windows 2003, you need to sign up for and pass three core exams (one client operating system and two networking) and one elective exam, for a total of four exams.

For the core exams/client operating system requirement of one required exam, you need to pass one of these two exams:

➤ Exam 70–210: Installing, Configuring, and Administering Microsoft Windows 2000 Professional

➤ Exam 70–270: Installing, Configuring, and Administering Microsoft Windows XP Professional

For the core exams/networking system requirement of two required exams, you need to pass both of these exams:

➤ Exam 70–290: Managing and Maintaining a Microsoft Windows Server 2003 Environment

➤ Exam 70–291: Implementing, Managing, and Maintaining a Microsoft Windows Server 2003 Network Infrastructure

For the one elective exam requirement, you need to take and pass one of the exams from the following list:

➤ Exam 70-086: Implementing and Supporting Microsoft Systems Management Server 2.0

➤ Exam 70-227: Installing, Configuring, and Administering Microsoft Internet Security and Acceleration (ISA) Server 2000, Enterprise Edition

➤ Exam 70-228: Installing, Configuring, and Administering Microsoft SQL Server 2000 Enterprise Edition

➤ Exam 70-284: Implementing and Managing Microsoft Exchange Server 2003

➤ Exam 70-299: Implementing and Administering Security in a Microsoft Windows Server 2003 Network

This is the most up-to-date list of electives at the time of this writing. It is safe to assume that as more exams become available on the 2003 track, they will be listed on the Microsoft Web site at `http://www.microsoft.com/ traincert/mcp/mcsa/windows2003/`.

Also, in place of the listed electives, you can substitute any of the following third-party certifications or certification combinations:

➤ Exam SY0-101: CompTIA Security+ (This single certification can be substituted for any of the listed electives.)

➤ CompTIA A+ and CompTIA Network+ (Both of these certifications are required as a substitution for any of the listed electives.)

➤ CompTIA A+ and CompTIA Server+ (Both of these certifications are required as a substitution for any of the listed electives.)

Candidates that are already MCSA-certified on Windows 2000 can take Exam 70-292: Managing and Maintaining a Microsoft Windows Server 2003 Environment for an MCSA Certified on Windows 2000 upgrade exam, as there are no additional core or elective exams required for an MCSA on Windows 2000 who passes Exam 70-292.

Exam 70-292 is required for an MCSA on W2K to upgrade to MCSA on Windows 2003, short of taking a mixture of the four exams, as just outlined.

Exam 70-292 is a standard exam, in that it is paid for at testing centers and can be retaken if the examinee does not pass it.

Microsoft Certified Systems Engineer (MCSE) on Windows 2000

To become a Microsoft Certified Systems Engineer (MCSE) on Windows 2000, you need to sign up for and pass five core exams total; four are operating system exams (one client operating system and three networking system) and one is a design exam. Two additional elective exams are also required, bringing the total exams needed for the full certification to seven.

You can find more information and details at `http://www.microsoft.com/ traincert/mcp/mcse/requirements.asp`. However, the following lists are offered as a summary of the requirements. For the four required operating system exams, candidates need to take and pass the following exams:

➤ *Core exams/client operating system*—One of the following two is required:

    ➤ Exam 70–210: Installing, Configuring, and Administering Microsoft Windows 2000 Professional

    ➤ Exam 70–270: Installing, Configuring, and Administering Microsoft Windows XP Professional

➤ *Core exams/networking system*—All three of the following are required:

> ➤ Exam 70-215: Installing, Configuring, and Administering Microsoft Windows 2000 Server

> ➤ Exam 70-216: Implementing and Administering a Microsoft Windows 2000 Network Infrastructure

> ➤ Exam 70-217: Implementing and Administering a Microsoft Windows 2000 Directory Services Infrastructure

Examinees who took and passed Windows NT 4.0 Exams 70-067, 70-068, and 70-073 had the option to take Exam 70-240 (Microsoft Windows 2000 Accelerated Exam for MCPs Certified on Microsoft Windows NT 4.0) when it was active. If they passed the 70-240 exam, they are not required to take and pass the individual core/client operating system and networking system exams listed previously. Exam 70-240 is no longer available.

For the core exams/design exam requirement, you need to take and pass one of the exams from the following list:

➤ Exam 70-219: Designing a Microsoft Windows 2000 Directory Services Infrastructure

➤ Exam 70-220: Designing Security for a Microsoft Windows 2000 Network

➤ Exam 70-221: Designing a Microsoft Windows 2000 Network Infrastructure

➤ Exam 70-226: Designing Highly Available Web Solutions with Microsoft Windows 2000 Server Technologies

➤ Exam 70-297: Designing a Microsoft Windows Server 2003 Active Directory and Network Infrastructure

➤ Exam 70-298: Designing Security for a Microsoft Windows Server 2003 Network

For the elective exam requirement, you need to take and pass two of the exams from the following list:

➤ Exam 70-019: Designing and Implementing Data Warehouses with Microsoft SQL Server 7.0

➤ Exam 70-028: Administering Microsoft SQL Server 7.0

➤ Exam 70-029: Designing and Implementing Databases with Microsoft SQL Server 7.0

➤ Exam 70-086: Implementing and Supporting Microsoft Systems Management Server 2.0

➤ Exam 70-214: Implementing and Administering Security in a Microsoft Windows 2000 Network

➤ Exam 70-218: Managing a Microsoft Windows 2000 Network Environment

➤ Exam 70-219: Designing a Microsoft Windows 2000 Directory Services Infrastructure

➤ Exam 70-220: Designing Security for a Microsoft Windows 2000 Network

➤ Exam 70-221: Designing a Microsoft Windows 2000 Network Infrastructure

➤ Exam 70-222: Migrating from Microsoft Windows NT 4.0 to Microsoft Windows 2000

➤ Exam 70-223: Installing, Configuring, and Administering Microsoft Clustering Services by Using Microsoft Windows 2000 Advanced Server

➤ Exam 70-224: Installing, Configuring, and Administering Microsoft Exchange 2000 Server

➤ Exam 70-225: Designing and Deploying a Messaging Infrastructure with Microsoft Exchange 2000 Server

➤ Exam 70-226: Designing Highly Available Web Solutions with Microsoft Windows 2000 Server Technologies

➤ Exam 70-227: Installing, Configuring, and Administering Microsoft Internet Security and Acceleration (ISA) Server 2000 Enterprise Edition

➤ Exam 70-228: Installing, Configuring, and Administering Microsoft SQL Server 2000 Enterprise Edition

➤ Exam 70-229: Designing and Implementing Databases with Microsoft SQL Server 2000 Enterprise Edition

➤ Exam 70-230: Designing and Implementing Solutions with Microsoft BizTalk Server 2000 Enterprise Edition

➤ Exam 70-232: Implementing and Maintaining Highly Available Web Solutions with Microsoft Windows 2000 Server Technologies and Microsoft Application Center 2000

➤ Exam 70-234: Designing and Implementing Solutions with Microsoft Commerce Server 2000

➤ Exam 70-244: Supporting and Maintaining a Microsoft Windows NT Server 4.0 Network

This is the most up-to-date list of electives at the time of this writing.

Also, in place of one of these electives, you can substitute the following third-party certification:

➤ Exam SY0-101: CompTIA Security+

Microsoft Certified Systems Engineer: Security (MCSE: Security) on Windows 2000

To become a Microsoft Certified Systems Engineer: Security (MCSE: Security) on Windows 2000, you need to sign up for and pass four core exams and three security specialization exams, for a total of seven exams. You can find full information and details at `http://www.microsoft.com/traincert/mcp/mcsesecurity/windows2000.asp`. The following information is offered as a summary:

For the four required operating system exams, candidates need to take and pass the following exams:

➤ *Core exams/client operating system*—One of the following two is required:

   ➤ Exam 70–210: Installing, Configuring, and Administering Microsoft Windows 2000 Professional

   ➤ Exam 70–270: Installing, Configuring, and Administering Microsoft Windows XP Professional

➤ *Core exams/networking system*—All three of the following are required:

   ➤ Exam 70-215: Installing, Configuring, and Administering Microsoft Windows 2000 Server

   ➤ Exam 70-216: Implementing and Administering a Microsoft Windows 2000 Network Infrastructure

   ➤ Exam 70-217: Implementing and Administering a Microsoft Windows 2000 Directory Services Infrastructure

Examinees who took and passed Windows NT 4.0 Exams 70-067, 70-068, and 70-073 had the option to take Exam 70-240 (Microsoft Windows 2000 Accelerated Exam for MCPs Certified on Microsoft Windows NT 4.0) when it was active. If they passed the 70-240 exam, they are not required to take and pass the individual core/client operating system and networking system exams listed previously. Exam 70-240 is no longer available.

For the Security Specialization: Core Design exam requirement, currently only one exam is used:

➤ Exam 70-220: Designing Security for a Microsoft Windows 2000 Network

For the two Security Specialization: Core Security exams requirement, you need to take and pass this exam:

➤ Exam 70-214: Implementing and Administering Security in a Microsoft Windows 2000 Network

Also, you need to take and pass *one* of the following exams (passing both is *not* required):

➤ Exam 70-227: Installing, Configuring, and Administering Microsoft Internet Security and Acceleration (ISA) Server 2000, Enterprise Edition

➤ Exam SY0-101: CompTIA Security+

Microsoft Certified Systems Engineer (MCSE) on Windows 2003

To become a Microsoft Certified Systems Engineer (MCSE) on Windows 2003, you need to sign up for and pass four networking system exams, one client operating system exam, one design exam, and one elective exam. You can find full information and details at `http://www.microsoft.com/traincert/mcp/mcse/windows2003/`, but the following list offers a summary:

For the four required core exams/networking system exams, candidates need to take and pass all four of the following exams:

➤ Exam 70-290: Managing and Maintaining a Microsoft Windows Server 2003 Environment

➤ Exam 70-291: Implementing, Managing, and Maintaining a Microsoft Windows Server 2003 Network Infrastructure

➤ Exam 70-293: Planning and Maintaining a Microsoft Windows Server 2003 Network Infrastructure

➤ Exam 70-294: Planning, Implementing, and Maintaining a Microsoft Windows Server 2003 Active Directory Infrastructure

For the core exams/client operating system exam requirement, one of these two exams is required:

➤ Exam 70–210: Installing, Configuring, and Administering Microsoft Windows 2000 Professional

➤ Exam 70–270: Installing, Configuring, and Administering Microsoft Windows XP Professional

For the core exams/design exam requirement, you need to take and pass one of the exams from the following list:

➤ Exam 70-297: Designing a Microsoft Windows Server 2003 Active Directory and Network Infrastructure

➤ Exam 70-298: Designing Security for a Microsoft Windows Server 2003 Network

For the elective exam requirement, you need to take and pass one of the exams from the following list:

➤ Exam 70-086: Implementing and Supporting Microsoft Systems Management Server 2.0

➤ Exam 70-227: Installing, Configuring, and Administering Microsoft Internet Security and Acceleration (ISA) Server 2000, Enterprise Edition

➤ Exam 70-228: Installing, Configuring, and Administering Microsoft SQL Server 2000 Enterprise Edition

➤ Exam 70-229: Designing and Implementing Databases with Microsoft SQL Server 2000 Enterprise Edition

➤ Exam 70-232: Implementing and Maintaining Highly Available Web Solutions with Microsoft Windows 2000 Server Technologies and Microsoft Application Center 2000

➤ Exam 70-284: Implementing and Managing Microsoft Exchange Server 2003

➤ Exam 70-297: Designing a Microsoft Windows Server 2003 Active Directory and Network Infrastructure

➤ Exam 70-298: Designing Security for a Microsoft Windows Server 2003 Network

➤ Exam 70-299: Implementing and Administering Security in a Microsoft Windows Server 2003 Network

This is the most up-to-date list of electives at the time of this writing.

Also, in place of one of the previously listed electives, you can substitute the following third-party certification:

➤ Exam SY0-101: CompTIA Security+

Candidates who are already MCSE-certified on Windows 2000 can take Exam 70-292: Managing and Maintaining a Microsoft Windows Server 2003 Environment for an MCSA Certified on Windows 2000 upgrade exam, along with Exam 70-296: Planning, Implementing, and Maintaining a Microsoft Windows Server 2003 Environment for an MCSE Certified on Windows 2000, as no additional core or elective exams are required for an MCSA on Windows 2000 who passes Exam 70-292 and Exam 70-296. Both exams are required for an MCSE on W2K to upgrade to MCSE on Windows 2003, short of taking a mixture of the seven exams as outlined previously.

Exams 70-292 and 70-296 are standard exams, in that they are paid for at the testing centers and can be retaken if examinees do not pass them.

This is the most up-to-date list of electives at the time of this writing. It is safe to assume that as more exams become available on the 2003 track, they will be listed on the Microsoft Web site `http://www.microsoft.com/ traincert/mcp/mcse/windows2003/`.

The Ideal MCSE Candidate

The Windows Server 2003 MCSE certification exams are aimed at the current IT professional with at least two years of hands-on networking experience with Windows Server and client operating systems. His or her experience should involve implementing and administering these systems and designing a network infrastructure, and the candidate should have a moderate knowledge of Windows Server 2003.

As with any certification exam, Microsoft or other, more knowledge is required than can be gathered from any single source, whether it's a textbox, on-the-job experience, test prep, and so forth. The 70-293 Exam: Planning and Maintaining a Microsoft Windows Server 2003 Network Infrastructure measures your ability to implement, administer, and troubleshoot information systems that incorporate Windows Server 2003 in a networked capacity.

Your two years of hands-on experience working with the product should include a minimum of one year of experience in an environment consisting of more than 250 users in three or more physical locations. To get a full understanding of what this exam encompasses, your experience should also include dealing with and understanding how to administer network services and resources from file and print servers to proxy servers, how to implement firewalling techniques, how to configure Internet, intranet, and remote access connections, and how to manage client systems.

Put Yourself to the Test

The following series of questions and observations is designed to help you figure out how much work you must do to pursue Microsoft certification and what kinds of resources you should consult on your quest. Be absolutely honest in your answers; otherwise, you'll end up wasting money on exams you're not yet ready to take. There are no right or wrong answers, only steps along the path to certification. Only you can decide where you belong in the broad spectrum of aspiring candidates.

NOTE Hands-on experience with Microsoft products and technologies is an essential ingredient to Microsoft certification success.

Educational Background

1. Have you ever taken any computer-related classes? [Yes or No]

   If Yes, proceed to Question 2; if No, you might want to look into some form of study on basic computing.

2. Have you taken any classes on computer operating systems? [Yes or No]

   If Yes, you can probably handle the general information pertaining to planning, implementing, and maintaining the Window Server 2003 operating system. If you're rusty, brush up on basic operating system concepts and general computer security topics.

   If No, consider some basic reading in this area. One of the best places to look up general information is right in the Microsoft Windows Server 2003 help files on any system. They are also available online at http://www.microsoft.com.

3. Have you taken any Microsoft Official Curriculum classes at a Certified Training and Education Center (CTEC) or a community college that sponsors an IT Academy? [Yes or No]

If Yes, you can probably handle Microsoft terminology, concepts, and technologies (but brace yourself for frequent departures from normal usage and from what you see on the job).

If No, you might want to read one or two books in this topic area.

4. Have you taken a practice exam on your chosen test subject? [Yes or No]

If Yes, and you scored 80% or better on the first run through the practice questions, you're probably ready to tackle the real thing. If your score isn't above that threshold, keep at it with different question pools until you break that barrier.

If No, obtain all the free and low-budget practice tests you can find and get to work. Keep at it until you can break the passing threshold comfortably.

Hands-on Experience

The most important key to success on all Microsoft tests is hands-on experience. If I leave you with only one realization after taking this self-assessment, it should be that there's no substitute for time spent digging in with the product. Your experience can be in a test lab or on the job, and a mix of both is actually best.

Although there is no substitute for on-the-job training, your job and day-to-day responsibilities might not fully expose you to everything you need to know to pass a certification exam, no matter how long you have been working with a product. I know many NT 4 administrators with five years of experience who could not pass all the NT 4 MCSE exams now, even if they were still being offered, simply because the scope of their jobs is not broad enough to expose them to everything they would need to know to pass the exams. This is why a small home lab with a few used systems goes a long way. Many older Pentium II 400MHz systems with 192MB of RAM or more and 8 or 12GB hard drives can be found at depot centers for less than $75.00; I know because I spent that much (each) on six of them, and they all handled Windows Server 2003 just fine. I have two installed as domain controllers.

You can download objectives, practice exams, and other data about Microsoft exams from the Training and Certification page at **http://www.microsoft.com/ traincert/**. Use the Microsoft Certifications link to find specific exam information.

If you have the funds, or your employer will pay your way, consider taking a class at a Certified Training and Education Center (CTEC). In addition to classroom exposure to the topic of your choice, you usually get a copy of the software that is the focus of your course, along with a trial version of whatever operating system it needs, with the training materials for that class.

Not all CTECs are the same. You might assume that there's not much difference in accredited schools, but there is, so be sure to look around at different ones in your area and spend your or your company's money wisely.

Before you even think about taking any Microsoft exam, make sure you've spent enough time with the related software to understand how it is installed, configured, and used. This knowledge will help you in the exam—and in real life!

Testing Your Exam-Readiness

Whether you attend a formal class on a specific topic to get ready for an exam or use written materials to study on your own, some preparation for the Microsoft certification exams is essential. At $125 a try (whether you pass or fail), you want to do everything you can to pass on your first try. That's where studying comes in.

This book offers a self-assessment section so that you can evaluate your current knowledge of the material and get an indication of where you currently stand. Also, each chapter includes some practice questions, and the accompanying CD offers two 60-question practice exams. You can find a wealth of additional study guides and test preps from different authors and sources at the Exam Cram Web site http://www.informit.com/examcram2/index.asp.

For any subject, consider taking a class if you've tackled self-study materials, taken the test, and failed anyway. The opportunity to interact with an instructor and fellow students can make all the difference in the world, if you can afford the class. For information about Microsoft classes, visit the Training and Certification page at http://www.microsoft.com/traincert/ training/default.asp for a link to find training from Microsoft Certified Education Centers.

If you can't afford to take a class, you should still visit the Training page at http://www.microsoft.com/traincert/training/find/default.asp because it offers pointers to free practice exams and to MCP-approved study guides and other self-study tools. Even if you can't afford to spend much, you should still invest in some low-cost practice exams from commercial vendors.

Practice Makes Perfect

When it comes to assessing your test readiness, there is no better way than to take a good-quality practice exam and pass with a score of 80% or better. When I'm preparing, I shoot for 80% or more right from the beginning.

As mentioned, good quality at a fair price is what you should aim for if you are going to spend money. I cannot recommend spending $200 from a "top tier" company for 200 questions when there are adequate exams in the $40 range from some secondary practice exam companies. You could buy an exam from two or three of these secondary companies and still have a pool of 600 or more questions.

I also recommend reviewing all the questions after you complete your practice exam, even the questions you got correct. Make sure you know why an answer is correct and why the other choices for that question are wrong. Read the explanation to get more details. If any URLs and book references are included in the explanation, take the time to investigate them; you never know which tidbit of information you're going to recall at the testing center during the actual exam.

What's Next?

After you've assessed your readiness, undertaken the right background studies, obtained the hands-on experience that will help you understand the products and technologies at work, and reviewed the many sources of information to help you prepare for a test, you'll be ready to take a round of practice tests. When your scores come back positive enough to get you through the exam, you're ready to go after the real thing. If you follow the assessment regimen, you'll not only know what you need to study, but also when you're ready to make a test date at Prometric (http://www.prometric.com) or Virtual University Enterprises (VUE; http://www.vue.com). In the United States and Canada, tests are administered by Pearson VUE (Virtual University Enterprises) and by Prometric:

➤ *Pearson VUE*—You can sign up for a test through the company's Web site at http://www.vue.com/ms/ or by phone at 800-837-8734. If you live outside the United States and Canada, you need to check the company's Web site at http://www.vue.com/contact/ms/ for the applicable phone number.

➤ *Prometric*—You can sign up for a test through the company's Web site at `http://www.prometric.com` or by phone at 800-755-3926. If you live outside the United States and Canada, you need to check the company's Web site for the applicable phone number.

To cancel or reschedule any exam you've signed up for, you need to call before 7:00 p.m. eastern standard time the day before the scheduled test time, or you might be charged the fee.

When you want to schedule a test, you need to have the following information ready:

➤ Your full name and mailing address.

➤ Your Microsoft Test ID. (In the United States, it's your Social Security number; for other countries, you need to call ahead to find out what type of identification number is required to register for a test.)

➤ The name and number of the exam you want to take.

➤ A method of payment, such as a credit card or voucher.

After you sign up to take the test, you'll choose a testing center nearest your home or work, and choose a time and date available at the center. Most centers test from 9-to-5 hours during the day, although a few have testing times available on Saturdays and after 5:00 p.m.

On the day of your exam, you should plan to arrive at least 15 minutes early with two forms of identification. One form must be a photo ID, such as a valid driver's license, and the other can be a birth certificate or a credit card, for example. (Check with your testing center ahead of time to make sure you have the correct forms of ID.)

Good luck!

1

Microsoft Certification Exams

. . . .

Terms you'll need to understand:

✓ Multiple-choice question format
✓ Build-list-and-reorder question format
✓ Create-a-tree question format
✓ Drag-and-connect question format
✓ Select-and-place question format
✓ Hot area question format
✓ Active screen question format
✓ Case study question format
✓ Fixed-length test
✓ Simulation
✓ Adaptive test
✓ Short-form test

Techniques you'll need to master:

✓ Assessing your exam readiness
✓ Answering Microsoft's various question types
✓ Altering your test strategy depending on the exam format
✓ Practicing to make perfect
✓ Making the best use of the testing software
✓ Budgeting your time
✓ Guessing as a last resort

Exam taking is not an activity that most people look forward to, no matter how well prepared they might be. In most cases, familiarity helps offset test anxiety. In plain English, this means you probably won't be as nervous when you take your fourth or fifth Microsoft certification exam as you'll be when you take your first one.

Whether it's your first exam or your tenth, understanding the details of taking the new exams (how much time to spend on questions, the environment you'll be in, and so on) and the new exam software will help you concentrate on the material rather than on the setting. Likewise, mastering a few basic exam-taking skills should help you recognize—and perhaps even outfox— some of the tricks and snares you're bound to find in some exam questions.

This chapter, besides explaining the exam environment and software, describes some proven exam-taking strategies that you should be able to use to your advantage.

Assessing Exam Readiness

I strongly recommend that you read through and take the self-assessment included with this book. (It appears just before this chapter.) It helps you compare your knowledge base to the requirements for obtaining MCSA and MCSE certification on Windows Server 2003, and it also helps you identify parts of your background or experience that might be in need of improvement, enhancement, or further learning. If you get the right set of basics under your belt, obtaining Microsoft certification is that much easier.

After you've gone through the self-assessment, you can remedy those topical areas where your background or experience might not measure up to those of an ideal certification candidate. However, you can also tackle subject matter for individual tests at the same time, so you can continue making progress while you're catching up in some areas.

After you work through this *Exam Cram 2* series book, read the supplementary materials, and take the practice tests, you'll have a clear idea of when you should be ready to take the real exam. Although I strongly recommend that you keep practicing until your scores top the 75% mark, 80% is a good goal to give yourself some margin for error in a real exam situation (where stress plays more of a role than when you practice). After you hit that point, you should be ready to go. If you get through the practice exam in this book without attaining that score, however, you should keep taking practice tests and studying the materials until you get there. You'll find more pointers on how to study and prepare in the self-assessment.

At this point, it's time to look at the exam itself.

What to Expect at the Testing Center

When you arrive at the testing center where you scheduled your exam, you need to sign in with an exam coordinator. He or she asks you to show two forms of identification, one of which must be a photo ID. After you sign in and your time slot arrives, you are asked to deposit any books, bags, or other items you brought with you. Then you are escorted into a closed room.

All exams are completely closed book. In fact, you are not permitted to take anything with you into the testing area, but you are furnished with a blank sheet of paper and a pen or, in some cases, an erasable plastic sheet and an erasable pen. Before the exam, be sure to carefully review this book's Cram Sheet, located in the very front of the book. You should memorize as much of the important material as you can so that you can write that information on the blank sheet as soon as you are seated in front of the computer. You can refer to that piece of paper anytime you like during the test, but you must surrender the sheet when you leave the room.

You are given some time to compose yourself, to record important information, and to take a sample exam before you begin the real thing. I suggest taking the sample exam before taking your first certification exam, but because all exams are more or less identical in layout, behavior, and controls, you probably don't need to do so more than once.

Typically, the testing room is furnished with anywhere from one to six computers, and each workstation is separated from the others by dividers designed to keep anyone from seeing what's happening on someone else's computer. Most testing rooms feature a wall with a large picture window. This layout permits the exam coordinator to monitor the room, to prevent exam-takers from talking to one another, and to observe anything out of the ordinary. The exam coordinator will have already loaded the appropriate Microsoft certification exam—for this book, that's Exam 70-293: Planning and Maintaining a Microsoft Windows Server 2003 Network Infrastructure—and you are permitted to start as soon as you're seated in front of the computer.

All Microsoft certification exams allow a certain maximum amount of testing time. (This time is indicated on the exam by an onscreen timer clock, so you can check the time remaining whenever you like.) All Microsoft certification exams are computer generated. In addition to multiple choice, most exams contain select–and-place (drag-and-drop), create-a-tree (categorization and prioritization), drag-and-connect, and build-list-and-reorder (list prioritization) types of questions. Although this format might sound quite simple, the questions are constructed not only to check your mastery of basic facts and figures about Windows Server 2003, but also to require you to evaluate one or more sets of circumstances or requirements. Often, you are asked to give more than one answer to a question. Likewise, you might be asked to select the best or most effective solution to a problem from a range of choices, all of which are technically correct. Taking the exam is quite an adventure, and it involves real thinking. This book shows you what to expect and how to deal with the potential problems, puzzles, and predicaments.

Exam Layout and Design

Historically, there have been six types of question formats on Microsoft certification exams. These types of questions continue to appear on current Microsoft tests and they are discussed in the following sections:

➤ Multiple-choice, single answer

➤ Multiple-choice, multiple answers

➤ Build-list-and-reorder (list prioritization)

➤ Create-a-tree (categorization and prioritization)

➤ Drag-and-connect

➤ Select-and-place (drag-and-drop)

The Single-Answer and Multiple-Answer Multiple-Choice Question Formats

Some exam questions require you to select a single answer, whereas others ask you to select multiple correct answers. The following multiple-choice question requires you to select a single correct answer. Following the question is a brief summary of each potential answer and why it is right or wrong.

Question 1

You have three domains connected to an empty root domain under one contiguous domain name: **tutu.com**. This organization is formed into a forest arrangement, with a secondary domain called **frog.com**. How many schema masters exist for this arrangement?

- ○ A. 1
- ○ B. 2
- ○ C. 3
- ○ D. 4

The correct answer is A. This answer is correct because only one schema master is necessary for a forest arrangement. The other answers (B, C, and D) are misleading because they try to make you believe that schema masters might be in each domain or perhaps that you should have one for each contiguous namespace domain.

This sample question format corresponds closely to the Microsoft certification exam format. The only difference is that on the exam, the questions are not followed by answers and their explanations. To select an answer, you position the cursor over the option button next to the answer you want to select. Then you click the mouse button to select the answer.

Next, examine a question with one or more possible answers. This type of question provides check boxes rather than option buttons for marking all appropriate selections.

Question 2

What can you use to seize FSMO roles? (Choose two.)

- ❑ A. The **ntdsutil.exe** utility
- ❑ B. The Active Directory Users and Computers console
- ❑ C. The **secedit.exe** utility
- ❑ D. The **utilman.exe** utility

The correct answers are A and B. You can seize roles from a server that is still running through the Active Directory Users and Computers console, or in the case of a server failure, you can seize roles with the ntdsutil.exe utility. You use the secedit.exe utility to force Group Policies into play; therefore, answer C is incorrect. The utilman.exe tool manages accessibility settings in Windows Server 2003; therefore, answer D is incorrect.

This question requires two answers. Microsoft sometimes gives partial credit for partially correct answers. For Question 2, you have to mark the check boxes next to answers A and B to obtain credit for a correct answer. Notice that choosing the right answers also means knowing why the other answers are wrong.

The Build-List-and-Reorder Question Format

Questions in the build-list-and-reorder format present two lists of items—one on the left side and one on the right. To answer the question, you must move items from the list on the right to the list on the left. The final list must then be reordered into a specific order.

These questions generally sound like this: "From the following list of choices, pick the choices that answer the question. Arrange the list in a certain order." Question 3 shows an example of how they appear in this book; for an example of how they appear on the test, see Figure 1.1.

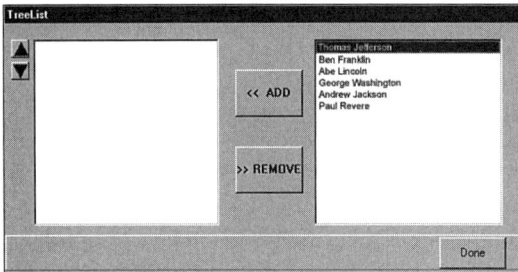

Figure 1.1   The format for build-list-and-reorder questions.

Question 3

From the following list of famous people, choose those who have been elected president of the United States. Arrange the list in the order in which the presidents served.

❍ 1. Thomas Jefferson

❍ 2. Ben Franklin

❍ 3. Abe Lincoln

❍ 4. George Washington

❍ 5. Andrew Jackson

❍ 6. Paul Revere

This is the correct answer:

1. George Washington

2. Thomas Jefferson

3. Andrew Jackson

4. Abe Lincoln

On an actual exam, the entire list of famous people would initially appear in the list on the right. You would move the four correct answers to the list on the left and then reorder the list on the left. Notice that the answer to Question 3 does not include all the items from the initial list. However, that might not always be the case.

To move an item from the right list to the left list on the exam, you first select the item by clicking it, and then click the Add button (left arrow). After you move an item from one list to the other, you can move the item back by selecting it and then clicking either the Add or Remove button. After you move items to the left list, you can move an item by selecting it and clicking the up or down arrow buttons.

The Create-a-Tree Question Format

Questions in the create-a-tree format also present two lists—one on the left side of the screen and one on the right. The list on the right consists of individual items, and the list on the left consists of nodes in a tree. To answer the question, you must move items from the list on the right to the correct node in the tree.

These questions can best be characterized as simply a matching exercise. Items from the list on the right are placed under the appropriate category in the list on the left. Question 4 shows an example of how they appear in this book; for a sample of how they appear on the test, see Figure 1.2.

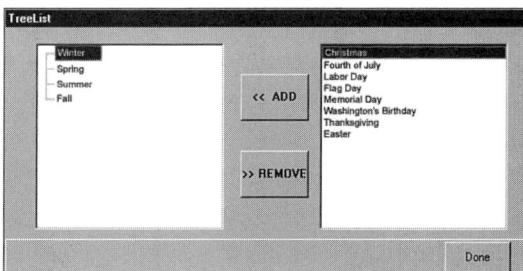

Figure 1.2   The create-a-tree question format.

Question 4

The calendar year is divided into four seasons:

Winter

Spring

Summer

Fall

Identify the season during which each of the following holidays occurs:

Christmas

Fourth of July

Labor Day

Flag Day

Memorial Day

Washington's Birthday

Thanksgiving

Easter

These are the correct answers:

➤ Winter

Christmas

Washington's Birthday

➤ Spring

Flag Day

Memorial Day

Easter

➤ Summer

Fourth of July

Labor Day

➤ Fall

Thanksgiving

In this case, you use all the items in the list. However, that might not always be the case.

To move an item from the right list to its correct location in the tree, you must first select the corresponding tree node by clicking it. Then you select the item to be moved and click the Add button. After you add one or more items to a tree node, a + icon appears to the left of the node name. You can click this icon to expand the node and view the items you have added. If you have added any item to the wrong tree node, you can remove it by selecting it and clicking the Remove button.

The Drag-and-Connect Question Format

Questions in the drag-and-connect format present a group of objects and a list of "connections." To answer the question, you must move the appropriate connections between the objects.

This type of question is best described by using graphics. Figure 1.3 shows an example.

Question 5

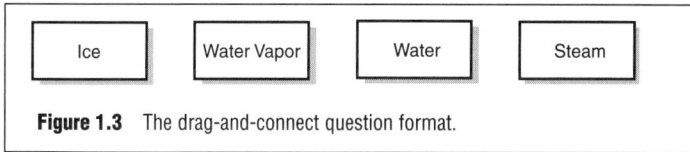

Figure 1.3   The drag-and-connect question format.

The correct answer is shown in Figure 1.4.

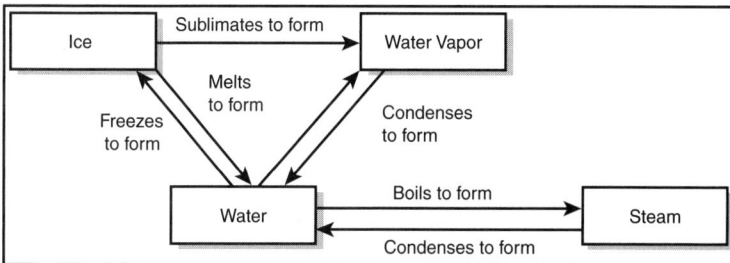

Figure 1.4   The answer to a drag-and-connect question format.

For this type of question, it's not necessary to use every object, and you can use each connection multiple times.

The Select-and-Place Question Format

Questions in the select-and-place (drag-and-drop) format present a diagram with blank boxes and a list of labels that you need to drag to correctly fill in the blank boxes. To answer these questions, you must move the labels to their correct positions on the diagram.

This type of question is best described by using graphics. Figure 1.5 shows an example.

Question 6

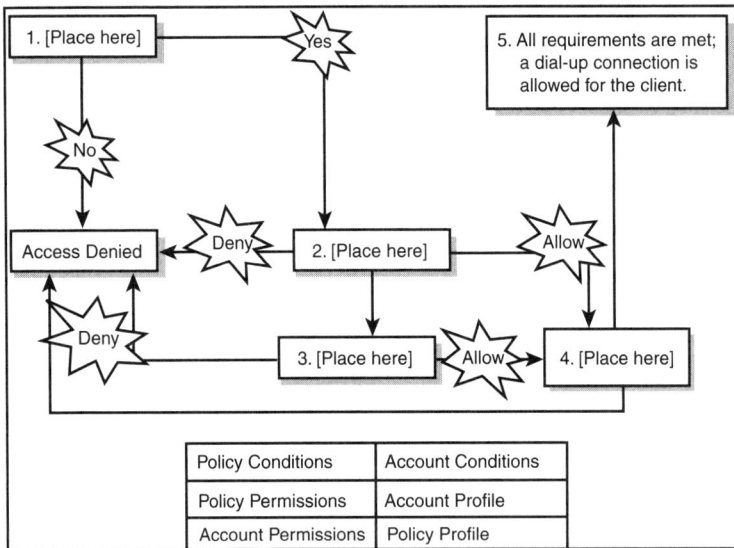

Figure 1.5   The select-and-place question format.

The correct answer is shown in Figure 1.6.

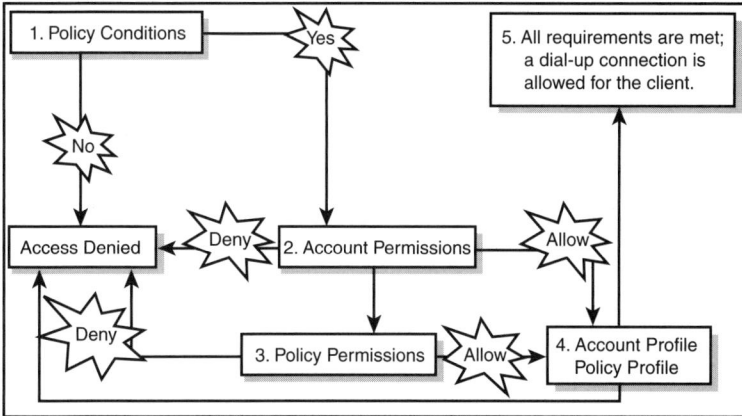

Figure 1.6 The answer to a select-and-place question format.

Design Exam Question Formats

The Windows 2000 MCSE track first introduced Microsoft's design series of exams. For the Windows Server 2003 MCSE track, design exams continue to be a core part of the curriculum. For the design exams, each exam consists entirely of a series of case studies, and the questions can be of six types. The MCSE design exams for the MCSE on Windows Server 2003 include the following:

➤ 70-229: Designing and Implementing Databases with Microsoft SQL Server 2000 Enterprise Edition

➤ 70-297: Designing a Microsoft Windows Server 2003 Active Directory and Network Infrastructure

➤ 70-298: Designing Security for a Microsoft Windows Server 2003 Network

For design exams, each case study or "testlet" presents a detailed problem that you must read and analyze. Figure 1.7 shows an example of what a case study looks like. You must select the different tabs in the case study to view the entire case.

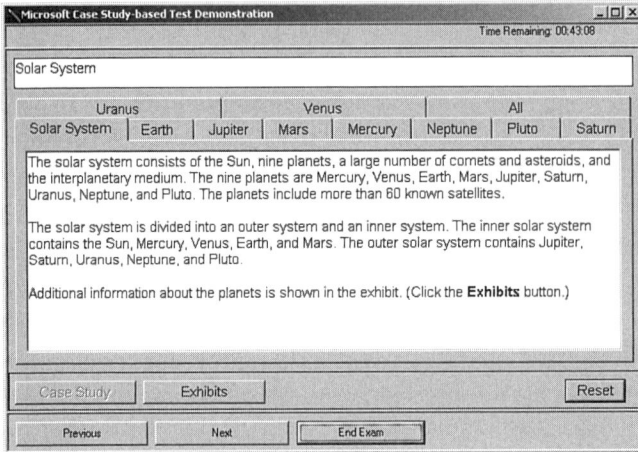

Figure 1.7   The format for case-study questions.

Following each case study is a set of questions related to the case study; these questions can be one of six types (which have been described previously). Careful attention to the details supplied in the case study is the key to success. You should be prepared to toggle between the case study and the questions frequently as you work. Some of the case studies include diagrams, which are called *exhibits*, that you'll need to examine closely to understand how to answer the questions.

After you complete a case study, you can review all the questions and your answers. However, after you move on to the next case study, you might not be able to return to the previous case study to make any changes.

For the MCSA and MCSE core exams and the upgrade exams, the same six types of questions can appear, but you are not likely to encounter complex multi-question case studies. The MCSA/MCSE core exams and upgrade exams for the Windows Server 2003 track include the following:

➤ 70-290: Managing and Maintaining a Microsoft Windows Server 2003 Environment

➤ 70-291: Implementing, Managing, and Maintaining a Microsoft Windows Server 2003 Network Infrastructure

➤ 70-292: Managing and Maintaining a Microsoft Windows Server 2003 Environment for an MCSA Certified on Windows 2000

➤ 70-293: Planning and Maintaining a Microsoft Windows Server 2003 Network Infrastructure

➤ 70-294: Planning, Implementing, and Maintaining a Microsoft Windows Server 2003 Active Directory Infrastructure

➤ 70-296: Planning, Implementing, and Maintaining a Microsoft Windows Server 2003 Environment for an MCSE Certified on Windows 2000

New Exam Question Formats

Microsoft is introducing several new question types in addition to the more traditional types of questions that are still widely used on all Microsoft exams. Microsoft thoroughly researched and tested these new, innovative question types before choosing to include them in many of the newer exams for the MCSA/MCSE on the Windows 2000 track and for the MCSA/MCSE on the Windows Server 2003 track. These new question types are as follows:

➤ Hot area questions

➤ Active screen questions

➤ New drag-and-drop–type questions

➤ Simulation questions

Hot Area Question Types

Hot area questions ask you to indicate the correct answer by selecting one or more elements in a graphic. For example, you might be asked to select multiple objects within a list, as shown in Figure 1.8.

Active Screen Question Types

Active screen questions ask you to configure a dialog box by modifying one or more elements. These types of questions offer a realistic interface in which you must correctly configure various settings, just as you would in the actual software product. For example, you might be asked to select the correct option in a drop-down list box, as shown in Figure 1.9.

New Drag-and-Drop Question Types

New drag-and-drop questions ask you to drag source elements to their corresponding targets within a work area. These types of questions test your knowledge of specific concepts and their definitions or descriptions. For example, you might be asked to match a description of a computer program to the actual software application, as shown in Figure 1.10.

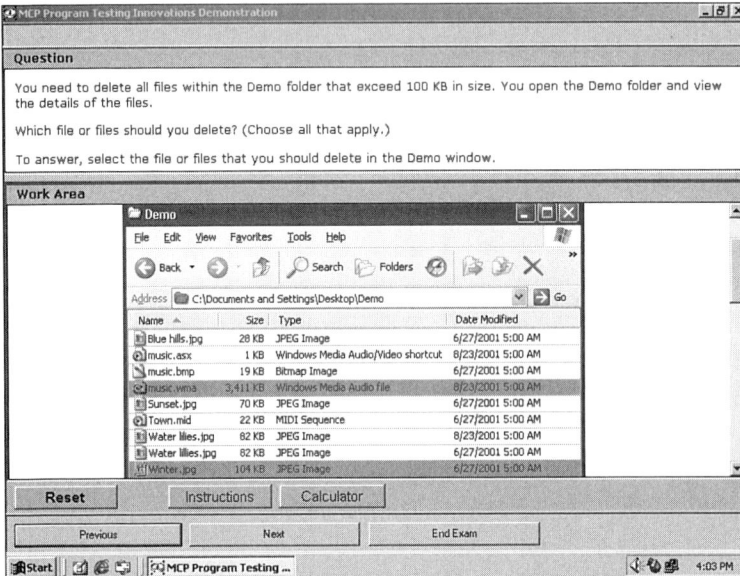

Figure 1.8 Selecting objects in a list box to answer a hot area question.

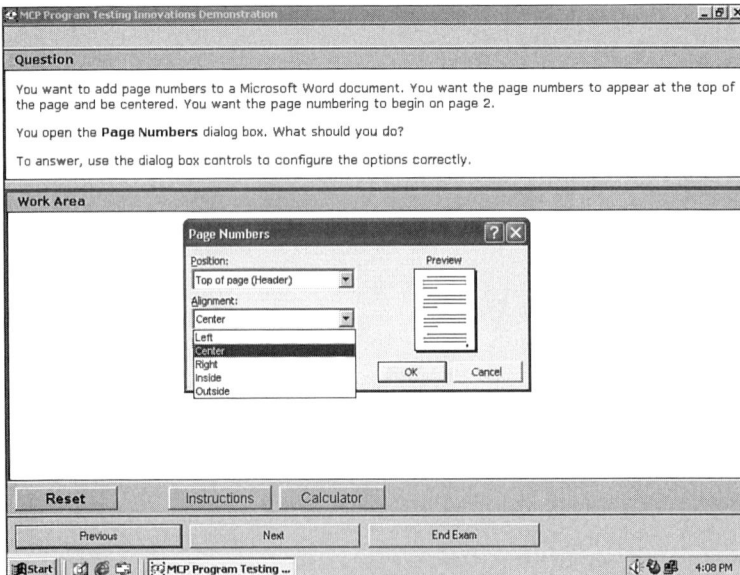

Figure 1.9 Configuring an option from a dialog box's drop-down list box to answer an active screen question.

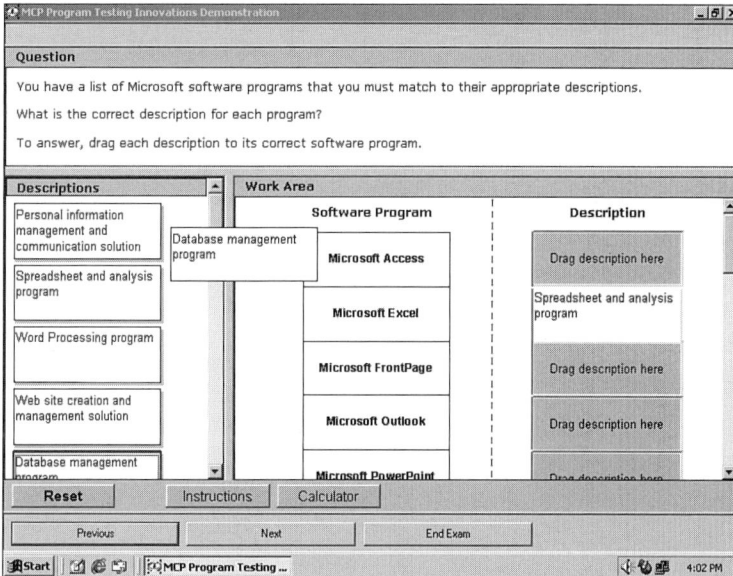

Figure 1.10   Using drag and drop to match the correct application description to each software program.

Simulation Question Types

Simulation questions ask you to indicate the correct answer by performing specific tasks, such as configuring and installing network adapters or drivers, configuring and controlling access to files, or troubleshooting hardware devices. Many of the tasks that systems administrators and systems engineers perform can be presented more accurately in simulations than in most traditional exam question types (see Figure 1.11).

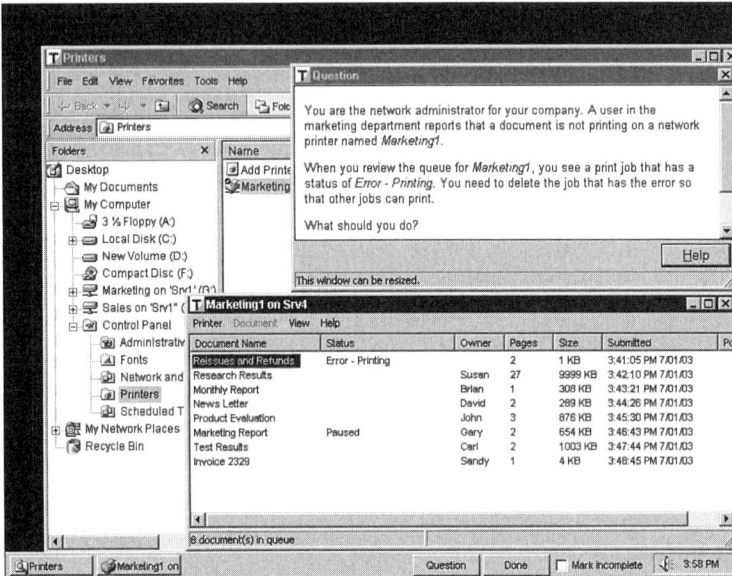

Figure 1.11   Answering a simulation question about troubleshooting a network printing problem.

Microsoft's Testing Formats

Currently, Microsoft uses four different testing formats:

➤ Fixed length

➤ Adaptive

➤ Short form

➤ Case study

Other Microsoft exams use advanced testing capabilities that might not be immediately apparent. Although the questions are primarily multiple-choice, the logic that drives them is more complex than that in older Microsoft tests, which use a fixed sequence of questions called a *fixed-length test*. Some questions have a sophisticated user interface, which Microsoft calls a *simulation*, to test your knowledge of the software and systems under consideration in a more-or-less "live" environment that behaves just like the real thing. You should review the Microsoft Training and Certification Web pages at http://www.microsoft.com/traincert for more information.

For some exams, Microsoft has turned to a well-known technique called *adaptive testing* to establish a test-taker's level of knowledge and product competence. Adaptive exams look the same as fixed-length exams, but they discover the level of difficulty at which a test-taker can correctly answer questions. Test-takers with differing levels of knowledge or ability, therefore, see different sets of questions; individuals with high levels of knowledge or ability are presented with a smaller set of more difficult questions, whereas individuals with lower levels of knowledge are given a larger set of easier questions. Two individuals might answer the same percentage of questions correctly, but the test-taker with a higher knowledge or ability level scores higher because his or her questions are worth more. Also, the lower-level test-taker will probably answer more questions than his or her more knowledgeable colleague. This explains why adaptive tests use ranges of values to define the number of questions and the amount of time it takes to complete the test.

Adaptive tests work by evaluating the test-taker's most recent answer. A correct answer leads to a more difficult question, and the test software's estimate of the test-taker's knowledge and ability level is raised. An incorrect answer leads to a less difficult question, and the test software's estimate of the test-taker's knowledge and ability level is lowered. This process continues until the test targets the test-taker's true ability level. The exam ends when the test-taker's level of accuracy meets a statistically acceptable value (in other words, when his or her performance demonstrates an acceptable level of knowledge and ability) or when the maximum number of items has been presented (in which case the test-taker is almost certain to fail).

Microsoft has also introduced a short-form test for its most popular tests. This test delivers 25 to 30 questions to its takers, giving them exactly 60 minutes to complete the exam. This type of exam is similar to a fixed-length test in that it allows readers to jump ahead or return to earlier questions and to cycle through the questions until the test is done. Microsoft does not use adaptive logic in short-form tests, but it claims that statistical analysis of the question pool is such that the 25 to 30 questions delivered during a short-form exam conclusively measure a test-taker's knowledge of the subject matter in much the same way as an adaptive test. You can think of the short-form test as a kind of "greatest hits" (that is, it covers the most important questions) version of an adaptive exam on the same topic.

NOTE Microsoft certification exams might use the adaptive-question format or the more traditional fixed-length question format. Historically, Microsoft tests have been primarily fixed-length format; however, the company seems to be moving in the direction of publishing more adaptive-question format exams.

Because you won't know which form the Microsoft exam might take, you should be prepared for an adaptive exam instead of a fixed-length or a short-form exam. The penalties for answering incorrectly are built into the test on an adaptive exam, whereas the layout remains the same for a fixed-length or short-form test, no matter how many questions you answer incorrectly.

> **TIP** The biggest difference between adaptive tests and fixed-length or short-form tests is that you can mark and revisit questions on fixed-length and short-form tests after you've read them. On an adaptive test, you must answer the question when it is presented, and you cannot return to that question later.

Strategies for Different Testing Formats

Before you choose a test-taking strategy, you must determine what type of test it is—fixed-length, short form, adaptive, or case study:

➤ Fixed-length tests consist of 50 to 70 questions with a check box for each question. You can mark these questions for review so that you can revisit one or more of the more challenging questions after you have completed the rest of the exam (provided that your exam time has not expired).

➤ Short-form tests have 25 to 30 questions with a check box for each question. You can mark these questions for review so that you can revisit one or more of the more challenging questions after you have completed the rest of the exam (provided that your exam time has not expired).

➤ Adaptive tests are identified in the introductory material of the test. Questions have no check boxes and can be viewed and answered only once. You cannot mark these questions for review at the end of the exam.

➤ Case-study tests consist of a tabbed window that allows you to navigate easily through the sections of the case.

> **TIP** You'll be able to tell for sure whether you are taking an adaptive, fixed-length, or short-form test by the first question. Fixed-length and short-form tests include a check box that allows you to mark the question for later review. Adaptive test questions include no such check box and can be viewed and answered only once.

The Fixed-Length and Short-Form Exam Strategy

One tactic that has worked well for many test-takers is to answer each question as well as you can before time expires on the exam. You will undoubtedly feel better equipped to answer some questions correctly than others; however, you should still select an answer to each question as you proceed through the exam. You should click the Mark for Review check box for any question that you are unsure of. In this way, at least you have answered all the questions in case you run out of time. Unanswered questions are automatically scored as incorrect; answers that are guessed at have at least some chance of being scored as correct. If time permits, after you have answered all questions, you can revisit each question that you have marked for review. This strategy also gives you an opportunity to gain some insight to questions you are unsure of by picking up clues from other questions on the exam.

> **TIP**
> Some people prefer to read over the exam completely before answering the trickier questions—sometimes, information supplied in later questions sheds more light on earlier questions. At other times, information you read in later questions might jog your memory about facts, figures, or behavior that helps you answer earlier questions. Either way, you could come out ahead if you answer only those questions on the first pass that you're absolutely confident about. However, be careful not to run out of time if you choose this strategy!

Fortunately, the Microsoft exam software for fixed-length and short-form tests makes the multiple-visit approach easy to implement. At the top-left corner of each question is a check box that permits you to mark that question for a later visit.

Here are some question-handling strategies that apply to fixed-length and short-form tests. Use them if you have the chance:

➤ When returning to a question after your initial read-through, read every word again; otherwise, your mind can miss important details. Sometimes, revisiting a question after turning your attention elsewhere lets you see something you missed, but the strong tendency is to see only what you've seen before. Avoid that tendency at all costs.

➤ If you return to a question more than twice, articulate to yourself what you don't understand about the question, why answers don't appear to make sense, or what appears to be missing. If you chew on the subject a while, your subconscious might provide the missing details, or you might notice a "trick" that points to the right answer.

As you work your way through the exam, another counter that Microsoft provides will come in handy—the number of questions completed and the number of questions outstanding. For fixed-length and short-form tests, it's wise to budget your time by making sure you've completed one-quarter of the questions when you're one-quarter of the way through the exam period and three-quarters of the questions three-quarters of the way through.

If you're not finished when only five minutes remain, use that time to guess your way through any remaining questions. Remember, guessing is potentially more valuable than not answering. Blank answers are always wrong, but a guess might turn out to be right. If you don't have a clue about any of the remaining questions, pick answers at random or choose all As, Bs, and so on. Questions left unanswered are counted as answered incorrectly, so a guess is better than nothing at all.

> At the very end of your exam period, you're better off guessing than leaving questions unanswered.

The Adaptive Exam Strategy

If there's one principle that applies to taking an adaptive test, it can be summed up as "Get it right the first time." You cannot elect to skip a question and move on to the next one when taking an adaptive test because the testing software uses your answer to the current question to select the question it presents next. Also, you cannot return to a question after you've moved on because the software gives you only one chance to answer the question. You can, however, take notes, and sometimes information supplied in earlier questions sheds more light on later questions.

Also, when you answer a question correctly, you are given a more difficult question next to help the software gauge your level of skill and ability. When you answer a question incorrectly, you are given a less difficult question, and the software lowers its current estimate of your skill and ability. This process continues until the program settles into a reasonably accurate estimate of what you know and can do, and it takes you, on average, somewhere between 15 and 30 questions to complete the test.

The good news is that if you know your stuff, you are likely to finish most adaptive tests in 30 minutes or so. The bad news is that you must *really* know your stuff to do your best on an adaptive test. That's because some questions are so convoluted, complex, or hard to follow that you're bound to miss one or two, at a minimum, even if you do know your stuff. So the more you know, the better you'll do, especially on an adaptive test, even accounting for the occasionally weird or unfathomable questions on these exams.

> Because you can't always tell in advance if a test is a fixed-length, short-form, or adaptive exam, you should prepare for the exam as though it were adaptive. That way, you're prepared to pass no matter what kind of test you take. If you do take a fixed-length or short-form test, however, you need to remember the tips from the preceding sections. These tips should help you perform even better on a fixed-length or short-form exam than on an adaptive test.

If you encounter a question on an adaptive test that you can't answer, you must guess an answer immediately. Because of how the software works, however, you might suffer for your guess on the next question if you guess right because you get a more difficult question next!

Case-Study Exam Strategy

As mentioned, the case study approach appears in Microsoft's design exams. These exams consist of a set of case studies that you must analyze so that you can answer related questions. Design exams include one or more case studies (tabbed topic areas), each of which is followed by 4 to 10 questions. The question types for design exams and for the four core Windows 2003 exams are multiple-choice, build-list-and-reorder, create-a-tree, drag-and-connect, and select-and-place. Depending on the test topic, some exams are totally case based, and others are not.

Most test-takers find that the case-study type of test used for the design exams (including Exams 70-229, 70-297, and 70-298) is the most difficult to master. When it comes to studying for a case-study test, your best bet is to approach each case study as a standalone test. The biggest challenge you're likely to encounter with this type of test is that you might feel as though you won't have enough time to get through all the cases that are presented.

> Each case study provides a lot of material that you need to read and study before you can effectively answer the questions that follow. The trick to taking a case-study exam is to first scan the case study to get the highlights. You should make sure you read the overview section of the case so that you understand the context of the problem at hand. Then you should quickly move on to scanning the questions.
>
> As you are scanning the questions, you should make mental notes so that you'll remember which sections of the case study you should focus on. Some case studies might supply a fair amount of extra information that you don't really need to answer the questions. The goal with this scanning approach is to avoid having to study and analyze material that is not completely relevant.

When studying a case, read the tabbed information carefully. It is important to answer every question. You can toggle back and forth from case to questions and from question to question within a case testlet. However, after you leave the case and move on, you might not be able to return to it. Therefore, you should take notes while reading useful information to help you when you tackle the test questions. It's hard to go wrong with this strategy when taking any kind of Microsoft certification test.

Question-Handling Strategies

For those questions that have only one right answer, usually two or three of the answers are obviously incorrect and two of the answers are plausible. Unless the answer leaps out at you (if it does, reread the question to look for a trick; sometimes those questions are the ones you're most likely to get wrong), begin the process of answering by eliminating the most obviously wrong answers.

You can usually immediately eliminate at least one answer of the possible choices for a question because it matches one of these conditions:

➤ The answer does not apply to the situation.

➤ The answer describes a nonexistent issue, an invalid option, or an imaginary state.

After you eliminate all the obviously wrong answers, you can apply your retained knowledge to eliminate more answers. You should look for items that sound correct but refer to actions, commands, or features that are not present or not available in the situation the question describes.

If you're still faced with a blind guess among two or more potentially correct answers, reread the question. Picture how each of the possible remaining answers would alter the situation. Be especially sensitive to terminology; sometimes the choice of words ("remove" instead of "disable") can make the difference between a right answer and a wrong one.

You should guess at an answer only after you've exhausted your ability to eliminate answers and you are still unclear about which remaining possibilities are correct. An unanswered question offers you no points, but guessing gives you at least some chance of getting a question right; just don't be too hasty when making a blind guess.

Numerous questions assume that the default behavior of a particular utility is in effect. If you know the defaults and understand what they mean, this knowledge can help you cut through many of the trickier questions. Simple "final" actions might be critical as well. If you must restart a utility before proposed changes take effect, a correct answer might require this step as well.

Mastering the Inner Game

In the final analysis, knowledge breeds confidence, and confidence breeds success. If you study the materials in this book carefully and review all the practice questions at the end of each chapter, you should become aware of the areas where you need additional learning and study.

After you've worked your way through the book, take the practice exams in the back of the book. Taking these tests provides a reality check and helps you identify areas for further study. Make sure you follow up and review materials related to the questions you miss on the practice exams before scheduling a real exam. Don't schedule your exam appointment until after you've thoroughly studied the material and you feel comfortable with the whole scope of the practice exams. You should score 80% or better on the practice exams before proceeding to the real thing. (Otherwise, obtain some additional practice tests so that you can keep trying until you hit this magic number.)

> **TIP**
> If you take a practice exam and don't get at least 70% to 80% of the questions correct, keep practicing. Microsoft offers links to practice-exam providers and self-assessment exams at **http://www.microsoft.com/traincert/mcpexams/prepare/**.

Armed with the information in this book and with the determination to augment your knowledge, you should be able to pass the certification exam. However, you need to work at it, or you'll spend the exam fee more than once before you finally pass. If you prepare seriously, you should do well.

The next section covers other sources that you can use to prepare for Microsoft certification exams.

Additional Resources

A good source of information about Microsoft certification exams comes from Microsoft itself. Because its products and technologies—and the exams that go with them—change frequently, the best place to go for exam-related information is online.

If you haven't already visited the Microsoft Training and Certification Web site, you should do so right now. Microsoft's Training and Certification home page resides at `http://www.microsoft.com/traincert` (see Figure 1.12).

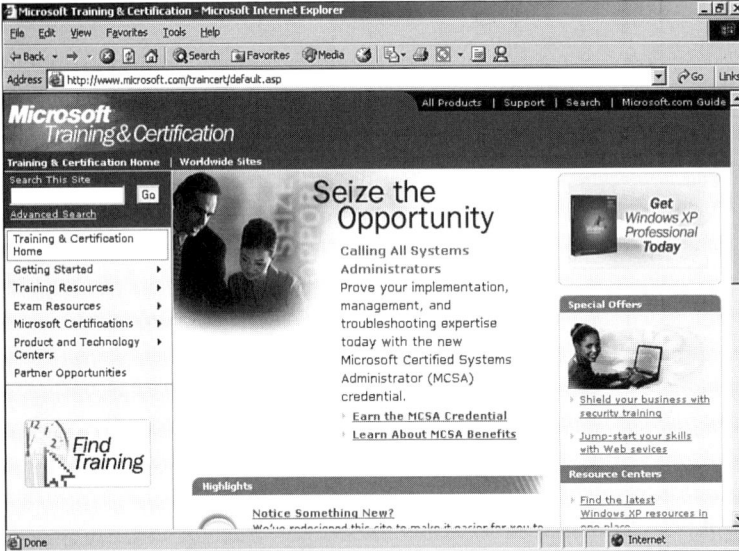

Figure 1.12 The Microsoft Training and Certification home page.

Coping with Change on the Web

Sooner or later, all the information in this book about the Microsoft Certified Professional pages and the other Web-based resources mentioned throughout the rest of this book will go stale or be replaced by newer information. In some cases, the URLs you find here might lead you to their replacements; in other cases, the URLs will go nowhere, leaving you with the dreaded "404 File not found" error message. When that happens, don't give up.

There's always a way to find what you want on the Web if you're willing to invest some time and energy. Most large or complex Web sites—and Microsoft's sites qualify on both counts—offer search engines. All of Microsoft's Web pages have a Search field at the top edge of the page. As long as you can get to Microsoft's site (it should stay at **http://www.microsoft.com** for a long time), you can use the Search field to find what you need.

The more focused you can make a search request, the more likely the results will include information you can use. For example, you can search for the string

```
"training and certification"
```

to produce a lot of data about the subject in general, but if you're looking for the preparation guide for Exam 70-293: Planning and Maintaining a Microsoft Windows Server 2003 Network Infrastructure, you'll be more likely to get there quickly if you use a search string similar to the following:

```
"Exam 70-293" AND "preparation guide"
```

Likewise, if you want to find the Training and Certification downloads, you should try a search string such as this:

```
"training and certification" AND "download page"
```

Finally, you should also use general search tools—such as **http://www.google.com**, **http://www.altavista.com**, and **http://www.excite.com**—to look for related information. Although Microsoft offers great information about its certification exams online, there are plenty of third-party sources of information and assistance that need not follow Microsoft's party line. Therefore, if you can't find something where the book says it lives, you should intensify your search.

Server Roles and Security

Terms you'll need to understand:

✓ Server roles
✓ Domain Name System (DNS) server
✓ Dynamic Host Configuration Protocol (DHCP) server
✓ Streaming media server
✓ Windows Internet Naming Service (WINS) server
✓ The **DCPROMO.EXE** program
✓ Active Directory Installation Wizard
✓ Security templates
✓ Microsoft Management Console (MMC)
✓ Post Office Protocol version 3 (POP3)
✓ The **WINPOP** command
✓ Internet Explorer Enhanced Security Configuration
✓ The **RUNAS** command

Techniques you'll need to master:

✓ Adding a role to a server
✓ Removing a role from a server
✓ Using Add/Remove Windows Components to add or remove a server role
✓ Installing domain controllers
✓ Applying default security templates
✓ Creating and using custom MMCs
✓ Configuring baseline environment security

Windows Server 2003 can have any number of different roles in the enterprise. The system could be deployed as a domain controller and, in that role, can also function as an Operations Master or a Global Catalog server. It could also be set up as a file server, a print server, or an application server, which includes setting the system up as an Internet Information Services (IIS) version 6 server. By installing it with the Post Office Protocol version 3 (POP3) and Simple Mail Transfer Protocol (SMTP) services, it could be set up as a mail server. You could also enable Terminal Services, configure the server as a streaming media server, or configure Routing and Remote Access Service (RRAS). The system could also be set up as a Domain Name System (DNS) server, a Dynamic Host Configuration Protocol (DHCP) server, or a Windows Internet Naming Service (WINS) server.

For the most part, this chapter reviews some DNS material as an overview and preparation for Exam 70-293: Planning and Maintaining a Microsoft Windows Server 2003 Network Infrastructure.

Regardless of which role you choose, you should carefully plan your server deployments so that those systems run only the services necessary for the server to perform its job. For example, there is usually no reason to enable RRAS on a file server or to install the NWLink protocol and bind it to the network adapters when NWLink is not needed on the network.

Editions of Windows Server 2003

You also need to choose which version of Windows Server 2003 is right for you. Windows Server 2003 Web Server Edition is designed specifically for low-end and entry-level Web hosting environments, providing a specific platform for deploying Web services and applications.

Using Windows Server 2003 Web Server Edition

Although Windows Server 2003 Web Server Edition can be installed with some of the same functionalities of the other OS versions, it is also limited in the following ways:

➤ The system can be set up as a virtual private network (VPN) server but with limited functionality. Connections are limited to one media type: Local area network (LAN), remote access (dial-up), direct cable connections, and Server Message Block (SMB) connections are limited to 10 simultaneous connections.

➤ It cannot be installed as part of server clusters via the operating system.

➤ It cannot be installed as a terminal server (a system that runs Remote Desktop for Administration).

➤ It cannot be installed as a file or print server for Macintosh systems.

➤ It does not have support for printer and fax sharing, nor does it support infrared devices.

➤ It cannot be deployed as a Remote Installation Service (RIS) server, nor can Internet Security and Acceleration (ISA) Server be installed on it for the system to perform as a firewall/proxy device.

➤ It cannot be established as a domain controller, a certification authority (CA), an Exchange server, a Microsoft SQL server, or a streaming media server.

➤ Remote Storage and Universal Description, Discovery, and Integration (UDDI) services are not available.

Windows Server 2003 Standard Edition is designed with the day-to-day needs of the average business in mind and is the progressive replacement for the Windows NT Server 4/Windows 2000 Server line of server operating systems.

Windows Server 2003 Enterprise Edition is designed specifically for the needs of larger organizations because their needs surpass the functional levels of Windows Server 2003 Standard Edition. Enterprise Edition is the progressive replacement for the Windows NT Server 4 Enterprise Edition/Windows 2000 Advanced Server line of server operating systems.

Windows Server 2003 Datacenter Edition is designed specifically for high-end hardware deployments that use business-critical and mission-critical applications requiring the highest levels of scalability and availability. Datacenter Edition is the progressive replacement for the Windows 2000 Datacenter Server line of operating systems.

The following list outlines the minimum system requirements and some additional information for Windows Server 2003 Standard Edition:

➤ The minimum supported processor speed is 133MHz.

➤ The minimum recommended processor speed is 550MHz

➤ Windows Server 2003 Standard Edition supports a maximum of four CPUs per server.

➤ The minimum supported amount of RAM is 128MB.

➤ The minimum recommended amount of RAM is 256MB.

➤ The maximum supported amount of RAM is 4GB.

➤ The minimum amount of space required for installation is approximately 1.5GB. Additional space might be needed under the following circumstances:

  ➤ When a FAT16 partition is in use, it requires 100MB to 200MB more free disk space than other supported file systems because of cluster sizes. NTFS is the recommended file system for any server deployment.

➤ If you are installing Windows Server 2003 Standard Edition from a network share, you need approximately 100MB to 200MB more space than if you ran the setup from the CD-ROM because Setup needs to use that space for temporary files associated with the installation. Also, the drive must have a formatted partition before the installation process starts so that those files can be copied. If the partition does not exist beforehand, the over-the-network installation fails.

➤ The amount of disk space required for the swapfile affects the initial partition's size because the swapfile is directly proportional to the amount of physical memory installed in the system. Larger amounts of RAM require a larger swapfile, so the minimum hard drive free space requirements must also increase.

➤ A VGA or higher resolution monitor is required, and an SVGA 800×600 or higher is recommended.

➤ A keyboard and mouse (or other pointing devices) are also minimum requirements.

The optional hardware list includes items such as CD-ROM or DVD drives, which are usually required only for local installations. The optional hardware list also includes a listing for network adapters and related cables from the Hardware Compatibility List (HCL).

Table 2.1 outlines the different requirement levels of the Windows Server 2003 family, as listed on the Microsoft Web site. This site (http://www.microsoft.com/windowsserver2003/evaluation/features/compareeditions.mspx) has another table that compares major features for each version.

Table 2.1 Windows Server 2003 Requirements				
Requirement	Standard Edition	Enterprise Edition	Datacenter Edition	Web Edition
Minimum CPU speed	133MHz	133MHz for x86-based computers 733MHz for Itanium-based computers	400MHz for x86-based computers 733MHz for Itanium-based computers	133MHz

(continued)

Table 2.1 Windows Server 2003 Requirements *(continued)*				
Requirement	Standard Edition	Enterprise Edition	Datacenter Edition	Web Edition
Recommended CPU speed	550MHz	733MHz	733MHz	550MHz
Minimum RAM	128MB	128MB	512MB	128MB
Recommended minimum RAM	256MB	256MB	1GB	256MB
Maximum RAM	4GB	32GB for x86-based computers 64GB for Itanium-based computers	64GB for x86-based computers 512GB for Itanium-based computers	2GB
Multiprocessor support	Up to 4	Up to 8	Minimum 8 required Maximum 64	Up to 2
Disk space for setup	1.5GB	1.5GB for x86-based computers 2.0GB for Itanium-based computers	1.5GB for x86-based computers 2.0GB for Itanium-based computers	1.5GB

The 64-bit versions of Windows Server 2003—Enterprise Edition and Datacenter Edition—can be installed only on 64-bit Intel Itanium-based hardware platforms. They can't be installed on 32-bit hardware platforms.

> There is a known issue with some Intel Pentium Pro or Pentium II Processors in which Windows Server 2003 sees only one processor, regardless of how many are physically installed. You can find additional information on this issue at the end of the chapter in the "Need to Know More?" section.

If you elect to upgrade your current server operating system, you need to be aware that the Setup program automatically installs Windows Server 2003 into the same folder as the currently installed operating system, regardless of its naming convention.

You can perform direct upgrades to Windows Server 2003 from the following versions of Windows:

➤ Windows NT Server 4.0 with Service Pack 5 or later

➤ Windows NT Server 4.0, Terminal Server Edition, with Service Pack 5 or later

➤ Windows 2000 Server

Remote Storage is not included with Windows Server 2003 Standard Edition. If you are using Windows 2000 Server with Remote Storage, you can't upgrade the system to Windows Server 2003 Standard Edition. You have the option to upgrade to Windows Server 2003 Enterprise Edition, which has Remote Storage included; remove Remote Storage through Add/Remove Programs in Control Panel from your currently installed version of Windows 2000 Server, and then upgrade to Windows Server 2003 Standard Edition; or install Windows Server 2003 Standard Edition as a new installation, which effectively sets it up as a dual-boot system.

You cannot upgrade from Windows 9x, Me, Windows NT Workstation, Windows 2000 Professional, or Windows XP Home or Professional directly to any Windows Server 2003 version. (Clean installations from within those existing operating systems to other partitions or over the existing partition are allowed.)

Also, if you have Windows NT 4.0 Server Enterprise Edition running Service Pack 5 or later, you can upgrade directly to Windows Server 2003 Enterprise Edition, but not to Windows Server 2003 Standard Edition. A clean installation to Windows Server 2003 Standard Edition is available. If you have a version of Windows NT earlier than 4.0, such as Windows NT Server 3.x, you cannot upgrade directly to any product in the Windows Server 2003 family. You can upgrade to Windows NT 4.0, apply Service Pack 5, and then perform a direct upgrade, but this method is not recommended.

Server Roles in Windows Server 2003

Server roles in Windows Server 2003 enable you, as the administrator, to configure specific roles for your system. To do this, you start the Configure Your Server Wizard through the Manage Your Server window.

Depending on your settings, the Manage Your Server window (see Figure 2.1) might be automatically available at login. If it's not, you can find it on the Start menu under All Programs, Administrative Tools.

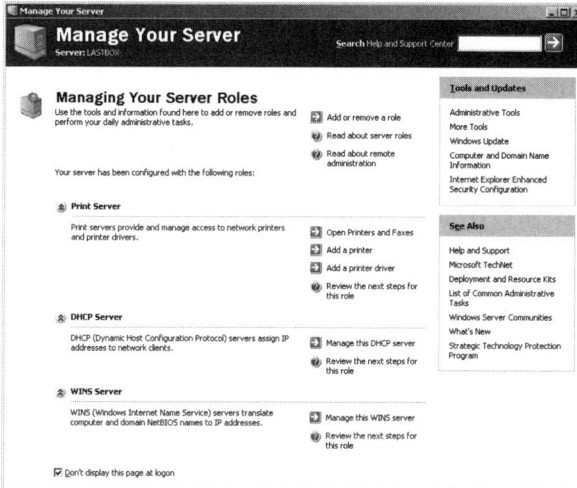

Figure 2.1 You configure your server role through the Manage Your Server window.

In this window, you can add a role to your existing server, which enables you to configure it for a specific task. You can also manage the current role from this window. You can pick one of the following listed roles, all of which are self-explanatory by their titles:

➤ File server

➤ Print server

➤ Application server

➤ Mail server

➤ Terminal server

➤ Remote access/VPN server

➤ Domain controller

➤ DNS server

➤ DHCP server

➤ Streaming media server

➤ WINS server

The steps for configuring a server in any role are straightforward; however, they do vary from one role to the other.

To start the Configure Your Server Wizard, click Add or remove a role in the main Manage Your Server window (refer to Figure 2.1). After you have read the onscreen information, ensured that all the network connections are verified, and have the necessary installation path information (or the CD) to the Windows Server 2003 setup files, click the Next button to continue.

The setup wizard then tests your available and enabled network connections and brings you to the Server Role page. From this point, you can set up the server for one or more roles. To set up a second or third role for a server, you need to run the Configure Your Server Wizard again; only one role can be established at a time.

If you need to install any additional software or services, you are prompted on other pages of the wizard. The Summary of Selections page shows the options you elected to install for the server role and continues with the role configuration. After the process is completed, the final page of the Configure Your Server Wizard is displayed.

Domain Controller Role

Configuring your system with the Configure Your Server Wizard is the same as doing it manually. Using the wizard, select the domain controller role. The wizard then runs DCPROMO.EXE to start the Active Directory Installation Wizard, which is discussed next.

Domain Controller Installation Overview

The actual process of configuring your Windows Server 2003 system as a domain controller is fairly straightforward; however, it should be noted that a lot of behind-the-scenes planning often goes on before configuration. There are also subtle differences in the process, depending on whether the system is to be a new domain controller in a new forest, a member of an existing forest, or a new domain or a domain controller in an existing domain.

To configure your server as a domain controller, log on locally to the Windows Server 2003 system you want to promote to the role of domain controller, and run DCPROMO (from the command line or from Start, Run) to start the Active Directory Installation Wizard. (You could also use the Configure Your Server Wizard, but it's not necessary.)

> **NOTE**
> To run **DCPROMO**, you must be logged on to the system as a local administrator. To join the server to an existing domain, you must have Domain Administrator rights (or higher rights, such as Enterprise Administrator, or have been delegated the permissions needed to complete the task) to successfully complete the installation and add the domain controller to the domain.

After you move past the Welcome window, how you continue with the installation depends on your current environment and where this new domain controller needs to fit in your environment.

In the Domain Controller Type page, you can install the domain controller for a new domain or install it as an additional domain controller in an existing domain. If you choose an existing domain, the installation continues from this point, as you are adding this server as a peer domain controller in an existing domain. This allows the necessary services to be installed and enabled so that the system can function as a domain controller after Active Directory has been installed and updated.

If you choose to install the domain controller in a new domain, DCPROMO prompts you in the Create New Domain page, asking whether this new domain should be installed as a new child domain or a new domain tree. If you choose to create a new child domain, the installation wizard continues, prompting you for a name for the domain and database locations.

If you decide to install this domain controller as a new domain tree, DCPROMO prompts you to select whether you are installing the domain controller in an existing forest or a new forest of domain trees. Regardless of your choice, the installation wizard continues to the New Domain Name page, which is where you enter the name of the new domain.

> **NOTE**   The only real difference in the process depends on whether you are installing the server in an existing forest or a new forest. If you are installing the server in an existing forest, schema and configuration information is copied from the forest into the new domain tree. If you are installing the server in a new forest, the schema and configuration information must be created.

Next, in the NetBIOS Domain Name page, verify the NetBIOS name for the domain for backward-compatibility with legacy systems. This means that a domain name of gunderville.com entered in the New Domain Name text box would show up as gunderville in the NetBIOS Domain Name text box. As with all NetBIOS entries, the NetBIOS domain name is limited to a maximum of 15 characters (with one additional special hidden character). That means a NetBIOS domain name of thecityofgunderville.com would default to the NetBIOS name of THECITYOFGUNDER because the number of characters exceeds the allowed maximum.

In the Database and Log Folders page, the installation wizard prompts you to choose a path for the installation location of the database and log folders. You can accept the listed defaults, enter a new path manually, or browse to a new location.

NOTE

The default location for the database and database log files is **systemroot\NTDS**. Whenever possible, you should choose an installation path for the database and the log files so that they are installed on different physical hard drives for the best performance.

In the Shared System Volume page, the installation wizard prompts you to choose a path for the installation location of the shared system volume. You can accept the listed default path, enter a new path manually, or browse to a new location.

The shared system volume stores scripts and domain-level Group Policy objects for the domain and, in certain instances, the entire enterprise. (This organization depends on whether this server holds any Flexible Single Masters of Operation roles—also known as Operations Masters—for the forest.) The default installation path for the shared system volume is `system-root\SYSVOL`, and the partition must be formatted with NTFS version 5 at a minimum. The version of NTFS used with Windows NT 4 Server (now referred to as version 4) cannot be used.

NOTE

Normally, you run into the NTFS issue only during the upgrade of a domain controller running Windows NT Server 4 with less than Service Pack 4; in most cases, the installation wizard asks you to upgrade the file system to NTFS version 5. (This is usually found only in upgrades from NT Server 4 to 2000 Server.)

One of the minimum system requirements for upgrading Windows NT Server 4 directly to Windows Server 2003 is that the system needs to be running with Service Pack 5 or later installed. **DCPROMO** is designed to not complete the installation if it detects anything lower.

Next, in the DNS Registration Diagnostics page, the DNS server that is authoritative for this forest is displayed. If the DNS server cannot be contacted because of a network issue or if there is no available DNS server to use, you are given the option to install and configure DNS on this server. You then need to configure this server's TCP/IP properties to use this DNS installation as its preferred DNS server.

Next, in the Permissions page, you need to select one of the following options:

➤ Permissions Compatible with Pre-Windows 2000 Server Operating Systems

➤ Permissions Compatible Only with Windows 2000 or Windows Server 2003 Operating Systems

Using Permissions Compatible Only with Windows 2000 or Windows Server 2003 Operating Systems is the recommended option.

NOTE

Choosing the option to set permissions compatible with pre-Windows 2000 Server operating systems is used only for backward-compatibility in certain instances. It weakens the security structure for the entire environment because it causes the installation wizard to add the Everyone group to the Pre-Windows 2000 Compatible group. This setting is undesirable because "everyone" includes anonymous users who have logged on to a network without any additional identification or authentication. For a new forest, choosing this option weakens the default security for the entire forest.

So far in this wizard, you have been gathering data and configuring installation parameters. When you reach the Summary page and click Next, continuing from this point actually installs Active Directory. After restarting, the server will be running as a domain controller.

Securing Domain Controllers: Security Templates

When a new domain controller is installed on a Windows Server 2003 system, the default template (DC Security.inf) is applied through the use of Group Policy objects linked to the Domain Controllers Organizational Unit (OU).

To change the level of security for domain controllers, you must apply the Securedc.inf security template, which increases the default security, or the Hisecdc.inf template, which maximizes the security settings. You can also set these templates manually by creating your own security template. You might want to create your own template if you need settings that the available templates do not provide or you need to customize the settings in some way. Follow these steps to create a custom template:

1. Open Active Directory Users and Computers, and select the Domain Controllers OU.

2. Right-click Domain Controllers, and choose Properties.

3. In the Group Policy tab, you can select the default policy (or disable the default policy and create a new one), and click the Edit button.

4. When the Group Policy Object Editor opens, expand Computer Configuration and then Windows Settings. Select Security Settings.

5. Right-click Security Settings and choose Import Policy (see Figure 2.2), which enables you to choose from the available default templates and any others you have created or modified on your own.

Table 2.2 shows the policy's Password Policy section with the default settings from each template available for domain controllers.

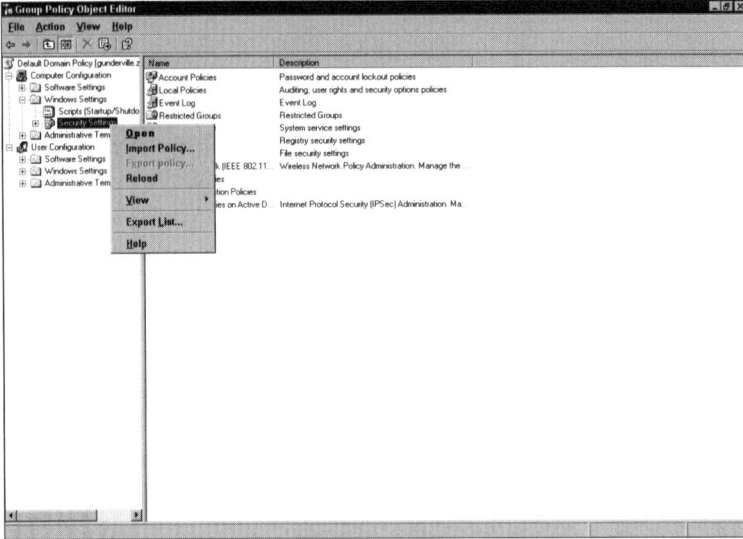

Figure 2.2 Right-click Security Settings to import security policies.

Password Policy	Default Template DC Security.inf	Secure Template Securedc.inf	High-Security Template Hisecdc.inf
Enforce password history	Not defined	24 passwords remembered	24 passwords remembered
Maximum password age	Not defined	42 days	42 days
Minimum password age	Not defined	2 days	2 days
Minimum password length	Not defined	8 characters	8 characters
Passwords must meet complexity requirements	Not defined	Enabled	Enabled
Store password using reversible encryption	Not defined	Disabled	Disabled

Table 2.2 Password Policy Settings from Security Templates

Table 2.3 shows the policy's Account Lockout Policy section with the default settings from each template.

Table 2.3 Account Lockout Policy Settings from Security Templates			
Account Lockout Policy	**Default Template DC Security.inf**	**Secure Template Securedc.inf**	**High-Security Template Hisecdc.inf**
Account lockout duration	Not defined	30 minutes	0
Account lockout threshold	Not defined	5 invalid logon attempts	5 invalid logon attempts
Reset account lockout counter after	Not defined	30 minutes	30 minutes

Table 2.4 shows the policy's Audit Policy section with the default settings from each template.

Table 2.4 Audit Policy Settings from Security Templates			
Audit Policy	**Default Template DC Security.inf**	**Secure Template Securedc.inf**	**High-Security Template Hisecdc.inf**
Audit account logon events	Not defined	Success/Failure	Success/Failure
Audit account management	Not defined	Success/Failure	Success/Failure
Audit directory services access	Not defined	Failure	Success/Failure
Audit logon events	Not defined	Success/Failure	Success/Failure
Audit object access	Not defined	No auditing	Success/Failure
Audit policy change	Not defined	Success/Failure	Success/Failure
Audit privilege use	Not defined	Failure	Success/Failure
Audit process tracking	Not defined	No auditing	No auditing
Audit system events	Not defined	No auditing	Success/Failure

By default, the policy's User Rights section is not defined in each template. Options for user rights include the following:

➤ Audit system events

➤ Access this computer from the network

➤ Add workstations to the domain

➤ Back up files and directories

➤ Bypass traverse checking

➤ Change system time

➤ Create a token object

➤ Create pagefile

➤ Create permanent shared objects

➤ Debug programs

➤ Force shutdown from a remote system

➤ Generate security audits

➤ Increase quotas

➤ Increase scheduling priority

➤ Load device drivers

➤ Lock pages in memory

➤ Log on locally

➤ Log on as a batch job

➤ Log on as a service

➤ Manage auditing and security log

➤ Modify firmware environment variables

➤ Profile a single process

➤ Profile system performance

➤ Replace a process level token

➤ Restore files and directories

➤ Shut down the system

➤ Take ownership of files and other objects

Table 2.5 shows the policy's Security Options section with the default settings from each template.

Table 2.5 Security Options Settings from Security Templates			
Security Options	Default Template DC Security.inf	Secure Template Securedc.inf	High-Security Template Hisecdc.inf
Accounts: Administrator account status	Not defined	Not defined	Not defined
Accounts: Guest account status	Not defined	Disabled	Disabled

(continued)

Table 2.5 Security Options Settings from Security Templates *(continued)*			
Security Options	**Default Template DC Security.inf**	**Secure Template Securedc.inf**	**High-Security Template Hisecdc.inf**
Accounts: Limit local account use of blank passwords to console logon only	Not defined	Not defined	Not defined
Accounts: Rename administrator account	Not defined	Not defined	Not defined
Accounts: Rename guest account	Not defined	Not defined	Not defined
Audit: Audit the access of global system objects	Not defined	Disabled	Disabled
Audit: Audit the use of backup and restore privilege	Not defined	Disabled	Disabled
Audit: Shut down system immediately if unable to log security audits	Not defined	Disabled	Disabled
Devices: Allow undock without having to log on	Not defined	Disabled	Disabled
Devices: Allowed to format and eject removable media	Not defined	Administrators	Administrators
Devices: Prevent users from installing printer drivers	Not defined	Enabled	Enabled
Devices: Restrict CD-ROM access to locally logged-on user only	Not defined	Enabled	Enabled
Devices: Restrict floppy access to locally logged-on user only	Not defined	Enabled	Enabled
Devices: Unsigned driver installation behavior	Not defined	Do not allow installation	Do not allow installation
Domain controller: Allow server operators to schedule tasks	Not defined	Disabled	Disabled

(continued)

Table 2.5   Security Options Settings from Security Templates *(continued)*

Security Options	Default Template DC Security.inf	Secure Template Securedc.inf	High-Security Template Hisecdc.inf
Domain controller: LDAP server signing requirements	Not defined	None	Require signing
Domain controller: Refuse machine account password changes	Not defined	Disabled	Disabled
Domain member: Digitally encrypt or sign secure channel data (always)	Not defined	Disabled	Enabled
Domain member: Digitally encrypt secure channel data (when possible)	Not defined	Enabled	Enabled
Domain member: Digitally sign secure channel data (when possible)	Not defined	Enabled	Enabled
Domain member: Disable machine account password changes	Not defined	Disabled	Disabled
Domain member: Maximum machine account password age	Not defined	30 days	30 days
Domain member: Require strong (Windows 2000 or later) session key	Not defined	Disabled	Enabled
Interactive logon: Do not display last user name	Not defined	Disabled	Enabled
Interactive logon: Do not require Ctrl+Alt+Del	Not defined	Disabled	Disabled
Interactive logon: Message text for users attempting to log on	Not defined		
Interactive logon: Message title for users attempting to log on	Not defined		

(continued)

Table 2.5 Security Options Settings from Security Templates *(continued)*			
Security Options	**Default Template DC Security.inf**	**Secure Template Securedc.inf**	**High-Security Template Hisecdc.inf**
Interactive logon: Number of previous logons to cache (in case domain controller is not available)	Not defined	10 logons	0 logons
Interactive logon: Prompt user to change password before expiration	Not defined	14 days	14 days
Interactive logon: Require domain controller authentication to unlock workstation	Not defined	Enabled	Enabled
Interactive logon: Require smart card	Not defined	Not defined	Not defined
Interactive logon: Smart card removal behavior	Not defined	Force logoff	Force logoff
Microsoft network client: Digitally sign communications (always)	Not defined	Disabled	Disabled
Microsoft network client: Digitally sign communications (if server agrees)	Not defined	Enabled	Enabled
Microsoft network client: Send unencrypted password to third-party SMB servers	Not defined	Disabled	Disabled
Microsoft network server: Amount of idle time required before suspending session	Not defined	15 minutes	15 minutes
Microsoft network server: Digitally sign communications (always)	Not defined	Disabled	Enabled

(continued)

Table 2.5 Security Options Settings from Security Templates *(continued)*			
Security Options	**Default Template DC Security.inf**	**Secure Template Securedc.inf**	**High-Security Template Hisecdc.inf**
Microsoft network server: Digitally sign communications (if client agrees)	Not defined	Enabled	Enabled
Microsoft network server: Disconnect clients when logon hours expire	Not defined	Enabled	Enabled
Network access: Allow anonymous SID/name translation	Not defined	Disabled	Disabled
Network access: Do not allow anonymous enumeration of SAM accounts	Not defined	Enabled	Enabled
Network access: Do not allow anonymous enumeration of SAM accounts and shares	Not defined	Enabled	Enabled
Network access: Do not allow storage of credentials or .NET Passports for network authentication	Not defined	Disabled	Enabled
Network access: Let Everyone permissions apply to anonymous users	Not defined	Disabled	Disabled
Network access: Named pipes that can be accessed anonymously	Not defined	Not defined	Not defined
Network access: Remotely accessible registry paths	Not defined	Not defined	Not defined
Network access: Remotely accessible registry paths and subpaths	Not defined	Not defined	Not defined
Network access: Restrict anonymous access to named pipes and shares	Not defined	Enabled	Enabled

(continued)

Table 2.5   Security Options Settings from Security Templates *(continued)*

Security Options	Default Template DC Security.inf	Secure Template Securedc.inf	High-Security Template Hisecdc.inf
Network access: Shares that can be accessed anonymously	Not defined	Not defined	Not defined
Network access: Sharing and security model for local accounts	Not defined	Not defined	Not defined
Network security: Do not store LAN Manager hash value on next password change	Not defined	Enabled	Enabled
Network security: Force logoff when logon hours expire	Not defined	Enabled	Enabled
Network security: LAN Manager authentication level	Not defined	Send NTLMv2 response only\ refuse LM	Send NTLMv2 response only\ refuse LM and NTLM
Network security: LDAP client signing requirements	Not defined	Negotiate signing	Negotiate signing
Network security: Minimum session security for NTLM SSP based (including secure RPC) clients	Not defined	No minimum	No minimum
Network security: Minimum session security for NTLM SSP based (including secure RPC) servers	Not defined	No minimum	No minimum
Recovery console: Allow automatic administrative logon	Not defined	Disabled	Disabled
Recovery console: Allow floppy copy and access o all drives and all folders	Not defined	Disabled	Disabled
Shutdown: Allow system to be shut down without having to log on	Not defined	Disabled	Disabled

(continued)

Table 2.5 Security Options Settings from Security Templates *(continued)*			
Security Options	**Default Template DC Security.inf**	**Secure Template Securedc.inf**	**High-Security Template Hisecdc.inf**
Shutdown: Clear virtual memory pagefile	Not defined	Disabled	Enabled
System cryptography: Force strong key protection for user keys stored on the computer	Not defined	Not defined	Not defined
System cryptography: Use FIPS compliant algorithms for encryption, hashing, and signing	Not defined	Not defined	Not defined
System objects: Default owner for objects created by members of the Administrators group	Not defined	Not defined	Not defined
System objects: Require case insensitivity for non-Windows subsystems	Not defined	Enabled	Enabled
System objects: Strengthen default permissions of internal system objects (e.g. symbolic links)	Not defined	Enabled	Enabled
System settings: Optional subsystems	Not defined	Not defined	Not defined
System settings: Use Certificate Rules on Windows executables for software restriction policies	Not defined	Not defined	Not defined

Memorizing everything laid out in these tables isn't critical. What you do need to know for the exam are the subtle differences between the templates—for example, Network security: LAN Manager authentication level is set to send NTLM response only by default, send NTLMv2 response only\refuse LM under the secure template, and send NTLMv2 response only\refuse LM and NTLM under the high-security template.

You also need to know that **Hisecdc.inf** causes issues with legacy clients because of configuration settings that refuse LAN Manager (LM) and NT LAN Manager (NTLM) authentication.

> You should also be aware that configuring the default domain controller policy, which is tied to the Domain Controllers OU (or any other policies linked to that OU) affect only the domain controllers in most cases. To make changes at the domain level and affect users and domain member systems, edit the default domain policy or other policies linked to the domain.

If you have found, for example, that using the Hisecdc.inf template in your enterprise has some undesired side effects that did not show up during testing, you can reapply the default template to the domain controllers and then choose the Securedc.inf template.

To apply the Securedc.inf template, perform the following steps:

1. Click Start, Run, type MMC, and click the OK button.

2. From within the MMC, choose File, Add/Remove Snap-in from the menu.

3. Click the Add button.

4. Click Security Configuration and Analysis, click the Add button, and click the Close button.

5. Click OK on the Add/Remove Snap-in dialog box.

6. In the left pane of the MMC, right-click Security Configuration and Analysis, choose Import Template.

7. In the Import Template From dialog box, browse to WINDOWS\security\templates, select the DC Security.inf template (see Figure 2.3), and click OK. (You also need to make sure you select the Clear this database before importing check box.)

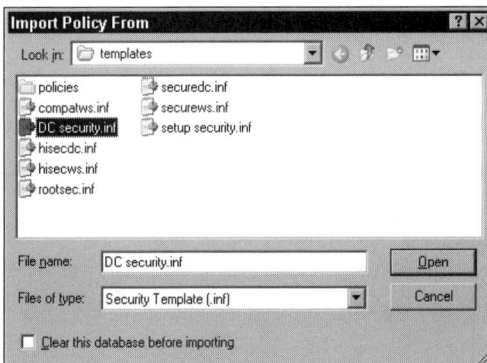

Figure 2.3 Applying the *DC Security.inf* template in the Import Template From dialog box.

Using Security Templates

In Window 2000, all basic templates are what can be applied to a system to reconfigure it to a baseline security configuration. They are also used on Windows NT 4 workstation (**Basicwk.inf**) and Windows NT Server 4 (**Basicsv.inf**) upgrades to bring the systems up to Windows 2000 security baselines.

When any Windows NT system is upgraded in place (not wiped clean), it retains all its previous and weaker security settings.

Clean installations (and Windows 9x upgrades to Windows 2000 Professional and XP Professional) run using the **Defltsv.inf** or **Defltwk.inf** templates as appropriate. If you want to reset security to baseline after installation, you cannot use the **Defltxx.inf** templates because they are not available. The **Basicxx.inf** templates should be used instead.

In Windows Server 2003, these templates have been replaced with the **DC Security.inf** template for domain controllers and the **Setup Security.inf** template for standard systems.

After you have opened the template, right-click Security Configuration and Analysis, and then click Configure Computer Now to configure the system with the default settings. (You can also choose Analyze Computer Now to simply review the difference between the current system configuration and the one the template would provide.)

When you choose Configure Computer Now, you need to use the specified default log file path, or choose a new one and click OK to continue. To specify a different log file path, type a valid path and filename in the Error Log File Path text box, and click OK.

When the configuration is done, you can view the changes that were made by right-clicking Security Configuration and Analysis, and then clicking View Log File.

The following code is a small sampling of the log; the full log is somewhat larger.

```
Log file: C:\Documents and Settings\Jasonz\
➥My Documents\Security\Logs\DC History.log
-------------------------------------------
Saturday, March 15, 2003 12:54:18 PM
----Configuration engine was initialized successfully.----
----Reading Configuration Template info...

----Configure User Rights...
User Rights configuration was completed successfully.

----Configure Group Membership...
Group Membership configuration was completed successfully.

----Configure Registry Keys...
Configure users\.default.
```

```
Configure users\.default\software\microsoft\netdde.
Configure machine\software.
```

Remote Access/VPN Server Role

Routing and Remote Access Service (RRAS) in Windows Server 2003 is installed by default when the operating system is installed, but it is not configured or enabled.

When you configure your server in the remote access/VPN server role, you can give remote users the proper access permission to access resources on the local area network (LAN) over a dial-up or DSL/cable connection.

When you run the Configure Your Server Wizard to set up your server as a remote access/VPN server, it starts the Routing and Remote Access Server Setup Wizard (see Figure 2.4).

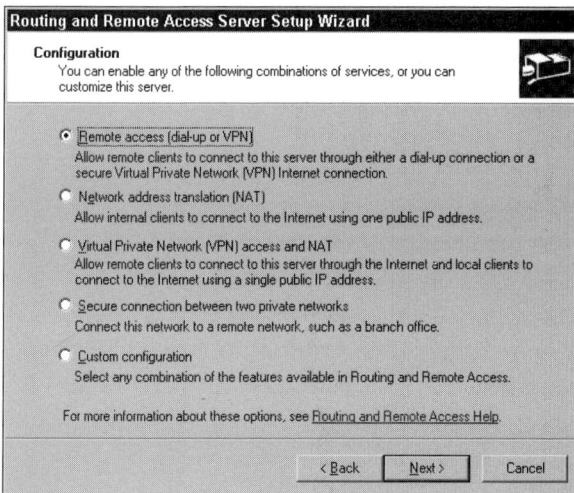

Figure 2.4   You can choose the types of connections to establish via the Configuration page of the Routing and Remote Access Server Setup Wizard.

NOTE   Chapter 4, "Planning, Implementing, and Maintaining Routing and Remote Access," covers this server role in depth.

File Server Role

The file server role for a Windows Server 2003 implementation is as simple as it sounds: a server role designed to enable administrators to set up a location for data to be stored and shared in the enterprise.

You use the Configure Your Server Wizard to step through the entire process and configure settings for disk quotas and the Indexing Service. You can also set up the shares themselves and permissions.

The File Server Disk Quotas page is where you enable disk quotas by selecting the Set up default disk quotas for new users of this server check box (see Figure 2.5).

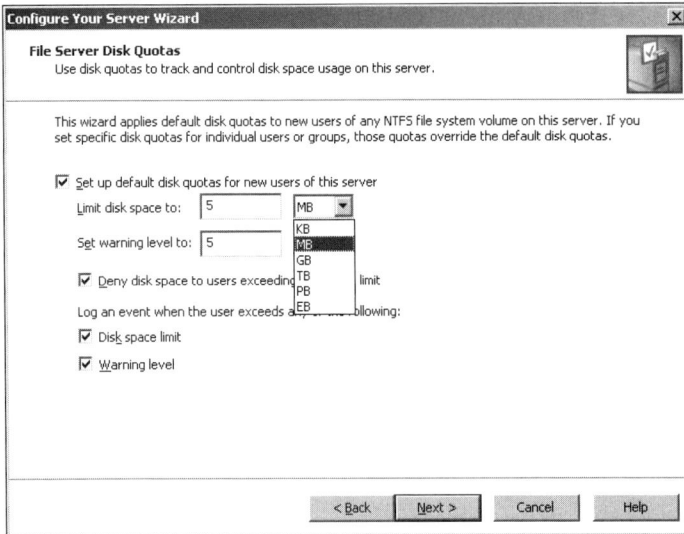

Figure 2.5 You can limit disk usage through the File Server Disk Quotas page.

After you enable quotas, you can limit the total space to any number of kilobytes, megabytes, gigabytes, terabytes, petabytes, and, finally, exabytes.

Measuring Space

As a point of reference, here's a breakdown of those disk space settings:

➤ A byte is a unit of data that is eight binary digits long; the digits, zeros and ones, make up the data.

➤ A kilobyte (KB) is 1,000 bytes (actually, 1,024 bytes).

➤ A megabyte (MB), the next available setting, is 1,000KB (or a million bytes, if you prefer), which is 1,048,576 bytes in true decimal notation.

➤ A gigabyte (GB), the next configurable parameter, is 1,000MB, or 2 to the 30th power, or 1,073,741,824 in decimal size, whichever you prefer.

➤ A terabyte (TB), the next setting, is computed as 2 to the 40th power or approximately 1,000GB. You might think this setting and the next couple of settings are somewhat outrageous, but when you consider that four of the largest IDE hard drives on the market today (which are 250GB) together make about 1TB and could all be placed inside a single end user system, it doesn't seem as off the wall as it did a year or so ago.

➤ A petabye (PB) is 2 to the 50th power bytes, the equivalent of approximately 1,000TB.

➤ An exabyte (EB) is currently the largest unit of measure for computer data storage. It equates to 2 to the 60th power bytes, which is 1,152,921,504,606,846,976 bytes in decimal size or, more simply, one billion gigabytes.

In NTFS, volumes larger than 2TB are possible, and the theoretical maximum limit is 16EB (18,446,744,073,709,551,616 bytes).

You can also set up a warning threshold numerically or by parameter (KB, MB, GB, and so on) so that a warning is sent when users approach their limits. For instance, if a user has a 100MB disk-writing limit, a warning could be set at 80MB.

To enforce the setting, you need to select the Deny disk space to users exceeding disk space limit check box. If you do not select this check box, users can continue writing to the disk.

Two other settings can be enabled on this page: the Disk space limit check box and the Warning level check box. Use these settings to configure the system logs to record each occurrence of these events.

NOTE

The total amount of disk space available to a user is calculated from actual file size before any type of compression. When a 100MB file is compressed down to 80MB, Windows counts the file's original 100MB toward the quota limit, for example.

Administrator level accounts are not limited to disk space limitations set in this manner. Regardless of the settings, they are not denied write access.

After you have configured any disk space limits (you can also opt to not choose any), you arrive at the File Server Indexing Service page (see Figure 2.6). Usually, leaving this setting disabled on a server is recommended because it affects performance; if only limited searches will be performed, leaving this option disabled makes sense. If the server can handle the load or there will be enough searches against the existing data, you can enable this option.

After you review the summary page of the options you have set and continue the role configuration process, the Share a Folder Wizard is displayed, where you can create new shares and paths to the shares (see Figure 2.7). You can also perform this action the "standard" way through Windows Explorer by right-clicking the folder you want to share and choosing Properties, and then electing to share the folder in the Sharing tab. In the next page (see Figure 2.8), you can supply a description for the share and configure offline settings for data in the share (whether the files should be made available when not connected to the network).

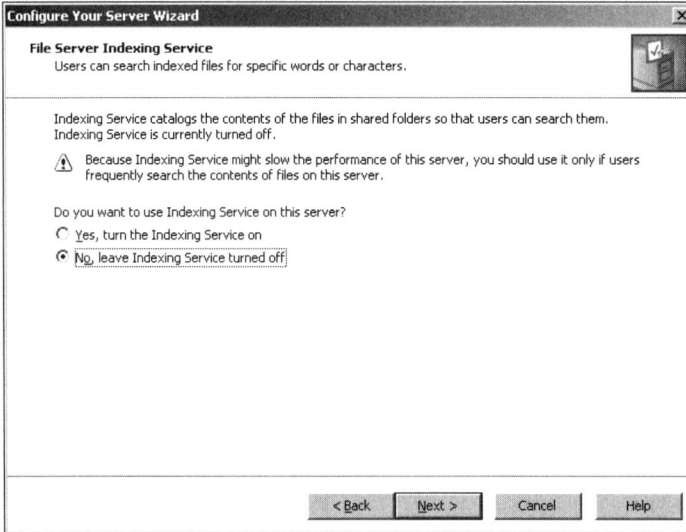

Figure 2.6 The File Server Indexing Service page is where you configure the Indexing Service.

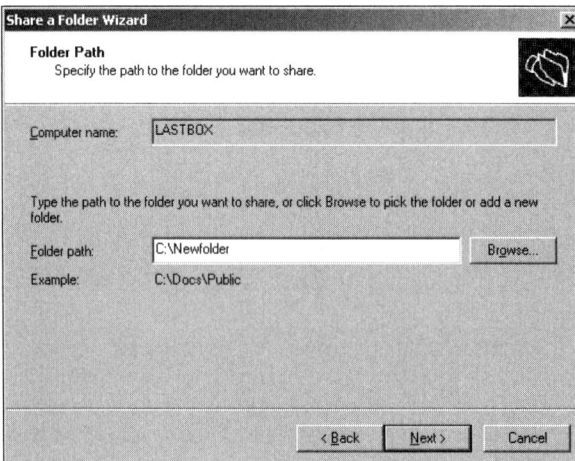

Figure 2.7 You can configure shares through the Folder Path page of the Share a Folder Wizard.

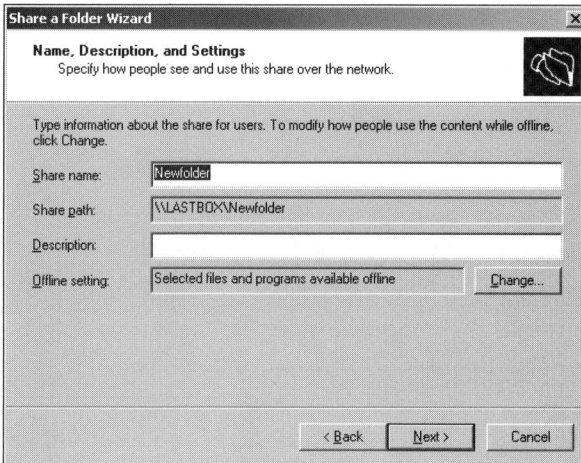

Figure 2.8   You can supply additional information about a share in the Name, Description, and Settings page of the Share a Folder Wizard.

Next is the Permissions page, where you set up permissions for a share. There are a few preconfigured settings (all users have Read access, Administrators have Full Control, and so on), and there is the option to configure your own access control. The initial setting is for share access, but you can customize the setting and set security permissions through NTFS. The final page is the summary page, which shows you that the share was successful and enables you to complete this process or run the wizard again to create another share (see Figure 2.9).

Figure 2.9   The Sharing was Successful page provides a summary about the newly created share.

NOTE

Regardless of whether you use the Configure Your Server Wizard, you set the server into a file server role as soon as you right-click on any share in Windows Explorer and choose to share a folder in the Sharing tab of the Properties dialog box.

Also, regardless of how the server got into the role of file server, when you use the Configure Your Server Wizard to remove the role, all shares on the server are removed by default, regardless of whether they were created via the wizard, manually, or a combination of both methods (see Figure 2.10).

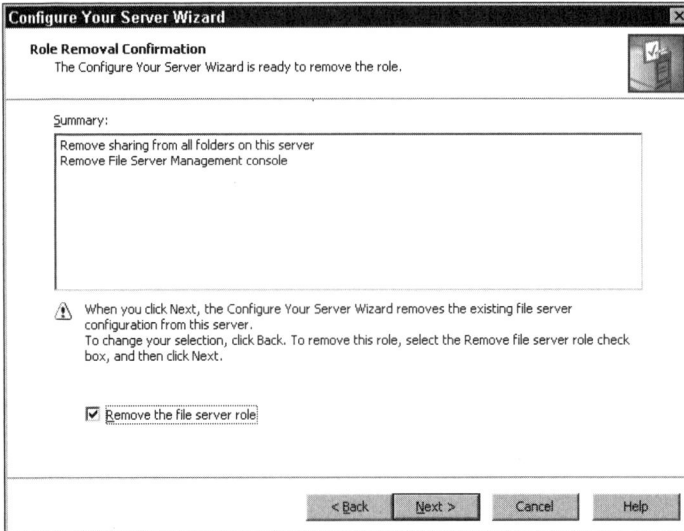

Configure Your Server Wizard ☒

Role Removal Confirmation
The Configure Your Server Wizard is ready to remove the role.

Summary:

Remove sharing from all folders on this server
Remove File Server Management console

⚠ When you click Next, the Configure Your Server Wizard removes the existing file server configuration from this server.
To change your selection, click Back. To remove this role, select the Remove file server role check box, and then click Next.

☑ Remove the file server role

< Back   Next >   Cancel   Help

Figure 2.10   All shares on the system are removed via the Role Removal Confirmation page.

Internet Information Services 6 Role

Unlike Windows 2000, which installs Internet Information Services (IIS) 5 by default, IIS 6 is not deployed on standard versions of Windows Server 2003 unless you explicitly choose to install it. You can install IIS 6 by using the Configure Your Server Wizard as outlined previously or by going to the Control Panel, choosing Add or Remove Programs, and choosing Add/Remove Windows Components.

If you use the Configure Your Server Wizard to enable the server's role as an application server, the wizard installs IIS 6. A quick look shows that only the World Wide Web service is installed. File Transfer Protocol (FTP), Network News Transfer Protocol (NNTP), and Simple Mail Transfer Protocol (SMTP) are not added by default when you establish the server role in this way.

If you want to add those other services, you must go to Add or Remove Programs and choose Add/Remove Windows Components. In the Windows Components dialog box, highlight Application Server, and click Details to choose Internet Information Services. Then highlight Internet Information Services and click Details to select just the services you want to install.

> **NOTE**
>
> You could perform your entire IIS installation (or any other Windows component, for that matter) using the Add or Remove Programs method if you want. Also, if you simply want to install everything associated with IIS, you could select the check box next to the name instead of drilling lower into the list by clicking Details.
>
> Installing only the services you need, and nothing else, is recommended. In most cases, even if you think you might need a service later, you should usually wait until you actually need a service to install it.

Under Windows 2000 Server, default security templates for Web servers as well as secure and high-security templates were deployed on IIS systems through the Group Policy linked to an OU where the accounts for IIS servers were found.

This deployment method is no longer applicable under Windows Server 2003. When you install IIS, it runs with almost everything disabled and almost fully locked down. At the end of the installation, about the only thing you can do with the server is have it respond to client requests and serve up static (HTML) content. Therefore, no other content, such as Active Server Pages (ASP), ASP.NET pages, WebDAV publishing, and FrontPage Server Extensions, can be hosted from the server until you explicitly enable it.

In fact, a new group policy setting, Prevent IIS from Installing, enables Domain and Enterprise Administrators to control which Windows Server 2003 systems are allowed to install IIS 6.

> **ALERT**
>
> For most Microsoft exams, you need to know other configuration tasks for IIS servers, such as configuring Internet Connection Firewall and setting proper access permissions for files and folders on the IIS server.
>
> This information is explained in more detail in the "Securing Servers: Standards and Best Practices" section of this chapter because these two specific actions are best practices across the board, not just when configuring an application server role.

Print Server Role

You can use the Configure Your Server Wizard to enable your server as a print server. After you select the print server role, the wizard displays the Printers and Printer Drivers page (see Figure 2.11), where you select which network clients should have printers installed. You can choose one of two options: Windows 2000 and Windows XP Clients Only or All Windows Clients.

Figure 2.11 The Printers and Printer Drivers page is where you can select how to handle printer drivers for network clients.

At this point, the Add Printer Wizard starts, and you step through the prompts of choosing a local printer or a network printer. You can specify the local printer yourself or let Plug and Play find it. You then have the option of choosing one of the local ports already available on the system or creating a new one (see Figure 2.12).

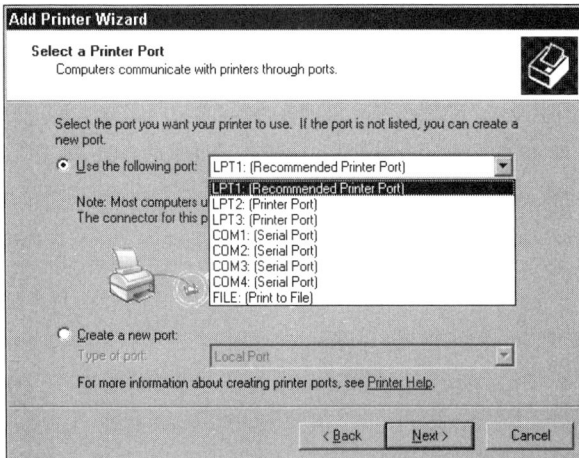

Figure 2.12 Use the Select a Printer Port page to specify a port for the printer or create a new one.

You then choose the make and model of the printer attached to the port you selected earlier. On Windows Server 2003 configurations, all printers added with the Add Printer Wizard are shared by default. If for some reason you do not want to share the printer, you must manually deselect this default option. If the server is a member of a domain, the printer is also published in Active Directory by default.

Configuring Printers

If you install printers by using the Add Printer Wizard and then use the Configure Your Server Wizard to remove the print server role, you will remove all the created printers on the server.

Also, note the terminology used for printers. A *printer* is the software driver for the print device connected to the system on a local port or over the network. There is a great deal of confusion on these terms because it is so common to say "I'm going to get my documents that I just printed on the 5SI laser printer." The technical term for this piece of hardware is *print device*.

Here is one way to remember these terms: The *print device* is the piece of hardware that physically prints on the paper. The term *printer* refers to the printer driver software, which allows the print job to be properly formatted for the print device that outputs the data to paper. You can also think of a printer as an icon in the Printers and Faxes Control Panel window.

Mail Server Role

When you run the Configure Your Server Wizard to set up your server in the mail server role, you can choose how your users are authenticated to the POP3 service: through the accounts that are local to the server, through Active Directory, or via an encrypted password file (see Figure 2.13).

This setting enables users to connect to the server and download email to their local systems by using Outlook, Outlook Express, or any other email client that supports POP3. After making your selection, the POP3 and SMTP services are installed on the local system.

After the process is completed, the Internet Information Services (IIS) Manager appears on the Administrative Tools menu. The IIS Manager enables administrators to configure the SMTP service that the Configure Your Server Wizard installed.

NOTE

The other IIS 6 components are not installed unless the server was already set up as an application server.

If you have previously run the Configure Your Server Wizard to install the server as an application server, the wizard would have enabled only the World Wide Web publishing service. SMTP, FTP, and NNTP are not added by default.

However, if you run the Configure Your Server Wizard to install the mail server role, you'll see that both POP3 and SMTP services are installed and enabled at completion of the installation.

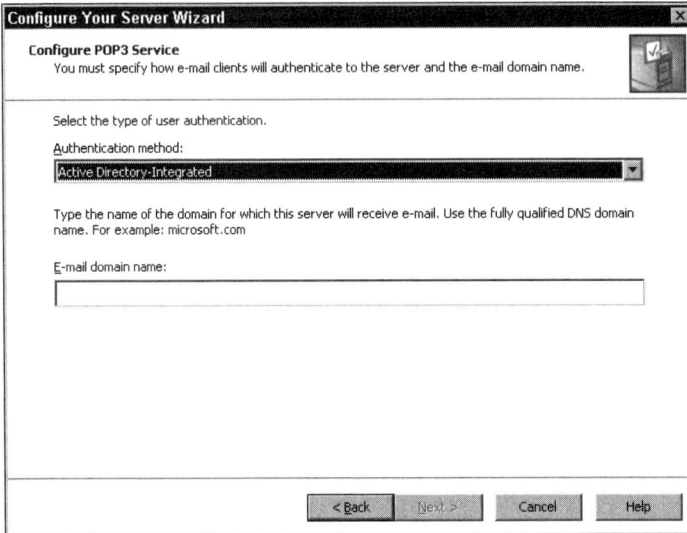

Figure 2.13 You configure how users are authenticated for mail service via the Configure POP3 Service page.

Configuring the SMTP service for this use is no different than any other SMTP configuration in Exchange Server 5.x, 2000, and 2003 or within IIS 4 and 5. Configuring the POP3 service is done through the POP3 Service MMC or through the command line by using WINPOP.

The usable WINPOP commands are as follows:

```
WINPOP.EXE <cmd> [<parameters>]
ADD, CHANGEPWD, CREATEQUOTAFILE, DEL ¦ DELETE, GET,
➥LIST, LOCK, MIGRATETOAD, SET, STAT, UNLOCK
Options:ADD <domainname> ¦ <user@domainname [/CREATEUSER <password>]>
CHANGEPWD <user@domainname> <new password>
CREATEQUOTAFILE <user@domainname> [/USER:user]
Note: Quota files are created by default when adding mailboxes
➥ (for SAM and AD authentication)
/USER: To specify a different user account the quota file will reference.
DEL ¦ DELETE <domainname> ¦ <user@domainname [/DELETEUSER]>
GET <property>
LIST [domainname]
LOCK <domainname ¦ user@domainname>
MIGRATETOAD <user@domainname>
SET <property> <value>
STAT [domainname]
UNLOCK <domainname ¦ user@domainname>
```

The POP3 Service MMC also enables you to perform all these actions through a graphical user interface (GUI). You can complete tasks such as setting the authentication method, configuring the POP3 mail store, and setting the mail server to require Secure Password Authentication in whatever way you're most comfortable working. You can also set the POP3 service state, the number of sockets, and the number of threads the service uses.

> You don't need to delve deeply into the POP3 Service from a server role perspective for the exam. You mainly need to know how it is installed, which is through the Configure Your Server Wizard or through Control Panel, Add or Remove Programs, Add/Remove Windows Components, Email Services. You also need to familiarize yourself with how to configure the services, whether you use **WINPOP** from the command line or the POP3 Service MMC.

Terminal Server Role

Like many of the other roles described so far, the terminal server role can be set up by running the Configure Your Server Wizard or through Control Panel, Add or Remove Programs, Add/Remove Windows Components, Terminal Server.

Note that when you install Terminal Services by running the Configure Your Server Wizard, you see a warning that the system will be rebooted as part of the installation process. There is no option to cancel the reboot until later; it occurs as part of the process. No forewarning is given about a reboot when you install the role through Control Panel; however, you are given the option to reboot later through a dialog box.

The installation process has changed since Windows 2000 Server, most noticeably in the capability to configure security modes for operating the terminal server and the lack of an option to install Terminal Services in Application or Remote Administration mode.

Remote Desktop for Administration is now used in place of the Terminal Services in Remote Administration mode. This new feature allows server administration from most systems on your network. No licenses are required, and up to two simultaneous remote connections are allowed in addition to someone logged in at the local console.

To enable Remote Desktop on a system, go to the Remote tab of the System Properties dialog box and select the Allow Users to Connect Remotely to This Computer check box (see Figure 2.14).

Running in the terminal server role, your server can operate in two security modes:

> ➤ *Full Security mode*—This mode is the default deployment of Terminal Services in Windows 2000 Server and Windows Server 2003. This configuration mode forces all applications that need to be installed and run by Terminal Services users to be written to run in the security context of

an ordinary user. Applications written so that a higher level of system permission is required do not operate properly (or at all). If they are necessary in the enterprise, require the system to be set up in Relaxed Security mode.

➤ *Relaxed Security mode*—This mode enables you to run programs that otherwise might not work under the higher settings of Full Security mode. Relaxed Security mode is also known as Windows NT 4.0/Terminal Server Edition permissions compatibility mode and runs in much the same manner; any user with a session can change certain files and some Registry settings because of the less rigorous security settings.

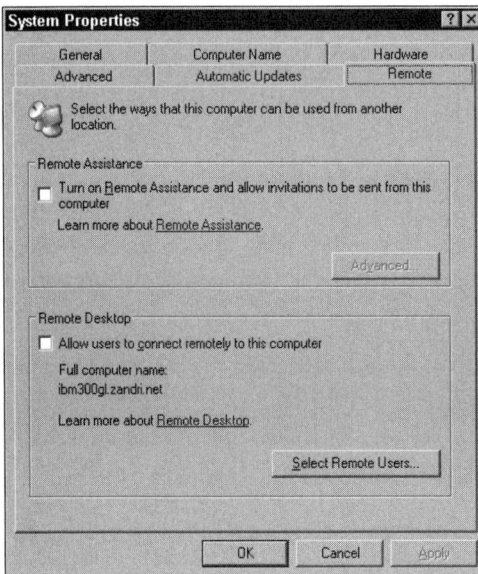

Figure 2.14   You can enable Remote Desktop on your Windows Server 2003 system via the Remote tab of the System Properties dialog box.

After the terminal server role has been established on the server, you need to configure two additional items: Internet Explorer Enhanced Security Configuration settings and configuring the Terminal Server License Server.

When you enable Internet Explorer Enhanced Security Configuration, users who log on as an administrator have high security settings configured for the Internet and local intranet security zones to disable scripts from running. The Microsoft Virtual Machine (VM) and Microsoft ActiveX controls are disabled. Users are also prevented from downloading files in these zones.

Medium security settings are configured for the trusted sites zone only, which effectively means that trusted sites, by default, are the only ones that allow Internet Explorer to completely render Web sites as they are actually designed. Although static HTML pages are usually not affected in the Internet and local intranet zones, pages designed with Microsoft VM and ActiveX controls are not displayed or don't function correctly.

The Terminal Server License Server must also be configured so that it continues to function normally after installation. When a server is set up in the terminal server role on a Windows Server 2003 system, it runs for only 120 days from the date of the first client logon without the license server in place. After that time, the system stops accepting connections from unlicensed clients.

The Terminal Server Licensing Service is installed via Control Panel, Add or Remove Programs, Add/Remove Windows Components, Terminal Server Licensing and can be enabled at the enterprise level, domain level, or workgroup level. After the service is installed, you can activate the Terminal Server License Server in the Terminal Server Licensing MMC. Right-click the Terminal Server License Server you want to activate, and choose Activate Server to start the Terminal Server License Server Activation Wizard. In the Connection Method page, click the Automatic Connection to Connect over the Internet link after providing the required information for your company.

After completing this process, you need to install the client access licenses (CALs) on the Terminal Server License Server for your clients to use when they connect to the terminal server. When a client makes a first-time connection to a terminal server, the server locates a Terminal Server License Server to issue a new CAL to the client.

DNS Server Role

You can set up the DNS server role by running the Configure Your Server Wizard or through Control Panel, Add or Remove Programs, Add/Remove Windows Components, Networking Services, Domain Name System (DNS). (To install DNS only, click the Networking Services option in the Components list, and click the Details button.)

Configuring IP Addresses

Before you begin installation, make sure the server on which you are configuring the service has been given a static IP address. Also, if the server, the DNS zone, or any systems joined to the domain this server is going to manage are going to be directly connected to the Internet, make sure the DNS name you are using is properly registered and can be resolved by DNS root servers.

It's one thing to set up a test lab or a very small environment by using **myhome.local** because your servers resolve names to the corresponding IP addresses. However, this name cannot be resolved by Internet DNS servers, and there is no way to handle the resolution outside your environment.

Also, if you decide to arbitrarily use a DNS name and then someone else registers the name later, you are forced to reconfigure your entire network so that it's not exposed directly to the Internet, or you need to rename the domains and forest to correct the problem. Planning and doing it right the first time go a long way toward saving you from future headaches.

If you opt to use the Configure Your Server Wizard, navigate to the Add or Remove Role prompt in the Manage Your Server window and then click DNS Server, which installs DNS and runs the Configure a DNS Server Wizard (see Figure 2.15).

Figure 2.15   You can install DNS via the Configure a DNS Server Wizard.

In the wizard's Configuration Action page, you can create a forward lookup zone only, a forward and reverse lookup zone, or root hints only.

NOTE   You can create lookup zone or root hints manually after the DNS service is installed by using the DNS MMC.

In the Primary Server Location page, you have the option to choose where the DNS and SRV records for your zone are maintained. You can choose the server you are configuring, which enables you to set up a primary forward lookup zone. You can also choose a secondary forward lookup zone, which is set up if another DNS server is authoritative for the zone, and the copy to be installed on this server should be a read-only copy.

Next, in the Zone name page, enter the name of the DNS zone you are enabling on this server, such as `cert.zandri.net` or `gunderville.com`.

The next page is the Zone File page, where you set the path of the standard primary or standard secondary DNS zone file. (The type depends on the answer you provided in the Primary Server Location page.)

In the Dynamic Update page (see Figure 2.16), notice that the default selection is Do not allow dynamic updates, as this is the most secure option when zones are set up as standard primary zones. (A standard secondary zone is a read-only copy and can't be edited directly.)

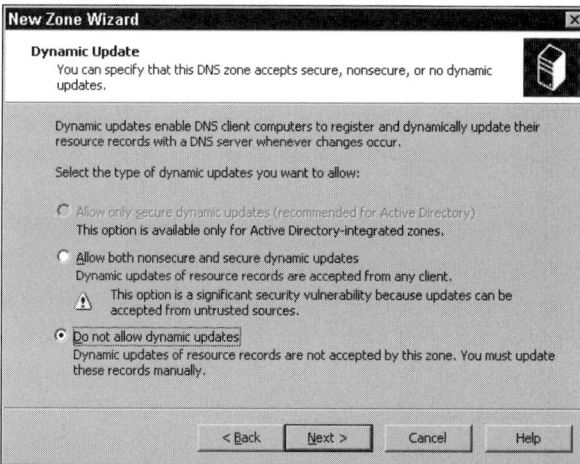

Figure 2.16   You can specify which type of updates to allow for your DNS zone via the Dynamic Update page.

In the Forwarders page, you can enter IP addresses to specify whether your DNS server should forward lookup queries to DNS servers outside your location to another DNS server in your enterprise, or whether it should forward lookup queries to an ISP-owned DNS server.

In the next page, Completing the Configure a DNS Server Wizard, you can click Back to change any of the settings or click the Finish button to complete the installation of the service as configured.

The Configure Your Server Wizard then displays the This Server Is Now a DNS Server page. If needed, you can review the installation logs at `systemroot\Debug\Configure Your Server.log`.

Under security information for DNS in "Need to Know More?" at the end of this chapter, the link supplied there takes you to a page listing a few of the typical threats your DNS infrastructure might be susceptible to, including denial-of-service (DoS) attacks, data modification, and DNS redirection. Proper setup and configuration of your DNS server provide some defense against these attacks; the rest is up to the defenses and firewalls enabled on your network.

> **NOTE** For more information on additional security against attacks for DNS servers and systems in general, see the "Securing Servers: Standards and Best Practices" section of this chapter.

DHCP Server Role

You can set up the DHCP server role by running the Configure Your Server Wizard or through Control Panel, Add or Remove Programs, Add/Remove Windows Components, Networking Services, Dynamic Host Configuration Protocol (DHCP). To install only DHCP, highlight Networking Services in the Components list, and click the Details button.

In the Manage Your Server window, click Add or Remove a Role, select DHCP Server, and then click Next. The Configure Your Server Wizard installs the DHCP service and starts the New Scope Wizard to configure a new IP address scope for your DHCP server.

In the Scope Name page, enter a name for the scope. In the Description text box, you can optionally enter a descriptive entry for the scope.

Next is the IP Address Range page, where you define the IP address range this particular scope will hand out to clients. To do this, type the IP address for the start of the range and the IP address for the end of the range. The wizard uses the IP address class denominator that you enter to determine the correct subnet mask in the Subnet Mask section. For example, the wizard knows that 131.15.0.1 is the start of the Class B range of addresses and sets the default subnet mask to 255.255.0.0. You can, if necessary, change the default address to another address in use in your environment.

NOTE Chapter 3, "Planning, Implementing, and Maintaining a Network Infrastructure," covers many of the TCP/IP addressing aspects that apply to DHCP configuration and IP addressing in general.

Excluding certain IP addresses in the Add Exclusions page configures the DHCP server to not lease these addresses to client systems. If the range of addresses in this scope is 199.168.1.5 through 199.168.1.254, and you want to exclude the 199.168.1.15 address (which belongs to a server with this address as a static entry, for example), enter the single address as an exclusion. If a range from this scope is dedicated as manually entered IP addresses for 10 printers on the floor where this scope is active, for example, enter the entire range as an exclusion, such as 199.168.1.21 through 199.168.1.30.

NOTE Another way of doing excluding IP addresses is to exclude the known range from the scope at the start. Then there is no reason to have entries in the Add Exclusions page.

If you know that you need to set up the scope for the 199.168.1.x address range and need 15 static IP addresses for servers and printers, you could always craft the valid range for the scope as 199.168.1.16 through 192.168.1.254. Then addresses 199.168.1.2 through 199.168.1.15 could be used for static systems, and you would have no entries in the Add Exclusions page.

After you have entered any exclusions necessary for this scope, you arrive at the Lease Duration page, where you can define the length of time (in days, hours, and minutes) a client can use an IP address from this scope.

The DHCP server leases IP addresses to its clients. Each lease has an expiration date and time; the default duration is eight days. The client must renew the lease if it will continue to use that IP address. Defining the lease's duration eases client administration, but this step is optional. If you leave all fields of the Lease Duration page blank and click Next, clients can still obtain IP addresses from the DHCP server.

In the Configure DHCP Options page, you can specify whether to configure additional DHCP options at this time. (If you decide not to, you can always return to the scope later and make these changes.) Using the default setting, Yes, is best, as one of the settings is the IP address of the router (default gateway), which allows clients that obtain a lease to have a default path out of their local subnet.

In the Configure DHCP Options section of the Domain Name and DNS Server page, you can assign DHCP clients the IP addresses of the preferred DNS servers they should use. You can also configure IP addresses of preferred NetBIOS name servers (WINS) for clients in the following page. Activating this newly created scope is the final step of setting up a DHCP server role.

Additional Notes on DHCP

After you set a subnet mask range for a DHCP scope, there is no going back to change it. The only way to change it is to delete the entire scope and re-create it with the correct subnet mask.

Windows Server 2003 requires that any Windows-based DHCP server running Windows 2000 or later be authorized to run on the network, the same as in Windows 2000 Server.

Nothing prevents Windows NT 4 DHCP services, other network operating systems hosting the DHCP service, or hardware devices running the DHCP service from responding to client requests.

Domain controllers handle the Active Directory database, and all domain members configured in the role of a DHCP server running Windows 2000 Server or Windows Server 2003 must be domain controllers or authorized to function in the Active Directory database.

Standalone Windows servers (non-domain members) can be configured as DHCP servers as long as they are not on a subnet with any authorized DHCP servers from a domain. Windows Server 2003 systems can run the DHCP service as standalone systems in a domain where Active Directory is not used, such as an NT 4 domain. For what it's worth, the Windows Server 2003 system could even be a member of this NT 4 domain and be allowed to offer IP addresses. This is one example of an exception to the Active Directory authorization requirement.

When a standalone DHCP server detects an authorized DHCP server, that Windows-based workgroup's DHCP server automatically stops leasing IP addresses to requesting DHCP clients.

When the DHCP service starts on a server that holds the DHCP server role, it sends out a **DHCPINFORM** broadcast message in an attempt to locate other DHCP servers. The other DHCP servers reply with a **DHCPACK** message and send the domain information to the starting DHCP server. The starting DHCP server then attempts to locate the SRV records for Active Directory in an effort to find the DHCP server's list of IP addresses that have been authorized in the domain as DHCP servers.

If the server finds its IP address in the authorized list, it finishes starting the service and responds to client requests. If it does not find its address in the authorized list, it does not start the DHCP service. The server is still online and active, but because the service does not complete the startup, it does not respond to client requests for IP addresses.

If Active Directory is not available, as with a standalone server in a workgroup, the initializing DHCP server can start if no other DHCP servers are running on the local subnet. If one is encountered, the standalone server stops its DHCP service; otherwise, it handles client requests.

The DHCP server continues to send the DHCPINFORM message every five minutes to check whether it is still authorized to function in the enterprise. If an administrator has not authorized the DHCP server, the server finds out at one of the five-minute intervals and stops its DHCP service, which prevents it from responding to client requests.

WINS Server Role

You can set up the Windows Internet Naming Service (WINS) server role by running the Configure Your Server Wizard or through Control Panel, Add or Remove Programs, Add/Remove Windows Components, Networking Services, Windows Internet Naming Service (WINS). To install only WINS, highlight Networking Services in the Components list, and click the Details button.

Of all the server roles discussed in this chapter, this one is the easiest to configure with the Configure Your Server Wizard. In the Manage Your Server window, click Add or Remove Role, and then choose WINS Server, which installs WINS. After this process is completed on the server end, the WINS server will be running on your network.

The setup wizard uses several default configuration parameters for how NetBIOS name records are managed in the WINS server database; these parameters are fine for most environments.

Removing the role is just as easy: Simply run the Configure Your Server Wizard a second time and choose WINS to remove the role.

> **NOTE**
>
> Originally, it was hoped during Windows 2000 builds that reliance on WINS would fade and the service could finally be retired. This was not the case and still isn't today, even as Windows Server 2003 hits the shelves. Because of legacy systems and backward-compatibility requirements for older software. NetBIOS name resolution and WINS services are still needed in many enterprises.

Securing Servers: Standards and Best Practices

When it comes to securing enterprise domain controllers and member servers in the enterprise, there are several considerations. Physical security plays a large role. The doors to the server room (or whatever room is being used to house the server) should be locked at all times by some means. Whether it's by key, smart card, or combination lock, the door should be locked and access to the room should be limited to those who need it. If someone needs access who does not normally have it, you can issue a temporary badge to the room or have someone with access to the room escort the person in and stay there until he or she leaves the room. When servers are installed in server racks in rooms with doors that close and lock, keeping them locked should be a standard practice, with the keys left in the charge of the responsible person.

Notes from the Field: Can You Be Too Secure?

In a nutshell, no. Many times I have been accused of being overzealous about mentioning security in the IT environment, but whenever possible, I try to bring the topic into the real world so that others see it the way I do.

"Lock server cabinets and the server room doors—isn't that overkill? It takes some extra time to relock things, especially server cabinet doors; it's just easier to leave them unlocked when the outer door to the room itself locks."

I respond by asking people if they have a garage for their cars or use a steering wheel lock, such as The Club, to secure their cars. They usually answer yes. When they do, I ask the following questions:

"Isn't locking your car doors inside your locked garage at home overkill? Doesn't putting The Club on your steering wheel take a little extra time? Why do it? The car doors are locked."

"It often deters someone who is considering the action" is the typical reply. I usually don't talk right away after this reply because my point often sinks in without any further effort from me.

One word of caution about locking up server cabinet doors: Make sure the doors have proper vents (that is, slotted doors), and make sure the servers are not susceptible to overheating. Just because the room is 68 degrees with a relative humidity of 50% doesn't mean that servers #5 and #6 in rack 12 are operating at that temperature.

Remember: With the doors closed, servers stacked in the rack with four to six drives spinning at 10,000RPM to 15,000RPM inside each system, and dual redundant power supplies engaged, the servers are throwing off quite a bit of heat. The systems in the center are insulated to a degree, but you often find that the center and upper systems catch all the rising heat, especially in an enclosed rack.

When it comes to securing domain controllers, ask why someone needs to log on locally at the console. This question is valid for many member servers as well. There should be a valid business reason (and proper change control) for working locally on a domain controller or any server system when most work can be done remotely with remote tools.

This brings me to my next point—limiting administrative access. Very few people should have Domain Administrator access, and even fewer should have Enterprise administrator permissions. Domain Administrator access should be limited to a select few people who need that level of access control over the domain. These users should also be trained and instructed (if they are not fully aware already) on the use of these domainwide unrestricted accounts.

They should not log in with administrative access to perform day-to-day work on their desktop systems and on servers except when necessary. More often than not, logging in on a daily basis with a standard user account (or perhaps a power user or server operator account) is usually good enough.

When additional rights are necessary, administrators can always run the Run As service to be authenticated to the services they need to access with their administrator account.

Power users on local systems can, by default, install programs that do not modify operating system files or install system services. They can also create and manage local user accounts and groups, stop and start system services, and modify resources on systems through the Control Panel.

Server operators can log on interactively to domain controllers and create and delete shared resources. They also have permissions to start and stop some domainwide services, back up and restore data, format disk drives, and shut down the system.

The RUNAS command enables you to run EXE and MMC programs as another user. In this way, you can run the program at a higher level of privilege than your current settings allow. The Run As service requires the Secondary Logon service to be running on the local system. To start the Run As service for Control Panel programs, you still need to hold the Shift key down, right-click the shortcut you want to run, and choose Run As. For other Start menu icons and actual EXEs from within Windows Explorer, you just need to right-click them to get RUNAS to appear on the shortcut menu. You can also issue the command from the Run dialog box or at a command prompt.

When providing Domain Administrator access, users should be given their own accounts so that if necessary, administrative actions can be traced back to the specific user. If everyone used the default Administrator account, there would be no way to know who performed a certain action because it could have been anyone with that account access. Best practices dictate that the default Administrator account should be renamed; use a complex password and limit access to that password for emergencies only.

Enterprise Administrator accounts should be handed out even more sparingly because they have Full Control permissions over all domains in the enterprise. They too should be assigned to just those users who need this level of access and protected even more rigorously.

Many white papers and KnowledgeBase articles state that Windows Server 2003 is "secure out of the box." I would counter that it is "more secure out of the box" because the only system that's truly secure is one that is "never taken out of the box." There have been great strides to make Windows Server 2003 as secure out of the box as possible. These efforts have brought the server operating system light years ahead of Windows NT Server 4 and Windows 2000 Server.

On the one hand, over half of the system services installed by default under the basic Windows Server 2003 installation are not enabled for automatic startup (instead, they're set to Manual) or are outright disabled. Most network services are not enabled until an administrator explicitly does so. With all these advances in default settings, it is still up to system administrators to have (or get) the required level of training and acquire the necessary level of knowledge to keep systems secure.

As mentioned earlier, there are a few steps you can take to limit system controls. In addition to limiting services on systems to only those who need them, you can, for example, take steps to allow only necessary traffic on your networks.

From an external to internal perspective, there is no need to allow certain port traffic through your firewall at the network's perimeter if this type of access is not necessary. You might use FTP (port 20 and 21) to push data from one segregated subnet to another on the WAN, but if you never cross the firewall to the public network (in or out), there is no need to have that port open full time. If organizational needs required opening this port, however, you could enable change controls to make the necessary configuration changes and then close the ports when they're no longer needed. Table 2.6 explains some of the more commonly used default Transmission Control Protocol (TCP) ports.

Table 2.6 Commonly Used TCP Ports	
Port Number	**Use**
7	ECHO
18	Message Send Protocol (MSP)
20	FTP - Data
21	FTP - Control
22	SSH Remote Login Protocol
23	Telnet
25	Simple Mail Transfer Protocol (SMTP)
29	MSG ICP
37	Time
42	Host Name Server (Nameserv)
43	WhoIs
49	Login Host Protocol (Login)
53	Domain Name System (DNS)
69	Trivial File Transfer Protocol (TFTP)

(continued)

Table 2.6 Commonly Used TCP Ports *(continued)*	
Port Number	Use
70	Gopher Services
79	Finger
80	HTTP
103	X.400 Standard
108	SNA Gateway Access Server
109	POP2
110	POP3
115	Simple File Transfer Protocol (SFTP)
118	SQL Services
119	Newsgroup (NNTP)
137	NetBIOS Name Service
139	NetBIOS Datagram Service
143	Internet Message Access Protocol (IMAP)
150	NetBIOS Session Service
156	SQL Server
161	Simple Network Management Protocol (SNMP)
179	Border Gateway Protocol (BGP)
190	Gateway Access Control Protocol (GACP)
194	Internet Relay Chat (IRC)
197	Directory Location Service (DLS)
389	Lightweight Directory Access Protocol (LDAP)
396	Novell NetWare over IP
443	HTTPS
444	Simple Network Paging Protocol (SNPP)
445	Microsoft-DS
458	Apple QuickTime
563	SNEWS
569	MSN
1080	Socks

If there is no reason to allow this port traffic, the outside firewalls should deny it. This is especially critical for demilitarized zone (DMZ) systems that Internet users access; you should have those firewalls finely tuned to only the necessary traffic, and you might want to consider blocking the ports on the servers themselves.

One method to stop traffic to specific servers is by using Internet Connection Firewall (ICF). For example, if you have an FTP server in the DMZ next to an IIS server, the FTP server could be subjected to port 80 attacks because the firewall allows that traffic to pass through to connect to the IIS server. If port 80 is open on the FTP server (it would be by default), the system could be compromised on that allowed port. You can configure ICF on the server to deny that traffic. To do that, follow these steps:

1. Open the Properties dialog box of your local area connection.

2. In the Advanced tab, select the check box in the Internet Connection Firewall section (see Figure 2.17). After selecting this option, the grayed out Settings button is available.

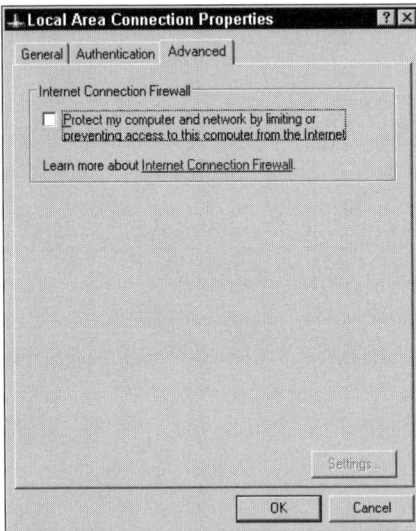

Figure 2.17 You can enable ICF in the Advanced tab of the Local Area Network Connection Properties dialog box.

3. Click the Settings button and, in the Services tab of the Advanced Settings dialog box (see Figure 2.18), configure the services you want to have access to the local system by selecting the corresponding check boxes. (By default, after ICF is enabled, no traffic is allowed to pass inward to the system.)

4. If a service or TCP port is not listed but required, you can add it by clicking the Add button and supplying the TCP port number, service name, and any other pertinent information.

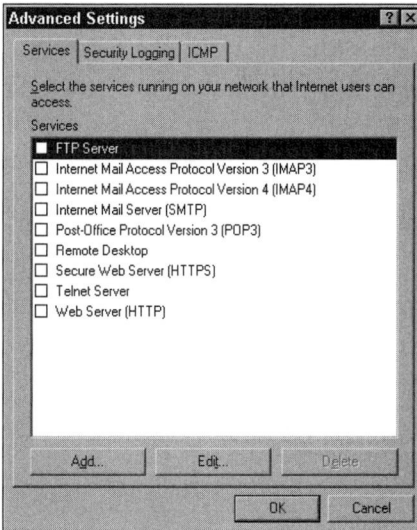

Figure 2.18   You can configure services to allow inbound traffic via the Services tab of the Advanced Settings dialog box.

ICF also enables you to set logging information on system attempts and Internet Control Message Protocol (ICMP) traffic behavior. Network cards on servers can also be configured to allow only specific traffic.

If you are concerned that ICF could be defeated, you can configure the TCP/IP protocol bound to the specific network card to allow only specific traffic. To do this, follow these steps:

1. Select the General tab in the Local Area Connection Properties dialog box.

2. Select Internet Protocol (TCP/IP) and click the Properties button (see Figure 2.19) to open the Internet Protocol Properties dialog box.

3. The Internet Protocol Properties dialog box has only the General tab. Click the Properties button to open the Advanced TCP/IP Settings dialog box. Select the Options tab and click TCP/IP Filtering (see Figure 2.20).

4. As you can see in the TCP/IP Filtering dialog box, by default, all traffic is permitted. To configure an adapter to permit only specific TCP and/or UDP traffic based on port number, select the Permit Only radio button above TCP Ports or UDP Ports (or both). You can also select the Enable TCP/IP Filtering (All Adapters) check box to enable these settings on all installed network adapters in the system that are bound to TCP/IP.

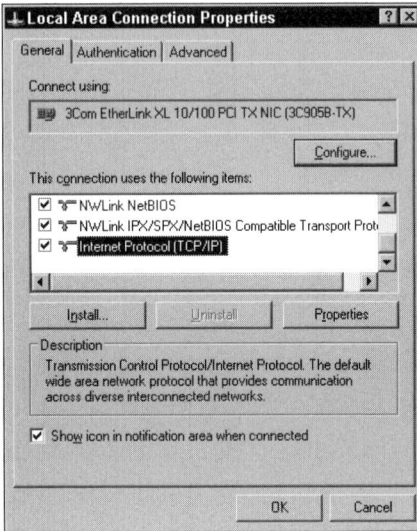

Figure 2.19 You can configure TCP/IP filtering by selecting TCP/IP in the list and clicking the Properties button.

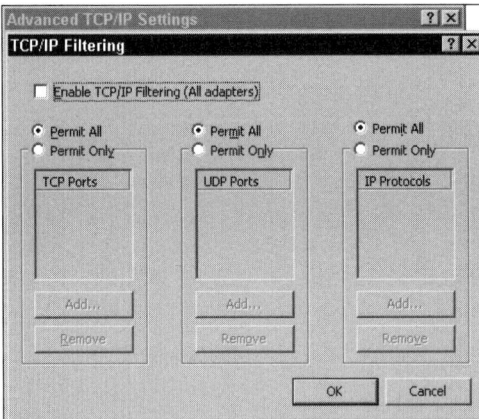

Figure 2.20 You configure TCP/IP filtering via the TCP/IP Filtering dialog box.

In discussions of local firewalling, ICF is often a main point of contention. You should be aware of the "old school" method of port filtering in the TCP/IP Filtering dialog box outlined in this section.

Note that limiting the IIS server to ports 80 and 443 or the SMTP server to port 25 traffic means that domain services, such as LDAP and DNS registration, are not available to these systems because they are blocking all but those listed allowed ports. Also, a port 80 attack using a known vulnerability on an unpatched Web server will be successful because Web traffic rides port 80, as do certain attacks.

Exam Prep Questions

Question 1

> What is the maximum number of server roles in any version of Windows Server 2003?
>
> ○ A. All versions of Windows Server 2003 can have any number of the available roles; the only limiting factor is system hardware.
>
> ○ B. All versions of Windows Server 2003 can have any number of the available roles, provided the roles are not overlapping in nature, such as IIS and POP3 (which both use the SMTP service). The only limiting factor is system hardware.
>
> ○ C. Windows Server 2003 Enterprise Edition and Datacenter Edition can have any number of the available roles; the only limiting factor is system hardware.
>
> ○ D. All versions of Windows Server 2003 except Web Server Edition can have any number of the available roles; the only limiting factor is system hardware.
>
> ○ E. All versions of Windows Server 2003 can have up to four of the available roles only.

The correct answer is D. All versions of Windows Server 2003 except Web Server Edition can have any number of the available roles; the only limiting factor is system hardware. Therefore, answers A, B, C, and E are incorrect.

Question 2

> Windows Server 2003 Web Server Edition is designed specifically for low-end and entry-level Web hosting environments. From the following list, choose all the roles that can be installed on Windows Server 2003 Web Server Edition. (Choose three.)
>
> ❑ A. Terminal server.
>
> ❑ B. Virtual private network (VPN) server.
>
> ❑ C. Streaming media server.
>
> ❑ D. File and print server.
>
> ❑ E. Domain controller.

The correct answers are B and D. Windows Server 2003 Web Server Edition can be installed with some of the same functionalities of the other OS versions. You can set the system up as a virtual private network (VPN) server, but in limited functionality. Connections are limited to one media type: Local area network (LAN), remote access (dial-up), and direct cable connection and Server Message Block (SMB) connections are limited to 10 simultaneous connections. Therefore, answer B is correct. The server can be set up as a file and print server; therefore, answer D is correct. The server cannot be installed as a terminal server or a streaming media server; therefore, answers A and C are incorrect. Windows Server 2003 Web Server Edition cannot be established as a domain controller; therefore, answer E is incorrect.

Question 3

When installing Windows Server 2003, a minimum amount of free hard drive space (approximately 1.5GB) is required for installation. Additional space—between 100MB and 200MB—might be required under which of the following circumstances? (Choose two.)

- ❏ A. When a FAT16 partition is in use.
- ❏ B. When a FAT32 partition is in use.
- ❏ C. When installing over the network.
- ❏ D. When installing via the Windows Server 2003 Setup floppy disks.
- ❏ E. When installing via Remote Installation Service.

The correct answers are A and C. The minimum amount of space required for installation is approximately 1.5GB. When a FAT16 partition is in use, it requires 100MB to 200MB more free disk space than other supported file systems because of cluster sizes. Therefore, answer A is correct. If you are installing Windows Server 2003 Standard Edition from a network share, you need approximately 100MB to 200MB more space than if you ran the setup from the CD because the Setup program needs to use that space for temporary files associated with the installation. Therefore, answer C is correct. FAT32 uses smaller cluster sizes and although it might require slightly more space than NTFS, it is not in the 100MB to 200MB range; therefore, answer B is incorrect. At this time, there is no floppy disk installation procedure because there are no Windows Server 2003 Setup floppy disks. Therefore, answer D is incorrect. An RIS installation does not require an additional 100-200MB; therefore, answer E is incorrect.

Question 4

When performing an upgrade installation to Windows Server 2003, which of the following operating systems can be directly upgraded without loss of features? (Choose four.)

❏ A. Windows NT Server 4.0 with Service Pack 4 or later.

❏ B. Windows NT Server 4.0 with Service Pack 5 or later.

❏ C. Windows NT Server 4.0, Terminal Server Edition, with Service Pack 4 or later.

❏ D. Windows NT Server 4.0, Terminal Server Edition, with Service Pack 5 or later.

❏ E. Windows 2000 Server with Service Pack 1 or later.

❏ F. Windows 2000 Server with Service Pack 2 or later.

The correct answers are B, D, E, and F. If you elect to upgrade your current server operating system, you need to be aware that the Setup program automatically installs Windows Server 2003 into the same folder as the currently installed operating system, regardless of its naming convention.

You can perform direct upgrades to Windows Server 2003 from the following versions of Windows:

➤ Windows NT Server 4.0 with Service Pack 5 or later

➤ Windows NT Server 4.0, Terminal Server Edition, with Service Pack 5 or later

➤ Windows 2000 Server

There are no service pack requirements for Windows 2000 Server; any version and service pack level of Windows 2000 can be directly upgraded to Windows Server 2003.

Question 5

> Configuring your system in the role of a domain controller with the Configure Your Server Wizard is just the same as doing it manually. In either case, what program do you run to convert a server to a domain controller?
>
> ○ A. **DCDIAG**
>
> ○ B. **DCPROMO**
>
> ○ C. **WINNT32.EXE**
>
> ○ D. **NTDSUTIL.EXE**
>
> ○ E. **SYSPREP**

The correct answer is B. With the Configure Your Server Wizard, you select the Domain Controller role. All the wizard does then is run DCPROMO.EXE to start the Active Directory Installation Wizard. If you want, you can perform this step manually from the Run dialog box or from a command prompt. DCDIAG is a command-line tool that analyzes the state of domain controllers in a forest or enterprise and reports any problems to assist in troubleshooting. Therefore, answer A is incorrect. Winnt32.exe is the program that runs to upgrade an existing operating system to a new one from within the running operating system and NtdsUtil.exe is used for the maintenance of the Active Directory store. It is also used to manage the Flexible Single Master Operations (FSMO) from the command line and can also be used to clean up metadata. Therefore, answers C and D are incorrect.

Question 6

> You are preparing to install a Windows Server 2003 system into a domain controller role for an existing domain. What are the minimum requirements needed to successfully complete this task? (Choose two.)
>
> ❑ A. DNS needs to be available on the network.
>
> ❑ B. You must have at least local administrative rights on the DNS server.
>
> ❑ C. DHCP needs to be available.
>
> ❑ D. You must have at least Domain Administrator rights.
>
> ❑ E. You must have at least local administrative rights on the Global Catalog server.

The correct answers are A and D. DNS needs to be available on the network. Without DNS, DCPROMO cannot successfully run. Therefore, answer A is correct. To join the server to an existing domain, you need to have Domain Administrator rights (or higher rights, such as Enterprise Administrator, or have been delegated the appropriate permissions to complete the task) to successfully complete the installation and add the domain controller to the domain. Therefore, answer D is correct. Although you must be logged on to the system as a local administrator, this does not allow a successful installation of Active Directory on the local server in an existing domain. Therefore, answer B is incorrect. DHCP is not a requirement for installing Active Directory. Therefore, answer C is incorrect. Rights on the Global Catalog server are not required to install a Windows Server 2003 system into a domain controller role for an existing domain; therefore, answer E is incorrect.

Question 7

You are preparing to install a Windows Server 2003 system into a domain controller role for an existing domain. What is the name of the default security template applied to all domain controllers in a domain, and how is it applied?

- ○ A. **Basicdc.inf** is applied through the use of Group Policy objects linked to the Domain Controllers OU.
- ○ B. **DC Security.inf** is applied through the use of Group Policy objects linked to the Domain Controllers OU.
- ○ C. **Basicdc.inf** is applied through the use of Group Policy objects linked to the Domain object.
- ○ D. **DC Security.inf** is applied through the use of Group Policy objects linked to the Domain object.
- ○ E. **Basicdc.inf** is applied through the use of Group Policy–enabled scripts.
- ○ F. **DC Security.inf** is applied through the use of Group Policy–enabled scripts.

The correct answer is B. When a new domain controller is installed on a Windows Server 2003 system, the default template, DC Security.inf, is applied through the use of Group Policy objects linked to the Domain Controllers OU. Therefore, all the other answers are incorrect.

Question 8

You have found that using a custom security template in your enterprise has caused some undesired side effects that did not show up during testing. You want to reapply the default template to the domain controllers through Group Policy objects and the Domain Controllers OU. Which tool is best suited for this task?

○ A. Security Configuration and Analysis.

○ B. Computer Management.

○ C. Active Directory Sites and Services.

○ D. Security Configuration and Analysis.

The correct answer is D. If a custom security template has caused some undesired side effects that did not show up during testing, you can reapply the default template to the domain controllers through Group Policy objects and the Domain Controllers OU by using the Security Configuration and Analysis snap-in. Choose Open Database, and import the DC Security.inf template. After you have opened the template, right-click Security Configuration and Analysis, and then click Configure Computer Now to configure the system with the default settings.

Active Directory Domains and Trusts is normally used to handle external or manually created trusts between domains. Therefore, answer A is incorrect. Computer Management is normally used to configure the local system services and hardware configuration. Therefore, answer B is incorrect. Active Directory Sites and Services is used to configure sites, replication between sites, and network protocols used for replication. Therefore, answer C is incorrect.

Question 9

You have been tasked with reviewing the resources of the **ACCTDATA** folder, which has been shared as **ATDATA** on **FILESRV3**. The permissions on the share are currently set as follows:

➤ Share Permissions

➤ Everyone—Full Control

➤ Accounting—Full Control

➤ Accounting Admin—Full Control

➤ Admins—Full Control

➤ Users—Full Control

➤ Guest—Full Control

The maximum level of share permissions that need to be set for the Accounting group is Read and Write. The maximum level of share permissions that need to be set for the Accounting Admin group is Modify.

You have decided to perform this task manually instead of through role assignment and have removed the file server role from the system by using the Configure Your Server Wizard. What effect, if any, will this action have on local NTFS settings for the **ACCTDATA** folder?

○ A. Removing the role will have no effect on NTFS settings.

○ B. Removing the role will remove all the current NTFS permissions.

○ C. Removing the role will remove the **ACCTDATA** folder.

○ D. Removing the role will remove the **ATDATA** share.

The correct answer is A. Whether or not you use the Configure Your Server Wizard, you set the server into a file server role as soon as you right-click any share in Windows Explorer and specify sharing a folder in the Sharing tab of the Properties dialog box.

Removing the file server role does not remove all the current NTFS permissions, as the file server role does not affect these security settings nor does it remove the ACCTDATA folder. Therefore, answers B and C are incorrect. Removing the role removes the ATDATA share, but the question asked what effect this would have on local NTFS settings for the ACCTDATA folder, so answer D is also incorrect.

Question 10

You have installed IIS 6 as a server role for your Windows Server 2003 system, which also holds the POP3 role, by using Add/Remove Windows components so that you could install FTP and NNTP services. These services are not added by default when you establish the server role with the Configure Your Server Wizard.

Which of the following services, if any, will be removed from the system if you remove the IIS6 role later by using the Configure Your Server Wizard?

○ A. SMTP

○ B. NNTP

○ C. FTP

○ D. WWW

○ E. All will be removed.

○ F. None will be removed.

The correct answer is D. If you use the Configure Your Server Wizard to remove the IIS role, you will remove only the WWW service. All the other services will remain; therefore, answers A, B, C, E, and F are incorrect.

Need To Know More?

Best practices for security: http://www.microsoft.com/technet/treeview/default.asp?url=/technet/prodtechnol/windowsserver2003/proddocs/server/sec_checklist.asp.

Locking down IIS: http://www.microsoft.com/technet/treeview/default.asp?url=/technet/prodtechnol/windowsserver2003/proddocs/server/sec_aboutsecurity.asp.

What's changed in Windows Server 2003: http://www.microsoft.com/technet/treeview/default.asp?url=/technet/prodtechnol/windowsserver2003/proddocs/server/gs_whatschanged.asp.

Windows Server 2003 system requirements: http://www.microsoft.com/windowsserver2003/evaluation/sysreqs/default.mspx.

Microsoft KnowledgeBase Article #319091: "Windows Server 2003 May Not Use Multiple Processors with Some Pentium Pro or Pentium II Processors": http://support.microsoft.com/default.aspx?scid=kb;en-us;319091.

Choosing between NTFS, FAT, and FAT32: http://www.microsoft.com/windowsxp/home/using/productdoc/en/default.asp?url=/WINDOWSXP/home/using/productdoc/en/choosing_between_NTFS_FAT_and_FAT32.asp.

File Manager displays maximum disk space of 1.99 GB: http://support.microsoft.com/default.aspx?scid=kb%3Ben-us%3B128794 (includes information on maximum file system sizes).

Windows NT file size and partition size limits: http://support.microsoft.com/default.aspx?scid=kb%3Ben-us%3B93496.

Security information for DNS: http://www.microsoft.com/technet/treeview/default.asp?url=/technet/prodtechnol/windowsserver2003/proddocs/server/sag_DNS_imp_Security.asp.

Authorizing a DHCP server in Active Directory: http://www.microsoft.com/windows2000/en/server/help/default.asp?url=/windows2000/en/server/help/sag_DHCP_pro_AuthorizeServerInDirectory.htm.

Authorizing DHCP servers: http://www.microsoft.com/windows2000/en/server/help/sag_DHCP_imp_AuthorizingServers.htm.

What's new in Active Directory: `http://www.microsoft.com/windowsserver2003/evaluation/overview/technologies/activedirectory.mspx`.

Upgrading from Windows 2000 Server to Windows Server 2003: `http://www.microsoft.com/windowsserver2003/evaluation/whyupgrade/win2k/default.mspx`.

Technical overview of Windows Server 2003 security services: `http://www.microsoft.com/windowsserver2003/techinfo/overview/security.mspx`.

The application server role: `http://www.microsoft.com/windowsserver2003/techinfo/serverroles/appserver/default.mspx`.

Securing the Windows Server 2003 application platform: `http://www.microsoft.com/windowsserver2003/techinfo/serverroles/appserver/secplat.mspx`.

For more articles on Windows Server 2003: `http://windows2003.2000trainers.com`.

To see a list of well-known IP port numbers: `http://www.iana.org/assignments/port-numbers`.

3

Planning, Implementing, and Maintaining a Network Infrastructure

. . . .

Terms you'll need to understand:

✓ TCP/IP version 4
✓ TCP/IP version 6
✓ Path Maximum Transmission Unit (PMTU)
✓ Dynamic Host Configuration Protocol (DHCP)
✓ Automatic Private IP Addressing (APIPA)
✓ Incremental zone transfer (IXFR)
✓ Full zone transfer (AXFR)
✓ Windows Internet Naming Service (WINS)

Techniques you'll need to master:

✓ Installing and configuring DNS, WINS, and DHCP
✓ Configuring clients to use Dynamic Update
✓ Configuring DHCP scopes and optional parameters
✓ Configuring ad analyzing IP addressing requirements

Transmission Control Protocol/Internet Protocol (TCP/IP) is a connection-oriented, Internet-standard, routable protocol in use on a majority of networks, including the Internet. The protocol suite supports connectivity across a number of dissimilar platforms and supports the main workload of most enterprises today that are designed in a client/server configuration.

Some subtle changes have been incorporated into the TCP/IP suite for Windows Server 2003. Internet Group Management Protocol (IGMP) version 3 adds support for source-based filtering and reporting while maintaining backward-compatibility with version 2. You can also use other settings so that systems can be configured to use an alternate, manually configured IP address instead of one that a Dynamic Host Configuration Protocol (DHCP) server provides. Autoconfiguration of the enabled network interface card (NIC) metric is also available; this feature determines the best routing metric for each interface's default gateway, based on its speed. Support for TCP/IP version 6 has also been added in Windows Server 2003.

These are some of the TCP/IP features that have been carried over from Windows 2000 Server:

➤ Binding multiple network adapters with different media types

➤ Logical and physical multihoming

➤ Internal IP routing

➤ Internet Control Message Protocol (ICMP) router discovery

➤ Ability to configure multiple default gateways

➤ TCP/IP over Asynchronous Transfer Mode (ATM)

➤ Dead gateway detection for TCP traffic

➤ Autodiscovery of Path Maximum Transmission Unit (PMTU) for TCP connections

➤ Data encryption and authentication encryption via Internet Protocol Security (IPSec)

➤ Automatic Private IP Addressing (APIPA), which allows clients to assign themselves a random IP address in the 169.254.0.0/16 range via subnet broadcast when they are configured to use DHCP and no server is available

➤ Quality of Service (QoS) mechanisms that reserve portions of the available bandwidth, allowing it to be prioritized for time-sensitive applications and transmissions

➤ Virtual private networks (VPNs)

> TCP scalable window sizes, including large TCP windows

> Selective Acknowledgments (SACK)

> Packet-level filtering

> NetBIOS over TCP/IP (NetBT)

TCP/IP Protocol Suite

TCP/IP is a network communication protocol suite. It can be used as a communications protocol on private networks and is the default protocol in use on the Internet. When you set up any system to have direct access to the Internet, whether it is via dial-up or a high-speed technology, your system needs to use TCP/IP whether it is a Windows-based system or not.

Also, if systems need to communicate to other TCP/IP systems on the local area network (LAN) or wide area network (WAN), they often use TCP/IP as well.

NOTE   Indirectly connected computers, such as those on a LAN that connect to the Internet via certain default gateways, certain types of routers, proxy servers, or other indirect means, do not necessarily need to use TCP/IP. They need use only the network protocol in use on the LAN, and that LAN protocol communicates with the directly connecting mechanism (default gateway, router, proxy server, or other direct device). That directly connected device needs to use the Internet default protocol of TCP/IP.

For Internet Security and Acceleration (ISA) servers, systems must use TCP/IP because it is the supported protocol for ISA.

TCP/IP is technically made up of two protocols. The upper layer, Transmission Control Protocol, is responsible for breaking data down into smaller packets to be transmitted over the network from a sending system (local and Internet), and the TCP layer on the receiving system reassembles the packets it receives into the original data structure. The lower layer, Internet Protocol, addresses each packet so that it gets delivered to the correct remote system. Each routing device on the network, be it a hardware router or a server system performing routing functions, checks the destination address to see where to forward the message.

The TCP/IP protocol suite maps to a four-layer conceptual model, which parallels the seven-layer Open Systems Interconnect (OSI) protocol model described in the following list:

➤ *Physical layer*—This layer defines the interface between the network medium (such as ethernet or token ring) and the hardware device (such as a NIC). Multiplexers, hubs, and repeaters are just a few examples of the components found at this layer of the OSI model.

➤ *Data Link layer*—This layer is divided into two sublayers: Logical Link Control (LLC), which handles error correction and flow control, and Media Access Control (MAC), which handles communication with the NIC. Bridges and switches are components that operate at this layer of the OSI model.

➤ *Network layer*—This layer translates logical network address and names to MAC addresses for routing data packets over a network. A number of protocols run at the Network layer, including IP, Address Resolution Protocol (ARP), Reverse ARP (RARP), Internet Control Message Protocol (ICMP), Routing Information Protocol (RIP), Open Shortest Path First (OSPF), IGMP, Internetwork Packet Exchange (IPX), NWLink (the Microsoft version of the IPX/SPX protocol suite), and NetBIOS Enhanced User Interface (NetBEUI). Brouters, routers, and some types of ATM switches can be found at this layer of the OSI model.

➤ *Transport layer*—This layer provides an additional connection below the Session layer and assists with managing some data flow control between hosts. Data is divided into packets on the sending node, and the receiving node's Transport layer reassembles the message from packets. This layer is also responsible for error checking to guarantee error-free data delivery, and requests a retransmission if necessary. It is also responsible for sending acknowledgments of successful transmissions back to the sending host. A number of protocols run at the Transport layer, including TCP, ARP, RARP, Sequenced Packet Exchange (SPX), and NWLink. Gateways and certain types of routers can be found at this layer of the OSI model.

➤ *Session layer*—This layer establishes, maintains, and ends sessions between transmitting hosts and controls which host can transmit data at a given interval and for how long. A number of protocols run at the Session layer, including Named Pipes, NetBIOS Names, Remote Procedure Calls (RPC), and Mail Slots. Gateways and certain types of proxy servers operate at this layer of the OSI model.

➤ *Presentation layer*—This layer translates data from the way applications understand it to the way networks understand it. It is responsible for protocol conversions, data encryption and decryption, and data compression and decompression when the network is considered. Gateways and certain types of redirectors operate at this layer of the OSI model. There are no protocols that normally operate in this layer of the OSI model.

➤ *Application layer*—This layer allows access to network services for applications specifically written to run over the network. Some protocols found at this OSI layer include File Transfer Protocol (FTP), Trivial FTP (TFTP), Bootstrap Protocol (BOOTP), Simple Network Management Protocol (SNMP), Simple Mail Transfer Protocol (SMTP), Telnet, NetWare Core Protocol (NCP), and Server Message Block (SMB).

The four-layer conceptual model for the TCP/IP protocol suite is as follows:

➤ *Network Interface layer*—This layer is responsible for putting bits on the wire and correlates closely with the OSI model's Physical layer and Data Link layer.

➤ *Internet layer*—This layer is responsible for encapsulating data packets into Internet datagrams. The Internet layer correlates, for the most part, with the OSI model's Network layer. Four Internet protocols operate at this layer:

➤IP supports connectionless packet delivery for all other protocols, such as TCP or User Datagram Protocol (UDP). IP does not guarantee packet arrival or correct packet sequence, nor does it acknowledge packet delivery. These tasks are left to the application using the network or higher-level protocols, such as TCP. IP is responsible for addressing and routing packets only; error correction is left to the application or to higher-level protocols.

➤ARP is responsible for mapping IP addresses to physical machine addresses called MAC addresses. IP broadcasts a special ARP inquiry packet containing the destination system's IP address, and that system replies by sending its physical address to the requester.

➤ICMP is charged with message control and error-reporting between network hosts. Higher-level protocols use this information to recover from transmission errors.

➤IGMP allows hosts to report their multicast group membership to multicast routers. With multicasting, hosts can send multicast traffic to a single MAC address, so multiple nodes can process the traffic.

➤ *Transport layer (also called Host-to-Host Transport)*—This layer basically (but not entirely) correlates with the OSI model's Transport layer. The two Transport layer protocols, TCP and UDP, provide communication sessions between systems.

➤ TCP is a connection-oriented protocol that guarantees data delivery by assigning a sequence number to each transmitted data segment so that the receiving host can send an acknowledgment (ACK) to verify that the data was received intact. If an ACK is not received or there was a transmission error, the data is sent again.

➤ UDP is a connectionless protocol that does not guarantee delivery or correct sequencing of packets. Applications that use UDP are typically tasked with the responsibility of ensuring data delivery because the protocol does not. UDP is often used instead of TCP because of its lower overhead. TFTP is an example of an application that uses UDP.

➤ *Application layer*—This layer is where network-aware applications operate. Network applications most commonly use two TCP/IP services, Winsock and the NetBT interface.

Internet Protocol Addressing Overview

IP version 4 (IPv4) addresses are made up of four 8-bit fields (*octets*)—32 bits total. There are five IPv4 address classes: A, B, C, D, and E.

IPv4 addresses consist of a network ID and a host ID. The *network ID* identifies the numeric network name of the physical network where the hosts exist. The *host ID* identifies the numeric network name of the individual TCP/IP host on a network. The numeric host ID must be unique on the internal network—that is, no two nodes on a network can have the same network ID and host ID.

NOTE

You can have two hosts with the same numeric IP hostname of 16.72.28 if one is on network 111 and another is on network 112. (The full IP addresses of these hosts would be 111.16.72.28 and 112.16.72.28. The subnet mask would be 255.0.0.0.)

A *subnet mask* is used to divide an entire TCP/IP address in an effort to define which part of the address is the network number and which part is the host system's numeric identifier. The bits in a subnet mask are set consecutively from left to right. For example, the subnet mask 255.128.0.0 is valid because all eight bits are set in the first two octets and the first bit of the next octet is also set (11111111.10000000.00000000.00000000). The subnet mask 255.64.0.0 is not valid because it has a "missing" bit, which is not allowed (11111111.01000000.00000000.00000000).

> **NOTE**
>
> Bit values are held to a specific order, from the Most Significant Bit (MSB) to the Least Significant Bit (LSB). From left to right, these designations are 128, 64, 32, 16, 8, 4, 2, and 1. Each bit that's set is noted by a "1" (showing that the bit is "on" or "enabled"), and bits are added together to give you the address. The IPv4 address 171.144.62.12 converts to a binary number of 10101011. 10010000.00111110.00001100 and a hexadecimal number of AB.90.3E.0C.

> **ALERT**
>
> You need to have a fairly good understanding of host IDs, network IDs, subnetting, and masks for just about any Microsoft certification exam. Any exams that introduce information about networking require you to have at least basic knowledge of TCP/IP addressing.

IP version 6 (IPv6) has been designed to overcome the current shortage of addresses under IPv4 and offers some changes to TCP/IP. Table 3.1 outlines some of the major differences between IPv4 and IPv6.

Table 3.1   Differences Between IPv4 and IPv6

Characteristic	IPv4	IPv6
Address length in bits	32	128
Header size in bytes	20 to 60	40
IPSec support	Optional	Required
Maximum Transmission Units (MTUs) in bytes	576	1280
QoS support	Yes	Yes, with more features
Fragmentation	Performed by hosts and routers	Performed by hosts only
Header checksum	Yes	No
Header options	Yes	No
Link-layer address resolution	Broadcast ARP frames	Multicast Neighbor Solicitation messages

(continued)

Table 3.1 Differences Between IPv4 and IPv6 *(continued)*		
Characteristic	**IPv4**	**IPv6**
Error reporting/diagnostic protocol	ICMP (for IPv4)	ICMPv6
Multicast group membership protocol	IGMP	Multicast Listener Discovery (MLD)
Support for router discovery	Optional	Required
Network layer broadcast	Yes	No
Host configuration	DHCP or manual	Automatic, DHCP, or manual
DNS record type used for name resolution	(A) record	AAAA record
DNS record type used for reverse name resolution	PTR records in **IN-ADDR.ARPA** domain	PTR records in **IP6.INT** domain

The original IP definitions set five classes of IP addresses, from A through E. (A, B, and C are for general-purpose use, D is used for multicasting, and E is reserved.) These classes made it possible to use one portion of the 32-bit IP address scheme for the network address and the remaining portion for nodes on the network.

In the past, some networks needed more addresses for systems than the 254 supplied by a Class C address, which was a major contribution to the shortage of IP addresses. Organizations often requested a Class B range that offered 65,534 available addresses rather than a few Class C ranges that might have suited their needs. The result was that many addresses within their allotted Class B blocks went unused.

However, Classless Inter-Domain Routing (CIDR) addressing is now used more often for IPv4 addressing schemes. It effectively "removes" the class from an address for the purpose of combining ranges, so it makes better use of the limited number of remaining available IPv4 addresses. A CIDR network address looks like this:

```
222.175.14.00/18
```

The network address is 222.175.14.00. The /18 specifies that the first 18 bits of the address are the network part of the address, which leaves the last 14 bits for the network hosts' address.

CIDR is supported by Border Gateway Protocol (BGP) and OSPF. Older gateway protocols, such as Exterior Gateway Protocol (EGP) and Routing

Information Protocol version 1 (RIPv1), do not support CIDR. Because CIDR supports multiple subnet masks per subnet, it requires routers that support more advanced interior routing protocols, such as RIPv2 and OSPF.

> **NOTE**
>
> A, B, and C classful networks support a single subnet mask and can use RIPv1.

Subnet Masks

Implementing subnets helps control network traffic and enables network administrators to create smaller collision domains. Every node on the same physical ethernet network sees all data packets sent out on the network, which results in multiple collisions and affects network performance. Routers or gateways separate networks into subnets. Subnet masks on each node allow nodes on the same subnetwork to continue communicating with one another and with the routers or gateways they use to send their messages.

Subnet masks enables you to identify the network ID and host (node) ID of an IP address. The following example is a default Class B subnet mask:

```
10110110.10100101.00110111.01100010 182.165.55.98
11111111.11111111.00000000.00000000 255.255.000.000
--------------------------------------------------
10110110.10100101.00000000.00000000 182.165.000.000
IP Address       : 182.165.55.98
Address Class    : B
Network Address  : 182.165.0.0

Subnet Address   : 182.165.48.0
Subnet Mask      : 255.255.240.0
Subnet bit mask  : 10nnnnnn.nnnnnnnn.nnnnhhhh.hhhhhhhh
Subnet Bits      : 20
Host Bits        : 12
Possible Number of Subnets : 16
Hosts per Subnet : 4094

Selected Subnet  : 182.165.0.0/255.255.240.0
Usable Addresses : 4094
    Host range   : 182.165.0.1  to  182.165.15.254
    Broadcast    : 182.165.15.255
```

To subnet networks further, more bits can be added to the subnet mask for a class of addresses.

The following example is a Class B address using an additional bit subnet mask of 240. Notice that instead of having the single subnet and 65,534 hosts per subnet allowed under the default subnet mask, you can have up to 16 subnets with up to 4,094 hosts per subnet by using a subnet mask of 255.255.240.000 (Table 3.2 shows a sample IP addressing scheme):

```
10110110.10100101.00110111.01100010 182.165.55.98
11111111.11111111.11110000.00000000 255.255.240.000 Subnet Mask
-------------------------------------------------------
IP Address       : 182.165.55.98
Address Class    : B
Network Address  : 182.165.0.0

Subnet Address   : 182.165.48.0
Subnet Mask      : 255.255.240.0
Subnet bit mask  : 10nnnnnn.nnnnnnnn.nnnnhhhh.hhhhhhhh
Subnet Bits      : 20
Host Bits        : 12
Possible Number of Subnets : 16
Hosts per Subnet : 4094

Selected Subnet  : 182.165.0.0/255.255.240.0
Usable Addresses : 4094
     Host range  : 182.165.0.1  to  182.165.15.254
     Broadcast   : 182.165.15.255
```

Table 3.2	Example of an IP Addressing Scheme			
Subnet	**Mask**	**Subnet Size**	**Host Range**	**Broadcast**
182.165.0.0	255.255.240.0	4094	182.165.0.1 to 182.165.15.254	182.165.15.255
182.165.16.0	255.255.240.0	4094	182.165.16.1 to 182.165.31.254	182.165.31.255
182.165.32.0	255.255.240.0	4094	182.165.32.1 to 182.165.47.254	182.165.47.255
182.165.48.0	255.255.240.0	4094	182.165.48.1 to 182.165.63.254	182.165.63.255
182.165.64.0	255.255.240.0	4094	182.165.64.1 to 182.165.79.254	182.165.79.255
182.165.80.0	255.255.240.0	4094	182.165.80.1 to 182.165.95.254	182.165.95.255
182.165.96.0	255.255.240.0	4094	182.165.96.1 to 182.165.111.254	182.165.111.255
182.165.112.0	255.255.240.0	4094	182.165.112.1 to 182.165.127.254	182.165.127.255
182.165.128.0	255.255.240.0	4094	182.165.128.1 to 182.165.143.254	182.165.143.255
182.165.144.0	255.255.240.0	4094	182.165.144.1 to 182.165.159.254	182.165.159.255

(continued)

Table 3.2 Example of an IP Addressing Scheme *(continued)*				
Subnet	Mask	Subnet Size	Host Range	Broadcast
182.165.160.0	255.255.240.0	4094	182.165.160.1 to 182.165.175.254	182.165.175.255
182.165.176.0	255.255.240.0	4094	182.165.176.1 to 182.165.191.254	182.165.191.255
182.165.192.0	255.255.240.0	4094	182.165.192.1 to 182.165.207.254	182.165.207.255
182.165.208.0	255.255.240.0	4094	182.165.208.1 to 182.165.223.254	182.165.223.255
182.165.224.0	255.255.240.0	4094	182.165.224.1 to 182.165.239.254	182.165.239.255
182.165.240.0	255.255.240.0	4094	182.165.240.1 to 182.165.255.254	182.165.255.255

When you use standard subnet masks in classful IP addressing schemes, you can plan how many hosts you can support per subnet and how many subnets are available for use. Table 3.3 shows classful IP addressing schemes and uses 255.x.0.0 as the default mask for Class A addresses, 255.255.x.0 as the default mask for Class B class addresses, and 255.255.255.x as the mask for Class C addresses. In these classes, the X is the subnet mask variable in the table's Subnet Mask column.

Table 3.3 Subnet Masking for Classful IP Addressing				
Subnet Mask	Number of Subnets in Classful Range	Number of Class A Hosts per Subnet	Number of Class B Hosts per Subnet	Number of Class C Hosts per Subnet
0	1	16,777,214	65,534	254
128	2	8,388,606	32,766	126
192	4	4,194,302	16,382	62
224	8	2,097,150	8,190	30
240	16	1,048,574	4,094	14
248	32	524,286	2,046	6
252	64	262,142	1,022	2
254	128	131,070	510	N/A
255	256	65,534	254	N/A

TCP/IP Class A Addresses

Class A addresses have an official start address of 0.0.0.0 and an official ending address of 127.255.255.255. However, the last usable client address in the range is 126.255.255.254, as the 127.*x.x.x* range is used for internal host loopback.

The full range of addresses that can be assigned to hosts is 1.0.0.1 to 126.255.255.254, with 126.255.255.255 as the broadcast address. The local host uses 0.0.0.0 when it has been configured to use a DHCP server but cannot reach one and cannot assign itself an address using APIPA. (This situation would be unusual.)

There are 126 Class A networks total, and each is allowed to have up to 16,777,214 hosts. Three IP network addresses are reserved for private networks as defined in Request for Comment (RFC) 1918. The Class A range is 10.0.0.0 to 10.255.255.255, with a subnet mask of 255.0.0.0.

These addresses can be used by anyone setting up internal IP networks, such as a lab or home LAN behind a Network Address Translation (NAT) server, proxy server, or router. It is always safe to use them because routers on the Internet never forward packets coming from these addresses.

TCP/IP Class B Addresses

The Class B range of IP addresses starts with address 128.0.0.0 and ends at address 191.255.255.255. IP addresses 128.0.0.1 to 191.255.255.254 are the usable range of Class B addresses for node assignment.

Three IP network addresses are reserved for private networks, as defined in RFC 1918. The Class B range is 172.16.0.0 to 172.31.255.255, with the subnet mask 255.240.0.0. These addresses can be used by anyone setting up internal IP networks, such as a lab or home LAN behind a NAT server, proxy server, or router. It is always safe to use these addresses because routers on the Internet never forward packets coming from these addresses.

TCP/IP Class C Addresses

The Class C range of IP addresses starts at address 192.0.0.0 and ends at 223.255.255.255. IP addresses 192.0.0.1 to 223.255.255.254 are the usable range of Class C addresses for node assignment.

Three IP network addresses are reserved for private networks, as defined in RFC 1918. The Class C range is 192.168.0.0 to 192.168.255.255, with the subnet mask 255.255.0.0. These addresses can be used by anyone setting up internal IP networks, such as a lab or home LAN behind a NAT server, proxy server, or router. It is always safe to use them because routers on the Internet never forward packets coming from these addresses.

TCP/IP Class D Addresses

The Class D IP addresses range from 224.0.0.0 through 239.255.255.255. Internet Assigned Numbers Authority (IANA) has set aside this range as a special class of addresses for multicast uses. ISPs are unable to allocate Class D address space to their customers because IANA is the only body through which these addresses can be allocated.

Allocation of Class D addresses is required only if you want to be a multicast source. You can still receive multicast data without needing a separate Class D address.

TCP/IP Class E Addresses

IANA has set aside Class E IP addresses from 240.0.0.0 to 254.255.255.255 as a special class of addresses for experimental and future use. The IP address 255.255.255.255 broadcasts to all hosts on the local network and, therefore, is not considered part of the Class E IP addresses.

Well-Known Ports

A number of well-known ports (0–1023) are used by different services on computers. For a single IP address on one system to offer all possible services to a network, each service must function on its own TCP or UDP port from that IP address.

You can find a helpful table at `http://www.networksorcery.com` that includes links to definitions and additional notes for some services. The following ports and associated protocols are the most important ones to remember:

➤ *20*—FTP—data

➤ *21*—FTP—control

➤ *22*—Secure Shell (SSH)

➤ *23*—Telnet

➤ *25*—SMTP

➤ *37*—Time Protocol (Time)

➤ *49*—Terminal Access Controller Access Control System (TACACS), TACACS+

➤ *53*—DNS

➤ *67*—BOOTP—server

➤ *68*—BOOTP—client

➤ *69*—TFTP

➤ *70*—Gopher

➤ *79*—Finger

➤ *80*—Hypertext Transfer Protocol (HTTP)

➤ *88*—Kerberos

➤ *109*—Post Office Protocol version 2 (POP2)

➤ *110*—Post Office Protocol version 3 (POP3)

➤ *115*—Simple File Transfer Protocol (SFTP)

➤ *119*—Network News Transfer Protocol (NNTP)

➤ *123*—Network Time Protocol (NTP)

➤ *137*—NetBIOS Name Service

➤ *138*—NetBIOS Datagram Service

➤ *139*—NetBIOS Session Service

➤ *143*—Internet Message Access Protocol (IMAP)

➤ *153*—Simple Gateway Monitoring Protocol (SGMP)

➤ *161*—SNMP

➤ *162*—SNMP—traps

➤ *179*—BGP

➤ *389*—Lightweight Directory Access Protocol (LDAP), Connectionless Lightweight X.500 Directory Access Protocol (CLDAP)

➤ *443*—HTTP over Secure Socket Layer/Transport Layer Security (SSL/TLS)—HTTPS

➤ *464*—Kerberos change/set password

➤ *500*—ISAKMP, Internet Key Exchange (IKE)

➤ *546*—DHCPv6 client

➤ *547*—DHCPv6 server

➤ *631*—Internet Printing Protocol (IPP)

TCP/IP Configuration and Optimization

So far you have learned about subnetting and configuring network systems in address class ranges in an effort to optimize TCP/IP configuration, but some other points should be mentioned as well. You need to be sure, above all else, that you understand your network configuration and behavior. Although you can take a few steps to fine-tune TCP/IP traffic, network topology plays a big role.

For TCP/IP specifically, there is the TCP/IP Receive Window Size setting, which is the buffer threshold for inbound packets. The default setting for ethernet networks is 17,520 bytes; when this threshold is met, the receiving system sends out an acknowledgement that the data has been received. This process of sending and acknowledging during a data transmission session repeats every 17,520 bytes until all data has been transmitted. As an administrator, you can adjust this acknowledgement setting to optimize transmissions.

Other settings on the network's Physical and Data Link layers are beyond normal administrative control. Maximum Transmission Units (MTUs), for example, are based on the type of network that is installed. For example, 16Mbps token-ring networks have an MTU setting of 17,914 bytes; 4Mbps token-ring networks have an MTU setting of 4,464 bytes. Ethernet deployments are limited to a 1,500 byte MTU setting. As an analogy, think of the MTU as an envelope in which data is carried.

The Maximum Segment Size (MSS) setting determines the largest segment that can be carried in the MTU. (Think of it as the pages of a letter in an envelope.) This setting also varies depending on the framework. Obviously, the MSS for token-ring networks will be larger than the MSS for ethernet networks.

Networks must consider application requirements when implementing certain services and protocols to optimize bandwidth. Quality of service (QoS) can also be implemented on networks to optimize bandwidth. The main issue on most networks is that all the associated networking equipment needs to support the Resource Reservation Protocol (RSVP). Networks also have certain application requirements to consider, such as the following:

➤ Routers forward traffic on a best-effort basis as they receive it. Video conferencing and streaming media suffer when available bandwidth is low.

➤ QoS Admission Control Service (QoS ACS) handles bandwidth on a subnet-to-subnet basis.

➤ Subnet Bandwidth Management (SBM) manages the use of network resources on a subnet.

➤ RSVP is a signaling protocol that enables sender and receiver systems to set up a reserved QoS session. RSVP messages carry the reservation request in an effort to maintain the QoS session. This is why each router and switch along the communication path between the sender and receiver needs to support RSVP.

➤ Traffic Control uses the packet classifier to separate packets into queues based on their priority. The Packet Scheduler manages the queues set up by the packet classifier.

TCP/IP Troubleshooting

Windows XP Professional and Windows Server 2003 offer several native programs that an administrator can use to troubleshoot TCP/IP issues. Some are full-fledged tools in their own right, such as FTP, but they can help in determining what might be affecting a TCP/IP network. Many of these TCP/IP troubleshooting tools are discussed in the sections that follow.

The PING Command

The PING command can be used to test network connectivity from a local system by sending an ICMP message to a remote host or gateway. On external networks such as the Internet, the use of PING might be somewhat limited, depending on how routers and firewalls are configured; many do not allow ICMP traffic. If the remote host receives the message, it responds with a reply message. PING notes the IP address, the number of bytes in the message, how long it took to reply (in milliseconds –], and the length of Time to Live (TTL) in seconds and shows any packet loss in terms of percentages, as shown here:

```
D:\>ping 192.168.1.225
Pinging 192.168.1.225 with 32 bytes of data:
Reply from 192.168.1.225: bytes=32 time<10ms TTL=128
Reply from 192.168.1.225: bytes=32 time<10ms TTL=128
Reply from 192.168.1.225: bytes=32 time<10ms TTL=128
Reply from 192.168.1.225: bytes=32 time<10ms TTL=128
Ping statistics for 192.168.1.225:
    Packets: Sent = 4, Received = 4, Lost = 0 (0% loss),
Approximate round trip times in milliseconds:
    Minimum = 0ms, Maximum =  0ms, Average =  0ms
Usage: ping [-t] [-a] [-n count] [-l size] [-f] [-i TTL] [-v TOS]
[-r count] [-s count] [[-j host-list] ¦ [-k host-list]]
[-w timeout] target_name
```

The following list describes the switches available for use with PING:

➤ -t—Ping the specified host until stopped. To see statistics and to continue, type Ctrl+Break; to stop, type Ctrl+C.

➤ -a—Resolve addresses to hostnames.

➤ -n count—The number of echo requests to send.

➤ -l size—Send buffer size.

➤ -f—Set the Don't Fragment flag in the packet.

➤ -i TTL—Time to Live.

➤ -v TOS—Type of Service.

➤ -r count—Record route for count hops.

➤ -s count—Timestamp for count hops.

➤ -j host-list—Loose source route along host list.

➤ -k host-list—Strict source route along host list.

➤ -w timeout—Time in milliseconds to wait for each reply.

The ARP Command

The ARP command displays and modifies the IP-to-physical address translation tables used by Address Resolution Protocol (ARP), as shown here:

```
ARP -s inet_addr eth_addr [if_addr]
ARP -d inet_addr [if_addr]
ARP -a [inet_addr] [-N if_addr]
```

The following list describes the switches available for use with ARP:

➤ -a—Displays current ARP entries by referencing the current protocol data. If inet_addr is specified, the IP and physical addresses for only the specified computer are displayed. If more than one network interface uses ARP, entries for each ARP table are displayed.

➤ -g—Same as -a.

➤ inet_addr—Specifies an Internet address.

➤ -N if_addr—Displays ARP entries for the network interface specified by if_addr.

➤ -d—Deletes the host specified by inet_addr. You can use * as a wildcard with inet_addr to delete all hosts.

➤ -s—Adds the host and associates the Internet address inet_addr with the physical (MAC) address.

➤ eth_addr—Uses the physical (MAC) address and is given as six hexadecimal bytes separated by hyphens.

➤ if_addr—Specifies the Internet address of the interface that should have its address translation table modified. If if_addr is not entered, the first applicable interface is used.

For example, the following code adds a static entry:

```
> arp -s 157.55.85.212 00-aa-00-62-c6-09 ....
```

The following displays the ARP table:

```
> arp -a
```

The **IPCONFIG** Command

IPCONFIG is a command-line tool for getting basic IP configuration information, including the IP address, subnet mask, and default gateway. The IPCONFIG /all switch produces a detailed configuration report for all interfaces on a system, including any configured remote access adapters, as shown here:

```
ipconfig [/? ¦ /all ¦ /renew [adapter] ¦ /release [adapter]
¦ /flushdns ¦ /displaydns ¦ /registerdns ¦ /showclassid adapter
¦ /setclassid adapter [classid] ]
```

The following list describes the switches available for use with IPCONFIG:

➤ /all—Display full configuration information.

➤ /release—Releases the IP address for the specified adapter.

➤ /renew—Renews the IP address for the specified adapter.

➤ /flushdns—Purges the DNS Resolver cache.

➤ /registerdns—Reregisters DNS names.

➤ /displaydns—Displays the contents of the DNS Resolver Cache.

➤ /showclassid—Displays all the DHCP class IDs allowed for adapter.

➤ /setclassid—Modifies the DHCP class ID.

The default is to display only the IP address, subnet mask, and default gateway for each adapter bound to TCP/IP. For /release and /renew, if no adapter name is specified, the IP address leases for all adapters bound to TCP/IP are released or renewed.

The **NBTSTAT** Command

NetBT Statistics (Nbtstat.exe) is a command-line tool that can be used to view and troubleshoot network NetBIOS over TCP/IP (NetBT) name resolution. It displays protocol statistics and current TCP/IP connections that are using NetBT.

NetBT resolves NetBIOS names to IP addresses by using several options for NetBIOS name resolution, including local cache lookup, WINS server query, broadcast, LMHOSTS and HOSTS file lookup, and DNS server query. It also displays protocol statistics and current TCP/IP connections using NetBT.

```
NBTSTAT [ [-a RemoteName] [-A IP address] [-c] [-n]
➥[-r] [-R] [-RR] [-s] [-S] [interval] ]
```

The following list describes the switches available for use with NBTSTAT:

➤ -a (adapter status)—Lists the remote machine's name table given its name.

➤ -A (adapter status)—Lists the remote machine's name table given its IP address.

➤ -c (cache)—Lists NBT's cache of remote (machine) names and their IP addresses.

➤ -n (names)—Lists local NetBIOS names.

➤ -r (resolved)—Lists names resolved by broadcast and via WINS.

➤ -R (Reload)—Purges and reloads the cache name table and reloads the #PRE tagged entries from the LMHOST file if any are present.

➤ -S (Sessions)—Lists the sessions table with the destination IP addresses.

➤ -s (sessions)—Lists the sessions table, converting destination IP addresses to computer NetBIOS names.

➤ -RR (ReleaseRefresh)—Sends Name Release packets to WINS and then starts Refresh.

➤ RemoteName—Remote host machine name.

➤ IP address—Dotted decimal representation of the IP address.

➤ interval—Redisplays selected statistics, pausing the number of seconds specified by interval between each display. Press Ctrl+C to stop redisplaying statistics.

The NETSTAT Command

NETSTAT (Netstat.exe) is a command-line tool that displays TCP/IP statistics and active connections to and from the local system. It can also display all connections and listening ports and has an option to display the number of bytes sent and received and any network packets dropped (if applicable).

NETSTAT [-a] [-e] [-n] [-o] [-s] [-p protocol] [-r] [interval]

The following list describes the switches available for use with NETSTAT:

➤ -a—Displays all connections and listening ports.

➤ -e—Displays ethernet statistics. Can be combined with the -s option.

➤ -n—Displays addresses and port numbers in numerical form.

➤ -o—Displays the owning process ID associated with each connection.

➤ -p protocol—Shows connections for the protocol specified by protocol, which can be TCP, UDP, TCPv6, or UDPv6. If used with the -s option to display per-protocol statistics, protocol can be any of the following: IP, IPv6, ICMP, ICMPv6, TCP, TCPv6, UDP, or UDPv6.

➤ -r—Displays the routing table.

➤ -s—Displays per-protocol statistics. By default, statistics are shown for IP, IPv6, ICMP, ICMPv6, TCP, TCPv6, UDP, and UDPv6; the -p option can be used to specify a subset of the default.

➤ interval—Redisplays selected statistics, pausing the number of seconds specified by interval between each display. Press Ctrl+C to stop redisplaying statistics. If this switch is omitted, NETSTAT prints the current configuration information once.

The **ROUTE** Command

The ROUTE command-line tool displays the current IP routing table for the local system, and it can be used to add or delete IP routes and to add persistent routes.

```
ROUTE [-f] [-p] [command] [destination] [MASK netmask]
➡[gateway] [METRIC metric] [IF interface]
```

The following list describes the switches available for use with ROUTE:

➤ -f—Clears the routing tables of all gateway entries. If it is used with one of the ROUTE commands (see the following list), the routing tables are cleared before running the command.

➤ -p—When used with the ADD command, it makes a route persistent across boots of the system. By default, routes are not preserved when the system is restarted. Ignored for all other commands, which always affect the appropriate persistent routes.

The following list describes the commands available for use with ROUTE:

➤ PRINT—Prints a route.

➤ ADD—Adds a route.

➤ DELETE—Deletes a route.

➤ CHANGE—Modifies an existing route.

➤ destination—Specifies the host.

➤ MASK—Specifies that the next parameter is the netmask value.

➤ netmask—Specifies a subnet mask value for this route entry. If not specified, it defaults to 255.255.255.255.

➤ gateway—Specifies the gateway.

➤ interface—Specifies the interface number for the specified route.

➤ METRIC—Specifies the metric—that is, the cost for the destination.

Names used for the destination command are looked up in the NETWORKS file on the local system. Names used for the gateway command are looked up in the HOSTS file on the local system. If the command is PRINT or DELETE, the destination or gateway can be a wildcard (*), or the gateway entry can be left blank. Invalid MASK entries, such as (DEST & MASK) != DEST, generate an error.

The **HOSTNAME** Command

HOSTNAME is a command-line tool for showing the local computer's hostname. It can be used for authentication purposes by the Remote Copy Protocol (RCP), Remote Shell (RSH), and Remote Execution (REXEC) tools.

The **TRACERT** Command

TRACERT is sometimes used to verify that IP addressing has been correctly configured on a client. It basically shows the route taken to reach a remote system.

```
tracert [-d] [-h maximum_hops] [-j host-list] [-w timeout] target_name
```

Here is a list of available switches for the TRACERT command:

➤ -d—Do not resolve addresses to hostnames.

➤ -h *maximum_hops*—Maximum number of hops to search for target.

➤ -j host-list—Loose source route along host list.

➤ -w *timeout*—Wait the number of milliseconds specified by *timeout* for each reply.

The **PATHPING** Command

Like TRACERT, PATHPING shows the route taken to reach a remote system, but PATHPING does so with more detail and offers more functionality.

```
pathping [-g host-list] [-h maximum_hops]
[-i address] [-n] [-p period] [-q num_queries]
[-w timeout] [-P] [-R] [-T] [-4] [-6] target_name
```

Here is a list of available switches for the PATHPING command:

➤ -g *host-list*—Loose source route along the host list.

➤ -h *maximum_hops*—Maximum number of hops to search for target.

➤ -i *address*—Use the specified source address.

➤ -n—Do not resolve addresses to hostnames.

➤ -p *period*—Wait the number of milliseconds specified by *period* between pings.

➤ -q *num_queries*—Number of queries per hop.

➤ -w *timeout*—Wait the number of milliseconds specified by *timeout* for each reply.

➤ -P—Test for RSVP PATH connectivity.

➤ -R—Test if each hop is RSVP aware.

➤ -T—Test connectivity to each hop with layer-2 priority tags.

➤ -4—Force using IPv4.

➤ -6—Force using IPv6.

The **FTP** Command

FTP is used to transfer files from system to system over TCP ports 20 and 21 (by default), but it can also help you diagnose problems on your TCP/IP network. By using Internet Explorer with FTP, users experience a Windows Explorer–type of GUI environment for the FTP file transfer by having features such as file and folder views, drag-and-drop, and copy-and-paste available.

The command-line FTP allows for more functionality. FTP is considered a connected session that uses TCP. FTP commands are as follows: !, delete, literal, prompt, send ?, debug, ls, put, status append, dir, mdelete, pwd, trace ascii, disconnect, mdir, quit, type, bell, get, mget, quote, user, binary, glob, mkdir, recv, verbose, bye, hash, mls, remotehelp, cd, help, mput, rename, close, lcd, open, and rmdir. Here is an example of the syntax:

```
FTP [-v] [-d] [-i] [-n] [-g] [-s:filename] [-a] [-w:windowsize] [-A] [host]
```

The following list explains the options you can use with the FTP command:

➤ -v—Suppresses display of remote server responses.

➤ -n—Suppresses auto-login at initial connection.

➤ -i—Turns off interactive prompting during multiple file transfers.

➤ -d—Enables debugging.

➤ -g—Disables filename globing.

➤ -s:*filename*—Specifies a text file containing FTP commands; the commands automatically run after FTP starts.

➤ -a—Use any local interface when binding a data connection.

➤ -A—Log in as anonymous.

➤ -w:*buffersize*—Overrides the default transfer buffer size of 4,096.

➤ *host*—Specifies the hostname or IP address of the remote host to connect to.

The **TFTP** Command

Trivial File Transfer Protocol allows for connectionless transfer of files to and from systems using UDP. Although TFTP is limited in functionality, there are still some command-line switches that can be used to tailor its performance:

```
TFTP [-i] host [GET ¦ PUT] source [destination]
```

Definitions for these switches are as follows:

➤ -i—Specifies binary image transfer mode (also called octet). In binary image mode, the file is moved literally byte by byte.

➤ *host*—Specifies the local or remote host by name.

➤ GET—Transfers the file destination on the remote host to the file source on the local host.

➤ PUT—Transfers the file source on the local host to the file destination on the remote host.

➤ *source*—Specifies the file to transfer.

➤ *destination*—Specifies where to transfer the file.

The **TELNET** Command

Telnet is a command-line terminal emulation program that enables an administrator to perform commands on a remote computer from a command window on a local system. Here is an example of the syntax:

```
telnet [-a] [-e char] [-f filename] [-l user] [-t term] [host] [port]
```

Definitions for TELNET switches are as follows:

➤ -a—Attempts automatic logon. Same as -1 option, except it uses the currently logged on user's name.

➤ -e *char*—Escape character to enter Telnet client prompt.

➤ -f *filename*—Filename for client-side logging.

➤ -l *user*—Specifies the username to log in with on the remote system. Requires that the remote system support the TELNET ENVIRON option.

➤ -t *term*—Specifies terminal type. Supported term types are vt100, vt52, ansi, and vtnt only.

➤ *host*—Specifies the hostname or IP address of the remote computer to connect to.

➤ *port*—Specifies a port number or service name.

The RCP Command

Remote Copy Protocol (RCP) uses TCP to copy files to and from systems running the RCP service. It can be scripted in a batch file and does not require a password. The remote host must be running the Remote Shell Daemon (RSHD) service, and the user's username must be configured in the remote host's .rhosts file. Microsoft's implementation of TCP/IP includes the RCP client software but not RSHD services. RCP is one of the r-commands available on all Unix systems.

RCP [-a ¦ -b] [-h] [-r] [*host*][*.user:*]*source* [*host*][*.user:*] *path\destination*

The following list explains the options you can use with the RCP command:

➤ -a—This is the default transfer mode that specifies ASCII transfer mode. This mode converts the end-of-line (EOL) characters to a carriage return for Unix and a carriage return/line feed for personal computers.

➤ -b—Specifies binary image transfer mode.

➤ -h—Transfers hidden files.

➤ -r—Copies the contents of all subdirectories; destination must be a directory.

➤ *host*—Specifies the local or remote host. If the host is specified as an IP address *or* if the hostname contains dots, you must specify the user.

➤ *.user:*—Specifies a username to use instead of the current username.

➤ *source*—Specifies the files to copy.

➤ *path\destination*—Specifies the path to the logon directory on the remote host.

The **RSH** Command

Remote Shell (RSH) enables clients to run commands directly on remote hosts running the RSH service without having to log on to the remote host. Microsoft's implementation of TCP/IP includes the RSH client software but not the RSH service. If a user on a computer running in a Windows domain tries to use RSH to run a command on a remote Unix server running RSH, the domain controller is required by the RSH client to resolve the user's username. RSH is one of the Unix r-commands that is available on all Unix systems.

The **REXEC** Command

Remote Execution (REXEC) runs commands on remote hosts running the REXEC service and authenticates the username on the remote host before executing the specified command.

```
REXEC host [-l username] [-n] command
```

The following list defines options to use with the REXEC command:

➤ *host*—Specifies the remote host on which to run the command.

➤ *-l username*—Specifies the username on the remote host.

➤ *-n*—Redirects the input of REXEC to NULL.

➤ *command*—Specifies the command to run.

Dynamic Host Configuration Protocol (DHCP)

By using the Dynamic Host Configuration Protocol (DHCP) service in Windows Server 2003, client systems can be automatically configured with IP addresses and other configurable parameters that allow them to operate on the network. To install the DHCP role on the server, refer to the "DHCP Server Role" section in Chapter 2, "Server Roles and Security."

After the server role has been established, you must authorize the DHCP server in Active Directory if it is installed on a member server. To do this, log in to the domain with administrative rights, run the DHCP MMC, and choose Action, Manage Authorized Servers from the menu. When the Manage Authorized Servers dialog box opens, you can then authorize the server.

DHCP and Domain Controllers

If you are installing the DHCP server role on a domain controller, the server should be automatically authorized the first time you add the server to the DHCP console. You can also use the Configure Your Server Wizard to install the DHCP role on your system, as outlined in Chapter 2, "Server Roles and Security."

Requiring DHCP servers from both the Windows 2000 Server and Windows Server 2003 families to be authorized in Active Directory introduces a certain level of stability to your network. Adding Active Directory authorization prevents Windows 2000 and 2003 servers from being brought online when they are not authorized and causing IP address allocation issues on the network.

The downside (for lack of a better term) is that nothing prevents Windows NT 4 DHCP servers, Unix DHCP servers, or hardware DHCP devices, such as routers that offer DHCP addresses, from being introduced onto the network.

Windows Server 2003 can provide IP addresses by using DHCP manual assignment, DHCP dynamic assignment, or Automatic Private IP Addressing (APIPA).

NOTE
In actuality, the DHCP client service supplies IP addresses when it attempts to contact the DHCP server and cannot get a response. Also, no default gateway is assigned to clients when APIPA is used. Because of this, clients using APIPA are limited to their own subnet.

Manual IP address assignment and DHCP manual address assignment are actually two different things. For manual IP address assignment, an administrator or similarly delegated person manually enters a static IP address and other information, such as the subnet mask and default gateway, DNS server, WINS server, and so forth.

DHCP manual address assignment dynamically assigns the same specific IP address from a scope of addresses to a specific DHCP client each time the client starts up by using the DHCP service. This enables administrators to automatically assign a static IP address to these systems without actually having to set each system with all the parameters (default gateway, DNS servers, and so on), as with manual IP address assignment.

DHCP automatic assignment dynamically assigns randomly available IP addresses from available scopes to all DHCP clients each time they start up by using the DHCP service. This allows administrators to automatically assign IP addresses to clients without actually having to set all the parameters (default gateway, DNS servers, and so on) for each system, as with manual IP address assignment.

DHCP servers are usually set up with multiple scopes, called a *superscope*, to work side by side with other DHCP servers in the enterprise. The DHCP lease process begins over UDP ports 67 and 68 as a broadcast message from the client system. For DHCP clients to successfully contact DHCP servers on remote networks, the IP routers must be RFC 1542 compliant. These routers support forwarding DHCP broadcasts off the local subnet. If the routers are not compliant, a DHCP Relay Agent must be in use on that subnet.

The DHCP Relay Agent is available through the Routing and Remote Access MMC on Windows Server 2003 (see Figure 3.1). Systems configured in the role of a DHCP server should not be configured as DHCP Relay Agents because both services use UDP ports 67 and 68 and degrade each other's services if they are installed together. On a single subnet, there is no practical need to do this because the DHCP server should simply respond to user requests on the subnet.

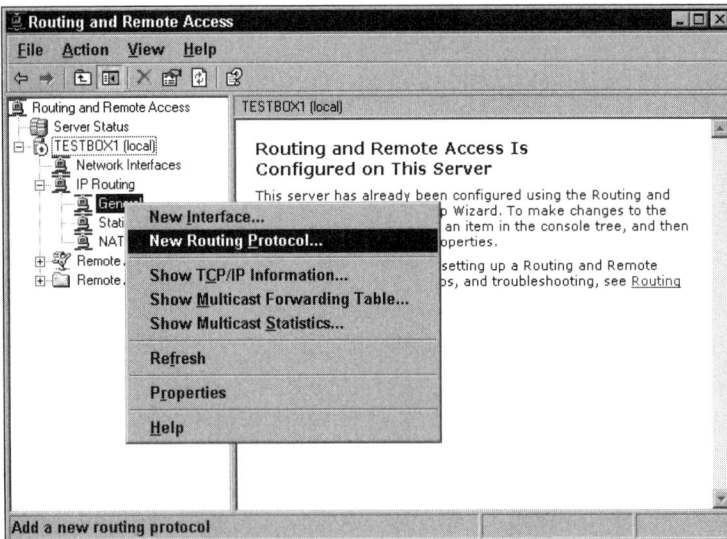

Figure 3.1 The first step in configuring the DHCP Relay Agent service in the Routing and Remote Access MMC.

Figure 3.2 shows the available routing protocols in the New Routing Protocol dialog box: DHCP Relay Agent, IGMP Router and Proxy, Open Shortest Path First (OSPF), and RIP Version 2 for Internet Protocol.

When a client first starts, it sends out a DHCPDISCOVER broadcast message to all addresses (255.255.255.255). The message contains the client's hardware (MAC) address and hostname. (The client also sends this message when its original lease has expired and cannot be renewed.) All available DHCP servers that are configured to respond receive the DHCPDISCOVER broadcast and send a DHCPOFFER broadcast message back with the following information:

➤ The client's hardware address

➤ An offered IP address

➤ Subnet mask

➤ Length of the lease

➤ A server identifier (the IP address of the offering DHCP server)

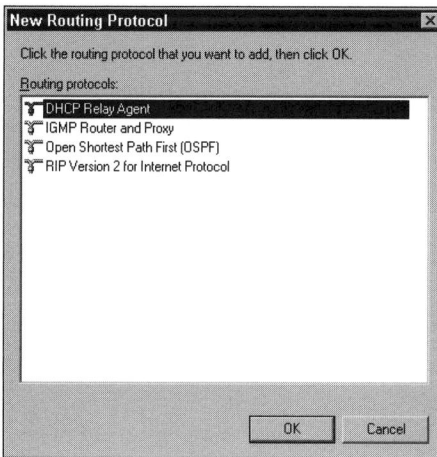

Figure 3.2 You can add routing protocols through the New Routing Protocol dialog box.

The DHCP client selects the IP address from the first offer it receives and responds with a DHCPREQUEST broadcast message that includes the IP address of the server whose offer was accepted. All the other DHCP servers then retract their lease offers and mark those addresses available for the next IP lease request.

The DHCP server whose lease was accepted responds with a DHCPACK broadcast message, which contains the valid lease period for that IP address and other configuration information outlined in the scope, such as router information (default gateway), subnet mask, and so forth. After the DHCP client receives this acknowledgment, TCP/IP is completely initialized, and the client can use the IP address for communication.

Automatic Private IP Addressing (APIPA)

When a DHCP client sends out the DHCPDISCOVER broadcast message, it waits one second for an offer. If the client does not receive a response from a DHCP server, it rebroadcasts the request three times at 9-, 13-, and 16-second intervals, with a random offset length of 0ms and 1000ms. If an offer is not received after the four requests, the client retries once every five minutes.

Beginning with Windows 98, DHCP clients can configure themselves by using APIPA and the DHCP client service. After the four attempts to receive an IP address have failed, the DHCP client auto-configures its IP address and subnet mask using the reserved Class B network address 169.254.0.0 and the subnet mask 255.255.0.0. No default gateway is used, so systems that use APIPA are not routable.

The DHCP client tests for an address conflict to make sure the IP address it has chosen is not already in use on the network. To do this, it broadcasts its selection from the range to the local subnet. If a conflict is found, the client selects another IP address and continues this process up to 10 attempts.

After the DHCP client makes sure the address it has chosen is not in conflict with another system on the subnet, it configures its network interface with the IP address. The client then continues to check for a response from the DHCP server every five minutes. If a DHCP server becomes available, the client drops its APIPA settings and uses the address the DHCP server offers at that time.

DHCP Relay Agent

When a DHCP client request for an IP address hits a non-RFC-1542–compliant router (meaning that the DHCPDISCOVER broadcast message can't be forwarded off the subnet), it fails to receive a response because the DHCP server never receives the DHCPDISCOVER broadcast message, and the client system configures itself with an APIPA address.

If a DHCP Relay Agent is in use on the subnet, it receives the DHCPDIS-COVER broadcast message and forwards (routes) the message off the subnet to the DHCP server. Subsequently, when the DHCP server responds with an address and the DHCP client selects the IP address, the client responds with a DHCPREQUEST broadcast message that includes the IP address of the server whose offer was accepted. Again, this DHCPREQUEST broad-cast message does not get out of this subnet unless a DHCP Relay Agent in use on the subnet can receive the DHCPREQUEST broadcast message and forward (route) the message off the subnet to the DHCP server.

Placement of DHCP Servers

DHCP servers should be located on at least one subnet on a LAN in a routed network. When the server needs to support clients on remote subnets separated by routers, the router should be RFC 1542 compliant, or a DHCP Relay Agent should be used to support forwarding DHCP traffic between the subnets.

When your network design allows more than one DHCP server to respond to requests, best practices dictate using the 80/20 rule, at a minimum, to divide the scope of addresses between the two DHCP servers. If Server 1 is configured to make available most of the addresses (approximately 80%) in the scope, Server 2 can be configured to make the remainder of the scope addresses (approximately 20%) available to clients.

> **NOTE**
>
> The 80/20 rule for splitting addresses available in the scope can be tailored to meet your environment's addressing needs.

DNS

The Windows Server 2003 DNS Service offers a number of new features and enhancements, and many of the Windows 2000 features have been carried over as well. For example, you can configure *conditional forwarders* on your Windows Server 2003 DNS server to forward all DNS queries for a specific domain name to an IP address of a specific DNS server or servers. Conditional forwarders can be used in both intranet and Internet queries.

You can also use forward-only servers when you need to manage the DNS traffic between your network and the Internet. To do this, you configure the firewall your network uses so that only one DNS server is allowed to communicate with the Internet. This requires you to configure the other DNS servers in your enterprise to forward queries they cannot resolve locally to the Internet-enabled DNS server in the DMZ so that the query can be resolved.

The Windows Server 2003 DNS service provides basic support of the DNS Security Extensions (DNSSEC) protocol defined in RFC 2535, which allows DNS servers to perform as secondary DNS servers for existing DNSSEC–compliant, secure zones. Windows Server 2003 DNS supports storing and loading DNSSEC-specific resource records (RRs).

Microsoft DNS is not a requirement for Active Directory, but it is recommended. Microsoft DNS on Windows Server 2003 is compliant with most of the RFC specifications used to define the DNS protocol and allows deploying Active Directory under other DNS implementations. The Windows Server 2003 DNS service supports the following features:

➤ IETF Internet-Draft "A DNS RR for specifying the location of services (DNS SRV)" (SRV records)

➤ Dynamic updates

➤ Secure dynamic update based on the General Security Service Transaction Signature (GSS-TSIG) algorithm

➤ WINS and WINS R (reverse) records

➤ Fast zone transfer

➤ Incremental zone transfer

➤ Support for UTF (eight-character encoding)

> **NOTE**
>
> Berkeley Internet Name Domain (BIND) DNS servers regard Active Directory–integrated zones as Standard Primary DNS zones. Active Directory–integrated zones can replicate DNS updates to other Active Directory–integrated zones or to Standard Secondary DNS zones. Because Active Directory–integrated zones can replicate DNS data to Standard Secondary DNS zones, you can use Active Directory–integrated zones with BIND servers hosting Standard Secondary DNS zones.

DNS is the primary naming convention for Windows 2000 and 2003 domains; it provides name resolution for client systems by translating computer names to IP addresses so that computers can locate each other. DNS domains and Active Directory domains can share a common naming structure; in many cases, they are identical, but they can also be completely different. For example, `Server1.gunderville.com` is a valid Windows domain name and could be the internal name for a host. If that same server were available to the Internet for access, it could also use that naming convention if it was available. The best analogy for correlating DNS names with IP addresses is using the phone book to look up someone's name (the DNS name, in other words) to find his or her area code and phone number (that is, the IP address).

There are two types of DNS lookup queries: forward and reverse. A *forward lookup query* resolves a DNS name to an IP address and is the most common DNS query. When you perform a forward lookup, such as entering `http://www.zandri.net` into a browser, your client looks up the Web site's IP address with the assistance of a DNS server behind the scenes. A *reverse lookup query* resolves an IP address to a name. A DNS name server can resolve a query only for a zone for which it has authority. When DNS servers receive a name resolution request, they attempt to locate the requested information in their own cache and local database.

DNS servers cache all external name resolution data for a specific interval called Time to Live (TTL). The default TTL for DNS resolution is one hour; for WINS lookups via DNS, the default is 15 minutes.

DNS administrators can adjust the default settings for the DNS cache by going to the zone's Properties dialog box and selecting the Start of Authority (SOA) tab. To change the 15-minute default setting for WINS, select the WINS tab and click the Advanced Settings button.

Configuring a shorter TTL interval ensures that DNS and WINS information is more up to date, but it also increases the load on your DNS server, your WINS server, and your network. You can increase the interval when network resources are a higher premium than "freshness" of name resolution.

Two types of queries can be performed in DNS: iterative and recursive. An *iterative query* happens when a client makes a DNS resolution query to a DNS server, and the server returns the best answer it can provide based on its local cache or stored zone data. If the server resolving the iterative query does not have an exact match for the name request, it provides a pointer to an authoritative server in another level of the domain namespace. The client system then queries that server, and continues this process until it locates a server that is authoritative for the requested name or until an error is returned, such as "name not found," or a timeout condition is met.

A *recursive query* happened when a client makes a DNS resolution query to a DNS server, and the server assumes the full workload and responsibility for providing a complete answer to the query. If the server cannot resolve the query from its own database, it performs separate iterative queries to other servers (on behalf of the client) to assist in resolving the recursive query. The server continues this process until it locates a server that is authoritative for the requested name or until an error is returned, such as "name not found," or a timeout condition is met.

In most cases, client computers send recursive queries to DNS servers, and usually the DNS server is set up to make iterative queries to supply an answer to the client. In the following query example, a client computer makes a request to a DNS server to resolve the Web address http://www.zandri.net:

1. The client computer generates a request for the IP address of www. zandri.net by sending a recursive query to the DNS server it is configured to use in its network configuration. (Call this server LOCAL-CFG.)

2. The LOCALCFG DNS server looks in its local database for an answer. If it finds that answer locally, it is returned to the client. Usually this happens only if the server is authoritative for the DNS zone in question or if it is hosting secondary zone files for other DNS zones. If the client is client1.zandri.net and is looking for www.zandri.net from DNS server localcfg.zandri.net, localcfg.zandri.net would likely have the required information in its own database.

   For the purposes of the remainder of this description, assume that the client looking for http://www.zandri.net is not going to find DNS resolution on the local DNS server and that LOCALCFG is not a member of the zandri.net domain and does not host secondary zone files for the zandri.net domain.

   NOTE The answer to this DNS query might be in the local cache if the DNS server recently looked up this resolution request for another client. In a large enterprise with many DNS clients connecting to the Internet, it would not be uncommon for many of the largest Internet sites to be almost constantly present in the local DNS server's cache, as clients throughout the enterprise commonly query for the name resolution of those servers.

3. If LOCALCFG is unable to locate an entry for www.zandri.net in its own database, it sends an iterative query to a DNS server that is authoritative for the root of the local domain. (Call this server LOCALROOT.)

4. If the LOCALROOT DNS server, which is authoritative for the root domain, has the answer in its local database, it sends a response to LOCALCFG. If the LOCALROOT DNS server is unable to locate an entry for www.zandri.net in its database, it sends a reply to the LOCAL-CFG DNS server with the IP address of a DNS server that is authoritative for the .net domain. (Call these servers DNSNETx; x would be the numerical designation of a particular server.)

   NOTE If the address ends in **.com**, IP addresses of DNS servers that are authoritative for the **.com** domain are sent. For addresses ending in **.org**, IP addresses of DNS servers that are authoritative for the **.org** domain are sent, and so on.

5. The LOCALCFG DNS server that received the client's recursive query sends an iterative query to the DNSNET server.

6. If the DNSNET server has an entry for `www.zandri.net` in its local cache, it returns the answer to the LOCALCFG DNS server. If DNSNET is unable to locate an entry for `www.zandri.net` in its database, it sends a reply to the LOCALCFG DNS server with the IP addresses of DNS servers that are authoritative for the `zandri.net` domain. (Call this server ZANDRIDNS.)

7. The LOCALCFG DNS server sends an iterative query to the ZANDRIDNS server.

8. The ZANDRIDNS server locates an entry for `www.zandri.net` in its database and sends a reply to the LOCALCFG DNS server with the IP address of `www.zandri.net`.

9. The LOCALCFG DNS server sends a reply to the client computer with the IP address of `www.zandri.net`, which allows that client's Web browser to display the Web page on `www.zandri.net`.

When DNS clients make a request for a reverse DNS lookup, they are effectively making a request to resolve a hostname of a known IP address. In the standard DNS namespace, there is no connection between hostnames and IP addresses, and only a thorough search of all domains allows for reverse resolution.

Often, DNS servers are called on to resolve the same query multiple times within a short time. As an example, if a number of AOL users (arguably the largest ISP in the world) get an email reporting that new articles have been posted to `www.2000trainers.com` and immediately go to this site to read the new articles, the AOL DNS servers must continually recall the resolved address many times within a short period and use their local cache to do so.

DNS servers cache resolved addresses for a specific duration, specified as the TTL in the returned data. The DNS server administrator of the zone containing the data decides on the TTL setting. Therefore, the administrator of the `2000trainers.com` domain and the DNS servers for that domain sets the TTL value. This value tells the resolving AOL DNS servers how long to hold that information in their cache. The lower the TTL, the "fresher" the resolution data is on the resolving AOL DNS servers.

After a DNS server caches data, it decreases the TTL from its original value so that it knows when to flush data from its cache. If another resolution query comes to the DNS server for the URL, the cached data is used and the TTL is reset (in most cases) to the original TTL. (The only time the TTL value isn't reset to its original value is if the administrator sets a different TTL.)

> **NOTE**
>
> In some instances, it is practical and perhaps necessary to disable recursion on certain DNS servers. If your enterprise has a number of internal-only DNS servers, it is not necessary for those servers to continue attempting to resolve **yahoo.com** for your clients, for example.
>
> By setting certain DNS servers to not perform recursive lookups, in effect external lookup resolutions would quickly fail (as they would not have local data for **yahoo.com**). This allows client systems to fail over to another DNS server they have been configured to use to resolve the external name. For this process to be effective, the other DNS server would have to be one that handles external lookups.

The `in-addr.arpa` domain was created to avoid query overloads on DNS servers. System names in the `in-addr.arpa` domain are listed by their respective IP addresses. Because IP addresses are designed so that they become more significant as you move from left to right in the address, and domain names get less significant from left to right, IP addresses in the `in-addr.arpa` domain are listed in reverse order.

Pointer (PTR) records are added to IP addresses and corresponding hostnames. To perform a successful reverse lookup of an IP address, such as 121.41.113.10, the DNS server performing the query looks for a PTR record for `10.113.41.121.inaddr.arpa`, which has the hostname and IP address 121.41.113.10.

DNS Zone Overview

A *DNS zone* is a contiguous portion of the domain namespace for which a DNS server has authority to resolve DNS queries. DNS namespaces are almost always divided into zones, which store name information about one or more DNS domains or portions of a DNS domain.

In the Windows Server 2003 Active Directory domain structure, there are three different zone types: Standard Primary zones, Standard Secondary zones, and stub zones. *Standard Primary zone* files contain a read/write version of the zone file that is stored in a standard text file. Any changes to the zone are recorded only in that file. Any other copies of that zone are Standard Secondary zone copies and are read-only.

A *Standard Secondary zone* file contains a read-only version of a Standard Primary zone file stored in a standard text file. Any changes to the zone are performed on the Primary zone file and replicated to the Secondary zone file. You create a Standard Secondary zone to make a copy of an existing

Standard Primary zone and its zone file, which allows the DNS name resolution workload to be distributed among multiple DNS servers, thus providing a certain level of fault tolerance and load balancing. Also, for remote sites, a Standard Secondary zone on that local site keeps local user systems from consuming unnecessary bandwidth by going over the WAN to query the DNS server. In most cases, local user systems are configured with the local DNS server that hosts the Standard Secondary zone as their primary DNS server, and perhaps another DNS server (at the main site) as a secondary DNS server.

Stub zones allow a DNS server that is authoritative for the parent zone to be kept aware of other authoritative DNS servers for its child DNS zones in an effort to maintain DNS name resolution parity. Configuring stub zones enables administrators to distribute a list of the authoritative DNS servers for a zone without using Standard Secondary zones. Stub zones do not serve the same purpose as Standard Secondary zones and should not be used explicitly for redundancy and load balancing.

Caching-only DNS servers perform name resolution on behalf of clients and then cache the resulting name resolutions. They are not configured to be authoritative for a DNS zone and do not store Standard Primary or Standard Secondary zones locally. Their local cache holds the most frequently requested names and associated IP addresses and are available for subsequent client queries. This helps reduce traffic across a WAN because a caching-only server attempts to locate information in its cache to resolve local client requests and queries across the WAN for name resolution only when the information needed to complete the name resolution request is not available.

Also, because a caching-only server does not maintain any zone files that need to be updated via replication, it does not generate any zone transfer traffic. Active Directory–integrated zones store DNS zone information in the Active Directory database rather than a text file. The Active Directory–integrated option is not available in the Change Zone Type dialog box unless the DNS server is also a domain controller. If the DNS server is not configured as a domain controller in your environment, the option to create the zone as Active Directory integrated is grayed out during the creation of the zone (see Figure 3.3).

When replication is considered for Standard zone types, Primary zones are the only read/write copy of the DNS zone database, and only one Standard Primary zone exists. You can replicate the zone to any number of Standard Secondary DNS zones as needed, and these zones are read-only copies of the zone information. The only place where updates to the DNS zone database can occur is on the Standard Primary copy of the zone. The changes recorded there are replicated incrementally by incremental zone transfer (IXFR) or by transferring the entire zone database via full zone transfer (AXFR).

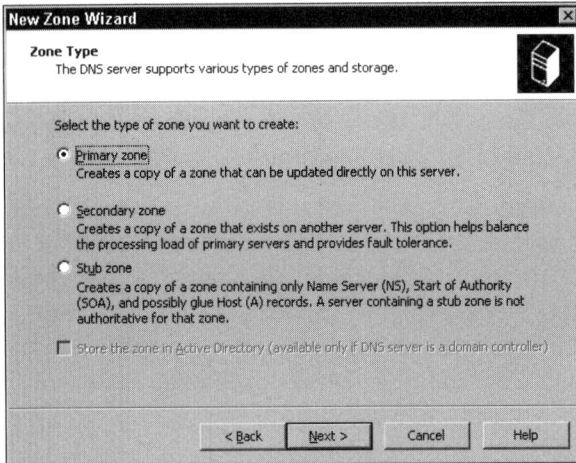

Figure 3.3 The option to create the DNS zone as Active Directory integrated is grayed out because the server is not installed in the role of a domain controller.

Although a Standard Primary DNS server with multiple Standard Secondary servers is fault tolerant and load-balanced to a degree, the loss of the Standard Primary DNS server prevents updates to the DNS database until an administrator can intervene. The administrator needs to repair the downed Standard Primary DNS server or promote a Standard Secondary DNS server to a Standard Primary DNS server. Name resolution still occurs with only the Standard Secondary servers functioning.

DNS zone transfers occur on a preconfigured basis, which is set to 15 minutes by default. This preconfigured basis is called a *refresh interval*, and its setting is found in the Start of Authority (SOA) tab of a zone's Properties dialog box. When the refresh interval expires, DNS servers request a copy of the current SOA record for their zone.

The DNS server then compares the serial number of the source DNS server's current SOA record with the serial number in its own local SOA record. If the responding DNS serial number is higher, the DNS server requests a zone transfer from the Primary DNS server. If a network issue or some other error prevents the zone transfer, the requesting DNS server retries the request for a zone transfer at a preconfigured interval, which is called a *retry interval* and is set to 10 minutes by default.

If the failure is persistent and a zone transfer cannot be completed, the requesting DNS server quits making requests for a zone transfer after the *expire interval* (default setting is one day) has been exceeded. Active Directory–integrated DNS zones store zone information in Active Directory and are multimaster in nature, which enables administrators to configure systems so that updates to the DNS database can occur on any domain controller hosting the DNS zone. This type of setup is fully load balanced and fault tolerant; the loss of any single DNS server does not affect DNS name resolution or updates to the DNS database because any DNS server can receive updates.

Because Active Directory–integrated zones store zone information in Active Directory, the DNS information is replicated along with other Active Directory data. This configuration also enables administrators to establish permissions using Access Control Lists (ACLs) to allow only authenticated systems, groups, or users to make updates to the DNS zone.

> **NOTE**
>
> ACL permissions to update the DNS zone are made in the DNS zone container within Active Directory and can be assigned for the entire DNS zone or for individual resource records within the zone. They can also be assigned to systems, groups, or users.

Active Directory–integrated zones can be configured for the following types of replication (see Figure 3.4):

➤ Replication can be configured so that all DNS servers in the Active Directory forest can replicate DNS zone data to all DNS servers running on domain controllers within the Active Directory forest. (For the most part, this is the Active Directory–integrated DNS zone replication in Windows 2000 Server.)

➤ Replication can be configured so that all DNS servers in the Active Directory domain can replicate DNS zone data to all DNS servers running on domain controllers in the local domain. This is the default Active Directory–integrated DNS zone replication setup in Windows Server 2003.

➤ Replication can be configured so that all domain controllers in the Active Directory domain can replicate DNS zone data to all domain controllers in the Active Directory domain. You can use this setting if you need Windows 2000 DNS servers to load a specific Active Directory zone.

➤ Replication can be configured so that all domain controllers in a specified application directory partition can replicate DNS zone data according to the replication scope of the specified application directory partition. For a zone to be stored in the specified application directory partition, the DNS server hosting the zone must be enlisted in the specified application directory partition.

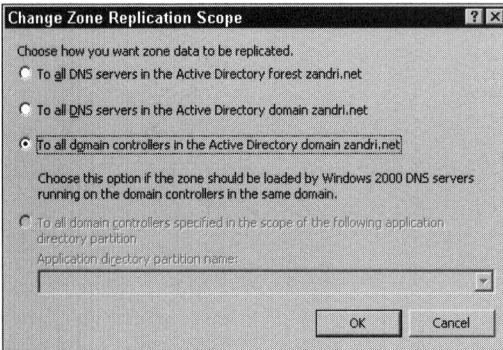

Figure 3.4 There are three options for changing the scope of DNS replication in Active Directory.

NOTE

Active Directory–integrated DNS zone data replicated to application directory partitions is not replicated to the forest's Global Catalog. The domain controller containing the Global Catalog can also host application directory partitions, but it does not replicate this data to its Global Catalog.

Active Directory–integrated DNS zone data replicated to domain partitions is replicated to all domain controllers in its Active Directory domain, and a portion of this data is stored in the Global Catalog. This setting is used to support Windows 2000.

TIP

The default configuration of the Windows Server 2003 DNS service allows zone transfers only to servers listed in a zone's Name Server (NS) resource records. Administrators can increase the security of the zone transfer process by changing the setting to allow zone transfers to the specified IP addresses of those servers only.

If DNS zone transfers must take place over a public network, such as the Internet, you can protect replication data by using VPNs and IPSec encryption. Using Active Directory–integrated zones exclusively for replicating DNS zone data adds another layer of security to zone transfers.

DNS zone files contain the name resolution data for a zone and include resource records with database entries containing various attributes of network systems. The most common resource records are discussed in the following sections.

(A) Records

Sometimes called host records or address records, *(A) records* contain the name–to–IP address mapping information used to map DNS domain names to a host IP address on the network. The following are examples of host or (A) records:

```
server1      IN A 121.41.113.10
localhost    IN A 127.0.0.1
```

Alias Records

Normally referred to as CNAME (canonical name) records, *Alias records* allow you to provide additional names to a server that already has a name in an (A) resource record. This is how a Web server with a name of Server1 in a domain of zandri.net "becomes" www.zandri.net, as far as DNS resolution is concerned: There is an Alias record referencing www.zandri.net to Server1.zandri.net. Here are some examples of using CNAME records:

```
www          CNAME Server1
ftp          CNAME Server1
```

MX (Mail Exchanger) Records

MX (Mail Exchanger) records specify which server email should be delivered to in a domain. When you have a mail server named Mailbox.zandri.net and you want all mail for all_users@zandri.net to be delivered to this mail server (named Mailbox in this example), the MX resource record must exist in the zone for Zandri.net and point to Mailbox.

NS (Name Server) Records

NS (Name Server) records designate DNS domain names for the servers that are authoritative for a DNS zone and can list additional name servers within the record. The following is an example of an NS record:

```
@ IN NS server2.zandri.net
```

The at symbol (@) in a database file indicates "this server" and the IN indicates an Internet record.

PTR (Pointer) Records

PTR (Pointer) records are used for reverse lookup queries that resolve IP addresses to names. Reverse lookup zones are created in the in-addr.arpa domain to designate a reverse mapping of a host IP address to a host DNS domain name.

As mentioned previously, to perform a successful reverse lookup of a IP address, such as 121.41.113.10, the DNS server performing the query looks for a PTR record for `10.113.41.121.in-addr.arpa`, which has the hostname and IP address 121.41.113.10. The PTR record for it looks like this:

```
10.113.41.121.in-addr.arpa. IN PTR Server1.Zandri.net.
```

Reverse lookup zones are not a requirement; they are an optional configuration for your DNS server in most cases. In certain situations, a reverse lookup zone might be required to verify the location of connecting clients.

SOA (Start of Authority) Records

SOA (Start of Authority) records indicate the starting point of authority for a DNS zone on a specific DNS server. The SOA record is the first resource record created when you add a new zone. The following is an example of an SOA record:

```
@ IN SOA server1.zandri.net. (
                        1        ; serial number
                        7200   ; refresh [2h]
                        900     ; retry [15m]
                        86400 ; expire [1d]
                        7200 ) ; min TTL [2h]
```

The at symbol (@) in a database file indicates "this server." `IN` indicates an Internet record. Any hostname not terminated with a period has the root domain appended. The @ symbol is replaced by a period in the administrator's email address. Parentheses must enclose line breaks that span more than one line. The `7200 ; refresh [2h]` shows a refresh interval of two hours, `900 ; retry [15m]` shows a retry interval of 15 minutes, `86400 ; expire [1d]` shows an expire interval of one day, and `7200 ; min TTL [2h]` shows a minimum TTL of two hours. Everything after a semicolon (;) is a comment, which is why line breaks are necessary.

SRV (Service) Records

Sometimes referred to as Service Location records, *SRV (Service) records* contain registered services within the zone so that clients can locate these services by using DNS. SRV records are mainly used to identify services in Active Directory.

The `CACHE.DNS` file contains the records of the root DNS servers. The cache file is basically the same on all name servers and must be present for a DNS server to handle a query outside its zone. The file provided by default with the Windows 2003 DNS server has current records for all the root servers on the Internet. This file is stored in the `%SystemRoot%\System32\Dns` folder when you install DNS on your Windows Server 2003 server.

If you are running DNS for internal use, not for connections for forwarding to the Internet, the CACHE.DNS file should be replaced to contain the name server's authoritative domains for the root of the private network. In certain situations, you replace the CACHE.DNS file in the %SystemRoot%\System32\Dns folder, and it does not update the root hints listed in the DNS Manager. This can happen because the DNS server is a domain controller configured to load zone data on startup from Active Directory and the Registry. If the root hints specified in Active Directory have been deleted, modified, incorrectly entered, or damaged, this behavior occurs. There is more information on CACHE.DNS in "Need To Know More?" at the end of this chapter.

Root hints consist of a list of resource records that the DNS service can use to locate other DNS servers that are authoritative for the root of the DNS domain namespace tree in your enterprise. For DNS servers that have been deployed to resolve names external to your environment, root hints host addresses for the Internet root servers. When a new server is added or removed from your DNS structure, administrators might need to update the root hints list.

For a current copy of the root hints file for Internet root servers, you can download a copy of the named.root file from ftp://ftp.internic.net/domain/. Figure 3.5 shows the DNS files you can download from InterNIC for DNS use.

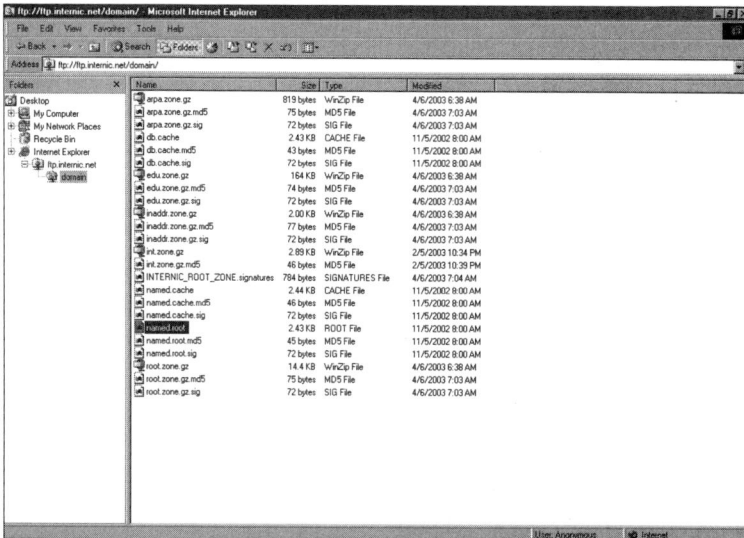

Figure 3.5 You can download DNS files from InterNIC to use with DNS.

You must take a number of considerations into account when you are planning your DNS namespace design. When setting up DNS in your environment, you should register a unique parent (second-level) DNS domain name that can be used for hosting your organization on the Internet, such as "zandri" in `zandri.net` or "2000trainers" in `2000trainers.com`. Even if you are not currently connected to the Internet via your proposed domain name or are not considering it in the near future, you should still make an effort to register your DNS domain name because you can't accurately predict what course your company might take in the future. If your company does decide to establish an Internet presence, you might find that the name you are currently using is registered to someone else. In that case, not only will you be unable to use it, but you will have to redesign your entire DNS deployment.

Also, you need to consider to which top-level domain name you will tie your second-level name. Table 3.4 shows the most common top-level domain names currently available on the Internet.

Table 3.4	Top-Level Domain Names	
Top-Level Name	**Description**	**Traditionally Used By:**
arpa	Run by Advanced Research Project Agency (ARPA). Used to register reverse mapping of IPv4 addresses assigned to DNS domain names for computers that use those addresses on the Internet.	The **in-addr.arpa** domain
com	For business and commercial use.	Businesses and corporations
edu	For educational use.	Public and private schools, colleges, and universities
gov	For use by government institutions.	Local, state, and federal government agencies
int	Reserved for international use. Currently planned for use in RFC 1886 to register reverse mapping of IPv6 addresses assigned by IANA to DNS domain names in the **ip6.int** domain for computers that use those addresses on the Internet.	The **ip6.int** domain

(continued)

Table 3.4	Top-Level Domain Names *(continued)*	
Top-Level Name	**Description**	**Traditionally Used By:**
mil	For use by military agencies.	Department of Defense (DoD), U.S. Navy, U.S. Army, U.S. Air Force, and other military agencies
net	For use by organizations that provide large-scale Internet or telephony-based service.	Large-scale Internet and telephone service providers
org	For use by noncommercial, nonprofit organizations.	Noncommercial, nonprofit organizations and charitable institutions

After your parent domain name is in place, you can configure other child names as needed. For example, `forums.2000trainers.com` can be created as a child of `2000trainers.com` for resources the forums section of `2000trainers` uses, and additional child domains could be established as needed. The domain might be broken down by geographical region, in which `us.forums.2000trainers.com` is one child domain and `canada.forums.2000trainers.com` is another.

Active Directory domains often correspond directly with DNS names. When choosing DNS names to use for Active Directory, starting with the registered DNS domain name suffix your organization has reserved for use on the Internet is best. Effectively, it means that internal and external namespaces are the same. For example, `zandri.net` is what you can reach from the Internet *and* the intranet. The main benefit is that users access one domain name when they need to find resources, regardless of where those resources exist.

This common naming scheme causes a certain amount of additional administration to make certain that appropriate DNS and SRV records are stored on internal and external DNS servers. You could also use a delegated namespace internally, so that `2000trainers.com` is reachable from the Internet and the Active Directory namespace is set up with something along the lines of `corp.2000trainers.com`.

This configuration offers better security because users and computers outside the organization cannot access the private DNS namespace from standard Internet connections with the proper segmentation of DNS zones. There is also less administrative overhead for DNS and SRV records, as the zones for both namespaces are independent of each other. This setup could cause some confusion for internal users, however, if they need to access certain network resources from the external domain.

Optionally, the entire internal Active Directory namespace can be totally separate from the external namespace, so that `zandri.net` is used from the Internet and `mcmcse.com` is used internally. This configuration also offers better security, as users and computers outside the organization cannot access the private DNS namespace from standard Internet connections with the proper segmentation of DNS zones. There is also less administrative overhead for DNS and SRV records because the zones for both namespaces are independent of each other. This setup could also cause confusion for internal users, however, if they need to access certain network resources from the external domain.

Optimizing DNS

Administrators can optimize DNS servers in the enterprise by disabling local subnet prioritization and round-robin rotation. *Local subnet prioritization* is used so that clients on the same subnet as the available DNS server, based on IP address location, have priority over other DNS clients. *Round-robin rotation* of available DNS servers provides network load balancing. Disabling either or both settings reduces and balances client response time, for the most part, across the entire enterprise. Both settings are enabled by default.

Other DNS configurations can be modified from their default settings in an effort to tailor preferences to a locale's specific needs. To adjust these settings, right-click the DNS server in the DNS MMC, choose Properties, and select the Advanced tab of the Properties dialog box. Table 3.5 shows the properties that can be configured and the default settings.

Table 3.5 Default DNS Settings in Windows 2003 Server	
Property	**Default Settings**
Disable recursion	Off
BIND secondaries	On
Fail on load if bad zone data	Off
Enable round robin	On
Enable netmask ordering	On
Secure cache against pollution	On
Name checking	Multibyte (UTF8)
Load zone data on startup	From Active Directory and Registry
Enable automatic scavenging of stale records	Off

Client Dynamic Updates and DHCP

You can configure DHCP servers in your enterprise to dynamically update DNS when the DHCP server assigns a DHCP client computer IP information, or you can allow clients to dynamically update DNS.

DNS clients running Windows 2000, Windows XP, and Windows Server 2003 operating systems can dynamically update DNS on startup. When DNS clients are allowed to update DNS, they connect to the DNS server on startup and automatically register the appropriate client information, such as the system IP address and the fully qualified domain name (FQDN), with the DNS server, regardless of whether their IP addresses are entered manually or assigned via DHCP.

To have clients dynamically update DNS, in the Network and Dial-up Connections dialog box, select the client's active network connection, and choose Properties. Select Internet Protocol (TCP/IP), and click the Properties button. In the General tab, click the Advanced button to open the Advanced TCP/IP Settings dialog box, and then select the DNS tab (see Figure 3.6).

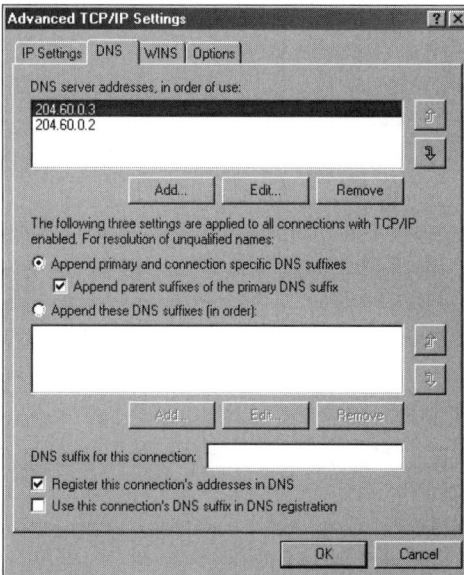

Figure 3.6 The Register this connection's addresses in DNS check box is enabled at the bottom of the Advanced TCP/IP Settings dialog box.

If you decide instead to configure the DHCP server to dynamically update DNS, you need to specify the DNS zones that the DHCP server is responsible for automatically updating. To do this, right-click the zone in the left pane and choose Properties. In the DNS tab (see Figure 3.7), select the Enable DNS dynamic updates according to the settings below check box. Then choose whether to allow the DHCP server to make the updates or to override client settings and always perform updates.

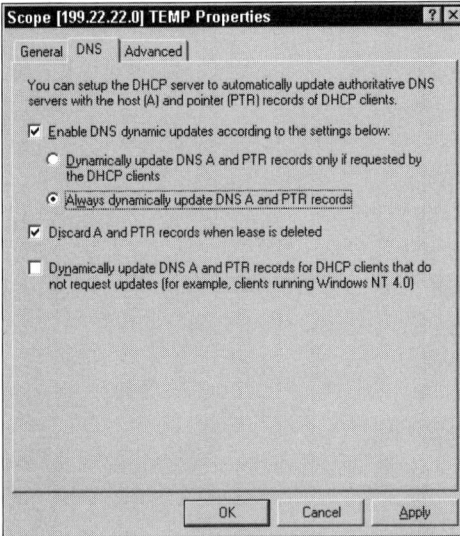

Figure 3.7 The Always dynamically update DNS A and PTR records option has been set.

You can also set the DHCP server to update A and PTR records of clients that do not make any dynamic update requests, such as Windows NT 4 systems. On the DNS server, you specify the DHCP server as the only computer authorized to update DNS entries.

If you use multiple Windows Server 2003 DHCP servers on your network and configure your zones to allow secure dynamic updates only, you need to add your DHCP servers to the built-in DnsUpdateProxyGroup to grant all your DHCP servers secure rights to perform updates for your DHCP clients. The default Discretionary Access Control List (DACL) entries on the DNS zones stored in Active Directory are as follows:

➤ Administrators have Allow settings for the following: Read, Write, Create All Child Objects, Special Permissions

➤ DnsAdmins have Allow settings for the following: Full Control, Read, Write, Create All Child Objects, Delete Child Objects

➤ Domain Admins have Allow settings for the following: Full Control, Read, Write, Create All Child Objects, Delete Child Objects

➤ Enterprise Admins have Allow settings for the following: Full Control, Read, Write, Create All Child Objects, Delete Child Objects

➤ Enterprise Domain Controllers have Allow settings for the following: Special Permissions

➤ Pre-Windows 2000 Compatible Access has Allow settings for the following: Special Permissions

➤ System has Allow settings for the following: Full Control, Read, Write, Create All Child Objects, Delete Child Objects

> **NOTE**
>
> When dealing with clients that dynamically update their own DNS records, host record registration often fails because the primary DNS suffix on the client machine does not match the DNS zone name. For example, say you have **gunderville.com** for the actual Active Directory domain and DNS domain, and the computer has a primary DNS suffix of **2000trainers.com**. This discrepancy causes the system to attempt to register at **2000trainers.com**, which it typically is not authorized to do.

WINS in the Mix

WINS is still around in Windows Server 2003 for backward-compatibility with older programs and client systems still used in some enterprises. You can add it to your Windows Server 2003 system through the Configure Your Server Wizard or by clicking Control Panel, Add or Remove Programs, Add/Remove Windows Components.

Only a couple of new features have been added to WINS (sometimes referred to as a *NetBIOS name server*) since the updates released in Windows 2000 Server. In Windows Server 2003, WINS has new filtering and search functions; to help you locate records, only those records that fit search criteria you have set are shown. Some of the available search filters include record owner, record type, NetBIOS name, and IP address with or without subnet mask.

When administrators are configuring a domain's replication strategy, they can define a list that controls the source of incoming name records during pull replication between WINS servers. They can also accept only name records owned by specific WINS servers during replication and exclude the name records of all other WINS servers.

The Windows Server 2003 DNS service enables administrators to configure WINS servers to look up hostnames not found in the DNS domain namespace. To do this, NetBIOS namespaces managed by WINS are checked, so systems that cannot query WINS directly can still resolve a system NetBIOS name to find the resource in WINS via DNS.

You can use WINS forward lookup resource records with a name query to WINS servers as a way to get further name resolution when machine names aren't found in DNS. The Windows Server 2003 WINS service supports WINS clients running on the following platforms:

➤ Windows Server 2003 (all versions including 64-bit)

➤ Windows XP (all versions including 64-bit)

➤ Windows Me

➤ Windows 2000 Server

➤ Windows 2000 Professional

➤ Windows NT Server

➤ Windows NT Workstation

➤ Windows 98

➤ Windows 95

➤ Windows for Workgroups

➤ Microsoft LAN Manager

➤ MS-DOS clients

➤ OS/2 clients

➤ Linux and Unix clients (with Samba installed)

WINS-enabled clients communicate with a WINS server to do the following:

➤ Register client names in the WINS database.

➤ Renew client names with the WINS database.

➤ Release client names from the WINS database.

➤ Resolve names by obtaining mappings from the WINS database for usernames, NetBIOS names, DNS names, and IP addresses.

Clients that are not WINS enabled can use some WINS services through the use of WINS proxies. *WINS proxies* are WINS clients configured on a specific subnet to act on behalf of other host computers that cannot use WINS directly to resolve NetBIOS names. NetBIOS names are 15 characters long, with a 16th reserved character that uniquely identifies a service the particular system is running.

WINS is mainly designed to resolve NetBIOS names to IP addresses, but in the past, this was often done via broadcast as well. Depending on system configuration and type, some systems use broadcasts only to resolve NetBIOS names on the network. You can configure a WINS proxy to listen on behalf of these systems and to query WINS for names not resolved by broadcast and send the resolution back to the querying client. Normally, WINS proxies are used only on networks that include NetBIOS broadcast-only (B-node) clients.

Systems that are configured to use WINS are normally configured as a hybrid (H-node) client, meaning they attempt to resolve NetBIOS names via a WINS server and then try a broadcast (B-node) if WINS is unsuccessful. Most systems can be configured to resolve NetBIOS names in one of four modes:

➤ *Broadcast (B-node)*—Clients use a broadcast only to resolve names. An enhanced B-node setting has the client use an LMHOST file as well. The hex value for this setting is 0x1.

➤ *Peer-to-Peer (P-node)*—Clients use WINS only to resolve names. The hex value for this setting is 0x2.

➤ *Mixed (M-node)*—Clients first use a broadcast in an attempt to resolve NetBIOS names. If this fails, they attempt the resolution via the WINS server. The hex value for this setting is 0x4.

➤ *Hybrid (H-node)*—Clients first use the WINS service in an attempt to resolve NetBIOS names. If this fails, they attempt the resolution via broadcast. The hex value for this setting is 0x8.

Enhanced B-node systems (specifically, others can be configured to use it as well) use the LMHOSTS file, a text file that is manually updated with NetBIOS name–to–IP address mapping information on a network. The file is located in the %SystemRoot%\System32\Drivers\Etc folder by default on Windows 2000, XP, and Server 2003 systems.

Additional information on LMHOSTS files is available in "Need To Know More?" at the end of this chapter. Using LMHOSTS files and manually updating them are usually administratively viable only when fewer than 25 systems total are in use. WINS is the best resolution in an environment with multiple subnets.

The following is a quick overview of the straight WINS registration process:

1. Systems receive their IP addresses from a DHCP server, which also configures them to use a specific WINS server or servers.

2. The client sends a name registration request directly to that WINS server.

3. If the system's NetBIOS name is not already in the WINS server's database, it is accepted as a new registration.

4. The name is entered with a new version ID, given a timestamp, and marked with the WINS server's owner ID. The timestamp is the length of time the system can use the name it has registered on the network.

5. A registration response is sent back to the registering client system from the WINS server with a TTL value equal to the timestamp recorded for the name.

The default renewal interval for WINS names is six days. Clients attempt to renew their registrations when 50% of the TTL value has elapsed. A name must be refreshed before this interval ends, or the WINS server force-releases it.

WINS servers support burst handling for name registration during peak traffic times. Name registration bursts normally occur first thing in the morning if a location has a set start time, and a large number of users come in to work at once and simultaneously start up their PCs.

WINS has a normal name registration operating threshold (called a *queue value*) of 500 by default. If registering systems stay below this value, they are handled via the normal registration process. If this queue value is exceeded, the WINS server responds to new client registration requests with a shorter lease threshold. The TTL is set much lower than the default six days (or whatever the current setting is), which forces clients to reregister with WINS.

The first 100 clients over the set queue value are given a TTL setting of five minutes on their names. The next 100 receive a TTL of 10 minutes, and so on, until a maximum of 50 minutes is reached. Then the 100-count process starts over at five minutes. As the load on the WINS server falls below the queue value, clients reregister and receive the full lease time for their NetBIOS names.

A single WINS server can handle up to 10,000 clients for NetBIOS name resolution requests, based on a decent CPU and adequate memory and disk throughput, but other factors need to be considered, such as fault tolerance, server hardware, other services running on the server, network topology, number of remote users, and so on.

WINS Replication

In most cases, especially in larger environments, multiple WINS servers are running. Some clients might be configured to use one WINS server, and other sets of clients might be configured to use another. This causes a problem if a client using WINS1 needs to resolve the name of a system that registered on WINS2. *Convergence time* is the time it takes to replicate a new entry in a WINS database to all the other WINS servers in the environment.

> **NOTE**
>
> When a client registers its name with a WINS server and an entry is made to that database, it is called an *originating update*. When that change is replicated to other WINS databases, it is referred to as a *replicated update*.

When planning placement and replication for WINS servers, you must decide on an acceptable convergence time for your network. Replication is used to synchronize WINS databases across the different WINS servers.

WINS servers are configured to sync with replication partners. Those partner WINS servers can be configured as pull partners, push partners, or a combination push/pull partner. *Pull partners* pull database entries from their WINS replica partners at a predetermined time. This means that no matter how many (or how few) changes have been made to the WINS database, at the time of pull replication, the server gets the updates. *Push partners* work off a quota number. When a WINS server has accrued a predetermined number of updates to its database, it pushes those changes out to its replication partners. In other words, push partners send updates out as soon as they have enough accumulated database updates, regardless of how long it has been since the last updates were sent.

There are issues with both designs. Pull partners, which might be configured to get databases only once every hour, are not properly updated during high-volume registration hours, such as the beginning of the workday. Push partners, which might be configured to replicate only when they have 300 new records, do nothing if the count stops at 153. The solution is to set up *push/pull partners*. These WINS servers are normally paired up, or if there are enough of them, configured in a hub and spoke setup to push and pull their changes among each other, thus solving both problems mentioned previously.

Exam Prep Questions

Question 1

Which OSI layer is responsible for translating logical network address and names, such as computer names, to their MAC addresses and for addressing and routing data packets over the network?

○ A. Transport layer

○ B. Physical layer

○ C. Network layer

○ D. Data Link layer

The correct answer is C. The Network layer is responsible for translating logical network address and names, such as computer names, to their MAC addresses and for addressing and routing data packets over the network. The Transport layer adds another connection below the Session layer and helps manage data flow control between nodes on the network. Therefore, answer A is incorrect. The Physical layer defines the interface between the medium and the device. Therefore, answer B is incorrect. The Data Link layer mainly handles error correction, flow control, and communication with the network adapter card. Therefore, answer D is incorrect.

Question 2

How is the division point between the network ID and the host ID of an IP address calculated?

○ A. The Internet Engineering Task Force (IETF) sets the standard for calculating the division point.

○ B. The Least Significant Bit (LSB) is used.

○ C. The Most Significant Bit (MSB) is used.

○ D. A subnet mask is used.

The correct answer is D. The division point between the network ID and the host ID is called the subnet mask. The subnet mask is used to determine where the network number in an IP address ends and the node number in an IP address begins. Therefore, answers A, B, and C are incorrect.

Question 3

Which routing protocols support Classless Inter-Domain Routing (CIDR)? (Choose two.)

❏ A. RIP version 2

❏ B. Open Shortest Path First (OSPF)

❏ C. RIP version 1

❏ D. Exterior Gateway Protocol

❏ E. Interior Gateway Protocol

The correct answers are A and B. CIDR is supported by RIP version 2 and OSPF routing. Because CIDR supports multiple subnet masks per subnet, it requires routers that support more advanced interior routing protocols, such as RIP version 2 and OSPF. CIDR isn't supported by RIP version 1 or EGP; therefore, answers C, D, and E are incorrect.

Question 4

Given the Class C IPv4 address range of 192.199.199.0, can you use a subnet mask of 255.255.255.240 and create at least 17 subnetworks with at least 13 hosts per subnet?

○ A. Yes, you can use a subnet mask of 255.255.255.240 and create at least 17 subnetworks with at least 13 hosts per subnet.

○ B. No, the subnet mask of 255.255.255.240 is invalid for the Class C version 4 IP address ranges.

○ C. 192.199.199.0 is not a Class C address range.

○ D. No, there would be less than 13 hosts per subnet.

○ E. No, there would be less than 17 subnetworks.

The correct answer is E. Given the Class C IPv4 address 192.199.199.0, you can use a subnet mask of 255.255.255.240 and create 16 subnetworks with 14 hosts per subnet. Because the question called for at least 17 subnetworks with at least 13 hosts per subnet, the only correct answer is E.

Question 5

Maximum Transmission Units (MTUs) are based on the type of network that is installed. What is the MTU of ethernet networks?

- ○ A. 1,460 bytes
- ○ B. 1,500 bytes
- ○ C. 4,464 bytes
- ○ D. 17,914 bytes

The correct answer is B. MTUs are based on the type of network that is installed. Ethernet deployments are limited to a 1,500 byte MTU. Therefore, answers A, C, and D are incorrect.

Question 6

How do you configure clients to use APIPA addressing?

- ○ A. APIPA addressing needs to be set manually in the Registry.
- ○ B. The client needs to be configured to obtain an IP address automatically.
- ○ C. The client needs to have the APIPA option selected in the IP Properties dialog box.
- ○ D. The DHCP server needs to have an APIPA scope configured and authorized.

The correct answer is B. To enable APIPA on clients, all you need to do is configure the client to use DHCP (obtain an IP address automatically). When the client starts up and cannot contact a DHCP server, it assigns itself an IP address from the reserved 169.254.0.0 range with a subnet mask of 255.255.0.0. No default gateway is used, and systems that use APIPA are not routable. Therefore, answers A, C, and D are incorrect.

Question 7

When a DHCP client request for an IP address hits a router that cannot forward the DHCPDISCOVER broadcast message, the client fails to receive a response from the DHCP server because the DHCP server never receives the DHCPDIS-COVER broadcast message. The client system configures itself with an APIPA address. What can be done to correct this problem? (Choose three.)

❏ A. Install an RFC 1452–compliant router.

❏ B. Install an RFC 1542–compliant router.

❏ C. Install DHCP Relay Agent on the client subnet.

❏ D. Install a local DHCP server.

❏ E. Install a DHCP Relay Agent on the DHCP server.

❏ F. Install a DHCP Relay Agent on the DHCP server subnet.

The correct answers are B, C, and D. When a DHCP client request for an IP address hits a non-RFC-1542–compliant router (meaning the DHCPDISCOVER broadcast message is not forwarded off the subnet), it fails to receive a response because the DHCP server never receives the DHCPDISCOVER broadcast message and the client system configures itself with an APIPA address. If a DHCP Relay Agent is in use on the subnet, it receives the DHCPDISCOVER broadcast message and routes the message off the subnet to the DHCP server. Subsequently, when the DHCP server responds with an address and the DHCP client selects the IP address, the client responds with a DHCPREQUEST broadcast message, which includes the IP address of the server that had its offer accepted. Again, this DHCPREQUEST broadcast message does not get out of this subnet unless a DHCP Relay Agent is in use on the subnet, and can receive the DHCPREQUEST broadcast message and forward (route) the message off the subnet to the DHCP server.

Question 8

What type of DNS resolution involves a query made from a client to a DNS server, and the server returns the best answer it can provide based on its local cache or stored zone data?

- ○ A. Recursive query
- ○ B. Iterative query
- ○ C. Forward query
- ○ D. Cache query

The correct answer is B. Two types of queries can be performed in DNS: iterative and recursive. The situation described in this scenario is an iterative query. A recursive query happens when a client makes a DNS resoluiotn query to a DNS server, and the server assumes the full workload and responsibility for providing a complere answer to the query, therfore, answer A is incorrect.

Question 9

What are some of the benefits of caching-only DNS servers? (Choose three.)

- ❑ A. Local sites that use them do not use WAN bandwidth for DNS resolutions.
- ❑ B. They hold a read/write copy of the DNS database on the local site.
- ❑ C. Replication is configurable for off hours, thus limiting the impact of zone transfer traffic.
- ❑ D. They do not produce any zone transfer traffic.
- ❑ E. They reduce traffic across a WAN because they attempt to locate information in their cache to resolve local client requests.

The correct answers are A, D, and E. Caching-only DNS servers perform name resolution on behalf of clients and then cache the resulting name resolutions. They are not configured to be authoritative for a DNS zone, and they do not store Standard Primary or Standard Secondary zones locally. Their local cache holds the most frequently requested names and associated IP addresses and are available for use by subsequent client queries.

Question 10

When clients dynamically update their own DNS records, what type of host record registration failures can occur?

○ A. Incorrect parent DNS suffix listed

○ B. Incorrect DNS suffix list entry appended

○ C. Incorrect secondary DNS suffix listed

○ D. Incorrect primary DNS suffix listed

The correct answer is D. When dealing with clients that dynamically update their own DNS records, host record registration often fails because the primary DNS suffix listed on the client machine does not match the DNS zone name. For example, the actual Active Directory domain and DNS domain is gunderville.com, but the computer has a primary DNS suffix listed as 2000trainers.com. This causes the system to attempt to register at 2000trainers.com, which it usually is not authorized to do.

Need To Know More?

TCP/IP Frequently Asked Questions: `http://www.itprc.com/tcpipfaq/default.htm`.

TCP/IP Protocol Suite—Questions and Answers: `http://www.geocities.com/SiliconValley/Vista/8672/network/`.

Microsoft Windows—IPv6: `http://www.microsoft.com/IPv6` and `http://www.microsoft.com/windowsserver2003/technologies/ipv6/default.mspx`.

RFC 2460: Internet Protocol, Version 6 (IPv6) Specification: `http://www.faqs.org/rfcs/rfc2460.html`.

TCP/IPv4 Configurable Registry Settings: `http://msdn.microsoft.com/library/default.asp?url=/library/en-us/wcetcpip/htm/cmconParametersConfigurableUsingRegistryEditor.asp`.

Automatic Windows 98/Me TCP/IP Addressing Without a DHCP Server: `http://support.microsoft.com/default.aspx?scid=KB;en-us;q220874`.

Planning DHCP Networks: `http://www.microsoft.com/windows2000/en/server/help/default.asp?url=/windows2000/en/server/help/sag_DHCP_imp_PlanningNetworks.htm`.

Domain Name System (DNS) Center: `http://www.microsoft.com/windows2000/technologies/communications/dns/`.

Domain Name System Security Extensions: `http://www.ietf.org/rfc/rfc2535.txt`.

Replacing Root Hints with the CACHE.DNS File: `http://support.microsoft.com/default.aspx?scid=KB;EN-US;Q249868&`.

How to Write an LMHOSTS File for Domain Validation and Other Name Resolution Issues: `http://support.microsoft.com/?kbid=180094`.

Domain Browsing with TCP/IP and LMHOSTS Files: `http://support.microsoft.com/?kbid=150800`.

LMHOSTS File Information and Predefined Keywords: `http://support.microsoft.com/?kbid=102725`.

Verify WINS Registration of Client NetBIOS Names: `http://www.microsoft.com/windows2000/en/server/help/default.asp?url=/windows2000/en/server/help/sag_WINS_pro_VerifyRegistration.htm`.

Registering Names in WINS: `http://www.microsoft.com/windows2000/en/server/help/sag_WINS_und_RegisteringNames.htm`.

Windows 2000 Server Windows Internet Naming Service (WINS) Overview: `http://www.microsoft.com/windows2000/techinfo/howitworks/communications/nameadrmgmt/wins.asp`.

Planning, Implementing, and Maintaining Routing and Remote Access

. . . .

Terms you'll need to understand

✓ Network Address Translation (NAT)

✓ Virtual private network (VPN)

✓ Routing and Remote Access Service (RRAS)

✓ Routing Information Protocol (RIP) versions 1 and 2

✓ Internet Connection Sharing (ICS)

✓ Internet Connection Firewall (ICF)

Techniques you'll need to master

✓ Installing and configuring Network Monitor

✓ Configuring System Monitor

✓ Configuring and troubleshooting DHCP client configurations

✓ Installing, configuring, and troubleshooting NAT

✓ Installing, configuring, and troubleshooting issues related to name resolution cache information

✓ Installing and configuring clients to connect to the Internet

✓ Installing and configuring clients to connect to remote networks

✓ Installing and configuring routing protocols

✓ Installing, configuring, and troubleshooting TCP/IP routing

✓ Configuring DHCP scopes and optional parameters

In Windows Server 2003, Routing and Remote Access Service (RRAS) enables administrators to set up and configure network services on wide area networks (WANs) and local area networks (LANs). RRAS can also be configured to provide services for virtual private networks (VPNs) and Network Address Translation (NAT). Before you take a look at the service itself, you should review basic routing and the routing tables of a local system.

Basic Routing

Any system on a network can perform a router's basic functions if it is properly configured to route between networks, even if it has only a single network interface card (NIC) installed. This one NIC must have two IP addresses bound to it (both from different networks), and a route must be identified in the routing table between the two networks. If the system meets these two requirements, when it receives packets from one network destined for the other, it can successfully pass the packets along.

To see the local routing table for a local system, enter ROUTE PRINT at a command prompt; the output is shown in Figure 4.1.

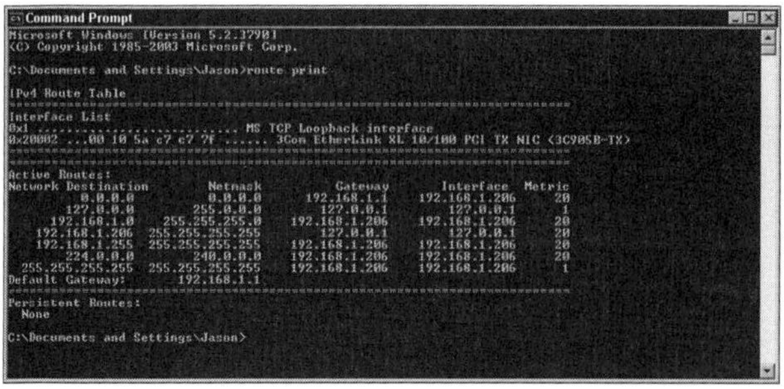

Figure 4.1 The local routing table as it appears on most Windows Server 2003 systems with a single NIC.

The columns in the Active Routes section have different functions:

➤ *Network Destination*—The addresses in this column are used as endpoints for network traffic.

➤ *Netmask (subnet mask)*—This column is used to divide which part of the listed IP address is the network's numeric name and which part is the intended host's numeric name.

➤ *Gateway*—This column denotes the default gateway address the host uses to send packets to other subnets.

➤ *Interface*—This column lists the IP address for the network adapter that the host system uses to transmit data over the network.

➤ *Metric*—This column assigns a cost to an interface and is usually considered when more than one network card is installed on a host; however, it can also be used to simply assign costs to different routes listed for a single NIC. A lower metric on a NIC or route denotes that it will be used preferentially. Other listings with higher metrics are used when the lowest cost route becomes unavailable.

> **NOTE**
>
> Considerations for setting metrics include factors such as hop count, which is the number of routers crossed from the sending host to the destination system; each router crossed is another hop added. Other factors, such as throughput and reliability of LAN and WAN connections (mainly considered based on their speed ratings) need to be considered as well.

When routes to other networks change because of temporary network failures or permanent changes in network paths, the corresponding routing entries on a router must be updated. Persistent routes on hosts entered into the local routing table must be deleted or at least updated. To add persistent routes to a host's local routing table, use the -p switch, as shown in the following lines in a command-prompt window:

```
route ADD -p 10.0.0.0 MASK 255.0.0.0  10.55.80.1 METRIC 1 IF 2
         destination^        ^mask       ^gateway   metric^   ^
                                                    Interface^
```

If you need to change this persistent setting because of a temporary update to the indicated routing path, enter the following:

```
route CHANGE -p 10.0.0.0 MASK 255.0.0.0  10.55.80.254 METRIC 1 IF 2
            destination^        ^mask       ^gateway   metric^   ^
                                                       Interface^
```

If the changes no longer require this host to hold a persistent route, delete the entry with the following command:

```
route DELETE -p 10.0.0.0 MASK 255.0.0.0  10.55.80.1 METRIC 1 IF 2
            destination^        ^mask       ^gateway   metric^   ^
                                                       Interface^
```

Routing and Remote Access

Using the Routing and Remote Access Microsoft Management Console (MMC) on a Windows Server 2003 system, you can manually add a static route by expanding the server in the left pane that will host the static route.

Under IP Routing, right-click Status Routes to create a new static route entry (see Figure 4.2).

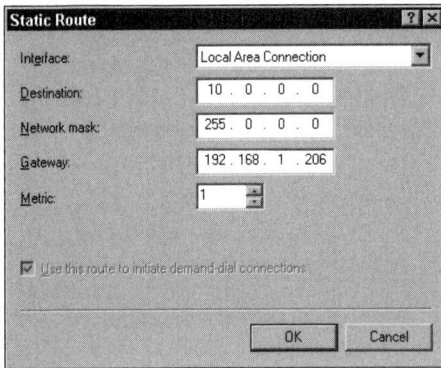

Figure 4.2 Adding a static route to the host system through the Routing and Remote Access MMC.

If you need to delete this static route later, simply right-click it in the right pane of the Routing and Remote Access MMC, and choose Delete from the shortcut menu.

With Windows 2000 and 2003 servers, you can enable the Routing and Remote Access Service and configure the server with routing protocols that can dynamically update routing information so that static entries do not have to be manually maintained. If a route changes for any reason—a temporary hardware failure, the removal or addition of another routing device, and so on—and static route entries are being performed, a network administrator must manually update the routing information wherever static records are stored.

To choose a new routing protocol, such as Open Shortest Path First (OSPF) or Routing Information Protocol (RIPv2), go to the Routing and Remote Access MMC and expand the server in the left pane that will function as the dynamic router. Under IP Routing, right-click General, and choose New Routing Protocol. You can then add a new protocol in the New Routing Protocol dialog box (see Figure 4.3).

Dynamic routing protocols, such as RIP versions 1 and 2 and OSPF, exchange information about their networks with other routers using the same dynamic routing protocols. RIP versions 1 and 2 are best used on medium-sized networks with about 50 routers maximum, and the maximum number of routers (hops) that any IP packet must cross is less than 16. Destination addresses that are 16 or more hops away are unreachable from RIP routers.

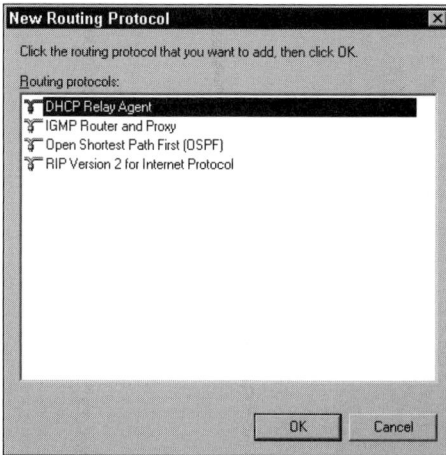

Figure 4.3 Adding a dynamic routing protocol in the Routing and Remote Access MMC.

Routing update announcements generated by RIP routers can cause unacceptable levels of network traffic when more than 50 RIP routers are in use. RIP routers maintain a routing table and periodically send updates to other RIP routers on the network with their routing information. RIPv1 uses IP broadcast packets for its announcements, and RIPv2 uses IP multicast packets for its announcements.

OSPF is a link-state protocol based on an algorithm that determines the shortest path between source and destination nodes on a routed network. OSPF routers maintain the routed network information in a link state database. As updates to information in the database and routing table are made, they are synchronized between other OSPF routers.

OSPF protocol is a better choice than either version of RIP when the network is designed with redundant paths between locales or when the number of subnets in the overall design is more than 50 routers. With Windows Server 2003, both RIPv2 and OSPF can be installed on a server running RRAS.

Routing Protocols and RRAS

With RRAS under Window 2000 Server, administrators could install RIPv1 outright. If you take a look at the available routing protocols to install in Figure 4.3, you will see that RIPv1 is absent; however, it is still available in the Incoming Packet Protocol list box shown in Figure 4.4.

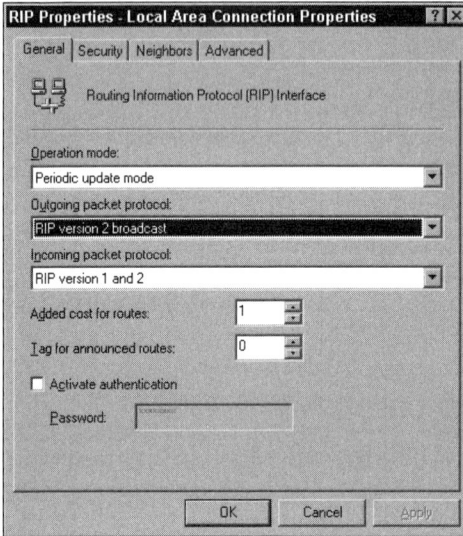

Figure 4.4 You can add RIPv1 in the RIP Properties dialog box.

RIPv1 is difficult to deploy in larger environments because it supports the main classes of IP addresses only and cannot use Classless Inter-Domain Routing (CIDR) or Variable Length Subnet Masks (VLSM).

RIPv1 is limited in security measures as well. Routers that exchange routing information using RIPv1 do not authenticate with each other, which could allow a Denial of Service (DoS) attack in which a hacker corrupts routing tables.

Also, because of the lack of proper security, RIP listeners can be placed on a network using RIPv1. This could allow someone to find out about the available networks in your enterprise.

On RIPv2 networks, routers broadcast their routing tables to other RIPv2 routers at predefined intervals via broadcast or multicast. RIPv2 supports simple password authentication, multicast announcements, CIDR, and VLSM. To configure RIPv1 or 2, set the outgoing packet protocol on the General tab to one of these options, depending on your design:

➤ RIP version 1 broadcast

➤ RIP version 2 broadcast

➤ RIP version 2 multicast

➤ Silent RIP

To complete the configuration, set the incoming packet protocol on the General tab to one of these, depending on your needs:

➤ Ignore incoming packets

➤ RIP version 1 and 2

➤ RIP version 1 only

➤ RIP version 2 only

If you need to enable authentication for your routers, select the Activate Authentication check box, and enter a password in the Password text box. All routers using RIPv2 to update each other must be configured in this way with the same password; otherwise, the route updates fail.

You can also configure additional security for RIP routers by setting the appropriate filters in the Security tab of the router's Properties dialog box. Select the appropriate radio button to accept all routes, to accept all routes from a given range of IP addresses that have been entered, or to ignore all routes from a given range of IP addresses that have been entered for incoming routes.

For outgoing routes, you can configure RIPv2 to announce all routes, to announce all routes from a given range of IP addresses that have been entered, or to not announce routes from a given range of IP addresses that have been entered (see Figure 4.5).

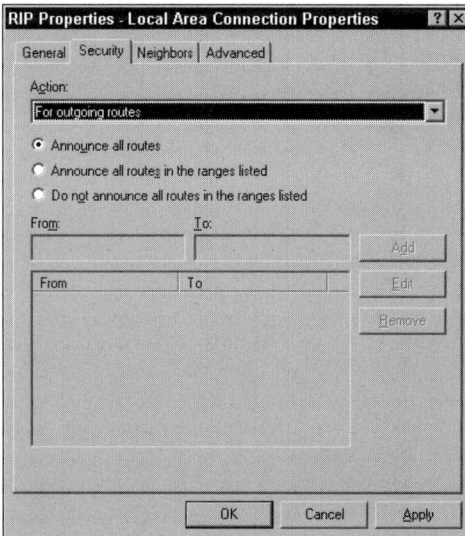

Figure 4.5 You can select actions to take for routing in the Security tab of the RIP Properties dialog box.

You can configure how this router responds to neighboring routers in the Neighbors tab of the RIP Properties dialog box. You can configure it to function by using broadcast and multicast only, using specific neighbors (notated by entering their IP addresses) in addition to broadcast and multicast, or by using only neighboring routers via the entered IP addresses.

In the Advanced tab, you can set timers for periodic updates by specifying the announcement interval in seconds (see Figure 4.6). You can also set the time before routes expire and the time before a route is removed by entering numeric values that denote seconds.

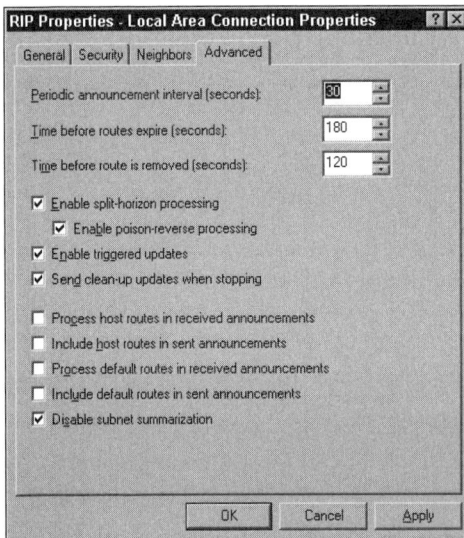

Figure 4.6 The settings shown in the Advanced tab of the RIP Properties dialog box are the default values.

Notice that the following options are enabled by default:

➤ *Split-horizon processing*—This route-advertising method prevents advertising routes in the same direction in which they were learned, which avoids routing loop situations.

➤ *Poison-reverse processing*—This option is used with split-horizon processing to improve RIP convergence by advertising all network IDs.

➤ *Triggered updates*—These route advertising methods advertise changes in the network topology as they occur, instead of waiting for the next scheduled interval.

➤ *Clean-up updates*—These updates are set when subnet summarization is being stopped and disabled.

The following options can also be set, if needed:

➤ Process Host Routes in Received Announcements

➤ Include Host Routes in Sent Announcements

➤ Process Default Routes in Received Announcements

➤ Include Default Routes in Sent Announcements

With OSPF, administrators can create an OSPF area by installing the OSPF protocol and then installing a new interface. To do this, right-click OSPF in the Routing and Remote Access MMC and choose New Interface, which enables OSPF for the selected network connection (see Figure 4.7).

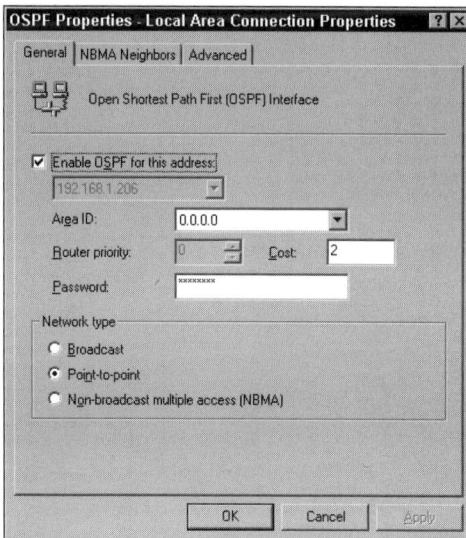

Figure 4.7 The OSPF Properties dialog box for an interface that has been configured. Because an OSPF area has not yet been assigned, the Area ID text box shows 0.0.0.0, which denotes a backbone area, not an actual IP address.

> OSPF is not available on Windows XP 64-bit edition and the 64-bit versions of Windows Server 2003. After all available interfaces on a system have been config- ured for OSPF, you will receive an error message if you attempt to choose New Interface again.

In the General tab, you can set the level of logging for the protocol with one of the following radio buttons:

➤ Log Errors Only

➤ Log Errors and Warnings

➤ Log the Maximum Amount of Information

➤ Disable Event Logging

To create an OSPF area, right-click OSPF and choose Properties to open the OSPF Properties dialog box. In the Areas tab, click the Add button to add an IP address. (Notice that the Enable Plaintext Password check box is selected by default.) Enter a destination IP address and a network mask in the Ranges text box.

> You can enable the OSPF area as a stub area by selecting the corresponding check box in the General tab. You cannot configure the default area ID of 0.0.0.0 as a stub area, and you cannot configure virtual links through stub areas.

To configure OSPF as an autonomous system boundary router that connects this router to another autonomous system or the Internet, select the Enable Autonomous System Boundary Router check box in the General tab of the OSPF Properties dialog box.

After you change this setting, the External Routing tab is enabled. Select the Accept routes from all route sources except those selected radio button or the Ignore routes from all route sources except those selected radio button (see Figure 4.8), depending on your requirements.

To enable route filters, click the Route Filters button in the External Routing tab. In the OSPF External Route Filters dialog box, select the Ignore Listed Routes radio button or the Accept Listed Routes radio button and enter the appropriate IP addresses in the Destination and Network Mask text boxes.

Notes from the Field

How you set up and configure RRAS and decide which routing protocols to use depend on the types of networking devices in your network, such as hubs, switches, and routers. Some switches operate at the Data Link layer (Layer 2) of the OSI model and form the borders of your collision domains. Bridges also work at Layer 2 and function in the same manner.

Network collisions occur when two hosts attempt to transmit data at the same time. A *collision domain* is a network segment in which all devices on that segment can "hear" when the collision happens. If a network design includes a switch at one end and a bridge at the other, for example, all hosts between those two network devices would be considered part of a single collision domain. Devices beyond the Layer 2 switch and bridge typically belong to a different collision domain.

Layer 2 switches and bridges do not form a border for *broadcast domains*, which are network segments in which all devices on those segments can hear broadcast and multicast messages. Broadcast and multicast frames are found at Layer 3 of the OSI model, so devices such as Layer 2 switches and bridges simply pass these packets along.

To create boarders for broadcast domains in an effort to segment which network devices hear broadcast messages, you need to use a Layer 3 switch or a router that operates at the Network layer of the OSI model. Network routing and switching devices can run in Full Duplex mode or Half Duplex mode.

Full Duplex devices allow two hosts on the same transmission medium at the same time. An everyday example of this type of transmission is the telephone: Both parties can speak and hear at the same time. Half Duplex devices allow only a single device to use the medium at a time. An everyday example of this type of transmission is the walkie-talkie: Only one person at a time can speak while the other listens. Whoever has the "speak and send" action at a certain point can be heard on any other walkie-talkie set to that frequency.

If one person presses the "talk" key at the same time as someone else, neither message is received by other units because both people are trying to access the same medium (frequency) at the same time. This is called a "collision," and both units must wait their turn to successfully transmit a message, just as two computers need to when they're on the same wire.

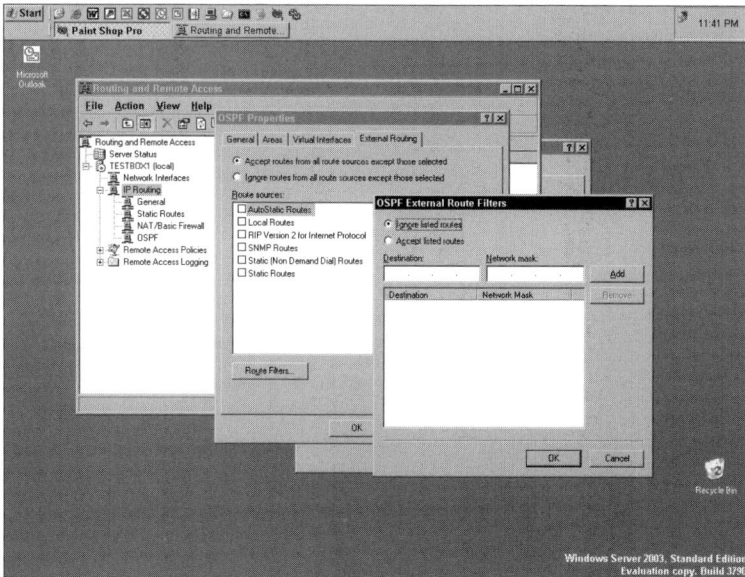

Figure 4.8   You can't use the External Routing tab until you have selected the Enable Autonomous System Boundary Router check box in the General tab.

Configuring for Internet Connectivity

To figure the best solution for connecting your environment to the Internet, you must consider your network's current configuration and the forecast for its future. Some typical considerations are growth, security, availability, and reliability.

Future growth can be built into a network by installing equipment such as routers, switches, and hubs with leftover open ports, which allows additional network devices to be quickly plugged in and configured for use as needed. Security is addressed on one level by locking rooms where switching and routing equipment are kept and by providing passwords to those devices only to those who absolutely need them. On additional levels, security is addressed by providing proper filtering of network traffic in and out of the network through the following filtering actions:

➤ *Application filtering*—Handles application traffic at the router or firewall.

➤ *Circuit-level filtering*—Enables inspection of Internet level sessions rather than the connections themselves or the packets transmitted.

➤ *Packet filtering*—Drops all packets except for those that are explicitly allowed.

➤ *Protocol filtering*—Drops specific protocol traffic from being forwarded out of identified ports on a particular networked device.

Additionally, you can further secure network resources by requiring users to authenticate before they gain any access to the network and to limit that access to users and groups based on the resources they need to perform their assigned tasks. This can be any type of limitation, from outright denial of access for resources that certain groups have no need of to allowing network logons only during permitted hours. If some network users never have a regular need to log on from 6 p.m. through 6 a.m. and all day on Saturday and Sunday, you could set logon restrictions for those users and groups.

Reliability is addressed by providing redundancy where needs are the most critical. Single points of failure can exist throughout a network, but at times these single points are not acceptable. It's one thing for a print server to go down because printing queues can be restarted or, if the server suffered a terminal crash, redirected during repairs and rebuild efforts. It's entirely different when the only Global Catalog server goes offline. For most deployments, clustering or redundant servers are recommended.

Clustered servers can be deployed so that a pair of physical servers (or larger cluster configurations) functions as a single virtual server. Clustering offers fault tolerance in the event of node failure, as the other node in a pair simply takes over the full load of all requests, and offers load balancing when the cluster is running in active/active mode, meaning both servers are online and servicing user requests for resources.

> **NOTE**   Windows Server 2003 Enterprise Edition and Datacenter Edition offer administrators the ability to configure two-node clusters, up to a total of eight-node clusters.

For Domain Name System (DNS) servers and domain controllers, having more than one of these servers available at the local site or over a WAN connection (locally is preferred) aids in fault tolerance. When one of the local servers fails, the other server running the same service assumes total responsibility for the network service being hosted. For example, assume that servers DNS1 and DNS2 are providing DNS services to a site, and some clients at that site are using DNS1 as a primary DNS server and DNS2 as a secondary DNS server. That means the other clients use DNS2 as their primary DNS server and DNS1 as their secondary DNS server. If DNS2 goes down, all clients are forced to use DNS1 until DNS2 becomes available again. Networked systems can be configured for Internet connectivity by using Internet Connection Sharing (ICS) or through an Internet Security and Acceleration (ISA) server.

Network Address Translation (NAT) is actually one of the protocols available on RRAS servers, but it is also used when Internet connectivity is configured through a Windows Server 2003 system using ICS. NAT can be used to share a single IP address or a small number of external IP addresses with a larger pool of internal systems by hiding the internal private address scheme from the Internet. The device performing the NAT service, be it an ISA server, RRAS server, or even a hardware device such as a router, holds a table of mappings between internal systems and externally accessed resources and vice versa.

What this means is that if you're using a host on the internal side of a NAT device and make a call to the Internet to access a remote Web site, when that Web server responds, the returning GET data makes it back to your system because the NAT device is keeping track of which internal host made the GET request of the remote Web server. The reverse is also true.

A GET call is nothing more than calling for a Web page. It's the function call your Web browser makes when you enter `http://www.gunderville.com` and the page is rendered in the browser window; in other words, you've told the browser to "get" the index page at the URL you've entered. If your NAT device receives a remote GET call coming into your private network for a Web server that is hosted, the NAT device knows to map <PUBLIC IP ADDRESS>:80 (:80 denotes the HTTP port number) to <PRIVATE IP ADDRESS>:80 to allow fetching the Web site.

> **NOTE**
>
> Currently, Internet Protocol Security (IPSec) does not support NAT by default; however, the Microsoft L2TP/IPSec VPN client includes support for a proposed extension of IPSec that supports NAT. The new behavior will be enabled whenever the client connects to a VPN server that also supports the proposed NAT-Traversal extensions for IPSec, as outlined in the IETF Internet drafts "UDP Encapsulation of IPSec Packets" (**http://www.ietf.org/Internet-drafts/draft-ietf-ipsec-udp-encaps-06.txt**) and "Negotiation of NAT-Traversal in the IKE" (**http://www.ietf.org/Internet-drafts/draft-ietf-ipsec-nat-t-ike-05.txt**). Microsoft plans to support these extensions in Windows Server 2003.

Internet Connection Sharing (ICS) also uses NAT when it is the main Internet connection point for a home or small office. All other systems on the small LAN use the one system configured for ICS as an access point (think "router" or "default gateway") to the Internet.

This is accomplished by allowing the system configured as the ICS point to obtain the necessary DHCP or fixed external IP address for access to the Internet. Also, clients on the LAN must use IP addresses from the private IP address ranges, which allows them to connect to the ICS system and route calls to the Internet through its installed interface. The private range of IP addressing assigned to clients using an ICS system is assigned directly from the ICS system. This includes any necessary DNS information as well.

> **NOTE**
>
> If the system configured to host the ICS service has multiple connections to internal LANs, you need to bridge the connections before you enable ICS so that all the different subnets can use the host system.

An administrator must set up and configure an interface for NAT when it is used for RRAS. To do this, right-click NAT/Basic Firewall in the Routing and Remote Access MMC tree pane, and then choose New Interface. Under Interfaces, select the interface you want to add, and then click OK. You are then left with a couple of options.

If the chosen interface is connected to the Internet, select the Public Interface Connected to the Internet radio button and click the Enable NAT on This Interface check box in the NAT/Basic Firewall tab. In a high-security environment, you should make sure your public interface is protected with packet filters by selecting the Enable a Basic Firewall on This Interface check box. If this interface connects to a small private network, select the Private Interface Connected to Private Network radio button in the NAT/Basic Firewall tab instead (see Figure 4.9).

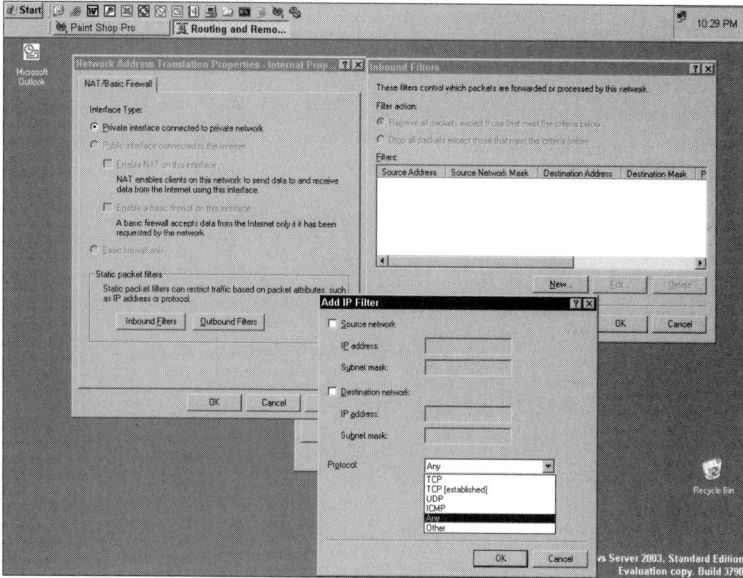

Figure 4.9   The Add IP Filter dialog box enables you to add a new filter to control which packets are accepted and forwarded or denied by the filter.

Under Routing and Remote Access Services in the Routing and Remote Access MMC tree pane, you can find the NAT/Basic Firewall Service installed by default in the IP Routing section. Right-click NAT/Basic Firewall Service and choose Properties to review general information that includes the default event log setting of Log Errors Only. You can change this setting to Log Errors and Warnings, Log the Maximum Amount of Information, or Disable Event Logging.

In the Translation tab, the default setting for Remove TCP Mapping After (Minutes) is set to 1440 (24 hours) and Remove UDP Mapping After (Minutes) is set for 1 minute. In the Address Assignment tab, you can set the NAT configuration so that clients are automatically assigned IP addresses by using DHCP addressing. To do this, select the Automatically Assign IP Addresses by Using the DHCP Allocator check box.

One of the features of Microsoft ISA Server is that it can function using NAT, just like RRAS and ICS. ISA Server can also use NAT to connect a private LAN to the Internet while protecting private network resources and internal IP addressing schemes from external access. It supports many additional features in an effort to ensure extra security for LANs.

ISA Server Enterprise Edition can be used in a cluster deployment to provide fault tolerance and load balancing and has the following additional security features:

➤ Firewalled configuration that supports packet-level, circuit-level, and application-level traffic screening.

➤ Stateful inspection of packets that traverse the firewall by protocol and connection.

➤ Dynamic packet filtering, which opens ports only as needed.

➤ Supports applications using Secure Network Address Translation (SecureNAT), predefined protocols, and application filters.

➤ Hardening of the ISA server via security templates.

➤ Integrated intrusion detection based on technology from Internet Security Systems (ISS), which has been designed to identify and respond to commonly known network attacks.

➤ Provides secure server publishing for Web servers, email servers, and application servers and protects from external attacks by allowing only authorized traffic.

➤ Prevents unauthorized access to mail servers for all services, including Simple Mail Transfer Protocol (SMTP) relaying, and stops certain email messages with attachments at the gateway via content screening.

After you have implemented the method your enterprise is going to use for configuring Internet connectivity, there is always the issue of troubleshooting connectivity problems. In many instances, the tools included in the TCP/IP suite can be used to assist with troubleshooting any network connectivity problems, through the LAN or WAN and even over the Internet.

NOTE Chapter 3, "Planning, Implementing, and Maintaining a Network Infrastructure," discusses many troubleshooting tools. Refer to this chapter for more information on which tools you could use for different types of troubleshooting.

You can also use Network Monitor to view and detect problems on LANs. Network Monitor is not installed on Windows Server 2003 by default. If you want to use it, perform the following steps:

1. Click Start, Control Panel, Add or Remove Programs.

2. Click Add/Remove Windows Components.

3. When the Windows Components Wizard opens, highlight Management and Monitoring Tools in the Components list, and click the Details button.

4. Select the Network Monitor Tools check box, and click OK.

5. Click Next. After Network Monitor has been configured, click Finish.

6. Close the Add or Remove Programs applet. Network Monitor then appears in the Administrative Tools section of the Start menu.

As with most component additions to a system, you must be a member of the Administrators group or have been delegated the necessary authority to perform this action on the local system. Domain and Enterprise Administrators can also install tools on the system if the server is a member of a domain. After Network Monitor is installed, you can gather information that can be used to identify baseline network loads of the client system and troubleshoot problems from the network adapter of the local system.

NOTE

If you want to expand the level of network monitoring beyond the local system, you need to install the Network Monitor component that ships with Microsoft Systems Management Server. That version of Network Monitor can capture frames sent to or from any system where the Network Monitor driver is installed.

Network Monitor can be set up with specific triggers so that it automatically starts capturing information when certain conditions are met. Captures can also be set up to use filters to "record" only specific network information in the capture.

System Monitor, which can be found in the Performance MMC, is much like Network Monitor, in that it allows you to baseline and review the performance and response of the local system or other systems on a network, depending on how it's configured. The main difference is that Network Monitor enables you to review the network performance, and System Monitor (in the Performance MMC) enables you to review the overall system performance beyond just the networking component.

The data that can be collected via System Monitor is categorized into performance objects, performance counters, and performance object instances.

Performance objects are the counters associated with a resource or service that can be monitored, such as output from the system processor or the browser service.

Performance counters are directly associated with a performance object. The corresponding values associated with the PhysicalDisk counter are values such as Average Disk Bytes/Read, Average Disk Bytes/Write, and so forth, and are not found under the Processor Object because they aren't relevant.

The output data from performance counters for particular performance objects can be collected and viewed in real time, or it can be written to a performance log file or an SQL database for analysis. The information can also be stored in HTML format and viewed using Internet Explorer.

Configuring Virtual Private Networking

Windows Server 2003 Routing and Remote Access Service enables administrators to configure the system for virtual private network (VPN) access for remote clients. VPN connections can be established by using the Point-to-Point Tunneling Protocol (PPTP) and secured by PPTP's own built-in PPP encryption. You can also use Layer Two Tunneling Protocol (L2TP) with Internet Protocol Security (IPSec) to secure the transmitted data. Administrators using Windows Server 2003 can create up to 1,000 PPTP ports and 1,000 L2TP ports to be available for connecting clients.

> **NOTE**
>
> VPN server support for PPTP is built into members of the Windows Server 2003 family, including Web Edition. The Web Edition of the server operating system can accept only one VPN connection at a time, regardless of how many PPTP ports and L2TP ports are configured.

PPTP uses PPP authentication, compression, and encryption mechanisms and has been around since the Windows NT 4.0 days. It is installed on the system as part of the TCP/IP protocol suite. The default configuration for RRAS allows PPTP to be configured with five PPTP and five L2TP ports, but you can also choose the VPN option, which automatically creates 128 PPTP and 128 L2TP ports.

Microsoft Point-to-Point Encryption (MPPE) is what provides the primary VPN encapsulation and encryption of data for PPTP VPN connections. Three levels of encryption are provided for PPTP and IPSec. The first is *basic encryption* (MPPE 40-bit), which is often used for backward-compatibility with older operating systems and other countries where high encryption is not available. Basic encryption can use IPSec Data Encryption

Standard (DES) or MPPE 40-bit data encryption. It is no longer considered a high level of encryption and can now be broken fairly easily.

Strong encryption (MPPE 56-bit) uses IPSec DES or MPPE 56-bit data encryption to secure the data. It's used when some level of security is required but security overhead needs to be minimized. This scheme is harder to break than its 40-bit cousin, but it has been done.

The strongest level of security comes from IPSec Triple DES (3DES) or MPPE 128-bit data encryption, which is the most secure level provided to data from within the operating system. This encryption scheme offers the highest level of security for data, but results in the highest overhead on system hardware; however, most of today's mid-range and high-end systems can readily handle this load.

PPTP does not require a Public Key Infrastructure (PKI) to issue computer certificates to connecting clients; L2TP does, however, unless a shared key is used in a client/server connection.

The transmitted data is encrypted with MPPE, using encryption keys generated from the Microsoft Challenge Handshake Authentication Protocol (MS-CHAP), MS-CHAP version 2 (MS-CHAP v2), or Extensible Authentication Protocol-Transport Layer Security (EAP-TLS) authentication process, depending on which one is in use for your configuration. VPN clients must use the same encryption schemes for the data to be encrypted and decrypted.

For L2TP and data security and confidentiality, IPSec, not MPPE, protects and validates the transmitted data. Both L2TP and IPSec must be supported by the VPN client and VPN server for the data to be encrypted and decrypted when this configuration is in use.

Client support for L2TP and PPTP is built into the Windows XP remote access client by default. On the server side, it's built into all members of the Windows Server 2003 family.

Data encrypted with L2TP uses DES or 3DES encryption by using encryption keys supplied by the Internet Key Exchange (IKE) negotiation process. IKE is a protocol that establishes the security association (SA) between two communicating systems over IPSec.

For a better understanding of all the potential clients that might be connecting to your Windows Server 2003 VPN server, the following list outlines the Microsoft clients and their supported tunneling protocols and authentication methods:

> ➤ Windows Server 2003 systems, Windows XP Home Edition and Professional systems, and Windows 2000 Server systems and Professional workstations can be configured to use PPTP or L2TP.

> ➤ By default, Windows NT 4 Workstation and Server operating systems as well as Windows Me, 98, and 95 (using the Windows Dial-Up Networking 1.3 Performance and Security Upgrade for Windows 95) can connect to the VPN server using only PPTP; L2TP is not supported unless the Microsoft L2TP/IPSec VPN client is installed.

> ➤ Windows Server 2003 systems, Windows XP Home Edition and Professional systems, and Windows 2000 Server systems and Professional workstations can be configured to use Password Authentication Protocol (PAP), Shiva Password Authentication Protocol (SPAP), CHAP, MS-CHAP, MS-CHAP v2, and EAP remote access authentication protocols.

> ➤ Windows NT 4 Workstation and Server operating systems as well as Windows 98 (Service Pack 1 and later) and Windows 95 (using the Dial-Up Networking 1.4 Upgrade) can connect using everything mentioned in this list, except EAP; these clients cannot use this remote access authentication protocol.

PAP sends all the supplied credentials over the wire in clear text and, therefore, provides no protection against unauthorized access of the information being transmitted. Anyone running a networking scanner in promiscuous mode can read the information being sent. PAP, the least secure of the authentication protocols, is often used only when clients and servers cannot negotiate a more secure confirmation.

SPAP is an older, proprietary, two-way reversible encryption mechanism originally designed by Shiva. (Intel acquired Shiva Corporation in February 1999.) When server and client systems use this hardware solution, Shiva encrypts the password data sent between the client and server.

CHAP, explained in more detail in RFC 1334, is sometimes referred to as "MD5–CHAP." This challenge-response authentication protocol uses the MD5 message-digest algorithm for a one-way encryption scheme on the response from the client system. Remote access servers return a challenge to client systems that attempt to make a connection. When the remote access client receives the challenge, it sends a response containing the username and a one-way encryption of the challenge string, the session identifier, and the password so that the remote access server can check the response and verify whether the information supplied is valid. If the supplied username and password information is valid and the remote connecting system and end user have the proper rights to make the connection, permission is granted.

VPN and RRAS servers can be configured to use MS-CHAP (sometimes referred to as "MS-CHAP v1") and MPPE (described in RFC 3078) to encrypt data between the client and server.

MS-CHAP v1 is a nonreversible, encrypted password authentication protocol that RRAS and VPN servers use to send a challenge to the connecting remote access client. This challenge consists of a session identifier and an arbitrary challenge string. When the connecting client receives the challenge, it responds by supplying the username of the user attempting the connection and a nonreversible encryption of the challenge string, the session identifier, and the password. If the supplied response information is valid and the remote connecting system and end user have the proper rights to make the connection, permission is granted at this point.

MS-CHAP v1 has some issues that make it less secure than its MS-CHAP v2 cousin. Less secure LAN Manager challenge responses are used for backward-compatibility with legacy RRAS and VPN clients. Also, in 40-bit encrypted connections, the user password cannot be longer than 14 characters, or the connection is denied automatically because the remainder of the password cannot be parsed. This affects all types of VPN and RRAS sessions. Not only are challenge responses less secure, but so are any password changes made using the encrypted password authentication protocol. (MS-CHAP v2 no longer allows LAN Manager–encoded challenge responses or password changes for this reason.)

MS-CHAP v1 uses only one-way authentication, so the client has no way to ascertain whether it has actually connected to the correct VPN server or to a rogue system that is allowing the authentication. MS-CHAP v2 provides two-way, mutual authentication, which allows the remote access client to verify that the VPN server it's connecting to is the correct system.

MS-CHAP v2 uses stronger initial data encryption keys based on the user's password and an arbitrary challenge string that varies each time the user connects. Windows 2000 dial-up and VPN connections can use MS-CHAP v2. Systems running Windows NT 4 and Windows 98 can use MS-CHAP v2 authentication for VPN connections only.

Exam Prep Questions

Question 1

You are the Web hosting administrator for your company's e-commerce environment, and you need to configure a single internal persistent static route to your internal subnet of 50.0.0.0 /8 on the internal NIC only. The server is using an internal IP address of 199.168.1.225 and an external address of 12.155.34.66.

You go to a command prompt and enter the following:

```
C:\>route add 50.0.0.0 mask 255.0.0.0 12.155.34.66
```

Which of the following steps have been met? (Choose two.)

❑ A. A static entry has been established.

❑ B. A persistent static entry has been established.

❑ C. The static route to your internal subnet of 50.0.0.0 /8 has been correctly configured.

❑ D. The static route to your internal subnet of 50.0.0.0 /8 has not been correctly configured.

❑ E. An incorrect persistent static entry has been established.

The correct answers are A and D. A static entry has been established. However, the entry is not on the correct route, as it has been tied to the external IP address, and the task called for it to be tied to the internal address. Also, although it is a static entry, it has not been made persistent. When you add a route using the ROUTE ADD command, you need to use the -p switch to make the route persistent, or it is removed when the system restarts. By default, manually entered routes are not rebuilt when the system is restarted unless they are configured as persistent.

Question 2

You are the network administrator for your Windows Server 2003 mixed-mode domain, and you have been tasked with solving the issue of routing in your environment. Currently, you use static routing, but now that your network has expanded, this method has become unmanageable.

You have decided to review the available dynamic routing protocols: RIPv1, RIPv2, and OSPF. For a network that has a little more than 30 routing points and up to 17 hops between the farthest segments, which of the following options is the best choice?

○ A. RIPv1

○ B. RIPv2

○ C. OSPF

○ D. Both RIPv1 and RIPv2 can be used.

○ E. All three routing protocols could be used.

The correct answer is C. RIPv1 and RIPv2 are best used on medium-sized networks with about 50 routers maximum, and the maximum number of routers (hops) that any IP packet must cross is less than 16.

When using any version of RIP, you need to consider that the update announcements generated by RIP routers can cause unacceptable levels of network traffic when more than 50 RIP routers are in use. In this scenario, there is less cause for concern because there are fewer than 30 routing points. The main reason this will not work is that there are 17 hops between the farthest segments. Destination addresses that are 16 or more hops away are unreachable from RIP routers.

OSPF is a link-state protocol based on an algorithm that determines the shortest path between source and destination nodes on a routed network, which is a better choice than either version of RIP when you are considering routing 17 hops between the farthest segments of a network.

Question 3

You are the network administrator for your Windows Server 2003 domain, and you have been tasked with solving the issue of routing in your environment. You have decided to use RIPv1 as your network's dynamic routing protocol, and you would like to configure router broadcasts by using multicast announcements. Your addressing scheme uses the CIDR address of 128.211.0.0 / 21. Which of the following answers are the most relevant to the information supplied? (Choose two.)

❏ A. RIPv1 routers use multicast announcements.

❏ B. RIPv1 routers use broadcast announcements.

❏ C. RIPv1 routers do not support CIDR.

❏ D. RIPv1 routers support CIDR.

❏ E. RIPv1 routers support CIDR only in native-mode forests.

The correct answers are B and C. RIPv1 is difficult to deploy in larger environments because it supports the main classes of IP addresses only and cannot use Classless Inter-Domain Routing (CIDR) or Variable Length Subnet Masks (VLSM). RIPv1 is limited in security measures as well. Routers that exchange routing information using RIPv1 do not authenticate with each other, which could allow a Denial of Service (DoS) attack in which a hacker corrupts routing tables. RIPv2 network routers broadcast their routing tables to other RIPv2 routers at predefined intervals via broadcast or multicast. RIPv1 uses broadcast only.

Question 4

> You are considering a Data Link layer switch on your LAN in an effort to form a border on your broadcast and collision domains to limit the traffic in two different locations.
>
> Location 1 has four Windows XP Professional workstations and one Windows Server 2003 system connected to HUB1, which is connected directly to HUB2.
>
> Location 2 has three Windows 2000 Professional workstations, one Windows 2000 Server system, and one Windows NT 4 server running Service Pack 5 (SP5). These systems are connected to HUB2, which is directly connected to HUB1.
>
> You install the Data Link layer switch and connect HUB1 to port 1 on the switch and HUB2 to port 15 on the switch. What are the end results of your actions? (Choose two.)
>
> ❑ A. Location 1 and Location 2 will be part of the same broadcast domain.
>
> ❑ B. Location 1 and Location 2 will be in different broadcast domains.
>
> ❑ C. Location 1 and Location 2 will be part of the same collision domain.
>
> ❑ D. Location 1 and Location 2 will be in different collision domains.
>
> ❑ E. Location 1 and Location 2 are in different subnets.

The correct answers are A and D. Bridges and switches operate at the Data Link layer (Layer 2) of the OSI model and automatically forward all broadcast traffic received; therefore, Location 1 and Location 2 will be part of the same broadcast domain.

Although Layer 2 switches can be found at the borders of collision domains, they do not form a border of a broadcast domain. Because Layer 2 switches do form the borders of collision domains, Location 1 and Location 2 will be in different collision domains. Only Network layer/Layer 3 devices, such as routers or Layer 3 switches, form a border of a broadcast domain.

Question 5

You are the network administrator for your Windows Server 2003 environment. You have been tasked with connecting three branch offices to your main office, all of which are in the same city. Branch 1 has four Windows XP Professional workstations and one Windows Server 2003 system connected locally by a hub.

Branch 2 has five Windows 2000 Professional and XP Professional workstations, one Windows 2000 Server system, and one Windows NT 4 server running SP6a. These systems are also connected locally by a hub.

Branch 3 has seven Windows 2000 Professional and XP Professional workstations, two Windows 2000 servers, one Windows Server 2003 system, and three Windows NT 4 servers running SP6a. These systems are also connected locally by a hub.

The main office is identical in layout to Branch 3, except that its Windows NT 4 servers have been retired. You have decided to use Layer 3 switches at the main office and the branch offices to connect all the systems. What is the result of your actions?

- ○ A. The solution will not work; routers will be needed.
- ○ B. The offices will be in different broadcast domains.
- ○ C. The offices will be in the same collision domain.
- ○ D. The offices will be in the same broadcast domain.

The correct answer is B. Because Network layer/Layer 3 devices, such as routers or Layer 3 switches, form a border of a broadcast domain, the offices will be in different broadcast domains. Routers are used to connect dissimilar LAN segments and to create smaller broadcast domains. Routers are better than switches for segmenting larger networks in an effort to improve performance and for connecting large LANs to WANs, but they are usually more expensive than similar performance switches.

Layer 3 switches route packets at Layer 3 and forward frames at Layer 2. They are very fast devices with minimal latency and are used primarily for LAN-based IP or IPX routing solutions. In most cases, Layer 3 switches are used to connect virtual LANs (VLANs) or to subdivide larger LANs into smaller broadcast domains; however, with very small branch offices, as in this example, this solution would work.

Question 6

You are the network administrator for your Windows Server 2003 domain. You have been tasked with connecting all three of your branch offices and your main office to the Internet. Branch 1 has five Windows XP Professional workstations, three Windows 2000 Professional workstations, and one Windows Server 2003 system connected locally by a Layer 3 switch. All the clients use manually assigned IP addresses.

Branch 2 has four Windows 2000 Professional workstations, four XP Professional workstations, one Windows 2000 server, and one Windows NT 4 server running SP6a. These systems are also connected locally by a Layer 3 switch. All the clients use manually assigned IP addresses.

Branch 3 has six Windows 2000 Professional workstations, five Windows XP Professional workstations, two Windows 2000 servers, one Windows Server 2003 system, and three Windows NT 4 servers running Service Pack 6a. These systems are also connected locally by a Layer 3 switch. All clients use manually assigned IP addresses.

The main office has five Windows 2000 Professional workstations, six XP Professional workstations, two Windows 2000 servers, and three Windows Server 2003 systems. These systems are also connected locally by a Layer 3 switch. All the clients use manually assigned IP addresses.

The four locations are all connected via private leased lines to a router at the main office. You have been asked to allow all the systems to have Internet connectivity. You need to ensure that all systems can connect to the Internet and that a moderate level of security is available for all systems from one centralized point. The method of security must be inclusive to all the hosts. You need to carry out the design efficiently with the least amount of administrative effort.

Which of the following actions could you take to complete this task as outlined? (Choose two.)

❑ A. Install ISA Server on one server and run it in firewall mode.

❑ B. Enable Internet Connection Sharing on one of the servers and allow all the systems to use that server as the default connection to the Internet.

❑ C. Install ISA Server on one server and run it in Integrated mode.

❑ D. Configure all the client systems to use APIPA. Configure the addresses with the ISA server as the default gateway.

❑ E. Configure all client systems to use APIPA. Configure the addresses with the ISA server as the proxy server in Internet Explorer.

❑ F. Configure the IP address of the ISA server as the proxy server in Internet Explorer on each client.

❑ G. Configure the IP address of the ISA server as the default gateway on each client.

❑ H. Enable Internet Connection Firewall on each client.

❑ I. Enable Internet Connection Sharing on each client.

The correct answers are C and F. By installing ISA Server on one server and running it in Integrated mode, you will be able to use the server as a proxy to the Internet for the hosts on the network and protect them from the Internet at the same time.

Configuring the IP address of the ISA server as the proxy server in Internet Explorer on each client is the only way to get all the systems connected to the Internet. Installing ISA Server on one server and running it in Firewall mode is not the best solution. Although it will protect the systems from a security standpoint, they will not be able to connect to the Internet.

Enabling Internet Connection Sharing on one of the servers and allowing all the systems to use that system as the default connection to the Internet is not necessarily the best option, as the systems are left unprotected from the Internet. Configuring all client systems to use APIPA would not work because APIPA does not use a default gateway, which would not allow the systems out of their subnets.

By configuring the IP address of the ISA server as the default gateway on each client, you prevent the systems from getting out of their current subnets. Enabling ICF on each client is not possible on all clients, as some of them are running legacy operating systems that do not have this option. The same is true for enabling ICS on each client.

Question 7

You are a domain administrator for your company, which hosts a mixed-mode Windows 2003 Active Directory forest. You have been tasked with setting up and configuring secured remote access to your intranet so that employees can successfully and securely access network resources from the field. Clients in use include Windows 2000 Professional running a mix of SP2 and SP3, Windows XP Professional running SP1, and a few Windows 98 and Windows NT 4 Workstation SP6a systems.

Which of the following authentication methods is the most secure and allows all workstations to authenticate users and prevent passwords from being "seen" on the wire?

- ○ A. Password Authentication Protocol (PAP)
- ○ B. Shiva Password Authentication Protocol (SPAP)
- ○ C. Challenge Handshake Authentication Protocol (CHAP)
- ○ D. Microsoft Challenge Handshake Authentication Protocol version 1 (MS-CHAP v1)
- ○ E. Microsoft Challenge Handshake Authentication Protocol version 2 (MS-CHAP v2)
- ○ F. Extensible Authentication Protocol (EAP)

The correct answer is D. MS-CHAP v1 functions in the same manner as CHAP; the server sends a challenge to the remote client that consists of a session ID and a challenge string. The remote client must return the username and a Message Digest 4 (MD4) hash of the challenge string, the session ID, and the MD4-hashed password.

MS-CHAP v1 requires only the MD4 hash of the password to validate the challenge response; it does not need the password available in plaintext, which is required in CHAP. In Windows 2000 and 2003, user passwords are stored as an MD4 hash and in a reversibly encrypted form. When CHAP is used, the remote access server decrypts the reversibly encrypted password to validate the remote access client's response.

The main reason MS-CHAP v1 must be used instead of the other protocols as "most secure" is that there are Windows 98 systems on the network. The DS Client Pack needs to be installed on Windows 95 or 98 systems to use NTLMv2. Windows Me and NT 4 systems running SP4 or later support NTLMv2 without additional modification.

MS-CHAP v2 is the Windows 2000 implementation of MS-CHAP. It does not support earlier Windows client versions, such as Windows NT 4 and Windows 9x. Although you should use MS-CHAP v2 whenever possible, it is not the correct answer to this question because of the legacy systems in use.

EAP is an authentication protocol that can be extended with additional authentication methods, such as SmartCards, biometrics, and certificate-based authentication.

All the other options require specific hardware for encryption, such as SPAP, or they do not provide any encryption at all, as in the case of PAP, which sends passwords as clear text.

Question 8

> You are the network administrator for **zandri.net**, which is a Windows Server 2003 native-mode domain. You have been reviewing authentication encryption solutions for remote field users, who consist mainly of your sales force using Windows NT 4, Windows 98, and Windows 2000 Professional clients on laptop systems. Of the following solutions, which can be used to encrypt authentication? (Choose two.)
>
> ❏ A. SHA
>
> ❏ B. MD5
>
> ❏ C. 40-bit DES
>
> ❏ D. 56-bit DES
>
> ❏ E. 3DES

The correct answers are A and B. Secure Hash Algorithm (SHA) is a 160-bit key authentication encryption method, and Message Digest 5 (MD5) is a standard authentication encryption method that uses a 128-bit key. Both methods encrypt authentication attempts, but they do not encrypt data. 40-bit DES uses a single 40-bit key, and 56-bit DES uses a single 56-bit key as part of their data encryption process. Both are used for smaller security concerns when system overhead is an issue. Both encryption processes do nothing to encrypt authentication attempts. 3DES uses three 56-bit keys and processes each data block three times, using a unique key each time as part of its data encryption process. It is often used in high-security situations and is also used for data only, as it, too, does not encrypt authentication attempts.

Question 9

You are the network administrator for **zandri.net**, which is a Windows Server 2003 native-mode domain. The systems in use between your main office and your branch offices are as follows:

Branch 1 has five Windows XP Professional workstations, three Windows 2000 Professional workstations, and one Windows Server 2003 system connected locally by one Windows Server 2003 system running Routing and Remote Access Service (RRAS). All the clients use manually assigned IP addresses.

Branch 2 has four Windows 2000 Professional workstations, four XP Professional workstations, one Windows 2000 server, and one Windows NT 4 server running SP6a. These systems are also connected locally by one Windows Server 2003 system running RRAS. All the clients use manually assigned IP addresses.

Branch 3 has six Windows 2000 Professional workstations, five XP Professional workstations, two Windows 2000 servers, one Windows Server 2003 system, and three Windows NT 4 servers running SP6a. These systems are also connected locally by one Windows Server 2003 system running RRAS. All the clients use manually assigned IP addresses.

The main office has five Windows 2000 Professional workstations, six XP Professional workstations, two Windows 2000 servers, and three Windows Server 2003 systems. These systems are also connected locally by one Windows Server 2003 system running RRAS. All the clients use manually assigned IP addresses.

Your primary objective is to provide a secure connection for all systems between your main office and your branch offices. One secondary objective is to provide a solution that is always available. The other secondary objective is to provide a solution that can work on all clients in all locations with the least amount of administrative effort.

You have decided to use L2TP and IPSec encryption in its default mode to provide the necessary security for your environment. All communications will be set to "require" security. What are the results of your efforts?

- ○ A. The primary and both secondary objectives have been satisfied.
- ○ B. The primary and one secondary objective have been satisfied.
- ○ C. Only the secondary objectives have been satisfied.
- ○ D. Only one secondary objective has been satisfied.
- ○ E. None of the objectives has been satisfied.

The correct answer is E. IPSec Transport mode authenticates and encrypts data flowing between any two computers running Windows 2000 Server or Windows Server 2003. It provides security for the network and can potentially support a secure connection with more than one other computer at a time. Transport mode is the default IPSec mode.

Using IPSec in Tunnel mode authenticates and encrypts data flowing within an IP tunnel that is created between two routers. Windows 2000 Server and Window Server 2003 requires RRAS to implement Tunnel mode for IPSec. You enable Tunnel mode in IPSec Management and configure Tunnel mode settings by supplying an IP address for each end of the tunnel. This encrypts all the data sent between any of the systems from one location to another via the two RRAS servers.

Your primary objective to provide a secure connection for all systems between your main office and your branch offices has not been met because you decided to use L2TP and IPSec encryption in its default mode to provide the necessary security for your environment. This configuration is set up in Transport mode, not Tunnel mode, which is what's needed.

The secondary objective of providing a solution that is always available has been met for all systems except the NT 4 systems. Forcing all communications to "require" security will encrypt all the data transferred between all hosts. With this deployment, the NT 4 systems will not be able to communicate with other systems.

The secondary objective of providing a solution that can work on all clients in all locations with the least amount of administrative effort has been met for all systems except the NT 4 systems. For those NT 4 systems to be able to use L2TP/IPSec, the Microsoft L2TP/IPSec VPN client needs to be installed so that those servers can use L2TP connections with IPSec.

Question 10

You are the network administrator for **zandri.net**, which is a Windows Server 2003 native-mode domain. You have identified Point-to-Point Tunneling Protocol (PPTP) as the secure VPN connection method for your sales users in the field when they need to connect to the main office over the Internet. The users will not call into the RRAS server directly; rather, they will call into a local ISP wherever they are traveling and use the Internet to make their connection to the RRAS server.

The laptop systems your sales force uses include Windows 98, Windows 2000, and Windows XP Professional. Your primary objective is to provide a secure connection for all systems between remote locations and your main office by way of the Internet. One secondary objective is to provide a solution that is always available. The other secondary objective is to provide a solution that has built-in encryption and works on IP-based infrastructures.

You have decided to use RRAS for your VPN solution and PPTP. What are the results of your efforts?

- ○ A. The primary and both secondary objectives have been satisfied.
- ○ B. The primary and one secondary objective have been satisfied.
- ○ C. Only the secondary objectives have been satisfied.
- ○ D. Only one secondary objective has been satisfied.
- ○ E. None of the objectives has been satisfied.

The correct answer is A. The primary and both secondary objectives have been satisfied. VPNs can use PPTP or L2TP to establish connections to RRAS servers on both the Windows 2000 Server and Windows Server 2003 platforms.

Both protocols can be configured to encapsulate data packets in an effort to securely send data over the Internet; however, L2TP needs to use IPSec to encrypt data because it does not have this capability built in. PPTP does have built-in encryption because it uses MPPE to encrypt data. PPTP can be used on IP-based networks only (which was all the question called for); it cannot use any other types. L2TP can be used on IP networks in addition to Frame Relay, X.25, or Asynchronous Transfer Mode (ATM) networks.

Need To Know More?

Go to the Windows Server 2003 area of TechNet (http://www.microsoft.com/technet/treeview/default.asp?url=/technet/prodtechnol/windowsserver2003/default.asp) and search on the following keywords: Network Monitor, route, PATHPING, System Monitor, Performance Console, Internet Connection Sharing (ICS), Network Address Translation (NAT), IP address ranges, services and ports, IP routing, Routing and Remote Access, unicast routing, multicast forwarding, remote access policies, RADIUS clients, RADIUS servers, L2TP, PPTP, IAS ports, IPSec troubleshooting, virtual private network (VPN), authentication methods, 802.1X authentication for wireless networks, PEAP, and SmartCard support.

Planning, Implementing, and Maintaining Server Availability

. . . .

Terms you'll need to understand:

✓ Network Load Balancing Manager (NLBM)
✓ Mean Time Between Failure (MTBF)
✓ Redundant array of independent (or inexpensive) disks (RAID)
✓ Automated System Recovery
✓ Shadow Copy

Techniques you'll need to master:

✓ Configuring servers to use Network Load Balancing
✓ Configuring servers to use the Microsoft Cluster Service
✓ Scheduling regular system backups with NTBACKUP
✓ Performing data restoration from backup sets with NTBACKUP
✓ Determining Mean Time Between Failures (MTBF)
✓ Understanding component load balancing
✓ Installing and configuring RAID sets
✓ Installing and configuring shadow copies on shared folders

Windows Server 2003 provides both the Cluster Service and Network Load Balancing for load balancing, high availability, and high reliability. Server systems and all their components have a rated reliability number (usually expressed in hours) called the *Mean Time Between Failure* (*MTBF*). The MTBF shows the measured failure rate of the system's individual components.

A high-availability server is expected to be available at all times: 7 days a week, 52 weeks a year. In effect, the system is built and deployed with the consideration that it would never be offline. This is, of course, not always true because every server needs to be shut down periodically for upgrades or to recover from system failures.

High-availability server deployments are normally undertaken as follows:

➤ Ensuring the longest span of time between hardware failures by referring to the MTBF ratings for hardware devices

➤ Installing and configuring the clustering services in the Windows Server 2003 operating system

➤ Third-party clustering solutions

Network Load Balancing

On the Windows NT Server platform, Network Load Balancing was known as the Windows NT Load Balancing Service (WLBS) and performed the same basic function it does today: providing higher availability for applications and faster response times from servers. Network Load Balancing works by distributing incoming IP traffic across a cluster of servers—up to 32 Windows Server 2003 systems—that share a single virtual IP address. It is available on all versions of Windows Server 2003. The service enables you to allocate incoming Transmission Control Protocol/Internet Protocol (TCP/IP) traffic between multiple servers so that applications and the servers that host them can handle traffic better and ensure a higher level of availability and throughput for users and system access.

Component Load Balancing is available under Microsoft Application Center 2000. These cluster designs allow growth and system availability by enabling COM+ applications to be distributed across up to 12 nodes. The cluster service is available on only the Enterprise and Datacenter Editions of Windows Server 2003. Under Windows 2000 Advanced Server, the maximum supported cluster size was two nodes; in Windows Server 2003 Enterprise

Edition, it's eight nodes. Windows 2000 Datacenter Server supported four node clusters; Windows Server 2003 Datacenter Edition supports eight.

> **NOTE** Component Load Balancing is a feature of Microsoft Application Center 2000. It is a standalone product not found in the Windows Server 2003 family of server operating systems. Server clusters cannot be made up of nodes running both Enterprise and Datacenter Editions of Windows Server 2003. All nodes must run either Datacenter Edition or Enterprise Edition. There cannot be a mix of both types.

When you're considering clustering services for a high-availability solution in your enterprise, think about whether the main focus should be on load balancing or fault tolerance when building clusters for your environment. Windows 2000 Server has two main types of cluster configurations: active/active clusters and active/passive clusters.

Active/active is an established pair in which either system responds to client requests. This design configuration allows for load balancing because the system with more available resources can respond better. To a degree, some fault tolerance is built into this design because a single node failure does not cause all the cluster's services to be lost.

In an Active/passive established pair, only one server responds to client requests; the job of the remaining server is to monitor the online system. If the twin system stops responding, the idle node comes fully online and responds to user service requests. This design is fault tolerant because unlike the active/active configuration, there is no shared load.

Implementing Network Load Balancing

After you decide to use Network Load Balancing to install and configure the clustering technology for your environment, follow these steps:

1. Log on as an administrator (or have this level of access on the system).

2. Open the Network Load Balancing Manager by typing `nlbmgr` at the command line.

3. Right-click Network Load Balancing Clusters, and choose New Cluster.

4. Enter the IP address and subnet mask of the cluster. Click Next.

5. Click the Add button to add virtual IP addresses used by the cluster. Click OK and then Next.

6. Enter the virtual IP address and subnet mask information. You can add any required port rules. Click Next.

7. Enter the name of a host that will be a member of the cluster, and click Connect. Available network adapters on the entered host are listed at the bottom of the dialog box. Click Next.

8. Choose the network adapter(s) you want to use for this Network Load Balancing configuration. Click Finish.

Now that the cluster has been created, you can add hosts in the future by opening the Network Load Balancing Manager, connecting to the existing cluster (if it is not shown), right-clicking the cluster, and choosing Add Host To Cluster. The remainder of the steps are the same as those for creating a new cluster: Enter a hostname, click Connect, and choose the network adapters that are available on the entered host. They are listed at the bottom of the dialog box, so you can choose the network adapter(s) you want to use for this Network Load Balancing configuration. After you complete these steps, the host will be part of this Network Load Balancing cluster.

If you need to drop a single node from a cluster, right-click the node in the Network Load Balancing Manager, and choose Delete Host. If you need to delete the entire Network Load Balancing cluster, right-click the cluster in the Network Load Balancing Manager, and choose Delete Cluster.

After you've finished setting up the entire Network Load Balancing cluster with the nodes you want to use, you need to configure additional settings, such as IP address, subnet mask, full Internet name, cluster operation mode, remote control, and password information, in the Cluster Parameters tab of the Cluster Properties dialog box.

Notes from the Field

There are many other things you need to know about Network Load Balancing that go beyond the scope of this book, but in this sidebar I've supplied some highlights you should focus on.

The Network Load Balancing Manager is the recommended way to configure Network Load Balancing. You also have the option to set up TCP/IP for Network Load Balancing by configuring the Network Load Balancing Properties dialog box through Network Connections.

You can connect to existing clusters in the Network Load Balancing Manager by choosing File, Load Host List from the menu, selecting any available host list text file, and clicking Open. You can also do this from the command line by entering the following:

```
nlbmgr /hostlist host-list
```

This command force-loads the hosts specified in the file into the Network Load Balancing Manager. Another point to remember about network configuration is that adapters can be configured in both unicast and Internet Group Management Protocol (IGMP) multicast mode.

Considering Systems for Network Load Balancing

Network Load Balancing is designed to work only on 10Mbps, 100Mbps, and gigabit ethernet network adapters. It is not compatible with Asynchronous Transfer Mode (ATM), ATM local area network (LAN) emulation, or token ring networks.

On x86-based 32-bit ethernet network configurations, Network Load Balancing uses from 750KB to 2MB of RAM per network adapter in a default configuration, which can vary as high as 27MB, depending on the network load. Configuration settings can be modified to allow using up to 84MB of memory.

On Itanium-based 64-bit ethernet network configurations, Network Load Balancing uses from 825KB to 2.5MB of RAM per network adapter in a default configuration, which can vary as high as 32MB, depending on the network load. Configuration settings can be modified to allow using up to 102MB of memory.

Network Load Balancing can be configured using only a single network adapter on a node. For the best possible cluster performance, however, you should install at least one additional network adapter on each Network Load Balancing node so that the first network adapter can be set to handle the network traffic addressed to the server as part of the Cluster Service. The second network adapter can be used for communication between nodes in the cluster.

The primary rationale for installing Network Load Balancing is to mitigate possible single points of failure that can interrupt your network services. Single points of failure can be hardware based, such as when a single router or a single server goes offline. They can also be caused by single external dependencies, such as the loss of public utilities. There are a number of ways to mitigate some single points of failure, depending on what they are.

When power for a server system is a concern, you can have redundant power supplies installed so that if one supply fails, another is running and can assume the full load for the system. You can also attach power to these redundant power supplies from separate electrical circuits in your building in an effort to prevent a circuit trip from becoming another single failure point.

Implementing a RAID Solution

For hard drive issues, there are hardware and software redundant array of independent (or inexpensive—both are correct) disks (RAID). On most

Windows Server 2003 systems, you deal with RAID 1 or 5 most of the time. RAID 0, which is often referred to as "stripe" or a "striping configuration," is just a stripe with no parity. It is available on Windows Server 2003 and considered a RAID build, but it has no parity or fault tolerance.

Hardware RAID is any type of RAID deployed on a computer system that is controlled at a hardware level, independent of the operating system. Before any type of operating system is installed on the system, the hardware-level RAID configuration is already configured on the system. Hardware RAID is designed and deployed so that when errors or configuration problems cause the loss of the operating system, recovering data is easier because the disk configuration is held on the hardware controller. (Sometimes the disk configuration is also stored on certain reserved sectors of the hard drives, depending on the controller's manufacturer and design.) The downside of a hardware RAID configuration is that loss of the hardware device makes data retrieval much more difficult. Because the operating system sees the combined space of all the drives as one logical structure, the hard drive configuration is unknown to the operating system (and any standard data recovery tools), thus increasing the difficulty of retrieving data.

In a software-based (by default, *software-based* means "derived from the operating system") RAID solution, the operating system creates and stores the logical structure of drives in the array. Direct access, such as booting from a floppy disk, an NTFS boot disk, or an installation CD, bypasses the operating system. In most cases, this bypassing does not allow access to data on the array because the operating system is not allowed to initialize and access the logical drive array it has created.

In a software-based RAID configuration, you don't need to be concerned about RAID-based hardware failure (such as a controller card); however, if you lose the operating system to the extent that its repair function cannot fix the problem, all the RAID data created by the operating system is usually lost.

A RAID 0 configuration makes it possible to use the total combined space of all drives without the loss of any available total space. That is, if five 20GB hard drives (totaling 100GB of space) are committed to a RAID 0 array, the total usable space is 100GB.

RAID 1 is deployed using a total of two drives. This configuration can sustain the loss of one drive and still allow the system's full operation. It is referred to as *disk mirroring* when two different hard drives are used on the same IDE, SCSI, or RAID controller. It's called *disk duplexing* when two different hard drives are used on two different IDE, SCSI, or RAID controllers.

There is no striping in this configuration (as you would see in a RAID 0 configuration); however, all data written to one disk is duplicated on the other. RAID 1's fault tolerance is based on of this duplicate data, which is the parity information used to maintain the system in the event of a drive failure.

A RAID 1 configuration effectively causes the "loss" of 50% of the total usable disk space because the second drive is committed to the parity writing of the array. When two 50GB hard drives totaling 100GB are installed in a system and then configured in a RAID 1 configuration, the total amount of disk space available for use is 50GB. The "lost" space is allotted for parity storage, which in this configuration is the total duplication of the first drive. A RAID 1 configuration can sustain the loss of its twin drive and still allow the system's full operation.

RAID 5, referred to as *striping with parity*, has some similarities to RAID 0; the main difference is that RAID 5 includes fault tolerance, and RAID 0 doesn't. RAID 5 data is divided into blocks ranging from 512 bytes to 64KB. The data is distributed across all disks in the array, with parity information being spread out and written to each drive. RAID 5 requires a minimum of three disks in its standard configuration.

A RAID 5 configuration makes it possible to use the total combined space of all drives, minus the total space of a single drive. That is, if five 20GB hard drives (totaling 100GB of space) are committed to a RAID 5 array, the total usable space is 80GB. The "lost" space is allotted for parity storage. A RAID 5 configuration can sustain the loss of one drive and still allow the system's full operation.

Clustering can help mitigate possible single points of failure in your environment. Although it does protect data availability, it cannot protect the data itself. Therefore, having a backup strategy is still important.

Backing Up Data

You have more options for backing up data in Windows Server 2003 from within the operating system than in previous versions of the operating system. The NTBACKUP utility is still available for administrators to set up and configure backups and offers five options to choose from. You can run NTBACKUP from the graphical user interface (GUI) or the command line. Note that even though you can perform a data backup from the command line, you cannot perform a restore. These are the available command-line switches for NTBACKUP:

➤ systemstate—Enables you to perform a normal or copy backup of the System State data.

➤ @bks file name—Enables you to set the backup selection filename (.bks file) to be used for this backup operation. The at (@) character must precede the name. An example of this usage is ntbackup backup @c:\monday.bks.

➤ /J {"job name"}—Identifies the job name to be used in the log file.

➤ /P {"pool name"}—Identifies the media pool from which you want to use media. If you select this command-line option, you cannot use the /A, /G, /F, or /T command-line switches.

➤ /G {"guid name"}—Overwrites or appends data to the specified media. You should not use this switch with the /P option.

➤ /T {"tape name"}—Overwrites or appends data to the specified media. You should not use this switch with the /P option.

➤ /N {"media name"}—Sets a new tape name. You should not use this switch with the /A option.

➤ /F {"file name"}—Enables you to enter the logical disk path and filename. You should not use this switch with the /P, /G, or /T options.

➤ /D {"set description"}—Enables you to identify the label for each backup set.

➤ /DS {"server name"}—Enables you to back up the directory service file for the specified Microsoft Exchange server.

➤ /IS {"server name"}—Enables you to back up the Information Store file for the specified Microsoft Exchange server.

➤ /A—Enables you to run an append operation on another backup. Either /G or /T must be used in combination with this switch. The /P option should not be used.

➤ /V:{yes¦no}—Verifies data after the backup is completed.

➤ /R:{yes¦no}—Restricts access to data on the backup media to the backup owner or members of the Administrators group.

➤ /L:{f¦s¦n}—Identifies the type of log file to use: f=full, s=summary, or n=none.

➤ /RS:{yes¦no}—Used to back up migrated data files located in Remote Storage. This option is not required to back up the local Removable Storage database (that contains the Remote Storage placeholder files). When you back up the %systemroot% folder, Backup automatically backs up the Removable Storage database as well.

➤ /HC:{on¦off}—Sets the use of hardware compression on backup media if it is available.

➤ /SNAP:{on¦off}—Identifies whether the backup is a volume shadow copy.

➤ /M {backup type}—Sets the backup type to normal, copy, differential, incremental, or daily.

Normal backups, also called full backups, are configured to back up all selected files and folders. A normal backup does not rely on backup markers, referred to as the *archive bit*, to determine which files to back up. The backup process simply backs up everything that's selected, regardless of the archive setting. A normal backup clears any existing archive bits it finds and marks all the backed up files as having been backed up. Normal backups are most efficient in the restoration process because the backed up files are the most current, and you do not need to restore multiple backup jobs. Their main drawback is the length of time it takes to perform the initial backup because this method takes the most time.

Copy backups are used to back up all selected files and folders. Like a normal or full backup, this backup process does not rely on the archive bit to determine which files to back up; it backs up everything selected. The copy backup, however, doesn't reset the archive bit as a normal backup does. If you need to back up files and folders and do not want to affect other backup types by resetting the archive bit, a copy backup is the best option. A copy backup is useful when you want a current backup but don't want to disrupt your backup rotation, such as performing an update, an upgrade, or system maintenance.

Daily backups are used to back up all selected files and folders that have changed during that particular day. This backup procedure also does not rely on or reset the archive bit.

Incremental backups back up only selected files and folders that have an archive bit set. That means if you select an entire partition, only the data that has changed is backed up. During an incremental backup, the archive bit is reset (turned off).

NOTE

When data is edited or changed after being backed up, the archive bit is turned on. Therefore, if a document was backed up during a normal backup on Sunday evening, the archive bit is turned off. If you made no changes to the document on Monday or Tuesday, there's no need for it to be backed up again by backup processes that focus on the archive bit, such as incremental backups.

If you open the file on Wednesday, edit it, and then save it, the archive bit is turned back on, which flags the incremental backup process to back up the data during the Wednesday night incremental backup. If you do not edit this file on Thursday, the incremental backup run on Thursday night does *not* back up this file again.

Incremental backups are normally used on a daily basis in between normal backups. For example, if you perform a normal backup Sunday night on an entire partition, you're backing up all the data on the entire partition, and the process backs up all available data and resets any archive bits it finds. On Monday night's incremental backup of the entire partition, the backup process backs up only those files that have changed since the Sunday normal backup, and as the data is backed up, the archive bits are turned off. Tuesday's incremental backup of the entire partition backs up only those files that have changed since the Monday incremental backup. During the Tuesday night backup, the data that has changed is backed up, and the archive bits are turned off. This process continues all week until another normal backup is run again on Sunday.

This process allows for quicker nightly backups of incrementally changed data from the previous day, but it does tend to lengthen the restoration process. If you need a restoration for all the backed up data from that partition on a Friday morning, you have to use the Sunday normal backup to restore the main bulk of the data and use each incremental tape, from Monday through Thursday, to restore all the required data.

Differential backups are normally used on a daily basis between normal backups. They back up only selected files and folders that have an archive bit set. That means if you select an entire partition, only the data that has changed is backed up. During a differential backup, the archive bit is not reset (is not turned off).

For example, if you perform a normal backup Sunday night on an entire partition, you are backing up all the data on the entire partition, and the process backs up all available data and resets any archive bits it finds. On Monday night's differential backup of the entire partition, the backup process backs up only those files that have changed since the Sunday normal backup. The archive bits are not reset (turned off). During Tuesday's incremental backup of the entire partition, all the changed files from Monday and Tuesday are backed up, even though Monday's changed data is already on the Monday tape. The Tuesday backup has all the differences in data from both Monday and Tuesday. Again, the differential backup process does not reset the archive bit. This process continues all week until another normal backup is run again on Sunday.

This process allows for quicker nightly backups of differentially changed data from Sunday's normal backup, but as each day passes, the backup process takes longer. However, it shortens any required restorations. If you need to restore all the backed up data from that partition on a Friday morning, you have to use the Sunday normal backup to restore the main bulk of the data and use only the *last* differential tape or media—in this case, the one from Thursday night—to restore all required data.

Using Automated System Recovery (ASR)

Another option in NTBACKUP is creating an Automated System Recovery (ASR) backup of your system, which creates a backup set of the System State data, system services, and all the disk configuration information on both basic and dynamic volumes.

ASR creates a startup disk, previously known as an Emergency Repair Disk (ERD, or RDISK from the NT 4 days), that contains information about the backup and how to accomplish a restore. New ASR startup disks should be created after any major change to the system so that the information is up to date.

> **NOTE**
> ASR backs up only the system files that are necessary to restart a failed system. You still need to have a separate, regular backup plan for the data on the system itself.
>
> For clusters, you need to run the Automated System Recovery Preparation Wizard on all nodes of the cluster and make sure the Cluster Service is running when you start each ASR backup. One of the nodes must be listed as the owner of the quorum resource while the wizard is running for this part of the ASR backup to be successful.

To create an ASR set, start NTBACKUP (see Figure 5.1) by clicking Start, Run and entering NTBACKUP or choosing All Programs, Accessories, System Tools, Backup.

The Backup Wizard or Restore Wizard should start by default unless they have been disabled. You can use the Backup Wizard to create an ASR set by selecting the All Information on This Computer option in the What Do You Want to Backup? section. You can also create the ASR set in advanced mode by clicking the Advanced Mode link in the Backup or Restore Wizard. After the ASR process starts, it creates a backup file that can be stored locally or remotely and recovery information that's stored on a floppy disk for emergency recovery (see Figure 5.2).

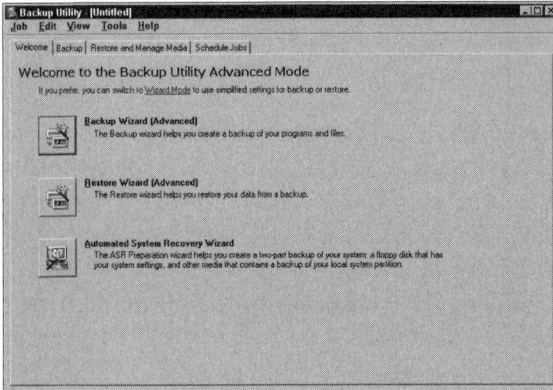

Figure 5.1 In the opening window of NTBACKUP, Automated System Recovery is the icon at the bottom.

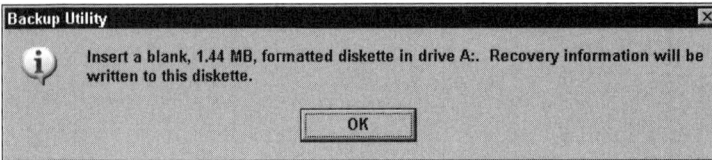

Figure 5.2 In this stage of creating an ASR set, the information required to restart a downed system is written to a floppy disk.

To recover from a system failure using Automated System Recovery, you need the ASR floppy disk, the most recent backup, and the operating system installation CD (or the network location of the operating system files used to build the system). From here, restart the failed system and press F2 when prompted at the beginning of the text-only mode section of Setup. When prompted, insert the ASR floppy disk to recover the system.

Using Shadow Copies

Windows Server 2003 includes the capability to create a *shadow copy*, which can be used on volumes and shared folders to help prevent unintentional loss of data caused by accidental deletions. By creating previous versions of the data at a specific point in time at predetermined time intervals, shadow copies enable users to return to their data at an earlier point in time to retrieve the document. For example, if a user is editing a PowerPoint presentation and deletes a few slides from the presentation and some images in the other remaining slides, and then saves and closes the presentation, there would be a problem if the user suddenly realized she still needs those slides and images. She would have to manually redo all the work in the presentation or have a previously backed up copy restored. With Shadow Copy, users can go back to a previously stored version of their data on their own, retrieve it—in this example, from a saved point before the deletions were made—and restore it for current use. Shadow copies are especially useful when deletions occur over the network and there is no Recycle Bin for users to recover the file.

NOTE

The name of the Shadow Copies of Shared Folders option is slightly misleading; it implies that you can apply shadow copies to specific folders on a volume. This option is enabled at the volume level only, however, so every shared folder on that volume is configured to use this feature after it is set. It also means that shadow copy settings are configured for the entire volume.

A shadow copy makes a copy of any changes in files that have occurred since the last shadow copy. Only the changes are copied, not the entire file, which is helpful because shadow copies don't normally take up as much disk space as the original file.

Using this feature does not eliminate the need to perform regular backups on your Windows Server 2003 systems; a full fault of your server, such as failure of the local hard drive, still causes a loss of data. The other key point to remember is that older shadow copies are periodically removed from the system when the maximum limit of shadow copies per volume is reached.

When using and configuring the Shadow Copy service, you need to determine the following settings:

➤ First, choose the volume that needs to be configured to use this service.

➤ Figure out the allocation of disk space needed for shadow copies and decide whether to use separate hard drives.

➤ Decide how often shadow copies should be created.

➤ Configure the maximum number of shadow copies per volume.

By default, the Shadow Copy service is configured to create shadow copies at 0700 and 1200, Monday through Friday, but administrators can reset this schedule to fit their needs. The default setting for volume space reserved for shadow copy use is 10% of the total volume size (not 10% of the volume's free space). Administrators can change this setting, too, but keep in mind that setting the limit too low causes the oldest shadow copies to be deleted regularly, often much sooner than the maximum number of shadow copies allowed per volume, because the volume's reserved space is being used up. Regardless of the amount of free space, the maximum number of shadow copies that can be created per volume is 64.

NOTE

Shadow copies can be configured on a volume only if you are logged in as an administrator. If you are logged in with an account that has a different level of access on the system, you can't see the Shadow Copies tab in the volume's Properties dialog box. To use the Shadow Copy service, volumes must be formatted with NTFS.

The Shadow Copy service is disabled by default; to enable it, go to the Shadow Copies tab in the applicable volume's Properties dialog box (see Figure 5.3).

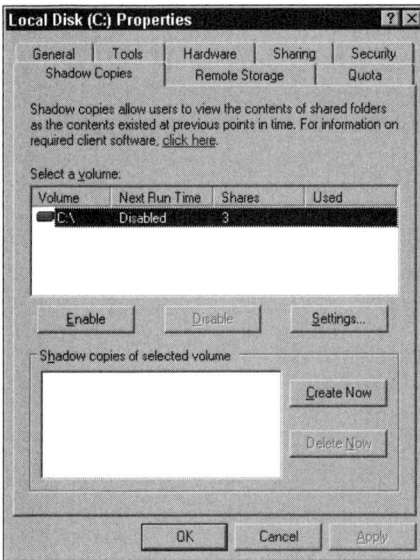

Figure 5.3 The Shadow Copies tab of the volume's Properties dialog box, shown in its default state.

If you want to make just a one-time shadow copy, click the Create Now button, which creates a single copy that appears in the Shadow Copies of Selected Volume list box at the bottom.

To enable default settings for the Shadow Copy service, click the Enable button. As shown in Figure 5.3, three shares are enabled for the Shadow Copy service. To change the default settings (see Figure 5.4), click the Settings button to open the Settings dialog box, where you can change parameters such as the default amount of drive space. To change the schedule for making shadow copies, click the Schedule button.

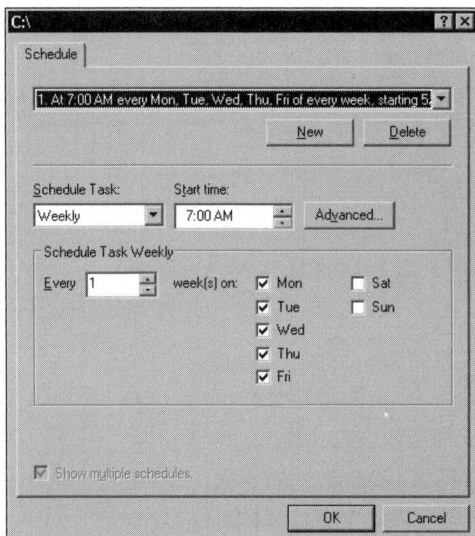

Figure 5.4   Changing the default settings for shadow copies in the Settings and Schedule dialog boxes.

Using Server Clusters

When you minimize the number of single points of failure in your network environment, as with Network Load Balancing, you also ensure maximum reliability and availability because a number of servers are running in a distributed fashion, performing the same core work. This is the main goal of a true server cluster, in which virtually interconnected multiple systems function as a single system to ensure maximum reliability and availability.

A server cluster running under Windows Server 2003 Enterprise or Datacenter Edition can be formed from two to eight nodes and can be configured in one of the following ways:

➤ *Single node server cluster*—A cluster configuration made up of a single node and configured with or without external cluster storage devices. When no external cluster storage device is used, the local drive is used as the cluster storage device.

➤ *Single quorum device server cluster*—A cluster configuration made up of two or more nodes; each node is attached to one or more cluster storage devices. The cluster configuration data is stored on a single cluster storage device.

➤ *Majority node set server cluster*—A cluster configuration with two or more nodes, each node may or may not be attached to one or more cluster storage devices. The cluster configuration data is stored on multiple disks across the cluster, and the Cluster Service makes sure this data is kept consistent across different disks.

Nodes that are part of a cluster configuration have one of the following five states assigned:

➤ *DOWN*—Assigned when the node is not actively participating in cluster operations.

➤ *JOINING*—Assigned when a node is in the process of becoming an active participant in cluster operations.

➤ *PAUSED*—Assigned when a node is actively engaged in some part of the cluster process but it cannot or has not taken ownership of any resource groups.

➤ *UP*—Assigned when a node is actively participating in all cluster operations.

➤ *UNKNOWN*—Assigned when the node's state cannot be determined.

After you have decided which type of cluster to use, you need to assign an IP address and a network name for the cluster. You must also allocate physical disk space for the local system and the clustered data (where the disk space is often located on a drive array).

You also need to consider the applications or services being hosted because some applications are cluster aware, meaning they can be fully utilized in a clustered environment; other applications are not and must be specifically configured to be used with clusters. In some situations, you might not be able to use a particular application in this type of configuration. If so, you need to determine which resources can fail over with the cluster and which will become unavailable because of a node failure. You also need to list any service dependencies for all applications on the cluster so that the Cluster Service enables the dependent services successfully. That way, the application or service can run after a failover.

There are also considerations for the server hardware and the network infrastructure supporting the cluster. Microsoft supports only the server cluster systems deployed with hardware listed in the Windows Catalog, including hardware components such as hard drives, network interface cards (NICs), and the like. Best practices dictate that the cluster configuration consist of identical storage hardware (drives, arrays, controllers, and so on) on all nodes in the cluster to help prevent potential compatibility and differential issues.

Implementing Clusters

All the hard drives that are allocated for the cluster need to be partitioned and formatted before adding the first node of the cluster. All partitions on the cluster drives must be formatted with NTFS, and all partitions on one disk are managed as one resource, which also includes the quorum resource. That means it doesn't matter how many drive letters are configured for the physical disk; when the set fails over, all the drive letters go.

Also, you need to be sure that hardware requirements for your hosted applications and services are scaled correctly. The hardware in place must provide the type of system response you require, such as ensuring fast disk access by installing fast, high-RPM drives with solid controller input. You should also optimize the configuration by making sure the paging file is sized correctly (not too large or to small) and resides on a separate local drive in each node to increase overall system performance.

Other considerations include the proper type and number of CPUs installed in the system and a sufficient amount of physical RAM. The quorum resource is a single resource per cluster that performs these tasks:

➤ A quorum resource allows the cluster to maintain its state and configuration independently of individual node failures by storing a constantly updated version of the cluster database and having it available to all nodes in the cluster.

➤ Cluster implementations can use one of two types of quorum resources at initial build and cannot be changed.

A quorum-device cluster requires a storage-class resource on a shared SCSI implementation or fiber-driven solution. The Window Server 2003 Cluster Service allows only physical disk resources to operate as quorum devices by default, but third-party solutions support other types of storage devices as quorum devices. The quorum disk should be at least 500MB, but you might need to increase this amount, depending on your environment's needs.

A majority node set server cluster is a type of cluster configuration that has two or more nodes; each node may or may not be attached to one or more cluster storage devices. The cluster configuration data is stored on multiple disks across the cluster, and the Cluster Service makes sure this data is kept consistent across different disks.

Other concerns that need to be addressed for your cluster setup are the design of the network where your cluster resides. All network adapters in each cluster node need to be bound to TCP/IP. Best practices also recommend that client-side network adapters, called *public network adapters*, should have NetBIOS over TCP/IP and NetBIOS enabled so that clients can browse to a virtual server by name. (NetBIOS should be disabled on the cluster-only side.) You should also make sure you are configuring NICs to specific settings and not leaving them on "auto-configure." If the network is half-duplex, you should force-set NICs that way. Flow control and media type should also be set to the same values on each adapter.

> **NOTE**
>
> A private network is set up for the sole use of internal cluster communication. In this setup, there is no client communication on the wire.
>
> A public network is set up and enabled so that client systems have access to the cluster's applications and services. In this setup, there is no internal cluster communication on the wire.
>
> A mixed (public and private) network allows using the networked connection for both internal cluster communication and client communication.

The Cluster Service doesn't support NWLink, AppleTalk, and NetBEUI. Clustering should be enabled on nodes that are member servers in the same domain with access to a domain controller. If any node needs to be configured as a domain controller, all the nodes should be configured as domain controllers.

If you want nodes to be domain controllers of their own domain, it is better to configure a *domainlet*, which is a small domain that contains no user accounts and no Global Catalog servers. Domain controllers in a domainlet do not have to authenticate users or provide global catalog lookup services to users or computers.

A domainlet includes only well-known policies and groups defined for all domains, such as Administrators, Domain Administrators, and service accounts required by the clusters it supports. When configuring an account to run the Cluster Service, you should select a domain account that's static across all nodes in the cluster. You must also verify that the TCP/IP configuration your nodes used in the network cluster is statically enabled on each NIC for the best performance.

You should follow some standard best practices for securing server clusters in your enterprise. As with all server systems deployed in your enterprise, you should restrict physical access to the server cluster to only trusted personnel. Physical access restrictions include the physical location of the server hardware and any associated networking infrastructure.

On the network side, you should use firewalling to protect your cluster from unauthorized access. Make sure the internal cluster communication is segmented from other networks. If the heartbeat messages exchanged between systems are disrupted—either intentionally by a denial-of-service (DoS) attack or accidentally through traffic overload of that network circuit—the failure might cause another node on the cluster to believe it needs to take over as an active resource. This takeover can potentially bring down the cluster if different nodes begin to fight over shared resources.

Any remote administration should be done only from trusted, secure computers. Additionally, the Cluster Service account should not be a member of the Domain Administrators group, and it should never be used to administer the cluster. To track events on the cluster's nodes, enable full auditing of security-related events in the cluster.

Understanding Cluster Management

On Windows Server 2003 cluster systems, you can use several different resource types to manage cluster resources. For example, the Physical Disk resource type manages disks on a cluster storage device and enables you to assign drive letters to disks or create mounted drives. When drive letter designations are used, they must be constant across all cluster nodes.

No more than one node at a time should use a cluster disk. Normally, the Cluster Service handles this, but if you install a new disk to a cluster or remove a disk from the cluster's control, the Cluster Service can't maintain control of the resource, and nodes might fight over the newly available resource.

Dynamic Host Configuration Protocol (DHCP) and Windows Internet Naming Service (WINS) provide network services to clients. Their resources can be configured to fail over if their databases are kept on a disk that is part of the cluster storage.

The Print Spooler resource is used to cluster print services that are available over the network and allows print jobs to be handed off to another node during system failover. The main exception to this rule is when the printer is connected by a local port on a node, such as LPT1. There is no way to fail over control of that printer because the system it's physically connected to has gone offline.

The File Share resource can be used to provide basic file sharing via the cluster for high availability. You can also use the File Share resource type to create a resource that manages a standalone distributed file system (DFS) root, but the File Share resource type cannot manage fault-tolerant DFS roots.

The Internet Protocol Address resource type manages IP addresses as cluster resources, which allow network clients to access groups as virtual servers. In a similar fashion, the Network Name resource type provides an alternate computer name on a network so that when the resource is included in a group with an IP address resource, network clients can access it as a virtual server by using this alternate computer name.

The Volume Shadow Copy Service Task resource type can be used to create jobs in the Scheduled Task folder that must run on the node currently hosting a particular resource group. This enables you to configure the scheduled task so that it can fail over from one cluster node to another.

Exam Prep Questions

Question 1

You are the Web hosting administrator for your company's e-commerce environment, and you need to configure Network Load Balancing across the four Web servers running Windows Server 2003 Web Edition. The sites the servers host offers dynamic, Active Server Pages (ASP) content. Each server hosts content for different sites.

The hardware design is a multiprocessor build with redundant, hot-swappable power supplies. Each system is also installed with a hot-swappable, 64-bit, dual-port, gigabit ethernet card. (An onboard NIC is used for internal cluster communication.) Spare sets of server hot-swap hardware are locked in a cabinet in the data center's server room.

Your primary objective is to deploy Network Load Balancing across the four Web servers. Your secondary objectives are eliminating any single point of failure on the four Web servers (concerning just the servers, not the surrounding network points, such as routers) and making sure that any system hardware failures can be dealt with quickly and with limited downtime. Which of these objectives were you able to meet?

- ○ A. The primary objective and both secondary objectives have been met.
- ○ B. The primary objective and one secondary objective have been met.
- ○ C. The primary objective has not been met. However, both secondary objectives have been met.
- ○ D. Only one secondary objective has been met.
- ○ E. None of the objectives has been met.

The correct answer is D. For the primary objective, although Network Load Balancing is available in all editions of Windows Server 2003, the service load-balances incoming IP traffic across clusters. This scenario is concerned with Windows Server 2003 Web Edition, which does not support clustering. Also, Network Load Balancing does not support ASP pages, as they are referred to as stateful content. For Web servers, a static Web page is an example of stateless content. Network Load Balancing clusters can process these types of requests.

The first secondary objective, eliminating any single point of failure on the four Web servers, was not met because of the installed hot-swappable, 64-bit, dual-port, gigabit ethernet card. If the PCI slot the card is in should fail, it would create a single point of failure. The other secondary objective, making sure hardware failures are dealt with quickly and with limited downtime, was met by using hot-swappable equipment and having spares on site.

Question 2

You are the server administrator for your company's domain. You need to configure the Cluster Service across the four servers running Windows Server 2003 Standard Edition that are configured as Web servers.

The sites the servers host offer dynamic ASP content. The systems' hardware design is a multiprocessor build with redundant, hot-swappable power supplies. Each system is also installed with two single-port, gigabit ethernet cards and two single-port 10/100 cards for internal cluster communication. Spare sets of server hot-swap hardware are locked in a cabinet in the data center's server room.

Your primary objective is to deploy the Cluster Service across the four Web servers. Your secondary objectives are eliminating any single point of failure on the four Web servers (concerning just the servers, not the surrounding network points, such as routers) and making sure that any hardware failures on the system can be dealt with quickly and with limited downtime. Which of these objectives were you able to meet?

- ○ A. The primary objective and both secondary objectives have been met.
- ○ B. The primary objective and one secondary objective have been met.
- ○ C. The primary objective has not been met. However, both secondary objectives have been met.
- ○ D. Only one secondary objective has been met.
- ○ E. None of the objectives has been met.

The correct answer is C. For the primary objective, although server clusters are available in Windows Server 2003 Enterprise and Datacenter Editions, they are not available in Standard Edition. The Cluster Service does support ASP pages and other stateful content, but the primary objective has not been met.

The first secondary objective, eliminating any single point of failure on the four Web servers, is met with the two single-port gigabit ethernet cards and the hot-swappable redundant power supplies.

The other secondary objective, making sure hardware failures can be dealt with quickly and with limited downtime, is met by using hot-swappable equipment and having spares on site.

Question 3

You are the system administrator for your server environment. Your backup strategy uses one normal backup and daily incremental backups. All servers in the environment have five 18GB, SCSI3, 10,000 RPM drives and are set up using hardware RAID 5 with an online (hot) spare and a mean rebuild time of 60 minutes. The normal backup is performed each Sunday morning at 4:00 a.m. EST and takes two hours.

Incremental backups are performed each day at 10:00 p.m., Monday through Friday. No full or incremental backups are performed on Saturday. The time needed for the incremental backups varies, but it never exceeds 75 minutes.

One of the servers has a hard disk failure at approximately 6:00 p.m. on Saturday. At 6:10 p.m., a second drive in the array fails. What needs to be done to bring the server back to working order so that users can access data?

○ A. The failed drives need to be replaced and data needs to be restored from the normal backup.

○ B. The failed drives need to be replaced and data needs to be restored from the normal backup and the last incremental backup.

○ C. The failed drives need to be replaced and data needs to be restored from the normal backup and all the incremental backups.

○ D. None of these options is necessary.

The correct answer is C. When you have an online (hot) spare configuration, an extra drive is kept powered up in the array for the purpose of failover. When a drive in the working array fails, data is rebuilt onto the hot spare from the parity information and inserted into the array. The array then takes the bad drive offline, and an administrator needs to replace the drive.

In this example, one of the active drives fails and 10 minutes later, a second drive dies. Because 10 minutes is not enough time to rebuild the array from the parity information to the hot spare, the array fails. To restore the server to working order so that users can access data, the failed drives need to be replaced, and data needs to be restored from the normal backup and all the incremental backups.

When your backup strategy uses one normal backup and daily incremental backups and you have to restore the system, first you must restore the last normal backup and then restore each successive day's incremental backup.

Question 4

You are the system administrator for your server environment. Your backup strategy uses one full backup and daily differential backups. All servers in the environment have five 18GB, SCSI3, 10,000 RPM drives and are set up using hardware RAID 5 with an online (hot) spare.

The full backup is performed each Sunday at 4:00 a.m. EST and takes two hours. Differential backups are performed each day at 10:00 p.m., Monday through Friday. No full or differential backups are performed on Saturday. The time needed for the differential backups varies, but it never exceeds 75 minutes.

One of the servers has a hard disk failure at approximately 6:00 p.m. on Saturday. At 6:10 p.m., a second drive in the array fails. What needs to be done to bring the server back to working order so that users can access data?

- ○ A. The failed drives need to be replaced and data needs to be restored from the full backup.
- ○ B. The failed drives need to be replaced and data needs to be restored from the full backup and the last differential backup.
- ○ C. The failed drives need to be replaced and data needs to be restored from the full backup and all the differential backups.
- ○ D. None of these options is needed.

The correct answer is B. When you have an online (hot) spare configuration, an extra drive is kept powered up in the array for the purpose of failover. When a drive in the working array fails, data is rebuilt onto the hot spare from the parity information and inserted into the array. The array then takes the bad drive offline, and an administrator needs to replace the drive.

In this example, one of the active drives fails, and 10 minutes later, a second drive dies. Because 10 minutes is not enough time to rebuild the array from the parity information to the hot spare, the array fails. To restore the server to working order so that users can access data, the failed drives need to be replaced and data needs to be restored from the full backup and the last differential backup.

When your backup strategy uses one full backup and daily differential backups and you have to restore the system, first you must restore the last full backup, and then restore the last differential backup.

In a differential backup, the backup software does not change the archive bit's status after making the backup. Therefore, differential backups don't leave behind any signs that they were done. The next differential backup that runs backs up all files from the previous backup and any new files that have changed because only the full backup changes the archive bit. In a restore situation, therefore, you need only the full backup tape and the last differential tape.

Question 5

You are the network administrator for your Windows Server 2003 environment. You have been tasked with configuring Network Load Balancing across the four servers running Windows Server 2003 Standard Edition that are configured as file and print services.

The systems' hardware design is a multiprocessor build with redundant, hot-swappable power supplies. Each system has two single-port, token ring NICS installed for internal cluster communication. Spare sets of server hot-swap hardware are locked in a cabinet in the data center's server room.

Your primary objective is to deploy Network Load Balancing across the four servers. Your secondary objectives are eliminating any single point of failure on the four servers and making sure that any hardware failures on the system can be dealt with quickly and with limited downtime. Which of these objectives were you able to meet?

○ A. The primary objective and both secondary objectives have been met.

○ B. The primary objective and one secondary objective have been met.

○ C. The primary objective has not been met. However, both secondary objectives have been met.

○ D. Only one secondary objective has been met.

○ E. None of the objectives has been met.

The correct answer is B. The key piece of information is that Network Load Balancing is designed to work on 10Mbps, 100Mbps, and gigabit ethernet network adapters only. It is not compatible with ATM, ATM LAN emulation, or token ring networks. That means you weren't able to meet the primary objective of deploying Network Load Balancing across the four servers.

The first secondary objective, eliminating any single point of failure on the four servers, was not met because of the installed token ring cards and their incompatibility with Network Load Balancing. The other secondary objective, making sure that hardware failures can be dealt with quickly and with limited downtime, was met by using hot-swappable equipment and having spares on site.

Question 6

You are the server operator for the WLFD02 system, which is a member of the **gunderville.com** domain. The server is a dual-processor system running Windows Server 2003 Standard Edition and formatted with three separate partitions. The C:\ partition is NTFS, the D:\ partition is FAT32, and the E:\ partition, where shared resources are kept, is also formatted with NTFS.

You have been asked to review the frequency of tape restorations of data and the main reasons these types of restores are required on WLFD02. You have found that many of them are caused by accidental deletions by users connected to the system over the network.

You determine the restoration time for deleted data is an average of 36 hours, from the time the user who deleted the data logs the help desk ticket to the time you close the ticket after restoring the data.

Your primary objective is configuring a way for users to recover their own deleted information. Your secondary objectives are reducing data restoration time and setting up a system for users to recover their own data with the least amount of administrative effort. You have decided to enable the Shadow Copy of Shared Folders option on WLFD02 by following these steps:

Log on with your local user account, which is a member of the Server Operators group on the local system, and enable shadow copies on the C:\ and E:\ partitions.

Change the default limit of 10% for the shadow copy's total size to 5% of the available drive space.

What are the results of your actions?

- ○ A. The primary objective and both secondary objectives have been met.
- ○ B. The primary objective and one secondary objective have been met.
- ○ C. The primary objective has not been met. However, both secondary objectives have been met.
- ○ D. Only one secondary objective has been met.
- ○ E. None of the objectives has been met.

The correct answer is E. The Shadow Copies of Shared Folders option is enabled at the volume level only, so every shared folder on that volume is configured to use this feature after it is set. The shadow copy configuration is also set for the entire volume.

The primary objective has not been met because you are not logged in as an administrator. Logging in with any other level of access means you can't see the Shadow Copies tab in the volume's Properties dialog box. Because you cannot enable this option, your secondary objective of reducing data restoration time has not been satisfied. The other secondary objective, setting up the primary objective with the least amount of administrative effort, has not been met, either. Volumes configured with the Shadow Copy service need to be formatted with NTFS.

The default setting for volume space reserved for shadow copy use is 10% of the total volume size (not 10% of the volume's free space). Administrators can change this setting, too, but setting the limit too low causes the oldest shadow copies to be deleted regularly, often much sooner than the maximum number of shadow copies allowed per volume, because the volume's reserved space is being used up.

Question 7

You are the server administrator for the WLFD07 system, which is a member of the **gunderville.com** domain. The server is a single-processor system running Windows Server 2003 Standard Edition and formatted with three separate partitions. The C:\ partition is NTFS, the D:\ partition is FAT32, and the E:\ partition, where shared resources are kept, is also formatted with NTFS.

You have been asked to review the frequency of tape restorations of data and the main reasons these types of restores are required on WLFD07. You have found that many of them are caused by accidental deletions by users connected to the system over the network.

You determine the restoration time for deleted data is an average of 48 hours, from the time the user who deleted the data logs the help desk ticket to the time you close the ticket after restoring the data.

Your primary objective is configuring a way for users to recover their own deleted information. Your secondary objectives are reducing data restoration time and setting up a system for users to recover their own data with the least amount of administrative effort. You have decided to enable the Shadow Copy of Shared Folders option on WLFD07 by following these steps: Log on with your local user account, which is a member of the Administrators group on the local system, and enable shadow copies on the C:\ and E:\ partitions.

Change the default limit of 10% for the shadow copy's total size to 5% of the available drive space.

What are the results of your actions?

- ○ A. The primary objective and both secondary objectives have been met.
- ○ B. The primary objective and one secondary objective have been met.
- ○ C. The primary objective has not been met. However, both secondary objectives have been met.
- ○ D. Only one secondary objective has been met.
- ○ E. None of the objectives has been met.

The correct answer is B. You have met the primary objective because you logged in as an administrator to enable the feature on the system. You also met the secondary objective of reducing data restoration time because shadow copies are an easier way for users to retrieve previous versions of their files than relying on data restoration via backup media.

However, you didn't meet the other secondary objective of setting up a user restoration method with the least amount of administrative effort because you went through the extra step of enabling shadow copies on the C:\ partition. The data that required shadow copying is located only on the E:\ partition, so there was no reason to enable this option on the C:\ partition.

Question 8

> You are the network administrator for **zandri.net**, which is a Windows Server 2003 native mode domain. You have been reviewing the steps for installing the Cluster Service on a pair of systems that are already running Windows Server 2003 Standard Edition. Your staff has already gathered the following information for you:
>
> Only a user account logged on as an administrator can perform the installation.
>
> One specific node should be selected for the initial installation.
>
> During the installation, the second node must be powered on to ensure that the shared drive array is "aware" that multiple servers will access the drive.
>
> Your staff has not been able to successfully deploy the Cluster Service on these systems. Which of the following reasons are the most likely explanation for this failure?
>
> ○ A. The issue is that there is only a pair of servers for the cluster; no fewer than four systems should be in use.
>
> ○ B. The issue is with the second node being powered on.
>
> ○ C. The issue is with Windows Server 2003 Standard Edition.
>
> ○ D. The issue is with using the Administrator account; the account used must be a Domain Administrator account.

The correct answer is C. The key reason this installation will not succeed is the operating system; Windows Server 2003 Standard Edition does not support clustering, so answer A is not correct. Installation must be performed by a user account logged on as an administrator, so answer D is not correct. One specific node should be selected for the initial installation.

During the installation, the second node must be powered off to ensure that the shared device does not become corrupt because of multiple computers accessing the drive, so answer B is not correct.

Question 9

You are the network administrator for **zandri.net**, which is a Windows Server 2003 native mode domain. You are currently troubleshooting a cluster configuration in your testing environment that is having intermediate failure issues.

Your four servers are running Windows Server 2003, Enterprise Edition. They are all running 933MHz processors (two per system) and are configured with two dual-port PCI add-on NICs and one NIC on the motherboard. The network cards for the public network are set up and enabled to auto-detect the network speed, as are the onboard NICs.

The main problem you are having with the cluster is that live nodes are being knocked offline and losing access to their resources. The Event Viewer logs show that at certain points in the day, two nodes are attempting to control the same resource. The logs also show lost heartbeat messages for nodes that are actively participating in cluster operations and listed as UP in the cluster manager.

The problem occurred more often on an older version of the network drivers (version 5.5) for the add-on cards. You have updated them to the recommended version, 5.56. A new version of the network card driver, 5.75, is available, but it has not been tested on Windows Server 2003. A firmware revision is also available for the system motherboard.

Which of the following course of actions should you attempt next?

- ○ A. Proceed with the firmware revision for the system motherboard.
- ○ B. Update the PCI NIC drivers in each node to version 5.75 only.
- ○ C. Configure each adapter in each node to the same values (Duplex Mode, Flow Control, and Media Type), and update the drivers to version 5.75.
- ○ D. Configure each adapter in each node to the same values (Duplex Mode, Flow Control, and Media Type). Do not update the drivers to version 5.75.

The correct answer is D. The properties of each adapter in each node (Duplex Mode, Flow Control, and Media Type) should be set to the same values and should not be set to auto-detect the network speed. If the adapters are allowed to detect the speed, some adapters might drop network packets while trying to determine the speed, and the incorrect speed, which is incompatible with some network hardware, might be used.

Having NICs set to auto-detect has the potential of disrupting network traffic to the clusters, and on the heartbeat network, it can cause intermittent network failures that could result in one node thinking another active node has gone offline, which could result in systems fighting over resources.

Also, you do not want to make two changes at once, such as changing the settings *and* updating the drivers. Updating the drivers alone did not correct the problem before, and the drivers have not yet been tested on Windows Server 2003, so this action is not recommended.

Question 10

You are the network administrator for **zandri.net**, which is a Windows Server 2003 native mode domain. You have identified four of your Windows Server 2003 systems to be installed as nodes and domain controllers of their own domain. What is the best way to configure these systems?

- ○ A. Configure a domainlet.
- ○ B. Configure the servers in a workgroup first and then add each one into one domain.
- ○ C. Configure the servers in a workgroup first and then add each one into different domains.
- ○ D. Configure the servers in a workgroup and add computer accounts for them in a single domain. Edit the network identification for each node so that each has a corresponding network ID to the domain where its account exists.

The correct answer is A. Clustering should be enabled on nodes that are member servers in the same domain with access to a domain controller. If any node needs to be configured as a domain controller, all nodes should be configured as domain controllers.

If you want nodes to be domain controllers of their own domain, it is better to configure a domainlet. Domain controllers in the domainlet do not have to authenticate users or provide global catalog lookup services to users or computers. The domainlet includes only well-known policies and groups defined for all domains, such as Administrators, Domain Administrators, and service accounts required by the clusters it supports.

Need To Know More?

Compare the Editions of Windows Server 2003: http://www.microsoft.com/windowsserver2003/evaluation/features/compareeditions.mspx.

Windows Server 2003 Server Cluster Architecture: http://www.microsoft.com/windowsserver2003/techinfo/overview/servercluster.mspx and http://www.microsoft.com/windowsserver2003/docs/ServerClustersArchitecture.doc.

Introducing Microsoft Cluster Service (MSCS) in the Windows Server 2003 Family: http://msdn.microsoft.com/library/default.asp?url=/library/en-us/dnnetserv/html/wns-introclustermscs.asp.

Technical Overview of Windows Server 2003 Clustering Services: http://www.microsoft.com/windowsserver2003/techinfo/overview/clustering.mspx and http://www.microsoft.com/windowsserver2003/docs/ClusteringOverview.doc.

Support WebCast: Windows Server 2003 Clustering: New Features: http://support.microsoft.com/default.aspx?scid=kb;en-us;810220&gssnb=1.

What's New in Clustering Technologies: http://www.microsoft.com/windowsserver2003/evaluation/overview/technologies/clustering.mspx.

Implementing Microsoft Windows Enterprise Server 2003 on ProLiant Packaged Clusters: ftp://ftp.compaq.com/pub/partners/microsoft/infolib/osintegration/ClusterWP5981-5629EN.pdf.

Dell PowerEdge Clusters and Microsoft Exchange Deployment: http://ftp.us.dell.com/app/2qSE-Pos.pdf and http://ftp.us.dell.com/app/ps2q03se.pdf.

High-Availability Clustering Capabilities in Windows Server 2003: http://www.dell.com/us/en/esg/topics/power_ps2q03se-kosacek.htm, http://ftp.us.dell.com/app/2qSE-Kos.pdf, and http://ftp.us.dell.com/app/ps2q03se.pdf.

Quorums in Microsoft Windows Server 2003 Clusters: http://www.microsoft.com/windowsserver2003/techinfo/overview/clusterquorums.mspx and http://www.microsoft.com/windowsserver2003/docs/ClusterQuorums.doc.

Microsoft Windows Clustering: Storage Area Networks: `http://www.microsoft.com/windowsserver2003/techinfo/overview/san.mspx` and `http://www.microsoft.com/windowsserver2003/docs/SAN.doc`.

Geographically Dispersed Clusters in Windows Server 2003: `http://www.microsoft.com/windowsserver2003/techinfo/overview/clustergeo.mspx`, `http://www.microsoft.com/windowsserver2003/docs/GDClusters.doc`, and `http://support.microsoft.com/newsgroups/default.aspx?NewsGroup=microsoft.public.windows.server.clustering&LEFT=1&ICP=GSS3&SLCID=US`.

Go to the Microsoft KnowledgeBase at `http://support.microsoft.com` and view the following articles:

> ➤ 324320—HOW TO: Use a FrontPage Web Site on a Clustered File Share

> ➤ 278007—Available Features in Windows Server 2003 Clusters

> ➤ 812877—Cluster Service Does Not Start After You Upgrade to Windows Server 2003, Enterprise Edition

> ➤ 307532—How to Troubleshoot the Cluster Service Account When It Modifies Computer Objects

> ➤ 811272—How to Perform a Rolling Upgrade of Windows Server 2003 Server Clusters

> ➤ 305813—How to Change the Cluster Service Account Password

> ➤ 301600—How to Configure Microsoft Distributed Transaction Coordinator on a Windows Server 2003 Cluster

> ➤ 301538—How to Upgrade a Microsoft Windows NT 4.0 Cluster to a Windows Server 2003 Cluster

> ➤ 285369—How to Configure Client-Side Caching on a Server Cluster

> ➤ 282227—How to Uninstall the Cluster Service on a Windows Server 2003 Cluster

> ➤ 816111—HOW TO: Perform Basic Network Load Balancing Procedures in Windows Server 2003

> ➤ 323437—HOW TO: Configure Network Load Balancing Parameters in Windows Server 2003

➤ 323431—HOW TO: Set Up TCP/IP for Network Load Balancing in Windows Server 2003

➤ 257937—HOW TO: Format an Existing Partition on a Shared Cluster Hard Disk:

Network Load Balancing: Security Best Practices for Windows 2000 and Windows Server 2003: http://www.microsoft.com/ technet/treeview/default.asp?url=/technet/prodtechnol/ windowsserver2003/maintain/security/nlbsecbp.asp.

Windows Clustering: Network Load Balancing Frequently Asked Questions (FAQ): http://www.microsoft.com/technet/treeview/ default.asp?url=/technet/prodtechnol/windowsserver2003/ support/netlbfaq.asp.

Server Cluster Frequently Asked Questions: http://www.microsoft.com/technet/treeview/default.asp?url=/ technet/prodtechnol/windowsserver2003/support/srcltfaq.asp.

Feature Highlights Sorter Results for Clustering: http:// www.microsoft.com/windowsserver2003/evaluation/features/ featuresorterresults.aspx?Technology=Clustering.

Planning for High Availability and Scalability: http://www. microsoft.com/technet/treeview/default.asp?url=/technet/ prodtechnol/windowsserver2003/proddocs/deployguide/config/ part2/rksrvhas.asp.

Windows Clustering Technologies—An Overview: http://www. microsoft.com/technet/treeview/default.asp?url=/technet/ prodtechnol/windowsserver2003/deploy/confeat/clustovw.asp.

Windows Clustering Technologies—Server Cluster Rolling Upgrade Procedures and Best Practices: http://www. microsoft.com/technet/treeview/default.asp?url=/technet/ prodtechnol/windowsserver2003/deploy/upgrdmigrate/ rollupnt.asp.

Server Clusters: Majority Node Sets (a.k.a. Quorum of Nodes): http://www.microsoft.com/technet/treeview/default.asp?url=/ technet/prodtechnol/windowsserver2003/deploy/confeat/ majnode.asp.

Server Clusters: Remote Setup, Unattended Installations and Image-based Installations: http://www.microsoft.com/technet/ treeview/default.asp?url=/technet/prodtechnol/ windowsserver2003/deploy/confeat/mscclust.asp.

Windows Cluster Technologies: Remote Setup, Unattended Installations and Image-based Installations of Network Load Balancing: `http://www.microsoft.com/technet/treeview/default.asp?url=/technet/prodtechnol/windowsserver2003/deploy/confeat/nlbclust.asp`.

Deploying Network Load Balancing: `http://www.microsoft.com/technet/treeview/default.asp?url=/technet/prodtechnol/windowsserver2003/proddocs/deployguide/config/part2/rksrvnlb.asp`.

Designing Server Clusters: `http://www.microsoft.com/technet/treeview/default.asp?url=/technet/prodtechnol/windowsserver2003/proddocs/deployguide/config/part2/rksrvdsc.asp`.

Network Load Balancing: Configuration Best Practices for Windows 2000 and Windows Server 2003: `http://www.microsoft.com/technet/treeview/default.asp?url=/technet/prodtechnol/windowsserver2003/maintain/operate/nlbbp.asp`.

Network Load Balancing: Security Best Practices for Windows 2000 and Windows Server 2003: `http://www.microsoft.com/technet/treeview/default.asp?url=/technet/prodtechnol/windowsserver2003/maintain/security/nlbsecbp.asp`.

Server Clusters: Backup and Recovery Best Practices for Windows Server 2003: `http://www.microsoft.com/technet/treeview/default.asp?url=/technet/prodtechnol/windowsserver2003/maintain/operate/sercbrbp.asp`.

Server Clusters: Cluster Configuration Best Practices for Windows Server 2003: `http://www.microsoft.com/technet/treeview/default.asp?url=/technet/prodtechnol/windowsserver2003/maintain/operate/scconbp.asp`.

Server Clusters: Network Configuration Best Practices for Windows 2000 and Windows Server 2003: `http://www.microsoft.com/technet/treeview/default.asp?url=/technet/prodtechnol/windowsserver2003/maintain/operate/clstntbp.asp`.

Server Clusters Overview: `http://www.microsoft.com/technet/treeview/default.asp?url=/technet/prodtechnol/windowsserver2003/proddocs/entserver/sag_mscs1concepts_2.asp`.

Planning and Maintaining Network Security

Terms you'll need to understand:

✓ Encapsulating Security Payload (ESP)
✓ Resultant Set of Policy (RSoP)
✓ Group Policy Management Console (GPMC)
✓ Internet Protocol Security (IPSec)

Techniques you'll need to master:

✓ Configuring protocol security in a heterogeneous client computer environment
✓ Configuring IPSec policies and settings
✓ Configuring and planning security for data transmissions
✓ Planning for network protocol security
✓ Planning an IPSec policy for secure network communications
✓ Planning secure network administration methods
✓ Secure data transmission between client computers to meet security requirements
✓ Securing data transmission by using IPSec
✓ Troubleshooting security for data transmission
✓ Using the IP Security Monitor MMC snap-in
✓ Using the Resultant Set of Policy (RSoP) MMC snap-in
✓ Implementing secure access between private networks

Windows Server 2003 has been designed as a more secure operating system out of the box. However, many features and services available in different versions of the operating system are not installed or enabled by default. As part of its secure computing initiative, Microsoft has been shifting away from ease of use toward securing the platform.

System Services

Table 6.1 shows the system services and their default configurations, including the Log On As account settings for a default installation of Windows Server 2003.

NOTE
Unless otherwise noted, the Startup type and Log On As accounts are the same for all members of the Windows Server 2003 family.

Table 6.1   Default Services and Their Settings

Service Name (Short Name)	Startup Type	Logs On As
Alerter	Disabled	Local Service
Application Layer Gateway (ALG)	Manual	Local Service
Application Management (AppMgmt)	Manual	Local System
Automatic Updates (wuauserv)	Automatic	Local System
Background Intelligent Transfer Service (BITS)	Manual	Local System
ClipBook (ClipSrv)	Disabled	Local System
COM+ Event System (EventSystem)	Manual/Started	Local System
COM+ System Application (COMSysApp)	Manual	Local System
Computer Browser (Browser)	Automatic/Started	Local System
Cryptographic Services (CryptSvc)	Automatic/Started	Local System
DHCP Client (DHCP)	Automatic/Started	Network Service
Distributed File System (DFS)	Automatic/Started	Local System
Distributed Link Tracking Client (TrkWks)	Automatic/Started	Local System
Distributed Link Tracking Server (TrkSvr)	Disabled	Local System
Distributed Transaction Coordinator (MSDTC)	Automatic/Started	Network Service
DNS Client (Dnscache)	Automatic/Started	Network Service
Error Reporting Service (ERSvc)	Automatic/Started	Local System

(continued)

Table 6.1 Default Services and Their Settings *(continued)*		
Service Name (Short Name)	**Startup Type**	**Logs On As**
Event Log (Eventlog)	Automatic/Started	Local System
File Replication (ntfrs)	Manual	Local System
Help and Support (helpsvc)	Automatic/Started	Local System
HTTP SSL (W3SSL)	Manual	Local System
Human Interface Device Access (HidServ)	Disabled	Local System
IIS Admin (IISADMIN)	Automatic/Started	Local System
IMAPI CD-Burning COM Service (ImapiService)	Disabled	Local System
Indexing Service (cisvc)	Manual	Local System
ICF/ICS (SharedAccess)	Disabled	Local System
Intersite Messaging (IsmServ)	Disabled	Local System
IPSec Services (PolicyAgent)	Automatic/Started	Local System
Kerberos Key Distribution Center (KDC)	Disabled	Local System
License Logging (LicenseService)	Disabled	Network Service
Logical Disk Manager (dmserver)	Automatic/Started	Local System
Logical Disk Manager Administrative Service (dmadmin)	Manual	Local System
Messenger (messenger)	Disabled	Local System
Microsoft Software Shadow Copy Provider (SWPRV)	Manual	Network Service
Net Logon (Netlogon)	Varies	Local System
NetMeeting Remote Desktop Sharing (mnmsrvc)	Disabled	Local System
Network Connections (Netman)	Manual/Started	Local System
Network DDE (NetDDE)	Disabled	Local System
Network DDE DSDM (NetDDEDSDM)	Disabled	Local System
Network Location Awareness (NLA)	Manual/Started	Local System
NT LM Security Support Provider (NtLmSsp)	Manual	Local System
Performance Logs and Alerts (SysmonLog)	Manual	Network Service
Plug and Play (PlugPlay)	Automatic/Started	Local System
Portable Media Serial Number (WmdmPmSp)	Manual	Local System
Print Spooler (Spooler)	Automatic/Started	Local System
Protected Storage (ProtectedStorage)	Automatic/Started	Local System
Remote Access Auto Connection Manager (RasAuto)	Manual	Local System

(continued)

Table 6.1   Default Services and Their Settings *(continued)*

Service Name (Short Name)	Startup Type	Logs On As
Remote Access Connection Manager (RasMan)	Manual	Local System
Remote Desktop Help Session Manager (RDSessMgr)	Manual	Local System
Remote Procedure Call (RpcSs)	Automatic/Started	Local System
Remote Procedure Call (RPC) Locator (RpcLocator)	Manual	Network Service
Remote Registry (RemoteRegistry)	Automatic/Started	Local Service
Removable Storage (NtmsSvc)	Manual	Local System
Resultant Set of Policy Provider (RsoPProv)	Manual	Local System
Routing and Remote Access (RemoteAccess)	Disabled	Local System
Secondary Logon (seclogon)	Automatic/Started	Local System
Security Accounts Manager (SamSs)	Automatic/Started	Local System
Server (lanmanserver)	Automatic/Started	Local System
Shell Hardware Detection (ShellHWDetection)	Automatic/Started	Local System
Simple Mail Transfer Protocol (SMTPSVC)	Automatic/Started	Local System
Smart Card (ScardSvr)	Manual	Local Service
Special Administration Console Helper (Sacsvr)	Manual	Local System
System Event Notification (SENS)	Automatic/Started	Local System
Task Scheduler (Schedule)	Automatic/Started	Local System
TCP/IP NetBIOS Helper (LmHosts)	Automatic/Started	Local Service
Telephony (TapiSrv)	Manual	Local System
Telnet (TlntSvr)	Disabled	Local System
Terminal Services (TermService)	Manual/Started	Local System
Terminal Services Session Directory (Tssdis)	Disabled	Local System
Themes (Themes)	Disabled	Local System
Uninterruptible Power Supply (UPS)	Manual	Local Service
Upload Manager (uploadmgr)	Manual	Local System
Virtual Disk Service (VDS)	Manual	Local System
Volume Shadow Copy (VSS)	Manual	Local System
WebClient (WebClient)	Disabled	Local Service
Windows Audio (AudioSrv)	Automatic/Started	Local System
Windows Image Acquisition (stisvc)	Disabled	Local System
Windows Installer (MSIServer)	Manual	Local System

(continued)

Table 6.1 Default Services and Their Settings *(continued)*		
Service Name (Short Name)	**Startup Type**	**Logs On As**
Windows Management Instrumentation (winmgmt)	Automatic/Started	Local System
Windows Management Instrumentation Driver Extensions (wmi)	Manual	Local System
Windows Time (W32time)	Automatic	Local System
WinHTTP Web Proxy Auto-Discovery Service (WinHttpAutoProxySvc)	Manual/Started	Local System
Wireless Configuration (WZCSVC)	Automatic/Started	Local System
WMI Performance Adapter (WmiApSrv)	Manual	Local System
Workstation (lanmanworkstation)	Automatic/Started	Local System
World Wide Web Publishing (W3SVC)	Automatic/Started	Local System

This new default configuration goes a long way toward preparing a formal level of security for Windows Server 2003 base installations, but many options beyond the defaults can be configured to further secure system deployments in the enterprise.

Internet Protocol Security (IPSec)

Almost any data transmitted on a network is vulnerable to some level of compromise. As most communications between systems are not secured, be it on a private network or across an open network such as the Internet, eavesdropping on the session and compromise of unencrypted data are possible. IPSec provides a security mechanism for ensuring the availability, integrity, and confidentiality of data.

IPSec can be deployed between two specific systems in an enterprise by using IPSec in Transport mode (the default mode). In Transport mode, IPSec encrypts only the IP payload, such as the Transmission Control Protocol (TCP) segments, a User Datagram Protocol (UDP) message, or the Internet Control Message Protocol (ICMP) message between two systems, when a security association has been established. All other communications to any other system in that environment might not require this secure level of communication and would not necessarily be set up to create a secure connection.

IPSec in Tunnel mode is often deployed in settings with two endpoints, such as a Routing and Remote Access Service (RRAS) server acting as a connection point from one site to another RRAS server at another site. The security association in this configuration is between both RRAS servers, which allows IPSec to encrypt the IP header and the payload. This encryption provides protection for all IP traffic leaving all systems on one site and traveling to systems on the other site. Regardless of the destination and recipient systems from either site, all traffic flow within that tunnel is encrypted.

In Windows Server 2003, Group Policies enable domain administrators to configure IPSec policies in a forest to be allocated at the site, domain, or Organizational Unit (OU) level as needed. IPSec Encapsulating Security Payload (ESP) can pass through Network Address Translation (NAT) devices that allow UDP traffic. This is done through the Internet Key Exchange (IKE) protocol, which automatically detects the presence of NAT devices and uses UDP–ESP encapsulation to allow IPSec traffic to pass through the NAT.

The use of NAT devices and UDP–ESP encapsulation allows businesses that want to use Layer Two Tunneling Protocol (L2TP)/IPSec in virtual private networks (VPNs) over untrusted networks, such as the Internet, to keep their clients behind NAT devices to establish secure connections back to the corporate network using IPSec-ESP Transport mode. The use of NAT devices and UDP–ESP encapsulation also makes it possible to set up and configure RRAS servers using IPSec in Tunnel mode when one of the two servers is behind a NAT device.

Implementing IPSec Policies

To add, edit, or remove IPSec policies, perform the following steps:

1. Start the IP Security Policy Management snap-in by clicking Start, Run, and entering MMC or by entering MMC at the command line.

2. After the console is open, choose File, Add/Remove Snap-in from the menu.

3. Click the Add button, choose the IP Security Policy Management snap-in from the Add Standalone Snap-in dialog box, and then click Add. The following three options for IPSec policies are then displayed (see Figure 6.1):

   ➤ *Local Computer*—Use this option to manage the local system only.

   ➤ *Active Directory Domain of Which This Computer Is a Member*—Use this option to manage IPSec policies for any domain members.

   ➤ *Another Active Directory Domain*—Use this option to manage IPSec policies for another domain.

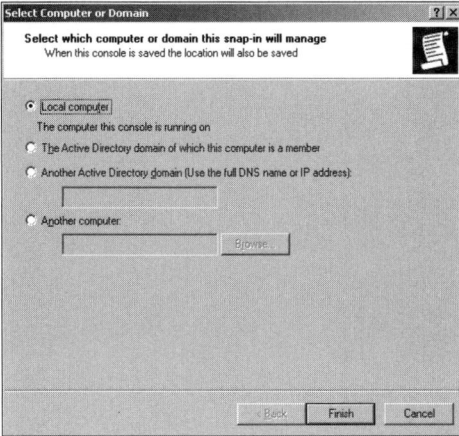

Figure 6.1   You must select how to apply the IPSec policy.

If you need to manage another local policy on a remote computer, you can select the Another Computer option. After making your selection, click the Finish button.

4. Click the Close button in the Add Standalone Snap-in dialog box. Then click OK in the Add/Remove Snap-in dialog box.

5. After creating this setup, you can add a new policy by going to the console tree and clicking IP Security Policies on <*SYSTEMNAME*>. Then choose Action, Create IP Security Policy from the menu, and follow the instructions in the IP Security Policy Wizard until the Properties dialog box for your new policy opens.

You can create or modify any rules for the policy in the Rules tab. To add a rule, use the Create IP Security Rule Wizard or add the rule manually. To use the wizard, you must confirm that the Use Add Wizard check box is selected on the policy you want to modify, click Add, and then follow the instructions after the wizard starts.

To add a rule manually, confirm that the Use Add Wizard check box is *not* selected, click Add, and then define settings in the IP Filter List, Filter Action, Authentication Methods, Tunnel Setting, and Connection Type tabs as needed.

To edit a rule, select the rule you want to edit, click the Edit button, and then modify the rule properties as needed (see Figure 6.2). To activate a rule, go to the Rules tab and select the check box next to the rule you want to activate. To deactivate a rule, simply clear the check box. To remove a rule, select the rule and then click Remove. To remove a policy that is no longer needed, highlight the policy and click Delete.

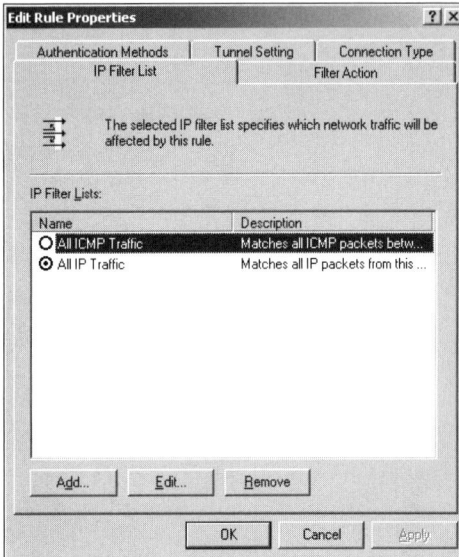

Figure 6.2 You can manage IP filter rules through the IP Security policy's rule properties.

To manage Active Directory–based IPSec policies, use an account that is a member of the Domain Administrators group or be assigned delegate authority for the domain. To manage local or remote IPSec policies for a system, use an account that is a member of the local Administrators group on that system.

A Word on Filters

The Negotiate Security filter action contains one or more security methods that are used in a specific order of preference during IKE negotiations. In security setups that include firewalls, proxy servers, or certain routers, you might have to enable the following settings so that IPSec traffic is not rejected:

For input filters:

➤ IP Protocol ID of 51 (0x33) for inbound IPSec Authentication Header traffic

➤ IP Protocol ID of 50 (0x32) for inbound IPSec ESP traffic

➤ UDP port 500 (0x1F4) for inbound Internet Security Association and Key Management Protocol (ISAKMP)/Oakley negotiation traffic

For output filters:

➤ IP Protocol ID of 51 (0x33) for outbound IPSec Authentication Header traffic

➤ IP Protocol ID of 50 (0x32) for outbound IPSec ESP traffic

➤ UDP port 500 (0x1F4) for outbound ISAKMP/Oakley negotiation traffic

The following three default policies are defined:

➤ *Client (Respond Only)*—This policy allows individual systems to secure their own communications at the request of the other system for secured communications. This policy contains the default response rule, which creates dynamic IPSec filters for inbound and outbound traffic based on the requested protocol and port traffic for the communication being secured.

➤ *Server (Request Security)*—This policy is configured so that systems can request secure IP communications whenever possible but allow unsecured IP communication if non–IPSec-aware computers or systems not configured via a Client (Respond Only) policy attempt a communications channel.

➤ *Secure Server (Require Security)*—This policy is used for systems that require secure communications. The filters for this policy require all communication from the given system to be secured, with the exception of the initial inbound communication request. When non–IPSec-aware computers or systems not configured via a Client (Respond Only) policy attempt a communications channel with this system, they are denied access because only secure communications channels are allowed to systems running this configuration.

To assign an IPSec policy, open Active Directory Users and Computers. Right-click the Active Directory object (domain or OU) where you need to assign the policy, and choose Properties. In the Properties dialog box, select the Group Policy tab. Then click Edit to open an existing Group Policy object that you want to edit, or click New to create a new one.

IPSec Authentication

IPSec uses three primary authentication methods: Kerberos V5, Certificates, and preshared secret keys, sometimes referred to as a *preshared secret*. The default authentication method in a domain is Kerberos V5, which verifies, by way of mutual authentication, the identity of the user and network services. It performs this verification by issuing tickets containing encrypted passwords to users during domain logon and system access. This password is used to confirm users' identities so that they can access requested network services seamlessly through pass-through authentication.

The Key Distribution Center (KDC) runs on each domain controller in your Active Directory domain and stores all client passwords and other account information. A user who logs on to a client system is authenticated to the KDC, which issues a special ticket-granting ticket (TGT) to the client. The client system uses the TGT to access the ticket-granting service (TGS), which in turn issues a service ticket to the client. The client then presents the service ticket to requested network services. The service ticket uses mutual authentication to prove the user's identity to the service and the service's identity to the user.

Kerberos V5 services are found on domain controllers and allow each domain controller in the domain to act as a KDC. The Kerberos client is installed on each system and uses Domain Name System (DNS) lookup to locate the nearest available domain controller—referred to as the *preferred KDC*—for that particular logon session. If the preferred KDC isn't available, the system locates another KDC via DNS lookup to provide the needed authentication.

Public key certificates can be used for IPSec via public key infrastructure when clients are in use that are not members of the same domain or when systems in use are running other operating systems that do not support Kerberos authentication, such as non-Microsoft operating systems and legacy Windows systems (Windows 95, for example).

Computers running Windows 2000, Windows XP, or the Windows Server 2003 family support X.509 Version 3 certificates, including computer certificates generated by commercial Certificate Authorities (CAs), which are often needed for public key certificate deployments.

IPSec can also use preshared keys for authentication when two systems attempting a security association use a shared secret key for authentication against an IPSec policy. In this scenario, information is encrypted before transmission on the sending system by using a session key during the initial security negotiation. The session key is created by using a Diffie-Hellman calculation and the preshared secret key. Information is decrypted on the recipient system with the same preshared key. One IPSec peer authenticates the other peer's packet by decryption and verification of the hash inside the packet. (The hash inside the packet is a hash of the preshared key.) If authentication fails, the security association is not established, and communication between the systems is not allowed.

To define one of these three IPSec authentication methods, perform the following steps:

1. Double-click the policy you want to modify in a saved or newly created IP Security Policies MMC and double-click the rule you want to modify.

2. In the Authentication Methods tab, click Add to add a method (if one is not already defined), or choose an existing method and then click the Edit button. Then select the authentication method you want to add or modify.

3. For authentication services in a Windows 2000 or Windows Server 2003 Active Directory domain or a trusted Active Directory domain, select the Active Directory Default (Kerberos V5 Protocol) option. To enable a public key certificate for authentication services, use the Use a Certificate from This Certification Authority option. If you decide to define a preshared key, select the Use This String (Preshared Key) option.

4. To delete methods you do not want to use, simply highlight them and click the Remove button. You can also rearrange the preference order of an authentication method by highlighting it and clicking the up or down arrows.

NOTE

IPSec polices are configured through a system's local policy or via Active Directory. IPSec policies that are configured and assigned via OUs take precedence over domain-level policies for computers that have accounts in that OU. An OU inherits the policies of its parent OU by default, unless inheritance is blocked or a policy is explicitly assigned to the child OU.

To specify IPSec connection types, go to the Connection Type tab and choose All Network Connections to set the connection type for all available network connections, Local Area Network (LAN) to set the connection type for all available LAN connections, or Remote Access to apply the rule to any available VPN or dial-up connections.

Implementing IPSec Rules

An IPSec policy consists of one or more rules that determine IPSec behavior and are configured on the Rules tab in the Properties dialog box of an IPSec policy. A filter list is configured on the IP Filter List tab in the Properties dialog box of an IPSec rule within an IPSec policy (refer back to Figure 6.2). This list contains one or more predefined packet filters describing the types of network traffic to be configured against a filter action for this rule.

To add, edit, or remove IP filter lists, select the policy you want to modify in a saved or newly created IP Security Policies MMC. Then double-click the rule containing the IP filter list you want to modify and go to the IP Filter List tab.

To add a new IP filter list, click the Add button. To modify an existing IP filter list, select the filter list you want to modify and then click the Edit button. To remove an IP filter list, highlight the filter list you want to remove and click the Remove button.

To configure a filter action, you use the Filter Action tab in the Properties dialog box of an IPSec rule within an IPSec policy (see Figure 6.3). You can set the type of action required (Permit, Block, or Negotiate Security) for packets that match the filter list.

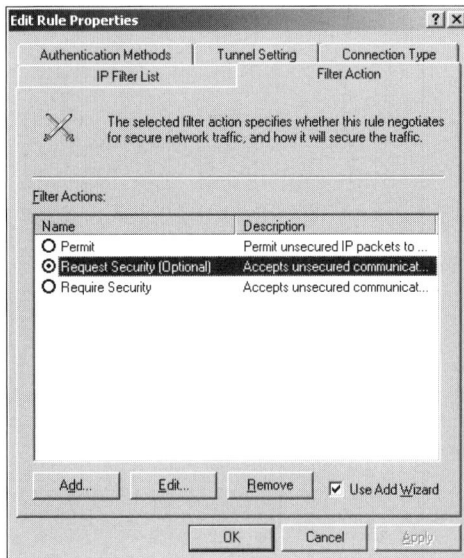

Figure 6.3 You can configure IP filter actions through the Filter Action tab in the IP Security policy's rule properties.

To add, edit, or remove IPSec filters, start the IP Security Policy Management snap-in by clicking Start, Run and entering MMC or typing MMC at the command line. Next, double-click the policy you want to modify and select the rule containing the IP filter list you want to modify.

In the IP Filter List tab, select the IP filter list containing the IPSec filter you want to modify and click the Add button to add a filter or the Edit button to make changes to an existing filter. To remove an existing filter, highlight it and then click the Remove button.

Some of the available options in the IP Filter Properties dialog box are described in the following list (see Figure 6.4):

➤ To secure packets from all IP addresses on the computer for which you are configuring this filter, select My IP Address.

➤ To secure packets from any computer, select Any IP Address.

➤ To secure packets from a DNS name specified in the hostname, select A Specific DNS Name.

➤ To secure packets from an IP address that you specify in the IP Address field, select the A Specific IP Address option.

➤ To secure packets from an IP subnet specified in the IP Address field and the subnet mask you specify in the Subnet Mask field, select the A Specific IP Subnet option.

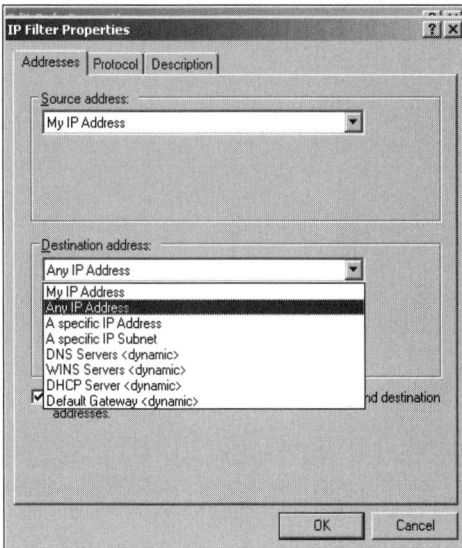

Figure 6.4   You can manage filters by IP address via the IP Filter Properties dialog box.

There are other options to secure packets from dynamically enabled network services, such as dynamic default gateway configurations, DNS, WINS, and DHCP. To configure these settings successfully, you must make the changes for both source and destination addresses.

> **NOTE**   To automatically create two filters based on configured filter settings going to and from the specific destination address, select the Mirrored check box. If the settings were created for a single filter configuration (to *or* from, but not both), clear the Mirrored check box.

> **TIP**   When you create a filter for an IPSec tunnel, clear the Mirrored check box because you need to create two separate filter lists. The first list handles outbound traffic, and the other describes inbound traffic. You also need to create two rules that use the inbound and outbound filter lists in your policy.

IPSec Troubleshooting Tools

Administrators can use a number of IPSec troubleshooting tools to assist them with their IPSec policy configurations.

IPSec Monitor

You can use the IPSec Monitor MMC to view details about an active IPSec policy that is applied to a domain or on the local system. You can also use it to search for all matches for filters of a specific traffic type in a domain or on the local system.

> **NOTE**
> When IPSec Monitor is used remotely, remote systems must be running the same version of the Windows operating system as the locally monitoring system. To perform monitoring by running **IPSECMON** on a remote system running a different version of Windows than your computer, use Remote Desktop Connection or Terminal Services instead.

You can also use the IPSec Monitor MMC to view details about IKE policies, negotiation policies, and active IPSec policy details. On systems in the Windows Server 2003 family, use the IP Security Monitor console and the `netsh ipsec static show gpoassignedpolicy` command from `netsh` to view the name of the active IPSec policy.

The netsh Command

A number of commands can be used with `netsh`. The following list describes the main options for its use. For more details, see "Need to Know More?" at the end of this chapter. To access help from the command line, use the syntax shown in this example:

```
C:\Documents and Settings\jzandri>netsh
netsh>help
```

The following commands are available:

➤ `..`—Goes up one context level.

➤ `?`—Displays a list of commands.

➤ `abort`—Discards changes made while in offline mode.

➤ `add`—Adds a configuration entry to a list of entries.

➤ `alias`—Adds an alias.

➤ `bridge`—Changes to the `netsh bridge` context.

➤ `bye`—Exits the program.

➤ `commit`—Commits changes made while in offline mode.

➤ `delete`—Deletes a configuration entry from a list of entries.

➤ `diag`—Changes to the `netsh diag` context.

➤ `dump`—Displays a configuration script.

➤ `exec`—Runs a script file.

➤ `exit`—Exits the program.

➤ `help`—Displays a list of commands.

➤ `interface`—Changes to the `netsh interface` context.

➤ `offline`—Sets the current mode to offline.

➤ `online`—Sets the current mode to online.

➤ `popd`—Pops a context from the stack.

➤ `pushd`—Pushes current context on the stack.

➤ `quit`—Exits the program.

➤ `ras`—Changes to the `netsh ras` context.

➤ `routing`—Changes to the `netsh routing` context.

➤ `set`—Updates configuration settings.

➤ `show`—Displays information.

➤ `unalias`—Deletes an alias.

The following subcontext is available:

`bridge diag interface ras routing`

To view help for a command, type the command, followed by a space, and then type `?`.

> On Windows 2000 systems you can use the **Netdiag.exe**, **netdiag /test:ipsec** command to view the name of the active IPSec policy. To review IPSec settings, you can go to the network connection's Properties dialog box and view the advanced options in the TCP/IP Properties dialog box. (Choose Start, Control Panel, Network Connections, Local Area Connection, and then click the Properties button.) The assigned IPSec policy displayed in the TCP/IP Properties dialog box is for the entire system, regardless of the number of NICs installed locally.

Resultant Set of Policy

You can use the Resultant Set of Policy (RSoP) MMC to review IPSec policy assignments for a computer or for members of a Group Policy container. To view IPSec policy assignments in the RSoP MMC, run a logging mode query, which is used for viewing IPSec policy assignments for a computer, or a planning mode query, which is used for viewing IPSec policy assignments for members of a Group Policy container.

The RSoP logging mode query can be used to view all IPSec policies assigned to a particular IPSec client. The query results display the precedence of each IPSec policy assignment and shows which IPSec policies are assigned but not being applied and which IPSec policy is being applied. The RSoP MMC also displays detailed settings, such as filter rules, filter actions, authentication methods, and so on, for the IPSec policy being applied.

The results shown in the RSoP MMC gives you a view of the policy settings being applied to the system. The RSoP planning mode query can be used to view all IPSec policies assigned to members of a Group Policy container by gathering names of the target user, computer, and domain controller from the Windows Management Instrumentation (WMI) repository on the domain controller. The query enables you to get an idea of the changes you can expect by moving systems from one OU to another. When you run a planning mode query, the RSoP MMC displays detailed policy settings for the IPSec policy being applied.

The Group Policy Management Console (GPMC) available in Windows Server 2003 is used for managing Group Policies. This combination MMC has the Active Directory Users and Computers, Active Directory Sites and Services, and Resultant Set of Policy snap-ins added by default.

With the new GPMC, administrators can now back up and restore Group Policy objects (GPOs) without having to bring a domain controller offline and perform an authoritative restore. You can also copy and import GPOs and WMI filters, get detailed information on GPO and RSoP data, and search GPOs.

You can also use the system Event Viewer and the Security Audit Logs to view any IPSec-related events logged for the policy agent. You should check the Security Audit Logs for Oakley informational messages and messages about failed IPSec communications. The following examples show System log messages related to IPSec and ISAKMP/Oakley that you can find in the Event Log. For example, the following message indicates whether an IPSec policy is in effect on the computer, specifies the source of the IPSec policy (local, domain), and indicates the Active Directory polling interval, if policy source is the domain.

```
System Log Informational Event 279
Source: PolicyAgent
Category: None
```

This message also specifies whether changes to an IPSec policy have been detected in the policy source. In this case, the text displayed is Updating IPSec Policy.

The following message indicates that PolicyAgent was unable to contact Active Directory for the domain in which the computer is a member:

```
System Log Error Event 284
Source: PolicyAgent
Category: None
```

These next examples are Security log messages related to IPSec and ISAKMP/Oakley. The following message indicates that an IPSec hard security association has been established. (Soft security associations are not audited.)

```
Security Log Success Audit event 541
Source: Security
Category: Logon/Logoff
```

The following message indicates that an IPSec hard or soft security association has ended:

```
Security Log Success Audit event 542
Source: Security
Category: Logon/Logoff
```

These next examples show some Application log messages related to IPSec and ISAKMP/Oakley. The following message indicates that the export client cannot generate domestic-strength key material; the resulting negotiation agrees only on export-strength key material:

```
Application Warning Event 541
Source: Oakley
Category: None
```

The following message indicates that the export client cannot perform encryption stronger than DES; the resulting negotiation agrees only on DES (provided the other computer can do DES):

```
Application Warning Event 542
Source: Oakley
Category: None
```

Exam Prep Questions

Question 1

You are the domain administrator for your Windows Server 2003 mixed mode domain. Clients in your domain consist of Windows 98, Windows Me, Windows 2000, and Windows XP Professional systems. You have been asked to config- ure and secure the IP traffic traveling from your headquarters to remote offices over an untrusted network, such as the Internet. You also need to configure a lower than standard level of data encryption because of backward-compatibility issues. Which of the following options is best suited to meet all your needs?

○ A. Layer Two Tunneling Protocol (L2TP) and IP Security (IPSec)

○ B. Layer Two Tunneling Protocol (L2TP) and Microsoft Point-to-Point Encryption (MPPE)

○ C. Point-to-Point Tunneling Protocol (PPTP) and IP Security (IPSec)

○ D. Point-to-Point Tunneling Protocol (PPTP) and Microsoft Point-to-Point Encryption (MPPE)

The correct answer is D. Authenticated Headers (AH) are used to digitally encrypt the source and destination ID addresses and the data to ensure that they have not been modified during their transit between hosts. AH address- es data integrity in this manner, but it does not encrypt data transmission.

Encapsulating Security Payload (ESP) is used to encrypt data packets and adds a nonencrypted header for packet routing. ESP does not guarantee the authenticity of header data, which is why it is often used in combination with AH to provide both authenticated headers and encrypted data payload. The Microsoft L2TP/IPSec VPN client allows systems running Windows 98, Windows Me, or Windows NT Workstation 4.0 to use L2TP and IPSec because those legacy operating systems cannot support L2TP and IPSec on their own.

Two forms of encryption are available: MPPE and IPSec. PPTP uses MPPE in 40-bit, 56-bit, or 128-bit encryption key strengths. The 40-bit key is nor- mally used for backward-compatibility and international settings. For VPN connections, Windows 2000 uses MPPE with PPTP and IPSec encryption with L2TP. L2TP over IPSec can use Data Encryption Standard (DES) with a 56-bit key and Triple DES (3DES), which uses three 56-bit keys.

Question 2

You are the domain administrator for your Windows Server 2003 mixed mode domain. Clients in your domain consist of Windows 98, Windows Me, Windows 2000, and Windows XP Professional systems. You have been asked to configure and secure the IP traffic traveling from your headquarters to remote offices over an untrusted network, such as the Internet.

Your solution must be able to be used on an IP network, be available to all clients in use, support header encryption and tunnel authentication, and provide encryption. Your primary objective is to secure IP traffic traversing an untrusted network in a manner that supports all clients in the environment. Your secondary objectives are carrying out these actions with the least amount of administrative effort and supporting the requirements for header encryption and tunnel authentication.

You decide to implement a strategy using L2TP and IPSec running in Transport mode and will enforce this security setting via the local security policy. What is the result of your actions?

- ○ A. The primary objective and both secondary objectives have been met.
- ○ B. The primary objective and one secondary objective have been met.
- ○ C. The primary objective has not been met. However, both secondary objectives have been met.
- ○ D. Only one secondary objective has been met.
- ○ E. None of the objectives has been met.

The correct answer is D. The Microsoft L2TP/IPSec VPN client needs to be installed for systems running Windows 98, Windows Me, or Windows NT Workstation 4.0 to use L2TP and IPSec because these legacy operating systems cannot support these protocols on their own when the configuration is set up in Transport mode. This means the primary objective has not been met.

Setting the IPSec policy via the local policy does not meet the secondary objective of least amount of administrative effort. The other secondary objective—addressing requirements for header encryption, tunnel authentication, and encryption—is met by using L2TP and IPSec, as L2TP can be used on IP, Frame Relay, X.25, or ATM-based networks. L2TP supports header encryption and tunnel authentication and does provide the needed encryption through the use of IPSec.

Question 3

You are the domain administrator for your Windows Server 2003 mixed mode domain. Clients in your domain consist of Windows 98, Windows ME, Windows 2000, and Windows XP Professional systems. You have been asked to config- ure and secure the IP traffic traveling from your headquarters to remote offices over an untrusted network, such as the Internet.

Your solution must be able to be used on an IP network, be available to all clients in use, support header encryption and tunnel authentication, and provide encryption. Your primary objective is to secure IP traffic traversing an untrust- ed network in a manner that supports all clients in the environment. Your sec- ondary objectives are carrying out these actions with the least amount of admin- istrative effort and supporting requirements for header encryption and tunnel authentication.

You decide to implement a strategy using L2TP and IPSec running in Tunnel mode between the headquarters' RRAS server and the server installed at the remote office in New York. You will enforce this security setting via the local security policies of those two servers. For legacy client systems to use this security solution, you will install the Microsoft L2TP/IPSec VPN client on the Windows 98, Me, and NT4 systems. What is the result of your actions?

- O A. The primary objective and both secondary objectives have been met.
- O B. The primary objective and one secondary objective have been met.
- O C. The primary objective has not been met. However, both secondary objectives have been met.
- O D. Only one secondary objective has been met.
- O E. None of the objectives has been met.

The correct answer is B. When your setup uses Tunnel mode, the two RRAS servers negotiate all security for the traffic, so the Microsoft L2TP/IPSec VPN client does not need to be installed on the legacy systems.

Regardless of this extra step, the primary objective of securing all the IP traf- fic traveling from your network over an untrusted network and supporting all clients in the environment has been met.

Setting the IPSec policy via the local policies of the two servers does meet the secondary objective of reducing administrative effort, as the traffic rules need to be deployed only on those two systems. However, you installed the Microsoft L2TP/IPSec VPN client on legacy systems when it wasn't neces- sary, so this secondary objective wasn't fully met.

The other secondary objective—addressing requirements for header encryp- tion, tunnel authentication, and encryption—is met by using L2TP and IPSec, as L2TP can be used on IP, Frame Relay, X.25, or ATM-based net- works.

Question 4

> You are the domain administrator for your single Windows Server 2003 mixed mode domain. The 200 clients in your domain consist of Windows 2000 and Windows XP Professional systems, and all are located in this office. You have been asked to configure systems in your environment to use Remote Assistance so that local help desk users can log on to local users' systems as needed. All Windows XP client systems are running Internet Connection Firewall (ICF).
>
> Your primary objective is to enable Remote Assistance for all client systems in your environment. Your secondary objectives are meeting your goals with the least amount of administrative effort and not altering the level of security on the LAN unless you need to.
>
> You decide to open port 3389 on the external firewall for the Remote Assistance traffic. You also open port 3389 on the Windows XP client systems running ICF. What is the result of your actions?
>
> ○ A. Remote Assistance will be enabled for all client systems in your environment, security will not be changed, and the steps taken involved the least amount of administrative effort.
>
> ○ B. Remote Assistance will not be enabled for all client systems in your environment, security will be changed, and the steps taken required extra administrative effort.
>
> ○ C. Remote Assistance will be enabled for all client systems in your environment, security will be changed, and the steps taken required extra administrative effort.
>
> ○ D. Remote Assistance will not be enabled for all client systems in your environment, security will be changed, and the steps taken involved the least amount of administrative effort.

The correct answer is B. Remote Assistance will not be enabled for all client systems in your environment because the Windows 2000 systems cannot be administered. (Windows 2000 could use Terminal Services in remote administrative mode, but these systems do not have Remote Assistance capabilities.)

Security will be changed by opening port 3389 on the firewall when it's not necessary. Although Remote Assistance offers do need to use port 3389, opening this port on the external firewall wasn't necessary because all systems are local; there was no indication in the question that Remote Assistance connections need to be made from outside this environment. Also, Windows XP ICF is designed to allow novice or expert requests to work if the novice or the expert is behind the firewall, so opening port 3389 on the Windows XP client systems manually is not required, either. These steps required extra administrative effort.

With Remote Assistance, users (regarded by the system as "novices") can allow a help desk user or another more experienced user to connect to their systems to assist them. This process can take place via Windows Messenger or through an invitation sent as an email or a file. When users who need assistance create invitation files on their computers, the HelpAssistant account is automatically enabled and an entry in the novice's table is created. The IP address and computer name configuration information, including requested port mapping from any Universal Plug-and-Play (UPnP) NAT servers on all interfaces, on the novice computer is obtained.

Question 5

You are the domain administrator for your single Windows Server 2003 mixed mode domain. The clients in your domain consist of Windows XP Professional systems, and all are located in this office. You have been asked to configure Remote Administration via Web access to manage the Windows Server 2003, Web Edition application servers by using a Web browser on a remote computer. Which of the following options best addresses what needs to be done?

○ A. Web Interface for Remote Administration needs to be installed because it is not installed by default in Windows Server 2003, Web Edition.

○ B. For the PDC emulator to be used in the domain for remote administration, Web Interface for Remote Administration needs to be installed on the PDC emulator because it is not installed by default.

○ C. Web Interface for Remote Administration does not need to be installed because it is installed by default in Windows Server 2003, Web Edition.

○ D. Web Interface for Remote Administration needs to be enabled on the PDC emulator; it is installed by default, but it is disabled.

The correct answer is C. When you need to manually install Web Interface for Remote Administration, go to Control Panel, Add/Remove Programs, and start the Windows Components Wizard. Select the Application Server check box, and then click Details.

Next, select the Internet Information Services (IIS) check box. In the Details section, select the World Wide Web Service check box and the Remote Administration (HTML) check box.

Web Interface for Remote Administration for an application server is installed by default in Windows Server 2003, Web Edition; on all other versions of Windows Server 2003, it must be manually installed. Installation of Remote Administration is not supported on domain controllers. Internet Explorer version 6.0 or later is recommended for Remote Administration.

Question 6

You are the domain administrator for your single Windows Server 2003 mixed mode domain. The clients in your domain consist of Windows XP Professional systems, and all are located in this office. You have been asked to configure Remote Administration to manage the Windows Server 2003 systems in your environment so that administrators can make remote connections to work on systems when they are unable to log on locally.

You must configure the server operating system so that it can have at least one network-administered connection and a locally logged on person working at the same time. How can you configure these Windows Server 2003 systems so that they can be administered remotely?

○ A. The operating system no longer has this type of remote administration functionality; a third-party option is required.

○ B. Enable Terminal Services.

○ C. Enable Remote Assistance.

○ D. Enable Remote Desktop.

The correct answer is D. For systems to accept remote connections, they need to run Windows NT 4 Terminal Server Edition, Windows 2000 Server with Terminal Services enabled in at least administrative mode, Windows XP Professional with Remote Desktop enabled, or Windows Server 2003 operating system with Remote Desktop enabled.

To open the Remote Desktop Connection interface, click Start, All Programs, Accessories, Communications, Remote Desktop Connection. On Windows XP and Server 2003 systems, you can also go to the System Properties dialog box and select the Remote tab.

Windows Server 2003 does not support Terminal Services in Remote Administration mode, as Windows 2000 Server did. For this functionality, you would use the Remote Desktop connection on the server system, which allows two remote administration connections to the server and one locally logged on session, just as Windows 2000 Server and Terminal Services in Remote Administration mode did.

Question 7

You are the server administrator for the WLFD01 system, which is a member of the **gunderville.com** domain. The server is a single-processor system running Windows Server 2003 Standard Edition and formatted with three separate partitions. The C:\ partition is NTFS, the D:\ partition is FAT32, and the E:\ partition, where shared resources are kept, is formatted with NTFS. You have been tasked with troubleshooting the existing Group Policies and polling their output based on site, domain, domain controller, and Organizational Unit (OU). In which mode is it best to run the Resultant Set of Policy MMC for this task?

○ A. Planning mode

○ B. Domain mode

○ C. Logging mode

○ D. Mixed mode

The correct answer is C. Resultant Set of Policy (RSoP) logging mode enables you to review policy settings that have been applied to computers and users and is optimized for discovering which policy settings are applied to a computer or user, discovering failed or overwritten policy settings, and reviewing how security groups affect policy settings. When you are logged on to a local system using a local user account, you can run a single RSoP logging mode query.

To run RSoP logging mode on a remote computer, you must be logged on as a member of the Domain Administrators or Enterprise Administrators security group or be delegated Generate Resultant Set of Policy (logging) rights.

When you run RSoP in planning mode, you can poll existing Group Policy objects (GPOs) for all policy settings that can be applied. This mode is best used under the following conditions:

You want to review the results of potential changes in policy settings if they are to be applied on a computer or user, domain, OU, or site.

The user is in Active Directory only (for example, a new account).

You want to test policy precedence when the user and the computer are in different security groups or different OUs.

You want to know what the results might be if the user or computer object is moved to a new location in the directory tree.

You need to simulate the results of policy application in a slow network situation or when loopback is used.

To run the tool in planning mode on a remote computer, you must be logged on as a member of the Domain Administrators or Enterprise Administrators security group or be delegated Generate Resultant Set of Policy (planning) rights.

Question 8

You are the server administrator for the **gunderville.com** domain and are reviewing some settings on the WLFD08 standalone system.

The server is a dual-processor system running Windows Server 2003 Standard Edition and is formatted with three separate partitions. The C:\ partition is NTFS, the D:\ partition is FAT32, and the E:\ partition, where the shared resources are kept, is formatted with NTFS.

You have been tasked with troubleshooting existing Group Policies and polling their output based on site, domain, domain controller, and OU. You need to determine the location of a settings conflict in all the policies enabled on the local system, as you have multiple GPOs linked at all levels of the hierarchy. Which of the following answers shows the correct order of execution for policy settings in WLFD08?

- ○ A. Local policy

- ○ B. Local policy, site-level policy, domain-level policy, domain controller policy (if the domain controller is left in the domain controller container), Organizational Unit policy

- ○ C. Site-level policy, domain-level policy, domain controller policy (if the domain controller is left in the domain controller container), Organizational Unit policy, local policy

- ○ D. Site-level policy, domain-level policy, domain controller policy (if the domain controller is left in the domain controller container), Organizational Unit policy

The correct answer is B. Policies are executed in the following order for a domain member: local policy, site-level policy, domain-level policy, domain controller policy (if the domain controller is left in the domain controller container), Organizational Unit policy. When a system is not a member of a domain, the only policy that gets applied is the local policy.

Question 9

You are the domain administrator for your single Windows Server 2003 domain. The 200 clients in your domain consist of Windows 2000 and Windows XP Professional systems, and all are located in this office. You have been asked to configure your environment with a security standard that uses IPSec so that systems outside your domain and non-Windows systems can set up a security association. Which of the following IPSec configurations enables you to do this with the least amount of administrative effort?

○ A. Kerberos V5

○ B. Preshared key

○ C. Preshared secret

○ D. Public key certificate

The correct answer is A. There are three primary authentication methods for IPSec, and the default authentication method for Windows Server 2003 domains is Kerberos V5. Kerberos V5 is used for an authentication method called dual verification, which is used to verify the identity of the user and network services.

Public key certificates are used to verify the identities of computers running non-Microsoft operating systems, standalone computers, clients that are not members of a trusted domain, or computers that are not running Kerberos V5. Preshared secrets and preshared keys are also capable of this verification, but they must be managed manually and are, therefore, much harder to administer and more susceptible to mishandling and compromise.

Question 10

You are the network administrator for **zandri.net**, which is a Windows Server 2003 domain. You have identified four of your Windows Server 2003 systems in the W2K3END OU that need to use IPSec for secure connections to other systems. What is the best way to configure these systems with the least amount of administrative effort and without affecting other systems in the environment? (Choose two.)

❑ A. Configure the policy to be distributed to the four systems via Active Directory policy at the domain level.

❑ B. Configure the policy to be distributed to the four systems via Active Directory policy at the OU level.

❑ C. Configure the policy to be distributed to the four systems via local policy.

❑ D. Configure the policy to be distributed to the four systems via local policy and via Active Directory policy at the domain level.

The correct answers are B and C. You need to choose whether you will deploy IPSec policies in your environment by using Active Directory or local policies. Active Directory should be used to deploy policies if you have a considerable number of computers that need to be grouped for IPSec assignment and when any manually applied deployment is simply not practical. It is also the best option to choose when you want to centralize your IPSec strategy for your environment.

You should limit deploying IPSec policies through local policies to settings with a very small number of computers that need to use IPSec or when centralization of IPSec is not a high priority. In a heterogeneous environment you can perform a mix of these deployments, in which some systems receive their settings via Active Directory and others receive the settings via local policy.

Need To Know More?

IP Security Protocol (IPSEC): `http://www.ietf.org/html.charters/ipsec-charter.html`.

How to Configure IPSec Tunneling in Windows Server 2003: `http://support.microsoft.com/?kbid=816514`.

Windows Server 2003 Deployment Kit: Deploying Network Services: `http://www.microsoft.com/downloads/details.aspx?displaylang=en&familyid=d91065ee-e618-4810-a036-de633f79872e`.

`http://download.microsoft.com/download/5/6/9/5695b3a2-bfbb-4638-8058-de94c3c5b7ff/Deploying_Network_Services.zip`.

Microsoft L2TP/IPSec VPN Client: `http://www.microsoft.com/windows2000/server/evaluation/news/bulletins/l2tpclient.asp` and `http://support.microsoft.com/default.aspx?scid=kb;en-us;325032`.

Description of the Microsoft L2TP/IPSec Virtual Private Networking Client for Earlier Clients: `http://support.microsoft.com/default.aspx?scid=kb;en-us;324915`.

IP Security for Windows 2000 Server: `http://www.microsoft.com/windows2000/techinfo/howitworks/security/ip_security.asp` and `http://www.microsoft.com/windows2000/docs/IPSecurity.doc`.

Step-by-Step Guide to Internet Protocol Security (IPSec): `http://www.microsoft.com/windows2000/techinfo/planning/security/ipsecsteps.asp`.

Using IPSec to Lock Down a Server: `http://www.microsoft.com/serviceproviders/columns/using_ipsec.asp`.

Active Directory Replication over Firewalls: `http://www.microsoft.com/serviceproviders/columns/config_ipsec_P63623.asp`.

Go to `http://www.microsoft.com/technet/` and search on the following terms: IP Security and Filtering, IKE Negotiation for IPSec Security Associations, Exploring Peer-to-Peer IPSec in Windows 2000, IPSec Best Practices, Establishing an IPSec Security Plan, IPSec Rules, Applying IPSec Policies, Remote Assistance Through a Firewall, Offer Remote Assistance Without an Invitation, Remote

Administration Using Terminal Services, Remote Administration Best Practices, Remote Desktops Snap-in, IPSec Architecture, IPSec Implementation, and Resultant Set of Policy.

Internet Protocol Security: `http://www.microsoft.com/windows2000/techinfo/reskit/en-us/default.asp?url=/windows2000/techinfo/reskit/en-us/cnet/cndb_ips_ddui.asp`.

Description of the IPSec Policy Created for L2TP/IPSec: `http://support.microsoft.com/default.aspx?scid=kb;en-us;248750`.

Windows 2000 Supports IP Address-Based IPSec Tunnels Only: `http://support.microsoft.com/default.aspx?scid=kb;en-us;248983`.

"Soft Associations" Between IPSec-Enabled and Non-IPSec-Enabled Computers: `http://support.microsoft.com/default.aspx?scid=kb;en-us;234580`.

IPSec Filter Action Option Does Not Preserve Changes: `http://support.microsoft.com/default.aspx?scid=kb;en-us;262079`.

Mutual Authentication Methods Supported for L2TP/IPSec: `http://support.microsoft.com/default.aspx?scid=kb;en-us;248711`.

IPSec Policy Is Applied After Being Deleted from a Group Policy: `http://support.microsoft.com/default.aspx?scid=kb;en-us;234320`.

How to Disable the Automatic L2TP/IPSec Policy: `http://support.microsoft.com/default.aspx?scid=kb;en-us;310109`.

IPSec Is Not Designed for Failover: `http://support.microsoft.com/default.aspx?scid=kb;en-us;306677`.

How to Configure a L2TP/IPSec Connection Using Preshared Key Authentication: `http://support.microsoft.com/default.aspx?scid=kb;EN-US;240262`.

Windows 2000-Based Virtual Private Networking: Supporting VPN Interoperability: `http://www.microsoft.com/windows2000/techinfo/howitworks/communications/remoteaccess/l2tp.asp` and `http://www.microsoft.com/windows2000/docs/vpninter.doc`.

Predefined IPSec Policies Documentation Errors in Windows 2000 Help: http://support.microsoft.com/default.aspx?scid=kb; en-us;253740.

IPSec and IP-to-IP Tunnels Do Not Work with Routing Protocols Such as RIP and OSPF: http://support.microsoft.com/ default.aspx?scid=kb;en-us;227523.

IPSec Default Policies May Overwrite Policies on an Imported Computer: http://support.microsoft.com/default.aspx?scid= kb;en-us;232817.

How to Use IPSec Monitor: http://support.microsoft.com/ default.aspx?scid=kb;en-us;313195.

IPSec Does Not Secure Kerberos Traffic Between Domain Controllers: http://support.microsoft.com/default.aspx?scid= kb;en-us;254728.

Client-to-Domain Controller and Domain Controller-to-Domain Controller IPSec Support: http://support.microsoft.com/ default.aspx?scid=kb;en-us;254949.

Virtual Private Networking with Windows Server 2003 Overview: http://www.microsoft.com/windowsserver2003/techinfo/ overview/vpnover.mspx and http://www.microsoft.com/ windowsserver2003/docs/vpnoverview.doc.

Virtual Private Networking with Windows Server 2003: Interoperability: http://www.microsoft.com/windowsserver2003/ techinfo/overview/vpninterop.mspx and http://www. microsoft.com/windowsserver2003/docs/vpninterop.doc.

Network Access Quarantine Control in Windows Server 2003: http://www.microsoft.com/windowsserver2003/techinfo/ overview/quarantine.mspx and http://www.microsoft.com/ windowsserver2003/docs/Quarantine.doc.

Connecting Remote Users to Your Network with Windows Server 2003: http://www.microsoft.com/windowsserver2003/ techinfo/overview/connectremote.mspx and http://www. microsoft.com/windowsserver2003/docs/connectremote.doc.

Administering Remote Assistance: http://www.microsoft.com/ technet/treeview/default.asp?url=/technet/prodtechnol/ windowsserver2003/proddocs/standard/ra_server_overview.asp.

Description of the Windows Messenger Reverse Connection Process Used by Remote Assistance: `http://support.microsoft.com/default.aspx?scid=kb%3Ben-us%3B306298`.

Supported Connection Scenarios for Remote Assistance: `http://support.microsoft.com/default.aspx?scid=kb%3Ben-us%3B301529`.

How to Use the Netsh.exe Tool and Command-Line Switches: `http://support.microsoft.com/?kbid=242468`.

Planning, Implementing, and Maintaining Security Infrastructure

. . . .

Terms you'll need to understand:

✓ Authentication protocols
✓ Point-to-Point Tunneling Protocol (PPTP)
✓ Rivest Shamir Adleman (RSA)
✓ Microsoft Point-to-Point Encryption (MPPE)
✓ Security Association (SA)
✓ Encryption
✓ Layer Two Tunneling Protocol (L2TP)
✓ IP Security (IPSec)
✓ Encapsulating Security Payload (ESP)
✓ Software Update Services (SUS)
✓ Microsoft Baseline Security Analyzer (MBSA)
✓ Background Intelligent Transfer Service (BITS)
✓ Remote Procedure Calls (RPC)
✓ Public Key Infrastructure (PKI)

Techniques you'll need to master:

✓ Planning a security update infrastructure
✓ Understanding the concepts of MBSA
✓ Understanding the concepts of Software Update Services

To keep desktop and server operating systems in an enterprise (or in a user's home, for that matter) up to date with the latest software updates from Microsoft, administrators and end users were tasked with monitoring the Windows product pages at the Microsoft Web site for individual updates as they were released and then manually downloading them when they were available. This often resulted in security hotfixes that were not deployed in a timely fashion or, in the worst-case scenario, not at all.

Many enterprises waited for semiregular Service Releases or Service Rollup Patches for updates to their systems, and some waited even longer, deploying updates and upgrades to their standard operating system deployment standards only when Service Packs were released. Although all these efforts are better than performing no updates at all, they were not the best security practices that could have been followed.

Microsoft has been shifting away from ease of use toward securing the platform over the past couple of years as part of its secure computing initiative. Windows Server 2003 is all about being more secure, from services being disabled or not installed by default to assisting users or system administrators with their efforts at keeping their systems up to date and patched.

Windows Update

Windows Update eases the administrative burden of maintaining systems by posting security fixes, critical updates, and critical drivers at http://windowsupdate.microsoft.com so that users and administrators can download them to their local operating systems. Microsoft releases updates on an as-needed basis. Often the "need" involves resolving known issues discovered in currently supported operating systems or in Internet Explorer, Office, and other supported products.

You can also download updates for hardware drivers from the Windows Update site; the Windows Hardware Quality Lab tests to ensure hardware compatibility with supported Microsoft operating systems and to determine which hardware qualifies for acceptance in the Designed for Windows Logo program. To ensure quality and compatibility with the operating system hardware drivers are designed to be installed on, the only hardware drivers available on the Windows Update site are the ones that Microsoft has tested extensively.

Critical updates made available via Windows Update are mainly security updates that solve recently discovered problems. There are also other recommended downloads for the operating system and Internet Explorer, and updates might include service packs available for installation (but not yet installed on the local system) and component updates, such as Windows Media Player.

An Installation History is used to keep track of what you've installed from Windows Update and reflects only the updates from the Windows Update site. If wholesale changes have been made to a system, such as restoring from backup or adding or removing services or software, these changes affect what items are listed on the Installation History page for that system. For a majority of the updates installed on a system, you can find their entries in the Registry at HKEY_LOCAL_MACHINE\SOFTWARE\Microsoft\Updates.

Administrators and users can visit the site as often as they want to choose updates for a local system and to find out whether any additional content has been posted since their last visit. At the site, users and system administrators can begin a manual scan of the local system for any available updates. They can also go to the update site via links in the Start menu or the Help and Support Center home page.

If you need to download updates for other computers that might not have direct Internet access, you can use the Windows Update Catalog, which has options for finding updates for Windows operating systems or driver updates for hardware devices.

Windows updates are available for the following Windows operating systems via the Windows Update site:

➤ Windows 98

➤ Windows 98 Second Edition

➤ Windows 2000 Professional

➤ Windows 2000 Server

➤ Windows 2000 Advanced Server

➤ Windows Me

➤ Windows XP

➤ Windows Server 2003

➤ 64-bit versions of Windows XP

➤ 64-bit versions of Server 2003

Windows 95 is no longer supported as of the end of 2001, and Windows NT 4 Workstation is no longer supported as of the end of June 2003, so no updates are available for download for these operating systems.

Using Windows Update depends on the type of browser you are using in addition to the operating systems just listed. You must be running Internet Explorer version 5 at a minimum to successfully access the available downloads.

Windows NT 4 Server will be supported (as of this writing) through the end of 2004; however, no update downloads are available on the Windows Update site. Downloads for Windows NT 4 Server must be performed manually, via Systems Management Server (SMS), or through a third-party solution.

At the Windows Update site, click the Scan for Updates link on the right side to scan your local system for updates, as shown in Figure 7.1.

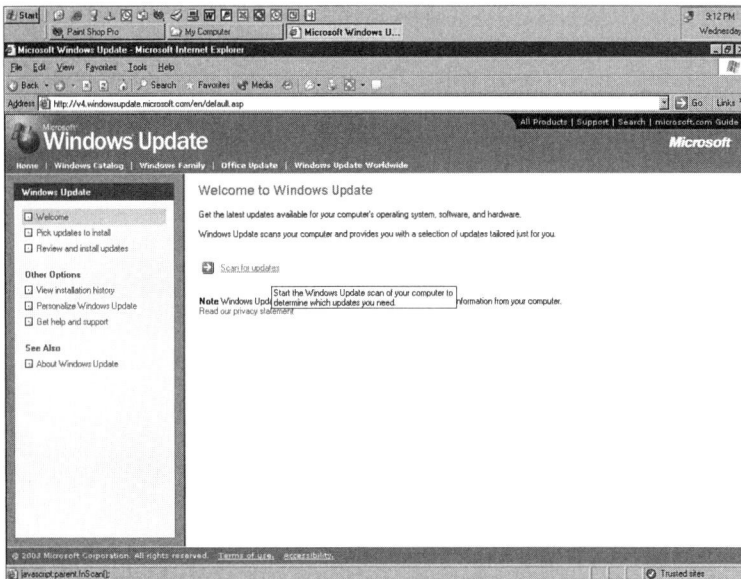

Figure 7.1 Beginning the scanning process for updates at the Windows Update site.

After the scan is complete, if your system needs any updates, a list of categories appears on the right after you click the Review and Install Updates link. The number of updates available in each category is noted in parentheses on the left.

Using RUNAS

The account used to scan the system should have administrative access to that system (see Figure 7.2). If you are not logged in locally with an account with administrative privileges on the local system, you can use the **RUNAS** command from the Windows Update shortcut on the Start menu or from a command line.

The syntax to start Windows Update from a command line is *<DRIVELETTER>:\>runas /user:<SYSTEM>\<USERNAME>* **wupdmgr.exe**. *<SYSTEM>* is the name of the local system, but it could also be a domain name where the administrative user account is located.

There is no way to supply password information as part of the command syntax; you must wait to be prompted to enter the information. The prompt looks like this:

```
Enter password for <SYSTEM>\<USERNAME>:
```

You could also use **RUNAS** to start Internet Explorer using the administrator account and then enter **http://windowsupdate.microsoft.com** in the address line.

This opens a dialog box where you enter the administrative credentials for the system, which could be a local Administrator account, a Domain Administrator account, or any account with delegated rights to perform this level of administrative action on the local system or on domain member systems within the domain.

After the secondary logon has been verified, a new browser window opens at the Windows Update site that allows updates to be installed at the required level of access.

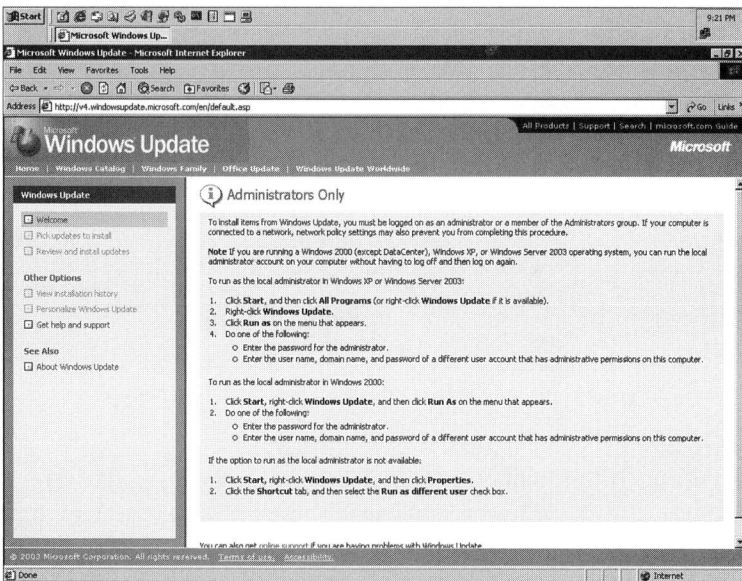

Figure 7.2   Scanning for updates at the Windows Update site requires administrative access.

As you can see in Figure 7.3, a number of updates are available on this machine running Windows 2000. The left pane shows 14 critical updates and service packs available to download, 9 recommended updates in the Windows 2000 section, and no driver updates.

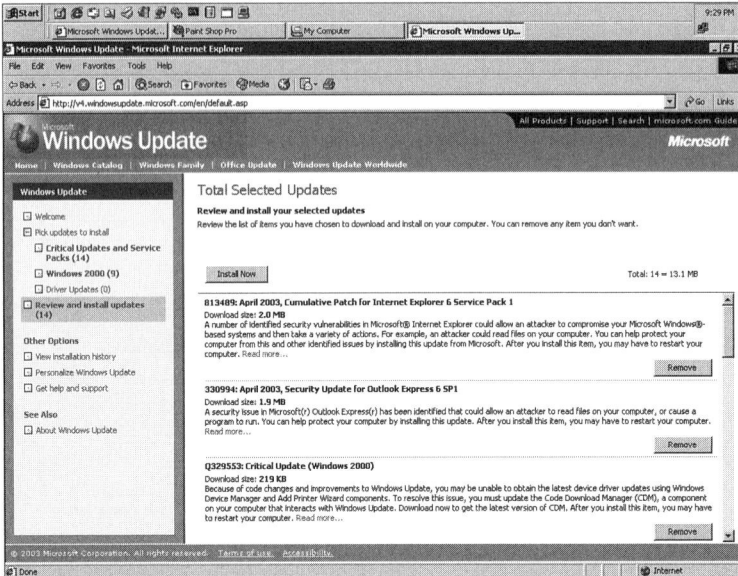

Figure 7.3 Results of the Windows Update scan.

On the right side, click Add to add the updates you want to install. In certain situations, such as when you choose critical updates, the Add button isn't displayed; by default, it's a selected addition for installation, as shown in Figure 7.3. Any selections you decide to skip show up the next time you return to the site and run the Scan for Updates option. Some updates you try to install need to be installed individually; if so, a prompt is displayed.

Each update has a brief description and a Read More link. If you need more information about an update, click this link and a new browser window opens directly to the Microsoft KnowledgeBase article for that update.

After downloading and installing the updates you have chosen, you see a message showing that the process is completed and asking you to restart your computer as the final step. You can also click the View Installation History link, as shown in Figure 7.4, to review what has been installed via Windows Update for this system. Any recently added updates would show up here as successfully installed.

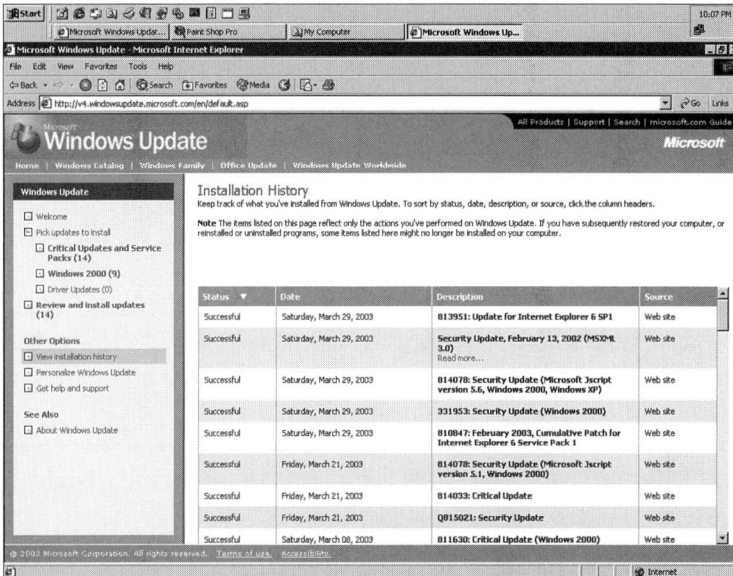

Figure 7.4   View installation history results from previous Windows Update scans.

Microsoft Baseline Security Analyzer

Microsoft Baseline Security Analyzer (MBSA) can perform local or remote scans of Windows systems for the purposes of categorizing the scanned system's current security configuration. The most recent release of MBSA, version 1.1.1 (as of this writing), can be installed and run on Windows 2000 Server and Professional systems as well as Windows XP Home Edition, Windows XP Professional, and Windows Server 2003.

MBSA cannot be installed on Windows NT 4.0 Server and Windows NT 4.0 Workstation, but those systems can be scanned over the network from another system. MBSA cannot be installed or run locally on Windows 95, 98, or Me systems; these systems cannot be scanned remotely from another host with MBSA installed, either.

With MBSA, you can scan systems for security configuration shortcomings within the operating system and scan additional services, such as Internet Information Services (IIS) 4.0 and 5.0, Internet Explorer versions 5.01 and higher, Microsoft SQL Server 7.0 and 2000, and Microsoft Office 2000 and

Office XP. MBSA 1.1.1 also scans for missing security updates for Windows NT 4.0, Windows 2000, Windows XP, and Windows Server 2003, along with updates missing from IIS 4.0 and 5.0, Internet Explorer 5.01 and higher, SQL Server 7.0 and 2000, Exchange 5.5 and 2000, and Windows Media Player 6.4 and higher.

Currently, MBSA is not localized for languages other than English. You can download it from `http://download.microsoft.com/download/8/e/e/8ee73487-4d36-4f7f-92f2-2bdc5c5385b3/mbsasetup.msi` and begin installing the tool by running the associated MSI file. After starting the installation, you are prompted to enter user information for this installation and indicate whether MBSA is to be installed for only your use or for anyone who uses the system, as shown in Figure 7.5.

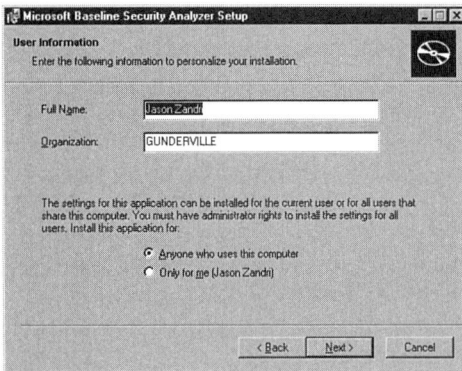

Figure 7.5 The User Information dialog box for MBSA installation.

> **NOTE**
>
> The account used to scan the system should have administrative access to that system. You can start MBSA by logging into an account that has local or Domain Administrator rights to the system or by using the **RUNAS** command to start MBSA with the appropriate user rights. Remote scans of other systems require the credentials for administrative access to the system.
>
> If you need to start the tool from the command line using **RUNAS**, you need to navigate to where the program is installed and then enter the following:
>
> ```
> <DRIVELETTER>:\Program Files\Microsoft Baseline Security
> Analyzer>
> [ic:ccc]RUNAS /user: <SYSTEM>\<USERNAME> mbsa
> ```
>
> At the secondary prompt, **Enter password for <SYSTEM>\<USERNAME>:**, supply the necessary password information for the administrator account.

After installing MBSA, you can choose to scan a single computer or more than one computer. For local scans to be successful, the Workstation service and Server service must be installed and running locally on the local system. To scan a remote machine, the scanning system must be running Windows

Server 2003, Windows 2000, or Windows XP with Internet Explorer (IE) 5.01 or later or an XML parser, such as MSXML version 3.0 SP2 or later.

MBSA can perform remote scans of systems running Windows NT 4.0 SP4 and above, Windows 2000, Windows XP, or Windows Server 2003. To perform remote scans of Windows XP systems, simple file sharing must be disabled. For remote scans to be successful on these systems, the Server service, Remote Registry service, and File and Print Sharing services must be enabled and running.

For a client system to be set up to perform remote scans on other clients, it must be running Windows Server 2003, Windows 2000, or Windows XP. The systems must also have IE 5.01 or later or MSXML version 3.0 SP2 or later. Additionally, IIS Common Files are required if IIS systems are being remotely scanned. Also, the Workstation service and Client for Microsoft Networks must be installed and running.

When you decide to scan a number of systems at once, you need to supply their domain names or IP address ranges, as shown in Figure 7.6.

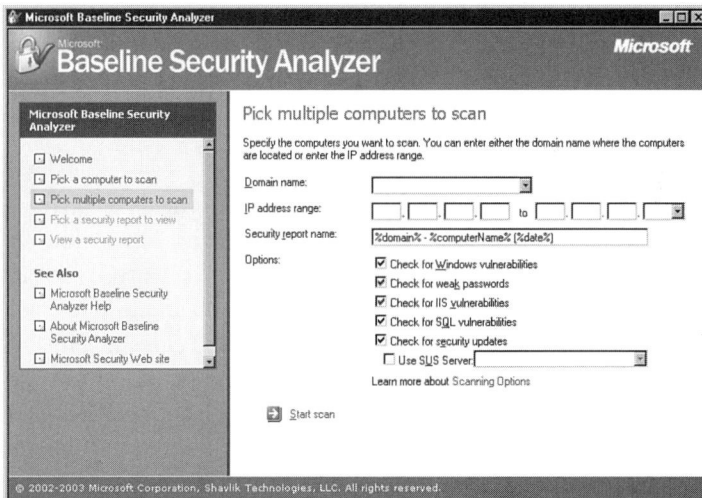

Figure 7.6 The Pick Multiple Computers to Scan window.

After entering location information for the systems, you can outline which parameters you want the analyzer to scan for. By default, all the following options are enabled:

➤ Check for Windows Vulnerabilities

➤ Check for Weak Passwords

➤ Check for IIS Vulnerabilities

➤ Check for SQL Vulnerabilities

➤ Check for Security Updates

The Windows vulnerabilities check scans for known security issues in Windows operating systems, such as the current status of the Guest account and whether MBSA detects the FAT32 file system in use. It also enumerates all available file shares and the number of members in the Administrators group. After the scan is finished, the output file provides instructions on best practices and workarounds for any problems found.

The weak passwords check scans systems for blank and weak passwords. This check might produce event log entries in the Security log, depending on whether auditing is enabled and whether additional time is available for this portion of the scan; the amount of available time depends on the number of accounts being scanned and the overall burden on the system hardware. Windows and SQL account password checks are not performed if the weak passwords option is not selected.

The scan for IIS vulnerability checks is normally performed on systems running IIS 4.0, 5.0, and 5.1 (for Windows XP systems) as well as version 6 under Windows Server 2003. MBSA also checks to see whether IIS Lockdown has been run on the scanned system. The output file provides instructions on best practices and workarounds for any problems found with the current IIS installation.

The scan for SQL vulnerability checks is normally performed for systems running SQL 7.0 and 2000 to root out possible security issues, such as whether Windows Authentication is being used or whether the SQL server is using SQL authentication or mixed mode. This scan also verifies the password status of the System Attendant (SA) account and the current status of SQL service account memberships. The output file outlines details of the SQL vulnerability checks and supplies instructions on best practices and workarounds for any problems.

The security updates check performed on the designated systems uses a version of the HFNetChk tool to detect any missing security updates. HFNetChk is available via the command line by running `mbsacli.exe /hf`.

Notes from the Field

HFNetChk uses an XML database that Microsoft continually updates when new security hotfixes are released. When a hotfix or other update, such as a Security Rollup Patch, is released, Microsoft makes that new fix available for download from the Microsoft download site. Also, the XML database is updated to include this newly released fix. The up-to-date XML database is automatically downloaded to the scanning system (unless you specify that HFNetChk not attempt an update to the file) to check the security update status on the machines being scanned.

The XML database, Mssecure.xml, is downloaded to the same folder as the MBSA executable. Subsequent updates are placed in that same folder. If any security updates in the XML database are not installed on the scanned machine, MBSA flags these updates in the security report and supplies links to downloads for the fixes, as shown in Figure 7.7.

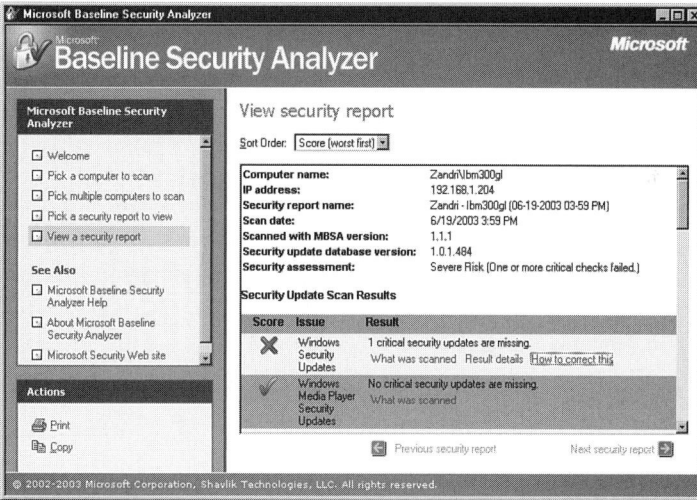

Figure 7.7   Missing security updates flagged in the output of an MBSA scan.

MBSA also offers an option to use Software Update Services (SUS) for checking systems against a list of approved updates from the local SUS server. (SUS is discussed in more depth in the next section.) If you select this option (shown previously in Figure 7.6), MBSA looks for missing security updates in a list of approved updates on the SUS server rather than the full list of available security updates in the Mssecure.xml file. All security updates marked as approved by the SUS Administrator, including updates that have been superseded, are scanned and reported by the MBSA tool.

Software Update Services Setup and Configuration

You can configure the Automatic Update client to use Software Update Services (SUS) rather than public update servers by manually changing the system Registry (not recommended) or using the system's Control Panel.

You can also configure settings through a local Group Policy on a standalone system or through a domain Group Policy object (GPO) for a domain member system.

The Automatic Update client software is included by default with the following Microsoft products:

➤ Software Update Services 1.0 Service Pack 1 (SP1)

➤ A standalone setup package (Windows Installer MSI package)

➤ Windows 2000 SP3

➤ Windows XP SP1

➤ Windows Server 2003 family of operating systems

If you're running an earlier version of Windows that supports automatic updates, you can download the component separately from the Microsoft Web site and install it on your system. You can find the available download by following `http://www.microsoft.com/windows2000/downloads/recommended/susclient/` to the download page.

The Automatic Update client software can be installed on the following operating systems if it's not already present:

➤ Windows 2000 Professional with SP2

➤ Windows 2000 Server with SP2

➤ Windows 2000 Advanced Server with SP2

➤ Windows XP Professional

➤ Windows XP Home Edition

When configuring the settings manually, an administrator needs to access the System Properties dialog box through Control Panel or by right-clicking My Computer and choosing Properties. Either method opens the dialog box to the Automatic Updates tab, as shown in Figure 7.8.

You can use this dialog box to configure update options for your system. You can notify users before any updates are downloaded and notify them before any updates are installed after the download is finished.

You can change the default settings so that the system automatically downloads any available updates whenever it's connected to the Internet. You can also notify users after the download is finished and updates are available to install. Given the choice, users can install updates immediately or later. To download updates automatically at a specified interval, select the

Automatically Download the Updates, and Install Them on the Schedule That I Specify radio button.

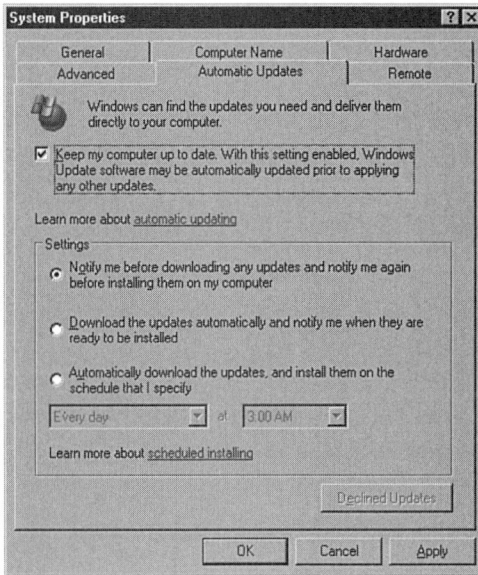

Figure 7.8 The Automatic Updates tab in the System Properties dialog box.

The Automatic Update client on Windows Server 2003 uses the Background Intelligent Transfer Service (BITS) built into the operating system. BITS allows downloading updates to the local system using only the available idle bandwidth so that update downloads do not unnecessarily slow down other network activity the client system might be engaged in. BITS runs on the local system, logs on with the local system account, and depends on Remote Procedure Calls (RPC) to function.

The Automatic Update client is available on Windows XP SP1 and Windows Server 2003 by default. If you are running Windows 2000 Server and Professional (SP2 or earlier) or the original release of Windows XP, you can download the Automatic Update client from the Microsoft Web site or have it automatically installed by applying the required service packs. The least amount of administrative effort (and the best security practice) involves testing and deploying service packs on your systems because one of the main goals of installing clients is to use the Windows Update site to remind you that those service packs need to be installed.

> **NOTE**
>
> Because the Automatic Update client can't be installed on Windows 98 and Me systems, you need to browse to the Windows Update site at **http://windowsupdate.microsoft.com** to perform manual scans on those systems, as outlined in the previous section.

For a client system using Automatic Update via the Windows Update site, the update process involves the Automatic Update client checking servers at the Windows Update Web site daily in an effort to download new update packages. The client then installs them automatically or notifies the user that the updates are available locally for installation.

SUS is a server component installed on your Windows 2000 Server or Windows Server 2003 system behind a secure firewall on your corporate network. It synchronizes with the public Windows Update site on behalf of your clients and is designed to support up to 15,000 clients. As the administrator, you can create an SUS distribution point for downloaded updates to be made available to clients in your environment in one of two ways:

➤ *Automatic*—You can create an automatic content distribution point on the server that synchronizes its content with content from the Windows Update site.

➤ *Manual*—Optionally, you can create a content distribution point on a server running IIS 5.0 or later.

The Automatic Update client is available by default on the following operating systems:

➤ Windows 2000 Professional with SP3 or later

➤ Windows 2000 Server with SP3 or later

➤ Windows XP Home Edition with SP1 or later

➤ Windows XP Professional with SP1 or later

➤ Windows Server 2003

Earlier versions of Windows 2000 and XP can be configured with the Automatic Update client through a separate download. From the standpoint of least administrative effort, installing service packs on the operating system rather than manually installing the client is recommended.

After the Automatic Update client is installed on systems, they can connect to a server running SUS on your internal network and receive any available updates from it instead of connecting to the Internet to download updates from the Microsoft site. As the administrator, you control which server each

Windows client should connect to for its updates (if you are running more than one SUS server across multiple sites) and schedule when the client should install critical updates. You can also decide which updates can be installed by allowing only approved updates to be made available to clients.

Currently, SUS allows distribution of Windows critical updates, critical security updates, and security rollups. It does not deploy service packs or driver updates, and it does not have a mechanism for deploying software packages outright, as Systems Management Server (SMS) does. SUS is based on clients going through the SUS server to download updates. Clients check with their registered SUS server (or the Windows Update site, if that is what they're configured to use) on a regular specified basis, such as once a night, for updates that are ready to be deployed. SMS 2.0 can be configured in many different ways and is predominantly deployed using push technology, in which updates ready to be deployed to SMS clients are pushed to them, instead of clients going through the server for update downloads.

The SUS server component can be installed on Windows 2000 Server or Windows Server 2003 systems and should meet the following system requirements:

➤ Pentium 700MHz or better processor

➤ 512MB of RAM

➤ 6GB of available hard disk space formatted with NTFS

➤ Windows 2000 Server with SP2 or later (the minimum requirement) or Windows Server 2003

➤ IIS 5.0 or later

➤ IE 5.5 or later

You can install SUS on your IIS-enabled server by downloading the software from http://www.microsoft.com/windows2003/windowsupdate/sus/default.asp. After the download is finished, run the sussetup.msi file to begin the installation and follow the menu prompts for a Typical installation. After the setup is complete, you can continue with the Setup Wizard to open the SUS Administration Web site in Internet Explorer.

When you install SUS on a computer running Windows 2000 Server, Windows Server 2003, or Microsoft Small Business Server 2000 with SP1, the IIS Lockdown v2.0 tool is also installed during setup, if it is not already installed on the local system, and includes URL Scanner v2.5.

The SUS updating procedure starts when the SUS server runs a scheduled synchronization with Windows Update and receives new packages of updates. The administrator then reviews the newly downloaded packages and establishes the severity and criticality of the updates for the enterprise. An administrator then deploys the updates on test systems so that they can be verified against standard desktop, laptop, and server build standards. This verification helps ready the new packages of updates for distribution in the enterprise.

After updates have been approved, clients configured to use Automatic Update and SUS check their SUS server daily and download any approved update packages from the SUS server that aren't already installed locally.

At the scheduled update time, SUS checks whether a user with appropriate permissions is logged on to run the update installation. By default, users need to be logged on using an account with administrator access (or the equivalent) to the local system.

NOTE

All files to be downloaded are digitally signed to ensure integrity and authenticity and to verify that the updates are actually from Microsoft and have not been tampered with. Automatic Update does not install files without this digital signature.

The Automatic Update client checks whether the newly applied updates require restarting the server or client; if so, it restarts the system after all packages are installed. If no restarts are needed, the installation simply ends. In either case, the updates are finished and Automatic Update waits for the next scheduled check before starting the process again.

After SUS is up and running, you must configure client systems to use SUS instead of attempting to use the Windows Update site. You can do this locally in a system's local policy (remembering that in a domain, local policy is overwritten by GPOs linked to the site, domain, and OU), in the Control Panel, or by using Group Policies (when multiple domain members need to be configured at once). The configuration of Automatic Update through linked GPOs always takes precedence over user-defined options and Automatic Update Control Panel options are grayed out on the target computer.

To configure the required settings via Group Policies, log on as Administrator to the domain, or open Active Directory Users and Computers using RUNAS and log on using an account with the required level of access. Right-click on the domain, choose Properties, and select the Group Policy tab, as shown in Figure 7.9.

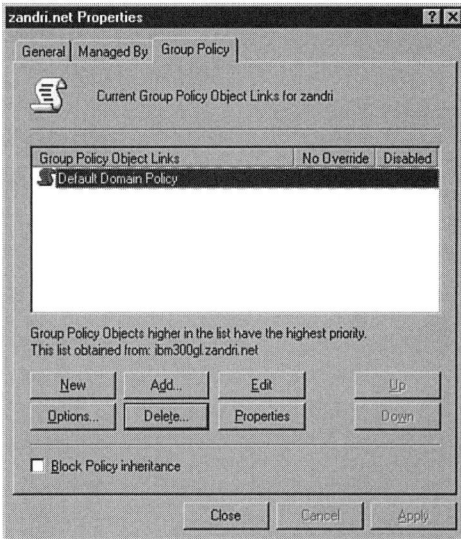

Figure 7.9   The Group Policy tab of the domain's Properties dialog box.

You could edit the default domain policy, but creating another policy for these types of secondary settings is usually recommended. To do this, click the New button and name the new policy that appears in the window. Then click the Edit button to make changes in the Group Policy window. In this window, expand the Computer Configuration node, and then expand Administrative Templates and Windows Components to reach the Windows Update item. The four available settings are shown in Figure 7.10.

In the pane on the right, double-click Configure Automatic Updates to enable the same settings for all systems in the domain. You can set domain-wide behavior to any of the following:

➤ *Notify for Download and Notify for Install*—This option notifies a logged-on administrative user before the download and before installing updates.

➤ *Auto Download and Notify for Install*—This option automatically begins downloading updates and then notifies a logged-on administrative user before installing updates.

➤ *Auto Download and Schedule the Install*—The Automatic Update client uses this option when it is configured to perform installations using the schedule listed in the policy's Properties dialog box.

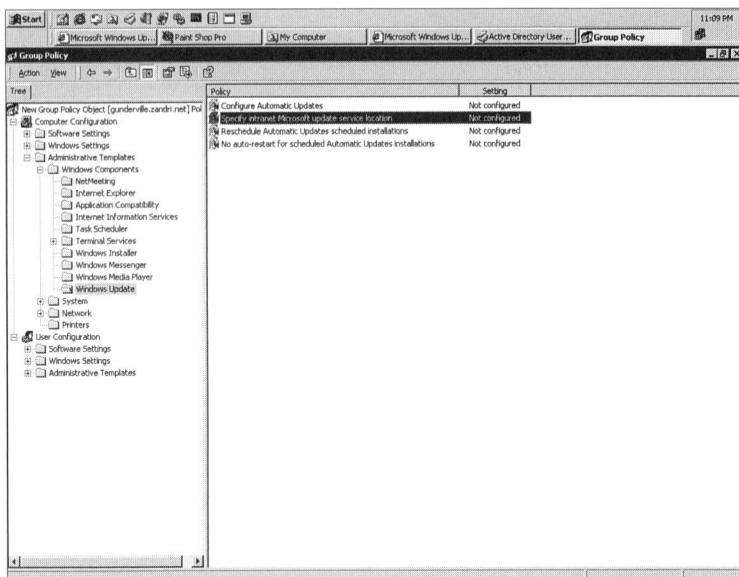

Figure 7.10   Windows Update settings listed in the Group Policy window.

Next, double-click the Specify Intranet Microsoft Update Service Location item and change its setting to Enabled. Enter the name of the internal SUS server that clients in the domain should use. You can use a server name, such as http://INT-SUS, or an IP address.

If you need to make these changes immediately, you could enter secedit /refreshpolicy machine_policy /enforce at a command prompt and press Enter, which refreshes the Group Policy; otherwise, you could wait for the next refresh interval for domain controllers, which is five minutes by default.

After either event has occurred, all your domain clients are configured through Group Policies to use Automatic Update in the manner you specified in the Configure Automatic Updates setting. These updates are performed against your internal SUS server, which is specified in the Specify Intranet Microsoft Update Service Location setting.

Software Update Services Synchronization

SUS administrators for your enterprise need to synchronize updates manually so that the SUS server is consistent with the content available on the

Windows Update site, or you need to set up the system to do it automatically. As new software updates are released and posted to the Windows Update download servers, they need to be downloaded to the local SUS server.

With automatic updates enabled on your SUS server, the administrator can review the available updates and then determine whether to approve them. After the administrator approves the updates, they are available at the next scheduled time for clients using Automatic Update. If the administrator decides that an update is not needed (for example, a fix for Exchange Server when Exchange is not in use), the update is not approved and is not made available to clients using Automatic Update.

With manual updates enabled, administrators must manually synchronize updates because they remain on the Windows Update site until administrators review them. You can synchronize the content on your SUS server from the Windows Update site, from another SUS server (often used when synchronizing from a remote location to a main location), or from a manually configured content distribution point on your network. To synchronize content from the Windows Update servers, select the Synchronize Directly from the Windows Update Servers option.

For a manual update, go to the SUS Web site, click Synchronize Server in the navigation bar, and click Synchronize Now. To synchronize content from another SUS server or a manually configured content distribution point, select the Synchronize from a Local Software Update Services Server option and enter the name of the synchronization server. This server can be another system you designate in your enterprise or a Windows Update server available at Microsoft.

During synchronization, existing content that is updated is marked on the Approve Updates page as "Updated." Administrators can customize the behavior for approved updates as follows:

➤ An approved item continues to be approved, even if it is updated during synchronization, as might be the case when a security update is being released again. This option is configured in the Set Options page by selecting the Automatically Approve New Versions of Previously Approved Updates option.

➤ An approved item is automatically unapproved if it's updated during synchronization. This setting is configured in the Set Options page by selecting the Do Not Automatically Approve New Versions of Previously Approved Updates. I Will Manually Approve These Later option. This setting is usually the safest bet because administrators can test the new update package before client computers download and install it.

After content from the Windows Update site is synchronized to the SUS servers in your environment, you can view the synchronization information on the SUS Web site. Each SUS server also maintains a synchronization log listing when the last synchronization was performed, any relevant success and failure notifications, and when the next synchronization is scheduled, if this option is enabled. The log also lists update packages that have been downloaded or updated since the last synchronization and denotes any update packages that failed synchronization. You can view the log in the administrator's Software Update Services window or by using any text editor.

Each SUS server also maintains an approval log to keep track of content that has been approved or not approved. The log has entries for times when the list of approved packages was changed, a list of items that changed, and a new list of approved items. You can view this log in the administrator's Software Update Services window or by using any text editor.

Exam Prep Questions

Question 1

You are the domain administrator for your Windows Server 2003 mixed mode domain. Currently, 12 Windows Server 2003 systems are in use in your enterprise; 3 of the 12 are installed as domain controllers. Clients in your domain consist of 102 Windows 98 systems, 22 Windows Me systems, 322 Windows NT 4 Workstations, 1,052 Windows 2000 Professional systems, 120 Windows 2000 Server systems, and 885 Windows XP Professional systems.

You have been asked to analyze the systems in your environment with Microsoft Baseline Security Analyzer (MBSA). You realize that MBSA won't be able to scan some systems, but you are required to scan as many systems as possible for your report at the next security staff meeting. You are performing all scans remotely from a single console. What is the total number of systems that can be scanned successfully across the network?

- ○ A. 2,069
- ○ B. 2,091
- ○ C. 2,391
- ○ D. 2,493

The correct answer is C. MBSA version 1.1.1 can scan a local system running Windows Server 2003, Windows 2000, or Windows XP. The systems also need Internet Explorer 5.01 or later installed or MSXML version 3.0 SP2 or later installed. MBSA also performs remote scans of systems running Windows NT 4.0 SP4 and later, Windows 2000, Windows XP, or Windows Server 2003. To perform remote scans of Windows XP systems, simple file sharing needs to be disabled.

For a client system to perform remote scans on other clients, it must be running Windows Server 2003, Windows 2000, or Windows XP. IE 5.01 or later or MSXML version 3.0 SP2 or later must be installed, and IIS Common Files are required if IIS systems are being scanned remotely. Also, the Workstation service and Client for Microsoft Networks need to be installed and running.

MBSA scans systems running Windows NT 4.0, Windows 2000, Windows XP, Windows Server 2003, IIS 4.0 and 5.0, SQL Server 7.0 and 2000, IE 5.01 and later, and Office 2000 and 2002.

MBSA also scans for missing security updates for Windows NT 4.0, Windows 2000, Windows XP, Windows Server 2003, IIS 4.0 and 5.0, SQL Server 7.0 and

2000, IE 5.01 and later, Exchange 5.5 and 2000, and Windows Media Player 6.4 and later. MBSA cannot be installed locally on Windows NT 4.0 systems, but remote scans of these systems can still be performed.

Question 2

You are the domain administrator for **gunderville.com**. Currently, 12 Windows Server 2003 systems installed as domain controllers are in use in your enterprise. Clients in your domain consist of 67 Windows 98 systems, 89 Windows NT 4 Workstations, 898 Windows 2000 Professional systems, 1,005 Windows XP Professional systems, 120 Windows 2000 Server systems, and 45 Window Server 2003 systems.

For security reasons, File and Print Sharing is not enabled on any system. All systems connect to the Internet via an Internet Security and Acceleration (ISA) server at the company's headquarters. You have been asked to perform a security analysis of systems in your environment.

Your primary objective is to run application vulnerability checks on Microsoft Office 2000 and XP for all systems in your enterprise. Your secondary objectives are to scan all systems remotely with the least amount of administrative effort and without altering the current network configuration or client setup.

You install MBSA version 1.1.1, which supports local and remote scanning for Windows Server 2003, on a Windows Server 2003 server in your domain. From this system, you will attempt to remotely run checks for known application vulnerabilities in Microsoft Office 2000 and XP. What is the result of your actions?

- ○ A. The primary objective and both secondary objectives have been met.
- ○ B. The primary objective and one secondary objective have been met.
- ○ C. The primary objective has not been met. However, both secondary objectives have been met.
- ○ D. Only one secondary objective has been met.
- ○ E. None of the objectives has been met.

The correct answer is E. Your primary objective cannot be met because MBSA cannot scan Windows 98 systems locally or remotely, and you can run only remote scans on Windows NT 4 systems. Your secondary objectives cannot be met because not all systems can be scanned remotely or locally, as the Windows 98 systems cannot be scanned. Also, there is an issue with the current network configuration/client setup. To scan any of the systems, the Server service, Remote Registry service, and File and Print Sharing services must be enabled and running on all systems; in this scenario, File and Print Sharing is turned off.

MBSA version 1.1.1 can scan a local system running Windows Server 2003, Windows 2000, or Windows XP. The systems also need IE 5.01 or later or MSXML version 3.0 SP2 or later. For local scans to be successful, the Workstation service and Server service need to be installed and running locally.

MBSA also performs remote scans of systems running Windows NT 4.0 SP4 and later, Windows 2000, Windows XP, or Windows Server 2003. To perform remote scans of Windows XP systems, simple file sharing needs to be disabled. For remote scans to be successful on these systems, the Server service, Remote Registry service, and File and Print Sharing services must be enabled and running.

For a client system to perform remote scans on other clients, it must be running Windows Server 2003, Windows 2000, or Windows XP. IE 5.01 or later or MSXML version 3.0 SP2 or later must be installed, and IIS Common Files are required if IIS systems are being scanned remotely. Also, the Workstation service and Client for Microsoft Networks need to be installed and running.

MBSA scans systems running Windows NT 4.0, Windows 2000, Windows XP, Windows Server 2003, IIS 4.0 and 5.0, SQL Server 7.0 and 2000, IE 5.01 and later, and Office 2000 and 2002. MBSA also scans for missing security updates for Windows NT 4.0, Windows 2000, Windows XP, Windows Server 2003, IIS 4.0 and 5.0, SQL Server 7.0 and 2000, IE 5.01 and later, Exchange 5.5 and 2000, and Windows Media Player 6.4 and later. MBSA cannot be installed locally on Windows NT 4.0 systems, but remote scans of these systems can still be performed.

Question 3

You are the domain administrator for **gunderville.com**. Currently, 64 Windows Server 2003 systems installed as domain controllers are in use in your enterprise. Clients in your domain consist of 67 Windows NT 4 Workstations, 989 Windows 2000 Professional systems, 5,001 Windows XP Professional systems, 145 Windows 2000 Server systems, and 415 Window Server 2003 systems.

You are currently reviewing migration plans of the Windows NT 4 Workstations and Windows 2000 Professional systems, which are to be upgraded to Windows XP Professional. For security reasons, all systems connect to the Internet via an ISA server at the company's headquarters. To decide whether to perform an upgrade or clean installation on these systems, you have been asked to perform a security check on the systems' current state to determine their status before upgrading the operating system.

Your primary objective is to perform a security analysis of these systems by checking whether accounts are using blank or simple passwords. Your secondary objectives are to carry out your task with the least amount of administrative effort and to report whether FTP and Telnet are present on the systems.

You decide to install MBSA version 1.1.1 on one of the Windows 2000 systems and scan the necessary systems over the network. What is the result of your actions?

- ○ A. The primary objective and both secondary objectives have been met.
- ○ B. The primary objective and one secondary objective have been met.
- ○ C. The primary objective has not been met. However, both secondary objectives have been met.
- ○ D. Only one secondary objective has been met.
- ○ E. None of the objectives has been met.

The correct answer is A. The primary objective can be met by using MBSA, which enables you to check all local user accounts for existing blank or simple passwords, such as having a password that's the same as the user account name or the local system's NetBIOS name. MBSA also checks for passwords of "password," "admin," or "administrator" and identifies any accounts that have been disabled or are currently locked out.

The secondary objectives have been met because you install MBSA on a single machine and run it against other systems as needed. Windows NT 4 systems can be scanned remotely, but not locally, so you must install MBSA on another system anyway. MBSA also reports whether FTP and Telnet are present. When the Check for Unnecessary Services part of the scan runs, it determines whether any services listed in the services.txt file are installed and running on the systems. The services.txt file is a configurable list of services that by default include MSFTPSVC (FTP), TlntSvr (Telnet),

W3SVC (WWW), and SMTPSVC (SMTP). You can add other services to the list simply by editing the file before the scan.

Question 4

> You are the domain administrator for your Windows Server 2003 mixed mode domain. Currently, 12 Windows Server 2003 systems are in use in your enterprise; 3 of the 12 are installed as domain controllers. Clients in your domain consist of 75 Windows NT 4 Workstations running Service Pack 6a, 1,052 Windows 2000 Professional systems running SP2, 120 Windows 2000 Server systems running SP2, and 885 Windows XP Professional systems running SP1. You have been asked to configure a software update solution for your environment.
>
> Your primary objective is to devise a single software update solution for all systems in the enterprise for security updates. Your secondary objectives are to carry out your task with the least amount of administrative effort and to devise a solution that supports scheduling the installation of downloaded content.
>
> You decide to deploy automated updates using the Automatic Update client. Part of the reason for using automated updates is to get all systems on a single software update solution for security updates, so you decide to deploy the Automatic Update client as a single installation and an independent installation only when absolutely necessary.
>
> You install SP3 on the Windows 2000 Professional systems running SP2 and the Windows 2000 Server systems. You leave the Windows XP Professional clients, Windows NT 4 clients, and Server 2003 clients at their current revision levels. What is the result of your actions?
>
> ○ A. The primary objective and both secondary objectives have been met.
>
> ○ B. The primary objective and one secondary objective have been met.
>
> ○ C. The primary objective has not been met. However, both secondary objectives have been met.
>
> ○ D. Only one secondary objective has been met.
>
> ○ E. None of the objectives has been met.

The correct answer is D. Your primary objective cannot be met when Windows NT 4 clients are in the mix. The Automatic Update client runs on Windows 2000 Professional, Windows 2000 Server, Windows 2000 Advanced Server (SP2 or higher), Windows XP Professional, Windows XP Home Edition, and all versions of Windows Server 2003. It cannot be installed on any other (legacy) versions of the Windows operating system.

The Automatic Update client enables administrators to provide support to systems in the domain and across the forest for downloading approved content from an SUS server that gets its updates from the Windows Update site.

It also allows scheduling the installation of downloaded content after administrator approval by configuring settings through the Group Policy window or by editing the local Registry.

The Automatic Update client software is included by default in Windows 2000 SP3, Windows XP SP1, and all versions of Windows Server 2003. It is also available for individual installation as a downloadable MSI setup package.

Your secondary objective of devising a solution that supports scheduling the installation of downloaded content has been met; however, the secondary objective of carrying out your task with the least amount of administrative effort has not been met because you cannot meet the primary objective.

Question 5

> You are the domain administrator for your Windows Server 2003 mixed mode domain. Clients in your domain consist of 1,662 Windows 2000 Professional systems running SP3, 120 Windows 2000 Server systems running SP3, and 885 Windows XP Professional systems running SP1. You have been asked to configure a software update solution for your environment.
>
> Your primary objective is to devise a single software update solution for all systems in the enterprise for security updates. The solution must allow administrative approval of all updates before they are deployed to any systems. Your secondary objectives are to carry out your task with the least amount of administrative effort and to devise a solution that supports scheduling the installation of downloaded content
>
> You decide to deploy automated updates via the Windows Update site, using the Automatic Update client. Update scheduling will be configured via GPOs linked at the domain level and at the Domain Controllers OU. What is the result of your actions?
>
> ○ A. The primary objective and both secondary objectives have been met.
>
> ○ B. The primary objective and one secondary objective have been met.
>
> ○ C. The primary objective has not been met. However, both secondary objectives have been met.
>
> ○ D. Only one secondary objective has been met.
>
> ○ E. None of the objectives has been met.

The correct answer is D. The Automatic Update client runs on Windows 2000 Professional, Windows 2000 Server, Windows 2000 Advanced Server (SP2 or higher), Windows XP Professional, Windows XP Home Edition, and all versions of Windows Server 2003. It cannot be installed on any other (legacy) versions of the Windows operating system.

The Automatic Update client is included by default in Windows 2000 SP3, Windows XP SP1, and all versions of Windows Server 2003. It is also available for individual installation as a downloadable MSI setup package. The Automatic Update client enables administrators to provide support to systems in the domain and across the forest for downloading approved content from an SUS server that gets its updates from the Windows Update site. If clients use the Windows Update site directly, there is no way for administrators to approve security updates. It is for this reason that the primary objective has not been met.

The solution for scheduling the installation of downloaded content does meet one of the secondary objectives; however, the secondary objective of carrying out your task with the least amount of administrative effort has not been met because you cannot meet the primary objective.

Question 6

You are the domain administrator for your Windows Server 2003 mixed mode domain. Currently, 18 Windows Server 2003 systems are in use in your enterprise; 8 of the 18 are installed as domain controllers. Clients in your domain consist of Windows 2000 Professional systems running SP3, Windows 2000 Server systems running SP3 and Windows XP Professional systems running SP1.

Your primary objective is to devise a software update solution that provides security updates and fixes for all systems in your enterprise, provides downloads of the latest Windows operating system and IE service packs, and allows administrative approval of all updates before they are deployed to any systems.

Your secondary objectives are to carry out your task with the least amount of administrative effort and to devise a solution that supports scheduling the installation of required downloaded content

You decide to deploy automated updates via the Windows Update site, using the Automatic Update client. Update scheduling will be configured via GPOs linked at the domain level and at the Domain Controllers OU. What is the result of your actions?

○ A. The primary objective and both secondary objectives have been met.

○ B. The primary objective and one secondary objective have been met.

○ C. The primary objective has not been met. However, both secondary objectives have been met.

○ D. Only one secondary objective has been met.

○ E. None of the objectives has been met.

The correct answer is E. The Automatic Update client runs on Windows 2000 Professional, Windows 2000 Server, Windows 2000 Advanced Server

(SP2 or higher), Windows XP Professional, Windows XP Home Edition, and all versions of Windows Server 2003. It cannot be installed on any other (legacy) versions of the Windows operating system.

The Automatic Update client enables administrators to provide support to systems in the domain and across the forest for downloading approved content from an SUS server that gets its updates from the Windows Update site. The following operating systems can go directly to the Windows Update site and download updates: Windows 98, Windows 98 SE, Windows 2000 Professional, Windows 2000 Server, Windows 2000 Advanced Server, Windows Me, Windows XP, and Windows Server 2003.

The updates on the Windows Update site include fixes and updates for the following categories: critical updates, recommended downloads, Windows tools and utilities, and Internet and multimedia updates. Additional Windows downloads are available, such as deployment guides and other software-related documentation.

Your primary objective has not been met because SUS doesn't support Windows NT or Windows 9x computers. The Windows Update site does allow Windows 98 clients to go to `http://v4.windowsupdate.microsoft.com/en/default.asp` and get updates, but the Automatic Update client cannot be used on local Windows 98 systems. SUS doesn't support Microsoft Office or Microsoft BackOffice products. SUS updates only the OS, IIS, and Internet Explorer and cannot be used to deploy service packs (so your objective of scheduling the installation of required downloaded content can't be met).

The solution for scheduling the installation of downloaded content does meet one of the secondary objectives; however, the secondary objective of carrying out your task with the least amount of administrative effort has not been met because you cannot meet the primary objective.

Question 7

You are the domain administrator for **gunderville.com**. Currently, 12 Windows Server 2003 systems are in use in your enterprise; 3 of the 12 are installed as domain controllers. Clients in your domain consist of Windows 98 Second Edition systems, Windows Me, Windows 2000 Professional systems running SP3, Windows 2000 Server systems running SP3, and Windows XP Professional systems running SP1.

Your primary objective is to devise an all-or-nothing software update solution that allows updating security updates and fixes for all systems in your enterprise and provides downloads of the latest Windows operating system and IE service packs.

Your secondary objectives are to carry out your task with the least amount of administrative effort and to devise a solution that supports scheduling the installation of required downloaded content.

You decide to deploy update services via the Windows Update site. Users will be asked to update their clients as required. What is the result of your actions?

- ○ A. The primary objective and both secondary objectives have been met.
- ○ B. The primary objective and one secondary objective have been met.
- ○ C. The primary objective has not been met. However, both secondary objectives have been met.
- ○ D. Only one secondary objective has been met.
- ○ E. None of the objectives has been met.

The correct answer is A. The following operating systems can go directly to the Windows Update site and download updates: Windows 98, Windows 98 SE, Windows 2000 Professional, Windows 2000 Server, Windows 2000 Advanced Server, Windows Me, Windows XP, and Windows Server 2003.

Having users update their clients via the Windows Update site is the only solution that meets the primary objective. The updates on the Windows Update site include fixes and updates for the following categories: critical updates, recommended downloads, Windows tools and utilities, and Internet and multimedia updates. Additional Windows downloads are available, such as deployment guides and other software-related documentation.

SUS doesn't support Windows NT or Windows 9x computers. The Windows Update site does allow Windows 98 clients to go to http://v4.windowsupdate.microsoft.com/en/default.asp and get updates, but the Automatic Update client cannot be used on local Windows 98 systems. SUS doesn't support Microsoft Office or Microsoft BackOffice products. SUS updates only the OS, IIS, and Internet Explorer and cannot be used to deploy service packs. These facts also contribute to meeting the secondary objectives.

Having users update their own clients isn't the most efficient or controlled method, nor does it seem like the least amount of administrative effort. However, considering that all clients need to be part of the solution, it does meet all the objectives.

Question 8

> You are the network administrator for **zandri.net**, which is a Windows Server 2003 native mode domain. You have been tasked with setting up and updating all desktop client systems in the local domain. You have decided to deploy Software Update Services (SUS) and need to specify the minimum system requirements for the server. Which of the following requirements are necessary for an SUS server build? (Choose four.)
>
> ❏ A. Pentium 500MHz or better processor
>
> ❏ B. Pentium 700MHz or better processor
>
> ❏ C. 256MB of RAM
>
> ❏ D. 512MB of RAM
>
> ❏ E. 768MB of RAM
>
> ❏ F. Windows 2000 Server with SP1 or later
>
> ❏ G. Windows 2000 Server with SP2 or later
>
> ❏ H. Windows Server 2003
>
> ❏ I. IE 5.0 or later
>
> ❏ J. IE 5.5 or later

The correct answers are B, D, G, and J. The SUS server component can be installed on Windows 2000 Server or Windows Server 2003 systems and should meet the following system requirements:

➤ Pentium 700MHz or better processor

➤ 512MB of RAM

➤ 6GB of available hard disk space formatted with NTFS

➤ Windows 2000 Server with SP2 or later or Windows Server 2003

➤ IIS 5.0 or later

➤ IE 5.5 or later

Although you might be able to install the SUS server component on other configurations, the preceding recommendations are the recognized minimum requirements.

Question 9

You are the network administrator for **zandri.net**, which is a Windows Server 2003 native mode domain. You have been tasked with setting up and updating all desktop client systems in the local domain. The current deployment of systems in your enterprise includes the following system configurations:

12 systems running Windows Server 2003

4 systems running Windows 2000 Server SP1

18 systems running Windows 2000 Server SP2

22 systems running Windows 2000 Server SP4

290 systems running Windows 2000 Professional SP1

638 systems running Windows 2000 Professional SP4

559 systems running Windows XP Professional SP1

You have decided to deploy SUS and need to identify which desktop client systems in the enterprise can use this software update solution. From the following selections, which desktop client systems can use SUS after being configured correctly? (Choose three.)

❏ A. 12 systems running Windows Server 2003

❏ B. 4 systems running Windows 2000 Server SP1

❏ C. 18 systems running Windows 2000 Server SP2

❏ D. 22 systems running Windows 2000 Server SP4

❏ E. 290 systems running Windows 2000 Professional SP1

❏ F. 638 systems running Windows 2000 Professional SP4

❏ G. 559 systems running Windows XP Professional SP1

The correct answers are E, F, and G. Although all these systems can be configured to use SUS, the question asked about desktop operating systems. Under that restriction, the only correct answers are systems running Windows 2000 Professional SP1, Windows 2000 Professional SP4, and Windows XP Professional SP1.

Although the systems running Windows 2000 Professional SP4 and Windows XP Professional SP1 are able to use SUS automatically, the systems running Windows 2000 Professional SP1 need to have the Automatic Update client installed separately. Installing the client isn't necessary if you are running Windows 2000 with SP3 or later or Windows XP SP1 or later because the client is included with those service packs. The Automatic Update client is required on the following systems, however:

➤ Windows 2000 Professional with SP2 or earlier

➤ Windows 2000 Server with SP2 or earlier

➤ Windows 2000 Advanced Server with SP2 or earlier

➤ Windows XP Professional (no service pack installed)

Question 10

You are the network administrator for **zandri.net**, which is a Windows Server 2003 native mode domain. You have been tasked with setting up and updating all systems in the local domain. The current deployment of systems in your enterprise includes the following system configurations:

12 systems running Windows Server 2003

4 systems running Windows 2000 Server SP1

18 systems running Windows 2000 Server SP2

22 systems running Windows 2000 Server SP4

9 systems running Windows NT4 Server SP6a

17 systems running Windows NT4 Workstation SP6a

290 systems running Windows 2000 Professional SP1

638 systems running Windows 2000 Professional SP4

245 systems running Windows XP Professional

You have decided to deploy SUS and need to identify which desktop client systems in the enterprise need special attention to use this software update solution. Of the following selections, which systems require special attention to use this software update solution? (Choose four.)

❑ A. 12 systems running Windows Server 2003

❑ B. 4 systems running Windows 2000 Server SP1

❑ C. 18 systems running Windows 2000 Server SP2

❑ D. 22 systems running Windows 2000 Server SP4

❑ E. 9 systems running Windows NT4 Server SP6a

❑ F. 17 systems running Windows NT4 Workstation SP6a

❑ G. 290 systems running Windows 2000 Professional SP1

❑ H. 638 systems running Windows 2000 Professional SP4

❑ I. 245 systems running Windows XP Professional

The correct answers are B, C, G, and I. Although all these systems can be configured to use SUS, with the exception of the Windows NT4 Server and Workstation systems (currently, nothing is available that allows these systems to be configured to use this solution), systems running Windows 2000 Server and Professional SP1, Windows 2000 Server SP2, and Windows XP Professional with no service pack installed need special attention because the Automatic Update client must be installed separately.

Installing the client isn't necessary if you are running Windows 2000 with SP3 or later or Windows XP SP1 or later because the client is included with those service packs. The Automatic Update client is required on the following systems, however:

➤ Windows 2000 Professional with SP2 or earlier

➤ Windows 2000 Server with SP2 or earlier

➤ Windows 2000 Advanced Server with SP2 or earlier

➤ Windows XP Professional (no service pack installed)

Need To Know More?

Software Update Services Overview: http://www.microsoft.com/windows2000/docs/SUSOverview.doc.

Deploying Microsoft Software Update Services: http://www.microsoft.com/windows2000/docs/SUS_Deployguide_sp1.doc.

Software Update Services Deployment White Paper: http://www.microsoft.com/windows2000/windowsupdate/sus/susdeployment.asp and http://www.microsoft.com/windows2000/docs/SUS_Deployguide_sp1.doc.

The Microsoft Network Security Hotfix Checker (Hfnetchk.exe) tool is available at http://support.microsoft.com/default.aspx?scid=kb%3Ben-us%3B303215.

Frequently Asked Questions about the Microsoft Network Security Hotfix Checker (Hfnetchk.exe) Tool: http://support.microsoft.com/default.aspx?scid=kb%3Ben-us%3B305385.

Go to http://www.microsoft.com/technet/ and search for the following terms: Microsoft Baseline Security Analyzer, virus protection strategies, security tool kit, UrlScan security tool, Software Update Services, Microsoft Systems Management Server, service packs, hotfixes, security patches, patch management, disaster recovery and incident response, Windows Update, configuring server roles, hardening systems and servers, IPSec, Lockdown, and security tools and checklists.

8

Practice Exam 1

Question 1

You are the domain administrator for your Windows 2000 Server domain and have been picked to work on the network design implementation of migrating your network from Windows 2000 Server to Windows Server 2003. Your design must require planners to take into consideration availability, reliability, scalability, performance, and security of all network resources.

Integration with the existing architecture is also required. You have been tasked with following Microsoft best practices in an effort to deploy a design that is fully supported. During the network design process, you must divide the work into separate phases to consolidate efforts and prevent more overlap than is necessary.

Which phase of the network design process takes into consideration all the requirements of a company and its users?

○ A. Conceptual design

○ B. Logical design

○ C. Physical design

○ D. Overview design

Question 2

You are the domain administrator for your Windows 2000 Server domain. You have been chosen to work on the network design implementation of migrating your network from Windows 2000 Server to Windows Server 2003. Your design must require planners to take into consideration availability, reliability, scalability, performance, and security of all network resources.

Integration with the existing architecture is also required, and you have been tasked with following Microsoft best practices in an effort to deploy a design that is fully supported. During the network design process, you must divide the work into separate phases to consolidate efforts and prevent more overlap than is necessary.

Which phase of the network design process begins to outline a solution for the company's needs?

○ A. Conceptual design

○ B. Logical design

○ C. Physical design

○ D. Overview design

Question 3

You are the domain administrator for **gunderville.com**. You are currently work-ing on the network design implementation of migrating your mixed NT 4/Windows 2000 Server network to Windows Server 2003.

You must plan and take into consideration the availability, reliability, scalability, performance, and security of all network resources. Integration with the exist-ing architecture is also required. You have been tasked with following Microsoft best practices in an effort to deploy a design that is fully supported.

During the design process, you must divide the work into separate phases to consolidate efforts and prevent more overlap than is necessary. You must also plan some of the details to include in your physical network diagram.

What information about your existing network topology should be detailed at this stage of planning the network's actual physical layout? (Choose three.)

❑ A. Analog lines should be noted.

❑ B. Digital lines should be noted.

❑ C. Wireless access points should be noted.

❑ D. Static IP addressing schemes should be listed and defined.

❑ E. Dynamic IP addressing schemes should be listed and defined.

❑ F. Subnet addressing schemes should be noted.

❑ G. DMZ addressing schemes should be noted.

Question 4

You are the domain administrator for **gunderville.com**. You are currently working on the network design implementation of migrating your mixed Windows NT 4/Windows 2000 Server network to Windows Server 2003. You must plan and take into consideration the availability, reliability, scalability, performance, and security of all network resources.

Integration with the existing architecture is also required. You have been tasked with following Microsoft best practices in an effort to deploy a design that is fully supported. During the design process, you must divide the work into separate phases to consolidate efforts and prevent more overlap than is necessary. You must also plan some of the details to include in your physical network diagram.

What information about your server services and server roles should be detailed at this stage? (Choose three.)

❏ A. Master browser (or any browser role)

❏ B. Gateway (default gateway)

❏ C. Schema master

❏ D. Internet Connection Firewall (ICF)

❏ E. Global Catalog

❏ F. Internet Connection Sharing (ICS)

❏ G. Router (Routing and Remote Access Service—RRAS)

Question 5

You are the domain administrator for **gunderville.com**. You have configured specific Windows Server 2003 systems to run on a restricted segment because they are all connected directly to the Internet.

You are performing TCP port filtering on these systems and using ICF to allow communications on only these TCP ports: 53, 67, 68, 80, 389, 443, 1723. All other TCP traffic, inbound and outbound, is being discarded.

What is the result of your actions? (Choose two.)

❏ A. These systems will not be able to resolve DNS names.

❏ B. These systems will not be able to obtain a valid DHCP address.

❏ C. These systems will not be able to call up Web sites via DNS name.

❏ D. These systems will not be able to call up Web sites via IP name.

❏ E. These systems will not be able to use Point-to-Point Tunneling Protocol (PPTP) control.

Question 6

You are a server administrator for the Web servers in your Windows Server 2003 domain and are troubleshooting a communications failure of an older application on a Web server that uses NetBIOS and the NetBIOS Session Service. You are fairly certain that the communications failure is caused by the way ICF is configured on the local system. Which TCP or UDP port setting should you enable on ICF to route out any potential issues with the NetBIOS Session Service?

○ A. UDP 136

○ B. TCP 137

○ C. UDP 138

○ D. UDP 139

Question 7

You are a server administrator for the Web servers in your Windows Server 2003 domain and are troubleshooting a communications failure of an older application on a Web server. The notes from the other technician assisting you with troubleshooting indicate that he is trying to verify the validity of some IPv4 addresses that are showing up in a trace he ran on the system. The older application seems to have been written to use a number of different IPv4 address formats. Which of the following are valid IPv4 addresses that this application could use? (Choose two.)

❏ A. 123.45.67.222

❏ B. 126.265.221.111

❏ C. 99.99.99.99

❏ D. 122.256.0.1

Question 8

You are a systems engineer for **gunderville.com** and are troubleshooting a communications failure of an application on one of the application servers. The notes from the other technician assisting you with troubleshooting indicate that he is trying to verify the validity of some IPv6 addresses showing up in a trace he ran on the system. The older application seems to have been written to use a number of different IPv6 address formats. Which of the following are valid IPv6 addresses that this application could use? (Choose four.)

❑ A. FEDC:BA98:7654:3210:FEDC:BA98:7654:3210

❑ B. ACEC:BG98:7654:3210:FEDC:BA98:7654:3210

❑ C. 1080:0:0:0:8:800:200C:417A

❑ D. 1080::8:800:200C:417A

❑ E. 5.40.161.101.256.255.0.0.80.191.119.8.13.201.78.118

❑ F. 0528:a165:ff00:50bf:7708:0dc9:4d76

Question 9

You are a network administrator for **gunderville.com**. You need to be able to subdivide your Class A IPv4 address range of 10.0.0.0 to generate the maximum number of subnets, using no more than 11 subnet bits. What is the maximum possible number of subnets you could create on the network?

○ A. 4

○ B. 5

○ C. 8

○ D. 6

Question 10

You are a network administrator for **gunderville.com**. You need to be able to subdivide your Class B IPv4 address range of 168.10.0.0 to generate the maximum number of subnets. Can you use a subnet mask of 255.255.248.0 to create at least 30 subnetworks with at least 2,048 hosts per subnet?

○ A. No, the subnet mask of 255.255.248.0 is invalid for Class B IPv4 address ranges.

○ B. No, there would be fewer than 30 subnetworks.

○ C. No, there would be fewer than 2,048 hosts per subnet.

○ D. 168.10.0.0 is not a Class B address range.

Question 11

You are a network administrator for your company's Windows Server 2003 domain. You are troubleshooting some configuration issues with the Class C IPv4 addressing scheme in use on your network. There are some client configuration problems and issues with lease expiration and not having enough addresses available for clients on your network. You are using a public address range of 192.199.199.0, and all clients have direct access to the Internet. What are your results if you use a subnet mask of 255.255.255.240 in an attempt to create at least 17 subnetworks with at least 13 hosts per subnet?

○ A. There would be more than 17 subnetworks.

○ B. You would not be able to successfully create the address range, as the mask is unusable.

○ C. There would be fewer than 13 hosts available per subnet.

○ D. There would be fewer than 17 subnetworks.

Question 12

You are a network administrator for **gunderville.com** and are configuring three separate subnets on your private network. You want to use classful IP addresses from the A, B, and C class ranges that are reserved for private networks in the IPv4 addressing scheme. Which ranges and subnet masks are valid IPv4 network addresses reserved for private networks? (Choose three.)

❏ A. 10.0.0.0–10.255.255.255 with the subnet mask 255.192.0.0

❏ B. 10.0.0.0–10.255.255.255 with the subnet mask 255.0.0.0

❏ C. 172.16.0.0–172.31.255.255 with the subnet mask 255.248.0.0

❏ D. 172.16.0.0–172.31.255.255 with the subnet mask 255.240.0.0

❏ E. 172.16.0.0–172.31.255.255 with the subnet mask 255.224.0.0

❏ F. 192.168.0.0–192.168.255.255 with the subnet mask 255.252.0.0

❏ G. 192.168.0.0–192.168.255.255 with the subnet mask 255.255.0.0

❏ H. 192.168.0.0–192.168.255.255 with the subnet mask 255.248.0.0

Question 13

You are a network administrator for **gunderville.com** working on some client configuration issues on your network. Your problems seem to stem from transmission and receiving errors between your client systems. Clients on your network are running a number of different operating systems, including Windows 98, Me, 2000, XP, and Server 2003.

You are currently working on a few test systems in your lab and want to review the default buffer setting threshold sizes for inbound packets for your token ring clients. You want to verify the threshold setting used when the receiving system sends an acknowledgement to the sending system that data has been received. Which of the following settings do you need to review?

○ A. TCP/IP Send Window Size

○ B. TCP/IP Receive Window Size

○ C. Maximum Transmission Unit

○ D. Maximum Segment Size

Question 14

You are the network administrator for your Windows 2003 Server domain. You are working with other team members on the network design upgrade to some network switching and routing equipment. Your design has outlined the requirements for service availability, reliability, performance, and security.

Integration with the existing architecture is also required, and you have been tasked with following Microsoft best practices in an effort to deploy a design that is fully supported.

You need to move away from your current design, which uses a connection-oriented dedicated circuit established for the duration of a transmission between clients, to one that is connectionless. Which of the following solutions should be presented for review?

○ A. Circuit-switching solution

○ B. Packet relay solution

○ C. Packet-switching solution

○ D. Circuit-routing solution

Question 15

You are the domain administrator for **zandri.net**. Clients in your domain consist of Windows 98 systems, Windows NT 4 workstations, Windows 2000 Professional systems, Windows XP Professional systems, Windows 2000 Server systems, and Window Server 2003 systems. Simple File Sharing is enabled on Windows XP Professional systems, and all systems connect to the Internet via a local RRAS to the company's headquarters.

You have been asked to perform a security analysis of systems in your environment. Your primary objective is to successfully scan all systems in the enterprise for application vulnerability checks against Microsoft Office XP.

Your secondary objectives are to successfully perform a remote scan of all systems with the least amount of administrative effort and to do so without altering the current network configuration or any individual settings on client systems.

You decide to install the Microsoft Baseline Security Analyzer (MBSA) version 1.1.1 to remotely run checks for known application vulnerabilities in Microsoft Office XP. What is the result of your actions?

- ○ A. The primary objective and both secondary objectives have been met.
- ○ B. The primary objective and one secondary objective have been met.
- ○ C. The primary objective has not been met. However, both secondary objectives have been met.
- ○ D. Only one secondary objective has been met.
- ○ E. None of the objectives has been met.

Question 16

You are the domain administrator for **zandri.net**. Clients in your domain consist of Windows 95 systems, Windows 98 systems, Windows NT 4 workstations, Windows XP Professional systems, and Window Server 2003 systems.

You have been asked to perform a security analysis of systems in your environment by documenting all the systems in your environment that can use Internet Connection Sharing (ICS).

From the following list, choose the operating systems deployed in your environment that can use ICS. (Choose two.)

- ❑ A. Windows 95
- ❑ B. Windows 98
- ❑ C. Windows NT
- ❑ D. Windows Me
- ❑ E. Windows 2000
- ❑ F. Windows XP

Question 17

You are the network administrator for **zandri.net**. Clients in your domain consist of Windows 95systems, Windows 98 systems, Windows NT 4 workstations, Windows XP Professional systems, and Window Server 2003 systems.

You have been tasked with determining the current utilization statistics on your network infrastructure and planning for future network growth. You are reviewing some ethernet cabling used in the enterprise, and you need to identify the existing cable runs that do not support 100Mbps throughput and mark it for replacement.

From the following list, identify the ethernet cable runs that support 100Mbps throughput. (Choose three.)

- ❑ A. 100BaseT4 CAT3 cable run
- ❑ B. 100BaseTX CAT5 cable run
- ❑ C. 10BaseT cable run
- ❑ D. 100BaseFX cable run
- ❑ E. 10Base5 cable run
- ❑ F. 10Base2 cable run

Question 18

You are the network administrator for **zandri.net**. Clients in your domain consist of Windows 95 systems, Windows 98 systems, Windows NT 4 workstations, Windows XP Professional systems, and Window Server 2003 systems. You have been tasked with configuring 13 Windows Server 2003 systems with persistent IP addresses.

You must also configure preferred DNS and WINS servers for the systems to use as well as a default gateway. You also need to set the NetBIOS Node Type to Hybrid mode (0x8).

What is best way to accomplish your task with the least amount of administrative effort?

- ○ A. Manual IP address assignment
- ○ B. DHCP automatic address assignment (using reservations)
- ○ C. DHCP automatic address assignment (using exclusions)
- ○ D. APIPA

Question 19

You are the network administrator for **zandri.net**. Clients in your domain consist of Windows 95 systems, Windows 98 systems, Windows NT 4 workstations, Windows XP Professional systems, and Window Server 2003 systems.

You have been tasked with configuring a dynamic routing protocol for use in your environment, which consists of multiple sites and access points. Although your network is designed with redundant paths between locations, the overall design has fewer than 20 routers and is not expected to grow much over the next three years. You also need to set up the appropriate number of collision domains so that no more than 200 clients are on the same subnet.

Which routing protocol is best for your network as it is currently designed?

- ○ A. Routing Information Protocol version 1 (RIPv1)
- ○ B. Routing Information Protocol version 2 (RIPv2)
- ○ C. Open Shortest Path First (OSPF)
- ○ D. Border Gateway Protocol (BGP)

Question 20

You are the network administrator for your Windows Server 2003 domain. The domain functional level has been configured to Windows Server 2003 interim mode. Clients in your domain consist of Windows NT 4 workstations, Windows 2000 systems, Windows XP Professional systems, and Window Server 2003 systems.

You have been tasked with configuring a dynamic routing protocol for use in your environment, which consists of multiple sites and access points. Although your network is designed with redundant paths between locations, the overall design has fewer than 20 routers and is not expected to grow much over the next three years. You also need to set up the appropriate number of collision domains so that no more than 200 clients are on the same subnet.

Which network devices can be used to set up collision domains in your enterprise? (Choose two.)

- ❑ A. Layer 2 switches
- ❑ B. Layer 3 switches
- ❑ C. Routers
- ❑ D. Bridges
- ❑ E. Hubs

Question 21

You are the network administrator for your Windows Server 2003 domain. The domain functional level has been configured for Windows Server 2003 interim mode. Clients in your domain consist of Windows NT 4 workstations, Windows 2000 systems, Windows XP Professional systems, and Window Server 2003 systems. You have been tasked with configuring a dynamic routing protocol for use in your environment, which consists of multiple sites and access points. Although your network is designed with redundant paths between locations, the overall design has fewer than 20 routers and is not expected to grow much over the next three years. You also need to set up the appropriate number of broadcast domains so that no more than 200 clients are on the same subnet.

Which network devices can be used to segment broadcast domains in your enterprise? (Choose two.)

❏ A. Layer 2 switches

❏ B. Layer 3 switches

❏ C. Routers

❏ D. Bridges

❏ E. Hubs

Question 22

You are the network administrator for your Windows Server 2003 domain. The domain functional level has been configured for Windows Server 2003 interim mode. Clients in your domain consist of Windows NT 4 workstations, Windows 2000 systems, Windows XP Professional systems, and Window Server 2003 systems. You have been tasked with setting up and configuring your network so that you can have specific workstations in the same broadcast domain, even though they are physically dispersed around your main site. What is the easiest way to implement this configuration?

○ A. Layer 2 switches

○ B. Layer 3 switches

○ C. Routers

○ D. Create a collision domain

Question 23

You are the network administrator for your Windows Server 2003 domain. The domain functional level has been configured to Windows Server 2003 interim mode. Clients in your domain consist of Windows NT 4 workstations, Windows 2000 systems, Windows XP Professional systems, and Window Server 2003 systems.

You are troubleshooting a connectivity issue with three users in a small remote office. Clients in the office are connected to an RRAS server through a local switch running in Full Duplex mode. The 16-port switch has numbered cable runs that go to each open wire jack at a workstation location. For example, port one on the switch is labeled as going to jack 1A, port two on the switch is labeled as going to jack 1B, and so on.

All three users have a desktop system, a laptop, and a developmental test workstation at their desk. Users one and two have all their systems connected to individual ports; user three has one system connected directly to a wall jack and the other two connected through a hub to the wall jack.

All three users have intermittent problems connecting to the main office, and the Internet user one has the largest number of connectivity issues, many of which include communications between local systems.

From the following choices, what is the most likely reason for user three's connectivity problems? (Choose two.)

❑ A. Layer 2 switches are being used.

❑ B. Layer 3 switches are being used.

❑ C. A virtual local area network (VLAN) is being used and is not configured correctly.

❑ D. A hub is being used.

❑ E. Full Duplex transmissions are being used, and Half Duplex should be used.

Question 24

You are the domain administrator in an enterprise with 25 Windows Server 2003 systems installed as domain controllers. Clients in your domain consist of Windows NT 4 workstations, Windows 2000 Professional systems, Windows XP Professional systems, Windows 2000 Server systems, and Window Server 2003 systems.

You are currently reviewing plans to upgrade the Windows NT 4 workstations and Windows 2000 Professional systems to Windows XP Professional. You have been tasked with performing a security check of the currently installed operating systems to determine the functional level of security before deciding whether to upgrade the operating system or perform a clean installation.

Your primary objective is to perform the security analysis by checking whether any user accounts are using blank or simple passwords.

Your secondary objectives are to perform this task with the least amount of administrative effort and to determine whether the W3SVC (WWW) and SMTPSVC (SMTP) services are installed and enabled on the systems.

You decide to install MBSA version 1.1.1 on a Windows 2000 system and scan the necessary systems over the network. What is the result of your actions?

- ○ A. The primary objective and both secondary objectives have been met.
- ○ B. The primary objective and one secondary objective have been met.
- ○ C. The primary objective has not been met. However, both secondary objectives have been met.
- ○ D. Only the primary objective has been met.

Question 25

You are the domain administrator in an enterprise with 25 Windows Server 2003 systems installed as domain controllers. Clients in your domain consist of Windows NT 4 workstations, Windows 2000 Professional systems, Windows XP Professional systems, Windows 2000 Server systems, and Window Server 2003 systems.

You are currently reviewing plans to upgrade the Windows NT 4 workstations and Windows 2000 Professional systems to Windows XP Professional.

You have been tasked with performing a security check of the currently installed operating systems to determine the functional level of security before deciding whether to upgrade the operating system or perform a clean installation.

Your primary objective is to perform the security analysis on all systems in question by checking whether any user accounts are using blank or simple passwords. Your secondary objectives are to perform this task with the least amount of administrative effort and to determine whether the W3SVC (WWW) and SMTPSVC (SMTP) services are installed and enabled on all systems in question.

You decide to install MBSA version 1.1.1 on each system to perform the scan. What is the result of your actions?

- ○ A. The primary objective and both secondary objectives have been met.
- ○ B. The primary objective and one secondary objective have been met.
- ○ C. The primary objective has not been met. However, both secondary objectives have been met.
- ○ D. None of the objectives has been met.

Question 26

You are the network administrator for your Windows Server 2003 domain. Clients in your domain consist of Windows NT 4 workstations, Windows 2000 Professional systems, Windows XP Professional systems, Windows 2000 Server systems, and Window Server 2003 systems.

You are considering a Layer 2 switch on your LAN to form a border on your broadcast and collision domains in an effort to limit the amount of traffic on two subnets.

Subnet one has four Windows XP Professional workstations, three Windows 2000 Professional workstations, one Windows 98 client and two Windows Server 2003 systems connected to HUB1 which is connected directly to HUB2.

Subnet two has two Windows 2000 Professional workstations, two Windows 2000 Servers and one Windows NT 4 Server. These systems are connected to HUB2 which is directly connected to HUB1.

You install the Layer 2 switch and connect HUB1 to port 1 of the switch and HUB2 port 15 on the switch. What is the end result of your actions? (Choose two.)

❑ A. Subnets one and two will be in different broadcast domains.

❑ B. Subnets one and two will be part of the same broadcast domain.

❑ C. Subnets one and two will be in different collision domains.

❑ D. Subnet one and two will be part of the same collision domain.

Question 27

You are the network administrator for your Windows Server 2003 domain; its domain functional level is currently running in Windows Server 2003 interim mode. You have been tasked with connecting three branch offices to the company's main headquarters.

Branch one has four Windows XP Professional workstations, four Windows 2000 Professional workstations, six Windows 98 clients, and two Windows Server 2003 systems connected locally by two hubs. HUB1 is connected to HUB2, and HUB2 connects to the Windows 2000 Server running RRAS. The Windows 2000 Server connects to the company's main headquarters.

Branch two has six Windows 2000 Professional workstations, seven Windows XP Professional workstations, two Windows 2000 Server systems, and one Windows NT 4 Server system running SP5. These systems are also connected locally by hubs. HUB2 is connected to HUB1, and HUB1 connects directly to the company's main headquarters via a private line.

Branch three has eight Windows 2000 Professional workstations, nine Windows XP Professional workstations, four Windows 98 clients, three Windows 2000 Server systems, one Windows Server 2003 system, and three Windows NT 4 Server systems running SP6a, all interconnected by hubs at this location. HUB3 is connected to HUB2, and HUB2 connects to HUB1, which connects directly to the company's main headquarters via a private line.

The main office has 9 Windows 2000 Professional workstations, 15 Windows XP Professional workstations, 4 Windows 2000 Server systems, and 4 Windows Server 2003 systems, all interconnected by hubs.

You have decided to use Layer 3 switches at the main office and the branch offices to connect all the systems. What is the result of your actions?

- ○ A. The solution will not work; routers will be needed.
- ○ B. The offices will be in the same collision domain.
- ○ C. The offices will be in the same broadcast domain.
- ○ D. The offices will be in different broadcast domains.

Question 28

You are the network administrator for **gunderville.com**. You have been tasked with connecting all three of your branch offices and your main office to the Internet.

Branch one has four Windows XP Professional workstations, four Windows 2000 Professional workstations, six Windows 98 clients, and two Windows Server 2003 systems. All clients use manually assigned IP addresses. They are connected locally by a Layer 3 switch and connected to the main office via private leased lines.

Branch two has six Windows 2000 Professional workstations, seven Windows XP Professional workstations, two Windows 2000 Server systems, and one Windows NT 4 Server system running SP5. All clients use manually assigned IP addresses. They are connected locally by a Layer 3 switch and connected to the main office via private leased lines.

Branch three has eight Windows 2000 Professional workstations, nine Windows XP Professional workstations, four Windows 98 clients, three Windows 2000 Server systems, one Windows Server 2003 system, and three Windows NT 4 Server systems running SP6a. All clients use manually assigned IP addresses. They are connected locally by a Layer 3 switch and connected to the main office via private leased lines.

The main office has 9 Windows 2000 Professional workstations, 15 Windows XP Professional workstations, 4 Windows 2000 Servers, and 4 Windows Server 2003 systems, all interconnected by hubs. All these clients use manually assigned IP addresses.

You have been asked to allow all systems to have Internet connectivity and to ensure that a moderate level of security is available for all systems in use. You have been asked to use the least amount of administrative effort and cost.

Which of the following actions could you take to complete this task as outlined? (Choose three.)

❑ A. Configure all the client systems to use APIPA. Configure the addresses with the ISA server as the proxy server in Internet Explorer.

❑ B. Configure the IP address of ISA server as the proxy server in Internet Explorer on each client.

❑ C. Install ISA Server on one server and run it in Integrated mode.

❑ D. Enable ICF on each client.

❑ E. Enable ICS on each client.

❑ F. Enable RRAS on one Windows 2000 server to connect to the Internet.

Question 29

You are the network administrator for **gunderville.com**. You have been tasked with securing your company's remote access solution. Clients in use include Windows 2000 Professional running a mix of SP2 and SP3, Windows XP Professional running SP1, and Windows 98 and Windows NT 4 workstation running SP6a with the Active Directory client installed.

Which of the following authentication methods is the most secure and allows all your users to authenticate securely without making any substantial changes to client deployments in the enterprise?

○ A. Password Authentication Protocol (PAP)

○ B. Shiva Password Authentication Protocol (SPAP)

○ C. Challenge Handshake Authentication Protocol (CHAP)

○ D. Microsoft Challenge Handshake Authentication Protocol version 1 (MS-CHAP v1)

Question 30

You are the network administrator for **gunderville.com**. You have been tasked with connecting all three of your branch offices and your main office to the Internet. DHCP is not in use on your network.

Branch one has four Windows XP Professional workstations, four Windows 2000 Professional workstations, six Windows 98 clients, and two Windows Server 2003 systems. All clients use manually assigned IP addresses. They are connected locally by a Layer 2 switch and connected to the main office via private leased lines.

Branch two has six Windows 2000 Professional workstations, seven Windows XP Professional workstations, two Windows 2000 Servers, and one Windows NT 4 Server running SP5. All clients use manually assigned IP addresses. They are connected locally by a Layer 2 switch and connected to the main office via private leased lines.

Branch three has eight Windows 2000 Professional workstations, nine Windows XP Professional workstations, four Windows 98 clients, three Windows 2000 servers, one Windows Server 2003 system, and three Windows NT 4 servers running SP6a. All the clients use manually assigned IP addresses. They are connected locally by a Layer 2 switch and connected to the main office via private leased lines.

The main office has 9 Windows 2000 Professional workstations, 15 Windows XP Professional workstations, 4 Windows 2000 servers, and 4 Windows Server 2003 systems, all interconnected by hubs. All these clients use manually assigned IP addresses.

You have been asked to allow all systems to have Internet connectivity and have decided to set up RRAS and enable Network Address Translation (NAT) for client systems.

What is the main reason this solution will not allow systems to connect to the Internet?

○ A. Static IP addressing is being used.

○ B. There is no DHCP server running.

○ C. The clients have not been configured to use the NAT system for DNS resolution.

○ D. Each location is segmented into different broadcast domains.

Question 31

You are the network administrator for **gunderville.com**. You have been tasked with connecting all three of your branch offices and your main office to the Internet.

Branch one has four Windows XP Professional workstations, four Windows 2000 Professional workstations, six Windows 98 clients, and two Windows Server 2003 systems. All clients have been configured to use DHCP. They are connected locally by a Layer 3 switch and connected to the main office via private leased lines.

Branch two has six Windows 2000 Professional workstations, seven Windows XP Professional workstations, two Windows 2000 servers, and one Windows NT 4 server running SP5. All clients have been configured to use DHCP. They are connected locally by a Layer 3 switch and connected to the main office via private leased lines.

Branch three has eight Windows 2000 Professional workstations, nine Windows XP Professional workstations, four Windows 98 clients, three Windows 2000 servers, one Windows Server 2003 system, and three Windows NT 4 servers running SP6a. All clients have been configured to use DHCP. They are connected locally by a Layer 3 switch and connected to the main office via private leased lines.

The main office has 9 Windows 2000 Professional workstations, 15 Windows XP Professional workstations, 4 Windows 2000 servers, and 4 Windows Server 2003 systems, all interconnected by hubs. All these clients are configured to use DHCP.

You have been asked to allow all systems to have Internet connectivity and have decided to set up one RRAS system at the main company headquarters and enable NAT for the client systems.

What is the main reason this solution will not allow systems to connect to the Internet?

○ A. Static IP addressing is being used.

○ B. There is no DHCP server running.

○ C. The clients have not been configured to use the NAT system for DNS resolution.

○ D. Each location is segmented into different broadcast domains.

Question 32

You are the network administrator for **gunderville.com**. You have been tasked with connecting all three of your branch offices and your main office to the Internet.

Branch one has four Windows XP Professional workstations, four Windows 2000 Professional workstations, six Windows 98 clients, and two Windows Server 2003 systems. There is a DNS server at this location that has not been configured as a forwarder, and all clients have been manually configured to use it for name resolution. All clients have been configured to use DHCP. They are connected locally by a Layer 2 switch and connected to the main office via private leased lines.

Branch two has six Windows 2000 Professional workstations, seven Windows XP Professional workstations, two Windows 2000 servers, and one Windows NT 4 server running SP5. There is a DNS server at this location that has not been configured as a forwarder, and all clients have been manually configured to use it for name resolution. All clients have been configured to use DHCP. They are connected locally by a Layer 2 switch and connected to the main office via private leased lines.

Branch three has eight Windows 2000 Professional workstations, nine Windows XP Professional workstations, four Windows 98 clients, three Windows 2000 servers, one Windows Server 2003 system, and three Windows NT 4 servers running SP6a. There is a DNS server at this location that has not been configured as a forwarder, and all clients have been manually configured to use it for name resolution. All clients have been configured to use DHCP. They are connected locally by a Layer 2 switch and connected to the main office via private leased lines.

The main office has 9 Windows 2000 Professional workstations, 15 Windows XP Professional workstations, 4 Windows 2000 servers, and 4 Windows Server 2003 systems, all interconnected by hubs. There is a DNS server at this location, and all clients have been manually configured to use it for name resolution. All these clients use DHCP.

You have been asked to allow all systems to have Internet connectivity and have decided to set up one RRAS system at the main company headquarters and enable NAT for client systems. You enable the NAT configuration to provide external DNS resolution for clients.

What is the main reason this solution will not allow systems to connect to the Internet?

○ A. Static IP addressing is being used.

○ B. There is no DHCP server running.

○ C. Clients have not been configured to use the NAT system for DNS resolution.

○ D. Each location is segmented into different broadcast domains.

Question 33

You are the network administrator for **gunderville.com**. You have been tasked with configuring all your branch offices and your main office to use DHCP.

Branch one has client systems running Windows XP Professional, Windows 2000 Professional, and Windows 98 and has two Windows Server 2003 systems. There is a DNS server at this location, and all clients must be configured to use it for name resolution. All clients have been configured to use DHCP (except for the Windows Server 2003 systems). They are connected locally by an old router to the main office via private leased lines.

Branch two has client systems running Windows XP Professional, Windows 2000 Professional, and Windows 98 and has two Windows 2000 servers and one Windows NT 4 server running SP5. There is a DNS server at this location, and all clients need to be configured to use it for name resolution. All clients have been configured to use DHCP (except for the Windows Server 2003 systems and the one Windows NT 4 server). They are connected locally by an old router to the main office via private leased lines. This router is configured to not forward broadcast messages.

The main office has client systems running Windows 2000 Professional and Windows XP Professional. It also has four Windows 2000 servers and four Windows Server 2003 systems, all interconnected by hubs internally. There is a DNS server at this location, and all clients need to be configured to use it for name resolution. All these clients (except for the Windows 2000 servers and Windows Server 2003 systems) use DHCP.

You have been asked to configure a DHCP server solution for your environment that allows all clients to obtain an IP address from a server hosting DHCP and that does not allow a single point of failure for addressing. Your configuration must also address your current business model needs, which require you to choose the least expensive option after ensuring no single point of failure. Which of the following is the best solution?

- ○ A. Deploy two DHCP servers at each location and use a 50/50 address rule for each scope between the two servers. Create one scope for each location.

- ○ B. Deploy three DHCP servers total and use a 33/33/34 address rule for each scope so that each DHCP server has addresses for its local scope and the two remote scopes.

- ○ C. Deploy three DHCP servers total and use an 80/10/10 address rule for each scope so that each DHCP server has addresses for its local scope and the two remote scopes.

- ○ D. Deploy two DHCP servers at the main office and use a 50/50 address rule for the scope. Configure two other systems to serve as relay agents, and create one scope for each location.

Question 34

You are the network administrator for your Windows Server 2003 domain running in interim mode. You have been tasked with configuring all your branch offices and your main office to use DHCP.

Branch one has client systems running Windows XP Professional, Windows 2000 Professional, and Windows 98 and has one DNS server. All clients need to be configured to use this DNS server for name resolution. All clients have been configured to use DHCP. They are connected locally by an old router to the main office via private leased lines. A newly installed on-demand interface is in use via a Linksys DSL router as a backup connection to the main office if the private leased line is unavailable. DHCP has been enabled on the device and configured to connect to the remote office only when the private leased line is unavailable.

Branch two has client systems running Windows XP Professional, Windows 2000 Professional, and Windows 98 and has one DNS server at this location. All clients must be configured to use this DNS server for name resolution. All clients have been configured to use DHCP (except for the Windows Server 2003 systems and the one Windows NT 4 server). They are connected locally by an old router to the main office via private leased lines. This router is configured to not forward broadcast messages. DHCP has been enabled on the device and configured to connect to the remote office only when the private leased line is unavailable.

The main office has client systems running Windows 2000 Professional and Windows XP Professional. It also has four Windows 2000 servers, four Windows Server 2003 systems, and two Windows NT 4 servers, all interconnected by hubs internally. A Windows Server 2003 system is configured as a DNS server at this location, and all clients need to be configured to use it for name resolution. All these clients (except for the Windows 2000 servers and Windows Server 2003 systems) use DHCP.

You have been asked to configure a DHCP server solution for your environment that allows all clients to obtain an IP address from DHCP and that does not allow a single point of failure for addressing. Your configuration must also address your current business model needs, which require you to choose the least expensive option after ensuring no single point of failure. Which of the following options is the best solution?

- ○ A. Deploy two DHCP servers at the main office and use a 50/50 address rule for the scope. Configure two other systems to serve as relay agents, and create one scope for each location.

- ○ B. Deploy three DHCP servers total and use a 33/33/34 address rule for each scope so that each DHCP server has addresses for its local scope and the two remote scopes.

- ○ C. Deploy three DHCP servers total and use an 80/10/10 address rule for each scope so that each DHCP server has addresses for its local scope and the two remote scopes.

○ D. Deploy one DHCP server with its own scope at each location and allow the DHCP service running on the demand-dial router to act as the backup.

○ E. None of the available choices meets all the question's needs.

Question 35

You are the network administrator for **gunderville.com**. You have been tasked with configuring all your branch offices and your main office to use DHCP.

Branch one has client systems running Windows XP Professional, Windows 2000 Professional, and Windows 98 and has two Windows Server 2003 systems. There is a DNS server at this location, and all clients must be configured to use it for name resolution. All clients have been configured to use DHCP (except for the Windows Server 2003 systems). They are connected locally by an RFC 1542–compliant router to the main office via a pair of private leased lines. Two different ISPs provide these leased lines.

Branch two has client systems running Windows XP Professional, Windows 2000 Professional, and Windows 98 and has two Windows 2000 servers and one Windows NT 4 SERVER running SP5. There is a DNS server at this location, and all clients need to be configured to use it for name resolution. All clients have been configured to use DHCP (except for the Windows Server 2003 systems and the Windows NT 4 server). They are connected locally by an RFC 1542–compliant router to the main office via a pair of private leased lines. Two different ISPs provide these leased lines.

The main office has client systems running Windows 2000 Professional and Windows XP Professional. It also has four Windows 2000 servers and four Windows Server 2003 systems, all interconnected by hubs internally. There is a DNS server at this location, and all clients need to be configured to use it for name resolution. All these clients (except for the Windows 2000 servers and Windows Server 2003 systems) use DHCP.

You have been asked to configure a DHCP server solution for your environment that allows all clients to obtain IP addresses from a server hosting DHCP and that does not allow a single point of failure for DHCP addressing. Your configuration must also address your current business model needs, which require you to choose the least expensive option after ensuring no single point of failure and to make sure the actions taken involve the least amount of administrative effort. Which of the following is the best solution?

○ A. Deploy two DHCP servers at each location and use a 50/50 address rule for the scope.

○ B. Deploy three DHCP servers total and use a 33/33/34 address rule for each scope so that each DHCP server has addresses for its local scope and the two remote scopes.

○ C. Deploy three DHCP servers total and use an 80/10/10 address rule for each scope so that each DHCP server has addresses for its local scope and the two remote scopes.

○ D. Deploy two DHCP servers at the main office and use a 50/50 address rule for the scope. Configure two other systems to serve as relay agents.

○ E. Deploy two DHCP servers at the main office and create three different scopes—one scope for each location. Use a 50/50 address rule for each scope.

Question 36

You are the network administrator for **gunderville.com**. You have been tasked with configuring all your existing client areas to use DHCP.

Area one has client systems running Windows XP Professional, Windows 2000 Professional, and Windows 98 and has two Windows Server 2003 systems. There is a DNS server in this area, and all clients have been manually configured to use it for name resolution. All clients have been configured to use DHCP (except for the Windows Server 2003 systems) and are connected in parallel by two hubs.

Area two has client systems running Windows XP Professional, Windows 2000 Professional, and Windows 98. It also has two Windows 2000 servers and one Windows NT 4 server running SP5. There is a DNS server in this area, and all clients have been manually configured to use it for name resolution. All clients have been configured to use DHCP (except for the Windows Server 2003 systems and the Windows NT 4 server) and are connected in parallel by two hubs.

Area three (the main server area) has client systems running Windows 2000 Professional and Windows XP Professional. It also has four Windows 2000 SERVERS and four Windows Server 2003 systems, all interconnected by hubs internally. There is a DNS server in this area, and all clients have been manually configured to use it for name resolution. All these clients (except for the Windows 2000 servers and Windows Server 2003 systems) use DHCP.

You have been asked to configure a DHCP server solution for your environment that allows all clients to obtain an IP address from a server hosting DHCP and that does not allow a single point of failure for addressing. Your configuration must also address your current business model needs, which require you to choose the least expensive option after ensuring no single point of failure and make sure the actions taken involve the least amount of administrative effort. Which of the following is the best solution?

○ A. Deploy three DHCP servers total (one in each area) and use a 33/33/34 address rule for each scope so that each DHCP server has addresses for its local scope and the two remote scopes.

○ B. Deploy two DHCP servers in the main server area and use a 50/50 address rule for the scope. Create one scope.

○ C. Deploy three DHCP servers in the main server area and use an 80/10/10 address rule for each scope so that each DHCP server has addresses for its local scope and the two remote scopes.

○ D. Deploy two DHCP servers in the main server area and use a 50/50 address rule for the scope. Configure two other systems to serve as relay agents.

Question 37

You are the network administrator for **gunderville.com**. You have been tasked with configuring all your branch offices and your main office to use DHCP.

Branch one has client systems running Windows XP Professional, Windows 2000 Professional, and Windows 98 and has two Windows Server 2003 systems. There is a DNS server at this location, and all clients must be configured to use it for name resolution. All clients have been configured to use DHCP and are connected locally by an old router to the main office via private leased lines. The two Windows Server 2003 systems have manually assigned static IP addresses, but you need to configure these systems to use DHCP and keep their current IP addresses.

Branch two has client systems running Windows XP Professional, Windows 2000 Professional, and Windows 98 and has two Windows 2000 servers. There is a DNS server at this location, and all clients need to be configured to use it for name resolution. All clients have been configured to use DHCP (except for the Windows Server 2003 systems and the Windows NT 4 server) and are connected locally by an old router to the main office via private leased lines. This router is configured to not forward broadcast messages. The two Windows 2000 Server systems have manually assigned static IP addresses, but you need to configure these systems to use DHCP and keep their current IP addresses.

The main office has client systems running Windows 2000 Professional and Windows XP Professional. It also has four Windows 2000 servers and four Windows Server 2003 systems, all interconnected by hubs internally. There is a DNS server at this location, and all clients need to be configured to use it for name resolution. All these clients (except for the Windows 2000 servers and Windows Server 2003 systems) use DHCP. The Windows Server 2003 systems and Windows 2000 servers have manually assigned static IP addresses, but you need to configure these systems to use DHCP and keep their current IP addresses.

You have been asked to configure a DHCP server solution for your environment that allows all clients to obtain an IP address from a server hosting DHCP and that does not allow a single point of failure for addressing. Your configuration must also address your current business model needs, which require you to choose the least expensive option after ensuring no single point of failure. Which of the following is the best solution?

○ A. Deploy two DHCP servers at each location and use a 50/50 address rule for each scope between the two servers. Create one scope for each location. Create the necessary IP address exclusions for the scope on both DHCP servers at each location.

○ B. Deploy three DHCP servers total and use a 33/33/34 address rule for each scope so that each DHCP server has addresses for its local scope and the two remote scopes. Create one scope for each location. Create the necessary client reservations for the scope on each DHCP server.

○ C. Deploy two DHCP servers at each location and use a 50/50 address
rule for each scope between the two servers. Create one scope for
each location. Create the necessary client reservations for the scope on
both DHCP servers at each location.

○ D. Deploy two DHCP servers at the main office and use a 50/50 address
rule for the scope. Configure two other systems to serve as relay
agents, and create one scope for each location. Create the necessary
client reservations for the scope on both DHCP servers.

Question 38

You are the network administrator for **gunderville.com**. You have been tasked
with configuring all your branch offices and your main office to use DHCP.

Branch one has client systems running Windows XP Professional, Windows
2000 Professional, and Windows 98 and has two Windows Server 2003 systems. There is a DNS server at this location, and all local clients need to be configured to use it for name resolution. All clients have been configured to use
DHCP. They are connected locally by a hub and connected to the main office via
two different RFC 1542–compliant routers via separate private leased lines. The
two Windows Server 2003 systems have manually assigned static IP addresses, but you need to configure these systems to use DHCP and keep their current IP addresses.

Branch two has client systems running Windows XP Professional, Windows
2000 Professional, and Windows 98 and has two Windows 2000 servers. There
is a DNS server at this location, and all local clients need to be configured to use
it for name resolution. All clients have been configured to use DHCP. They are
connected locally by a hub and connected to the main office via two different
RFC 1542–compliant routers via separate private leased lines. The two Windows
2000 Server systems have manually assigned static IP addresses, but you need
to configure these systems to use DHCP and keep their current IP addresses.

The main office has client systems running Windows 2000 Professional and
Windows XP Professional. It also has four Windows 2000 servers and four
Windows Server 2003 systems, all interconnected by hubs internally. There is a
DNS server at this location, and all clients need to be configured to use it for
name resolution. All these clients (except for the Windows 2000 servers and
Windows Server 2003 systems) are configured to use DHCP. The four Windows
Server 2003 systems and the four Windows 2000 servers have manually
assigned static IP addresses, but you need to configure these systems to use
DHCP and keep their current IP addresses.

You have been asked to configure a DHCP server solution for your environment
that allows all clients to obtain an IP address from a server hosting DHCP and
that does not allow a single point of failure for addressing. Your configuration
must also address your current business model needs, which require you to
choose the least expensive option after ensuring no single point of failure.

Which of the following is the best solution that uses the least amount of administrative effort?

○ A. Deploy two DHCP servers at each location, and use a 50/50 address rule for each scope between the two servers. Create one scope for each location. Create the necessary IP address exclusions for the scope on both DHCP servers at each location.

○ B. Deploy two DHCP servers at the main office. Create three different scopes (one for each location), and use a 50/50 address rule for each scope. Configure two other systems to serve as relay agents. Create the necessary client reservations for each scope on both DHCP servers.

○ C. Deploy two DHCP servers at each location, and use a 50/50 address rule for each scope between the two servers. Create one scope for each location. Create the necessary client reservations for the scope on both DHCP servers at each location.

○ D. Deploy two DHCP servers at the main office. Create three different scopes (one for each location), and use a 50/50 address rule for each scope. Create the necessary client reservations for each scope on both DHCP servers.

Question 39

You are the network administrator for **gunderville.com**. You have been tasked with configuring all your existing client areas to use DHCP.

Area one has client systems running Windows XP Professional, Windows 2000 Professional, and Windows 98 and has two Windows Server 2003 systems. There is a DNS server in this area, and all clients have been manually configured to use it for name resolution. All clients have been configured to use DHCP, and all are connected in parallel by two hubs. The two Windows Server 2003 systems have manually assigned static IP addresses, but you need to configure these systems to use DHCP and keep their current IP addresses.

Area two has client systems running Windows XP Professional, Windows 2000 Professional, and Windows 98 and has two Windows 2000 servers. There is a DNS server in this area, and all clients have been manually configured to use it for name resolution. All clients have been configured to use DHCP, and all are connected in parallel by two hubs. The two Windows 2000 Server systems have manually assigned static IP addresses, but you need to configure these systems to use DHCP and keep their current IP addresses.

Area three (the main server area) has client systems running Windows 2000 Professional and Windows XP Professional. It also has four Windows 2000 servers and four Windows Server 2003 systems, all interconnected by hubs internally. There is a DNS server in this area, and all clients have been manually configured to use it for name resolution. All clients use DHCP. The four Windows 2000 servers and four Windows Server 2003 systems have manually assigned static IP addresses, but you need to configure these systems to use DHCP and keep their current IP addresses.

You have been asked to configure a DHCP server solution for your environment that allows all clients to obtain an IP address from a server hosting the DHCP service and that does not allow a single point of failure for addressing. Your configuration must also address your current business model needs, which require you to choose the least expensive option after ensuring no single point of failure and make sure the actions taken involve the least amount of administrative effort. Which of the following is the best solution?

○ A. Deploy three DHCP servers total (one in each area) and use a 33/33/34 address rule for each scope so that each DHCP server has addresses for both its local scope and the two remote scopes. You need to create the necessary IP address exclusions on each DHCP server.

○ B. Deploy two DHCP servers in the main server area and use a 50/50 address rule for the scope. Create three different scopes for use—one scope for each location. You need to create the necessary client reservations on one DHCP server.

○ C. Deploy two DHCP servers in the main server area and use a 50/50 address rule for the scope, and configure two other systems to serve as relay agents. You need to create the necessary client reservations on both DHCP servers.

○ D. Deploy two DHCP servers in the main server area and use a 50/50 address rule for the scope. Create one scope for use. You need to create the necessary client reservations on both DHCP servers.

Question 40

You are the network administrator for **gunderville.com**. You have been tasked with configuring all your branch offices and your main office to use DHCP.

Branch one has client systems running Windows XP Professional, Windows 2000 Professional, and Windows 98 and has two Windows Server 2003 systems. There is a DNS server at this location, and all clients need to be configured to use it for name resolution. All clients have been configured to use DHCP and are connected locally by an old router to the main office via private leased lines. The two Windows Server 2003 systems have manually assigned static IP addresses.

Branch two has client systems running Windows XP Professional, Windows 2000 Professional, and Windows 98 and has two Windows 2000 servers. There is a DNS server at this location, and all clients need to be configured to use it for name resolution. All clients have been configured to use DHCP (except the Windows Server 2003 systems and the Windows NT 4 server). They are connected locally by an old router to the main office via private leased lines. This router is configured to not forward broadcast messages. The two Windows 2000 Server systems have manually assigned static IP addresses.

The main office has client systems running Windows 2000 Professional and Windows XP Professional. It also has four Windows 2000 servers and four Windows Server 2003 systems, all interconnected by hubs internally. There is a DNS server at this location, and all clients need to be configured to use it for name resolution. All these clients (except the Windows 2000 servers and Windows Server 2003 systems) use DHCP. The Windows Server 2003 systems and the Windows 2000 servers have manually assigned static IP addresses.

You have been asked to configure a DHCP server solution for your environment that allows all clients to obtain an IP address from a server hosting the DHCP service and that does not allow a single point of failure for addressing. Your configuration must also address your current business model needs, which require you to choose the least expensive option after ensuring no single point of failure. Which of the following is the best solution?

○ A. Deploy two DHCP servers at each location and use a 50/50 address rule for each scope between the two servers. Create one scope for each location. Create the necessary IP address exclusions for the scope on both DHCP servers at each location.

○ B. Deploy three DHCP servers total and use a 33/33/34 address rule for each scope so that each DHCP server has addresses for its local scope and the two remote scopes. Create one scope for each location. Create the necessary client reservations for the scope on each DHCP server.

○ C. Deploy two DHCP servers at each location and use a 50/50 address rule for each scope between the two servers. Create one scope for each location. Create the necessary client reservations for the scope on both DHCP servers at each location.

○ D. Deploy two DHCP servers at the main office and use a 50/50 address rule for the scope, and configure two other systems to serve as relay agents. Create one scope for each location. Create the necessary client reservations for the scope on both DHCP servers.

Question 41

You are the network administrator for **gunderville.com**. You have been tasked with configuring all your branch offices and your main office to use DHCP.

Branch one has client systems running Windows XP Professional, Windows 2000 Professional, and Windows 98 and has two Windows Server 2003 systems. There is a DNS server at this location, and all local clients need to be configured to use it for name resolution. All clients have been configured to use DHCP. They are connected locally by a hub and connected to the main office with two different RFC 1542–compliant routers via separate private leased lines. The two Windows Server 2003 systems have manually assigned static IP addresses.

Branch two has client systems running Windows XP Professional, Windows 2000 Professional, and Windows 98 and has two Windows 2000 servers. There is a DNS server at this location, and all local clients need to be configured to use it for name resolution. All clients have been configured to use DHCP. They are connected locally by a hub and connected to the main office with two different RFC 1542–compliant routers via separate private leased lines. The two Windows 2000 Server systems have manually assigned static IP addresses.

The main office has client systems running Windows 2000 Professional and Windows XP Professional. It also has four Windows 2000 servers and four Windows Server 2003 systems, all interconnected by hubs internally. There is a DNS server at this location, and all clients need to be configured to use it for name resolution. All these clients (except the Windows 2000 servers and Windows Server 2003 systems) are configured to use DHCP. The Windows Server 2003 systems and the Windows 2000 SERVERS have manually assigned static IP addresses.

You have been asked to configure a DHCP server solution for your environment that allows all clients to obtain an IP address from a server hosting DHCP and that does not allow a single point of failure for addressing. Your configuration must also address your current business model needs, which require you to choose the least expensive option after ensuring no single point of failure. Which of the following is the best solution?

○ A. Deploy two DHCP servers at each location and use a 50/50 address rule for each scope between the two servers. Create one scope for each location. Create the necessary IP address exclusions for the scope on both DHCP servers at each location.

○ B. Deploy two DHCP servers at the main office. Create three different scopes (one for each location) and use a 50/50 address rule for each scope. Configure two other systems to serve as relay agents. Create the necessary client reservations for each scope on both DHCP servers.

○ C. Deploy two DHCP servers at each location and use a 50/50 address rule for each scope between the two servers. Create one scope for each location. Create the necessary client reservations for the scope on both DHCP servers at each location.

○ D. Deploy two DHCP servers at the main office. Create three different scopes (one for each location) and use a 50/50 address rule for each scope. Create the necessary IP address exclusions for each scope on both DHCP servers.

Question 42

You are the network administrator for **gunderville.com**. You have been tasked with configuring all your existing client areas to use DHCP.

Area one has client systems running Windows XP Professional, Windows 2000 Professional, and Windows 98 and has two Windows Server 2003 systems. There is a DNS server in this area, and all clients have been manually configured to use it for name resolution. All clients have been configured to use DHCP, and all are connected in parallel by two hubs. The two Windows Server 2003 systems have manually assigned static IP addresses.

Area two has client systems running Windows XP Professional, Windows 2000 Professional, and Windows 98 and has two Windows 2000 servers. There is a DNS server in this area, and all clients have been manually configured to use it for name resolution. All clients have been configured to use DHCP, and all are connected in parallel by two hubs. The two Windows 2000 Server systems have manually assigned static IP addresses.

Area three (the main server area) has client systems running Windows 2000 Professional and Windows XP Professional. It also has four Windows 2000 servers and four Windows Server 2003 systems, all interconnected by hubs internally. There is a DNS server in this area, and all clients have been manually configured to use it for name resolution. All clients use DHCP. The Windows 2000 servers and Windows Server 2003 systems have manually assigned static IP addresses.

You have been asked to configure a DHCP server solution for your environment that allows all clients to obtain an IP address from a server hosting the DHCP service and that does not allow a single point of failure for addressing. Your configuration must also address your current business model needs, which require you to choose the least expensive option after ensuring no single point of failure and make sure the actions taken involve the least amount of administrative effort. Which of the following is the best solution?

- ○ A. Deploy three DHCP servers total (one in each area), and use a 33/33/34 address rule for each scope so that each DHCP server has addresses for its local scope and the two remote scopes. You need to create the necessary IP address exclusions on each of the DHCP servers.

- ○ B. Deploy two DHCP servers in the main server area and use a 50/50 address rule for the scope. Create three different scopes—one scope for each location. You need to create the necessary client reservations on one DHCP server.

- ○ C. Deploy two DHCP servers in the main server area and use a 50/50 address rule for the scope. Configure two other systems to serve as relay agents. You need to create the necessary client reservations on both DHCP servers.

- ○ D. Deploy two DHCP servers in the main server area and use a 50/50 address rule for the scope. Create one scope for use. You need to create the necessary IP address exclusions on both DHCP servers.

Question 43

You are the network architect for **gunderville.com**. You have been tasked with configuring all your existing client areas to use DHCP.

Area one has client systems running Windows XP Professional, Windows 2000 Professional, and Windows 98 and has two Windows Server 2003 systems. There is a DNS server in this area, and all clients have been manually configured to use it for name resolution. All clients have been configured to use DHCP, and all are connected in parallel by two hubs. The two Windows Server 2003 systems have manually assigned static IP addresses.

Area two has client systems running Windows XP Professional, Windows 2000 Professional, and Windows 98 and has two Windows 2000 servers. There is a DNS server in this area, and all clients have been manually configured to use it for name resolution. All clients have been configured to use DHCP, and all are connected in parallel by two hubs. The two Windows 2000 Server systems have manually assigned static IP addresses.

Area three (the main server area) has client systems running Windows 2000 Professional and Windows XP Professional. It also has four Windows 2000 servers and four Windows Server 2003 systems, all interconnected by hubs internally. This location is the only place with domain controllers for users to log in. There is a DNS server in this area, and all clients have been manually configured to use it for name resolution. All clients use DHCP. The Windows 2000 servers and Windows Server 2003 systems have manually assigned static IP addresses.

Your design calls for the installation of one DHCP server in each area that is not a member of the domain. After the systems engineers complete the server installation of one Windows Server 2003 system running DHCP, they assign it a dynamic IP address from its own scope and turn the system over to the administrator of the area. What is the result of this implementation?

○ A. The DHCP servers will be installed and be authorized in the domain.

○ B. The DHCP servers will be installed, but they will not be authorized in the domain because the DHCPINFORM messages cannot reach the domain controllers.

○ C. The DHCP servers will be installed, but they will not be authorized in the domain because the servers are using a dynamic address; they need to have a fixed IP address.

○ D. The DHCP servers will be installed, but they will not be authorized in the domain because the servers are using a dynamic address; they need to use an APIPA address for that subnet.

Question 44

You are the network architect for **gunderville.com**. You have been tasked with configuring all your existing branch offices to use DHCP.

Branch one has client systems running Windows XP Professional, Windows 2000 Professional, and Windows 98 and has two Windows Server 2003 systems. There is a DNS server in this area, and all clients have been manually configured to use it for name resolution. All clients have been configured to use DHCP. They are connected locally by a hub and connected in parallel by two routers to the company headquarters. Neither router meets the RFC 1542 specification. The two Windows Server 2003 systems have manually assigned static IP addresses.

Branch two has client systems running Windows XP Professional, Windows 2000 Professional, and Windows 98 and has two Windows 2000 servers. There is a DNS server in this area, and all clients have been manually configured to use it for name resolution. All clients have been configured to use DHCP. They are connected locally by a hub and connected in parallel by two routers to the company headquarters. Neither router meets the RFC 1542 specification. The two Windows 2000 Server systems have manually assigned static IP addresses.

The main server area at the company headquarters has client systems running Windows 2000 Professional and Windows XP Professional. It also has four Windows 2000 servers and four Windows Server 2003 systems, all interconnected by hubs internally. This location is the only place with domain controllers for users to log in. There is a DNS server in this area, and all clients have been manually configured to use it for name resolution. All clients use DHCP. The Windows 2000 servers and Windows Server 2003 systems have manually assigned static IP addresses.

Your design calls for the installation of one DHCP server in each area that is not a member of the domain. After the systems engineers complete the server installation of the Windows Server 2003 system running DHCP, they assign it a fixed IP address and turn the system over to the subnet administrator. What is the result of this implementation?

○ A. The DHCP servers will be installed and be authorized in the domain.

○ B. The DHCP servers will be installed, but they will not be authorized in the domain because the DHCPINFORM messages cannot reach the domain controllers.

○ C. The DHCP servers will be installed, but they will not be authorized in the domain because the servers are using a fixed address; they need to have a dynamic IP address from their own scope.

○ D. The DHCP servers will be installed, but they will not be authorized in the domain because the servers are using a fixed IP address; they need to use an APIPA address for that subnet.

Question 45

You are the network architect for **gunderville.com**. You have been tasked with configuring all your existing branch offices to use DHCP.

Branch one has client systems running Windows XP Professional, Windows 2000 Professional, and Windows 98 and has two Windows Server 2003 systems. There is a DNS server in this area, and all clients have been manually configured to use it for name resolution. All clients have been configured to use DHCP. They are connected locally by a hub and connected in parallel by two routers to the company headquarters. Neither router meets the RFC 1542 specification. The two Windows Server 2003 systems have manually assigned static IP addresses.

Branch two has client systems running Windows XP Professional, Windows 2000 Professional, and Windows 98 and has two Windows 2000 servers. There is a DNS server in this area, and all clients have been manually configured to use it for name resolution. All clients have been configured to use DHCP and all are connected locally by a hub and then in parallel by two routers back to the company headquarters. Neither router meets the RFC 1542 specification. The two Windows 2000 Server systems have manually assigned static IP addresses.

The main server area at the company headquarters has client systems running Windows 2000 Professional and Windows XP Professional. It also has four Windows 2000 servers and four Windows Server 2003 systems, all interconnected by hubs internally. This location is the only place with domain controllers for users to log in. There is a DNS server in this area, and all clients have been manually configured to use it for name resolution. All clients use DHCP. The Windows 2000 servers and Windows Server 2003 systems have manually assigned static IP addresses.

Your design calls for the installation of one DHCP server in each area that is not a member of the domain. Branch one and two will each have one DHCP relay agent installed.

After the systems engineers complete the server installation of a Windows Server 2003 system running DHCP, they assign it a fixed IP address and turn the system over to the administrator of the main server. This administrator is a member of the DHCP Administrators group and will authorize the DHCP server. What is the result of this implementation?

○ A. The DHCP servers will be installed and be authorized in the domain.

○ B. The DHCP servers will be installed, but they will not be authorized in the domain because the DHCPINFORM messages cannot reach the domain controllers.

○ C. The DHCP servers will be installed, but they will not be authorized in the domain because the administrator assigned cannot complete the task.

○ D. The DHCP servers will be installed, but they will not be authorized in the domain because the servers are using a fixed address; they need to use an APIPA address for that subnet.

Question 46

You are the network architect for **gunderville.com**. You have been tasked with planning and deploying Windows Server 2003 DNS servers on your network to replace the current BIND DNS service.

You have determined the number of zones that the DNS server named DNS1 is expected to host, and the size of the zone, and the approximate number of resource records to be used in the zone. Which of the following issues need to be addressed for this DNS server? (Choose three.)

❑ A. Whether the DNS server has more than one NIC installed.

❑ B. How many client requests the server needs to address.

❑ C. The number of subnets the DNS server is responsible for.

❑ D. The number of DHCP server authorization checks the DNS server needs to address.

❑ E. The number of Global Catalog server references the DNS server needs to address.

Question 47

You are the network architect for **gunderville.com**. You have been tasked with planning and deploying Windows Server 2003 DNS servers on your network to replace the current BIND DNS service.

You have determined the number of zones that the DNS server named DNS1 is expected to host, and the size of the zone, and the approximate number of resource records to be used in the zone.

You also need to assess the amount of RAM the DNS server needs, based on typical usage. Assuming 250,000 resource records (maximum) are needed for your environment, what is the expected amount of RAM the DNS service will use (beyond the minimum system requirements for the Windows Server 2003 operating system).

○ A. 10MB

○ B. 12MB

○ C. 15MB

○ D. 25MB

Question 48

You are the network architect for **gunderville.com**. You have been tasked with planning and deploying Windows Server 2003 DNS servers on your network to replace the current BIND DNS service.

You have determined the number of zones that the DNS server named DNS1 is expected to host, the size of the zone, and the approximate number of resource records to be used in the zone.

You also need to assess the physical placement of your DNS servers. For DNS1, the server is not expected to be promoted to a domain controller, as all the domain controllers have been deployed at this location. What other factors should you consider for DNS server placement? (Choose two.)

❏ A. What will happen if the local DNS server stops responding.

❏ B. What effects zone transfers will have on the network.

❏ C. The number of DHCP server authorization checks the DNS server needs to address.

❏ D. The number of Global Catalog server references the DNS server needs to address.

Question 49

You are the network architect for **gunderville.com**. You have been tasked with configuring all your existing branch offices to use DHCP.

Branch one has client systems running Windows XP Professional, Windows 2000 Professional, and Windows 98 and has two Windows Server 2003 systems. There are two DHCP servers on this site: DHCP1 and DHCP2.

You have created a scope and configured leasing IP addresses for six days. The scope uses a subnet mask of 255.255.255.0. Client reservations and the necessary IP address exclusions have been added to this scope.

Because of increased security issues, you have segmented certain networks and need to shorten the scope to a four-day lease. You also need to reconfigure the subnet mask to 255.255.255.224 in an effort to segment the network into smaller sections. Which of the following steps should you take to reconfigure this scope? Choose steps that accomplish this goal and require the least amount of administrative effort. (Choose four.)

- ❑ A. Delete the existing scope on both DHCP servers.
- ❑ B. Delete the existing scope on one DHCP server.
- ❑ C. Create a new scope on both DHCP servers.
- ❑ D. Create the client reservations as required on one DHCP server.
- ❑ E. Create the client reservations as required on both DHCP servers.
- ❑ F. Create the IP address exclusions as required on one DHCP server.
- ❑ G. Create the IP address exclusions as required on both DHCP servers.

Question 50

You are the network architect for **gunderville.com**. You have been tasked with planning and deploying Windows Server 2003 DNS servers on your network to replace the current BIND DNS service.

You need to determine which type of DNS server would work best for a remote office with a limited amount of available bandwidth. From the following choices, select the DNS server type that is best suited for this location.

- ○ A. Caching-only DNS server
- ○ B. Non-recursive DNS server
- ○ C. Forward-only DNS server
- ○ D. Conditional-forwarder DNS server

Question 51

You are the network architect for **gunderville.com**. You have been tasked with planning and deploying Windows Server 2003 DNS servers on your network to replace the current BIND DNS service.

You are reviewing a test installation of one Windows Server 2003 DNS server at a remote location. The DNS server has been configured to resolve a DNS query by using recursive lookup when it cannot resolve a DNS name lookup locally. Which of the following choices describes this type of DNS server implementation?

○ A. Caching-only DNS server

○ B. Non-recursive DNS server

○ C. Forward-only DNS server

○ D. Conditional-forwarder DNS server

Question 52

You are the network architect for your Windows Server 2003 domain, which is running at the domain functional level. You have been tasked with planning and deploying Windows Server 2003 DNS servers on your network to replace the current BIND DNS service.

You are reviewing a test installation of a Windows Server 2003 DNS server at a remote location. The DNS server has been configured to use low-level DNS security. Which of the following actions can be defined in this type of DNS implementation? (Choose four.)

❑ A. DNS can be stored in Active Directory–integrated zones but is not required.

❑ B. UDP and TCP port 53 are open on your network firewall.

❑ C. All DNS servers will be configured to use forwarders to point to a specific list of internal DNS servers when they cannot resolve names locally.

❑ D. The DNS servers limit zone transfers to servers listed in the name server (NS) resource records in their zones only. They will be configured to listen on specified IP addresses.

❑ E. Standard DNS resolution is performed by all DNS servers in your network, and all DNS servers are configured with root hints pointing to the root servers for the Internet.

❑ F. All DNS servers are configured to listen on all their IP addresses, and they will permit zone transfers to any server.

❑ G. Dynamic updating is allowed for all DNS zones, and cache pollution prevention is not enabled.

❑ H. Dynamic updating is not allowed for all DNS zones, and cache pollution prevention is enabled.

Question 53

You are the network architect for your Windows Server 2003 domain, which is running at the domain functional level. You have been tasked with planning and deploying Windows Server 2003 DNS servers on your network to replace the current BIND DNS service.

You are reviewing a test installation of a Windows Server 2003 DNS server at a remote location. The DNS server has been configured to use medium-level DNS security. Which of the following actions can be defined in this type of DNS implementation? (Choose three.)

❑ A. DNS can be stored in Active Directory–integrated zones but is not required.

❑ B. UDP and TCP port 53 are open on your network firewall.

❑ C. All DNS servers will be configured to use forwarders to point to a specific list of internal DNS servers when they cannot resolve names locally.

❑ D. The DNS servers limit zone transfers to servers listed in the name server (NS) resource records in their zones only. They will be configured to listen on specified IP addresses.

❑ E. Standard DNS resolution is performed by all DNS servers in your network, and all DNS servers are configured with root hints pointing to the root servers for the Internet.

Question 54

You are the network architect for your Windows Server 2003 domain, which is running at the domain functional level. You have been tasked with planning and deploying Windows Server 2003 DNS servers on your network to replace the current BIND DNS service.

You are reviewing some of the material on highly secure DNS server implementations. What are the two main points of consideration for these types of DNS servers? (Choose two.)

❑ A. Highly secure DNS servers are always installed as domain controllers.

❑ B. Highly secure DNS servers must never be installed as domain controllers.

❑ C. The DNS infrastructure needs to be configured with no Internet communication with internal DNS servers.

❑ D. The DNS infrastructure must allow secured Internet communication with internal DNS servers.

Question 55

You are the network architect for a new deployment of Windows Server 2003. You are currently in the planning stages of the DNS design for this new domain, and you need to consider the naming convention to be used before you implement a registered name for your company's use. Which of the following factors should you consider? (Choose three.)

❑ A. Whether to use RFC 1123 to define characters in the DNS namespace.

❑ B. Whether BIND or Windows Server 2003 DNS will be used.

❑ C. You need to register a unique domain name for your internal-only DNS name space.

❑ D. You need to register a unique domain name for your DNS namespace that will be exposed to the Internet.

❑ E. You need to conform to Internet naming standards for your internal-only DNS namespace.

❑ F. You need to conform to Internet naming standards for your DNS namespace that will be exposed to the Internet.

Question 56

You are the domain administrator for **gunderville.com**. You are currently troubleshooting an intermittent network connectivity problem between your main company headquarters and one of your branch offices.

Branch one has client systems running Windows XP Professional, Windows 2000 Professional, and Windows 98 and has two Windows Server 2003 systems. There is one DHCP server on this site, DHCP1. All systems on this site are interconnected by hubs and connected to the company headquarters via a router.

The company headquarters has client systems running Windows XP Professional, Windows 2000 Professional, and Windows 98 and has a few Windows Server 2003 systems. This site has two DHCP servers: DHCP7 and DHCP8. All systems on this site are interconnected by hubs and connected to the Internet via a Windows Server 2003 system running RRAS.

All systems at the company headquarters can successfully connect to one another and to the Internet, but they can no longer connect to the branch office. All systems at branch one can successfully connect to one another, but they cannot reach the company headquarters systems or the Internet.

Which of the following tools can be used to begin your troubleshooting efforts centered on client IP address issues? (Choose three.)

❑ A. **PING**

❑ B. **IPCONFIG**

❑ C. **NBTSTAT**

❑ D. **ROUTE**

❑ E. **PATHPING**

❑ F. **HOSTNAME**

Question 57

You are the domain administrator for **gunderville.com**. You are currently troubleshooting an intermittent network connectivity problem between your main company headquarters and one of your branch offices.

Branch one has client systems running Windows XP Professional, Windows 2000 Professional, and Windows 98 and has two Windows Server 2003 systems. There is one DHCP server on this site, DHCP1. All systems on this site are interconnected by hubs and connected to the company headquarters via a router.

The company headquarters has client systems running Windows XP Professional, Windows 2000 Professional, and Windows 98 and has a few Windows Server 2003 systems. There are two DHCP servers on this site: DHCP7 and DHCP8. All systems on this site are interconnected by hubs and connected to the Internet via a Windows Server 2003 system running RRAS.

All systems at the company headquarters can successfully connect to one another and to the Internet, but they can no longer connect to branch one. All systems at branch one can successfully connect to one another, but they cannot reach the company headquarters systems or the Internet.

You decide to test connectivity between systems at branch one and the default gateway to the company headquarters. Which simple tool is the best choice for testing connectivity?

○ A. **PING**

○ B. **IPCONFIG**

○ C. **NBTSTAT**

○ D. **ROUTE**

Question 58

You are the domain administrator for **gunderville.com**. You are currently troubleshooting an intermittent network connectivity problem between your main company headquarters and one of your branch offices.

Branch one has client systems running Windows XP Professional, Windows 2000 Professional, and Windows 98 and has two Windows Server 2003 systems. There is one DHCP server on this site, DHCP1. All systems on this site are interconnected by hubs and connected to the company headquarters via a router.

The company headquarters has client systems running Windows XP Professional, Windows 2000 Professional, and Windows 98 and has a few Windows Server 2003 systems. There are two DHCP servers on this site: DHCP7 and DHCP8. All systems on this site are interconnected by hubs and connected to the Internet via a Windows Server 2003 system running RRAS.

All systems at the company headquarters can successfully connect to one another and to the Internet, but they can no longer connect to branch one. All systems at branch one can successfully connect to one another, but they cannot reach the company headquarters systems or the Internet.

You decide to test connectivity between the systems at branch one and the default gateway to the company headquarters. You log in at WORKSTATION1, enter **PING LOCALHOST**, and receive the expected replies. You then PING WORKSTATION2, which is the next client system you're using for your testing, and receive the expected replies. You attempt to PING 157.199.23.1, which is the near side of the router that leads to the company headquarters, and you receive the following response:

```
Request timed out.
```

You log in at WORKSTATION2, enter **PING LOCALHOST**, and receive the expected replies. You then PING WORKSTATION1, which is the next client system you're using for your testing, and receive the expected replies. You attempt to PING 157.199.23.1, which is the near side of the router that leads to the company headquarters, and you receive the following response:

```
Request timed out.
```

You then call your counterpart at company headquarters and ask him if he can PING 157.199.24.1, which is the near side of the router that leads to branch office one. He receives the expected replies.

You ask him to PING 157.199.23.1, which is the near side of the router from your location but the far side from his location. He receives the expected replies.

You ask him to PING 157.199.25.1, which is the near side of the router from his location to the RRAS server. He receives the expected replies.

You ask him to PING RRAS1, which is the name of the RRAS server on the far side of the router. He receives the expected replies.

At this point, what appears to be the most likely cause of this problem?

○ A. Routing.

○ B. Name resolution.

○ C. Default gateway configuration from company headquarters to branch one.

○ D. IP address assignment.

○ E. Not enough troubleshooting has taken place to determine the most likely cause of this problem.

Question 59

You are the domain administrator for **gunderville.com**. You are currently troubleshooting an intermittent network connectivity problem between your main company headquarters and one of your branch offices.

Branch one has client systems running Windows XP Professional, Windows 2000 Professional, and Windows 98 and has two Windows Server 2003 systems. There is one DHCP server on this site, DHCP1. All systems on this site are interconnected by hubs and connected to the company headquarters via a router.

The company headquarters has client systems running Windows XP Professional, Windows 2000 Professional, and Windows 98 and has a few Windows Server 2003 systems. There are two DHCP servers on this site: DHCP7 and DHCP8. All systems on this site are interconnected by hubs and to the Internet via a Windows Server 2003 system running RRAS.

All systems at the company headquarters can successfully connect to one another and to the Internet, but they can no longer connect to branch one.

All systems at branch one can successfully connect to one another, but they cannot reach the company headquarters systems or the Internet.

You decide to test connectivity between the systems at branch one and the default gateway to the company headquarters.

You log in at WORKSTATION1, which is a Windows 2000 client, enter **PING LOCALHOST**, and receive the expected replies. You then decide to PING WORKSTATION2, which is the next client system you're testing, and receive the expected replies. You attempt to PING 157.199.23.1, which is the near side of the router that leads to the company headquarters, and you receive the following response:

```
Request timed out.
```

You log in at WORKSTATION2, which is a Windows XP system, enter **PING LOCALHOST**, and receive the expected replies. You then decide to PING WORK-STATION1, which is the next client system you're testing, and receive the expected replies. You attempt to PING 157.199.23.1, which is the near side of the router that leads to the company headquarters, and you receive the following response:

```
Request timed out.
```

You call your counterpart at the company headquarters and ask if he can PING 157.199.24.1, which is the near side of the router that leads to branch one. He receives the expected replies.

You ask him to PING 157.199.23.1, which is the near side of the router from your location but the far side from his. He receives the expected replies.

You ask him to PING 157.199.25.1, which is the near side of the router from his location to the RRAS server. He receives the expected replies.

You ask him to PING RRAS1, which is the name of the RRAS server on the far side of the router. He receives the expected replies.

You then decide to renew your IP address on WORKSTATION1 and WORKSTA-TION2.

How can you accomplish this task with the least amount of administrative effort?

○ A. Run **Winipcfg** on each client.

○ B. Run **Ipconfig /new /all** on each client.

○ C. Run **Ipconfig /release** and then **Ipconfig /renew** on each client.

○ D. Run **Winipcfg /release** and then **Winipcfg /renew** on each client.

Question 60

You are the domain administrator for **gunderville.com**. You are currently troubleshooting an intermittent network connectivity problem between your main company headquarters and one of your branch offices.

Branch one has client systems running Windows XP Professional, Windows 2000 Professional, and Windows 98 and has two Windows Server 2003 systems. There is one DHCP server on this site, DHCP1. All systems on this site are interconnected by hubs and connected to the company headquarters via a router.

The company headquarters has client systems running Windows XP Professional, Windows 2000 Professional, and Windows 98 and has a few Windows Server 2003 systems. There are two DHCP servers on this site: DHCP7 and DHCP8. All systems on this site are interconnected by hubs and to the Internet via a Windows Server 2003 system running RRAS.

All systems at the company headquarters can successfully connect to one another and to the Internet, but they can no longer connect to branch one.

All systems at branch one can successfully connect to one another, but they cannot reach the company headquarters systems or the Internet.

You decide to test connectivity between the systems at branch one and the default gateway to the company headquarters.

You log in at WORKSTATION1, enter **PING LOCALHOST**, and receive the expected replies. You then decide to PING WORKSTATION2, which is the next client system you're testing, and receive the expected replies. You attempt to PING 157.199.23.1, which is the near side of the router that leads to the company headquarters, and receive the following response:

```
Request timed out.
```

You log in at WORKSTATION2 and PING LOCALHOST and receive the expected replies. You then decide to PING WORKSTATION1, which is the next client system you're testing, and receive the expected replies. You attempt to PING 157.199.23.1, which is the near side of the router that leads to the company headquarters, and receive the following response:

```
Request timed out.
```

You then call your counterpart at the company headquarters and ask if he can PING 157.199.24.1, which is the near side of the router that leads to branch one. He receives the expected replies.

You ask him to PING 157.199.23.1, which is the near side of the router from your location but is the far side from his. He receives the expected replies.

You ask him to PING 157.199.25.1 which is the near side of the router from his location out to the Routing and Remote Access server. He receives the expected replies.

You ask him to PING RRAS1, which is the name of the RRAS server on the far side of the router. He receives the expected replies.

You then decide to renew your IP address on WORKSTATION1 and WORKSTATION2.

You have checked that the renewal of IP addressing was successful by using **IPCONFIG /all** and have received the following information on WORKSTATION1:

Host name: WORKSTATION1

Node type: Hybrid

IP routing enabled: No

WINS proxy enabled: No

Description: D-Link DFE-550TX fast ethernet 10/100 adapter

Physical address: 00-50-BA-F8-B5-93

DHCP enabled: Yes

IP address: 169.254.15.6

Subnet mask: 255.255.0.0

You attempt to PING the default gateway IP address of the router that leads to the company headquarters, but you are still receiving "Request timed out" responses. You can PING WORKSTATION2 with success.

From the following choices, what is the most likely reason you still cannot hit the default gateway by PINGing the IP address? (Please choose the single best answer.)

○ A. WINS proxy is not enabled.

○ B. IP routing is not enabled.

○ C. **Ipconfig /release** and **Ipconfig /renew** were not successful.

○ D. You are not receiving an IP address from the DHCP server.

9

Answers to
Practice Exam 1

1. A	**31.** D
2. B	**32.** C
3. A, B, C	**33.** A
4. C, E, G	**34.** E
5. C, D	**35.** E
6. D	**36.** B
7. A, C	**37.** C
8. A, C, D, F	**38.** D
9. C	**39.** D
10. C	**40.** A
11. D	**41.** D
12. B, D, G	**42.** D
13. B	**43.** C
14. C	**44.** B
15. E	**45.** C
16. B, F	**46.** A, B, C
17. A, B, D	**47.** D
18. B	**48.** A, B
19. C	**49.** A, C, E, G
20. A, D	**50.** A
21. B, D	**51.** C
22. B	**52.** B, E, F, G
23. D, E	**53.** C, D, E
24. A	**54.** A, C
25. D	**55.** A, D, F
26. B, C	**56.** A, B, E
27. D	**57.** A
28. B, C, F	**58.** E
29. D	**59.** C
30. A	**60.** D

Question 1

The correct answer is A. The conceptual design phase of the network design process takes into consideration all the company's requirements and the users' needs. The logical design phase only begins to outline a solution for the company's needs. The physical design phase outlines the services and technologies needed to meet the company's requirements and users' needs.

Question 2

The correct answer is B. The conceptual design phase of the network design process takes into consideration all the company's requirements and the users' needs. The logical design phase only begins to outline a solution for the company's needs. The physical design phase outlines the required services and technologies needed to service the company and end user needs. The physical design phase outlines the services and technologies needed to meet the company's requirements and users' needs.

Question 3

The correct answers are A, B, and C. When you are planning your physical network diagram, you must consider many factors; often they depend on your existing design and your future plans for the network. You should diagram generic physical equipment, such as your current wiring scheme and wiring types, which might include analog lines, wireless implementations (if any), Integrated Services Digital Network (ISDN) lines, Asymmetric Digital Subscriber Line (ADSL) lines, Integrate Digital Subscriber Line (IDSL) lines, Symmetric Digital Subscriber Line (SDSL) lines, fiber-optic cables, and so forth. Items such as static and dynamic IP addressing schemes and the subnet layout aren't normally included at this stage.

You should also include server information and details, such as the roles the system holds, the services it hosts on the network, the system's NetBIOS name, DNS name, and IP address. You should also indicate whether this server holds any major roles for the domain or forest and include the firmware levels of all your network devices and any special configuration requirements.

Question 4

The correct answers are C, E, and G. When you are planning details to include in your physical network diagram, you must consider many factors; often they depend on your existing design and your future plans for the network.

Your diagram should include generic physical equipment, such as your current wiring scheme. Items such as static and dynamic IP addressing schemes and the subnet layout aren't normally included at this stage.

You also need to outline where all your hubs, switches, routers, bridges, and proxy servers are on the network so that you can form a decent topology map. You should also indicate whether this server holds any major roles for the domain or forest and include the firmware levels of all your network devices and any special configuration requirements.

Question 5

The correct answers are C and D. The systems will not be able to call up Web sites via DNS name, and client systems will not be able to call up Web sites via IP name or DNS name because the high ports (above 1023) have been disabled. Ports above 1023 allow connections coming in from Web sites after traffic has left a system via port 80.

Question 6

The correct answer is D. There are three categories of NetBIOS services: the Name Service, the Session Service, and the Datagram Service. The NetBIOS name service uses TCP port 137 and allows an application to confirm its own NetBIOS name to make sure it is unique; therefore, answer B is incorrect. The NetBIOS datagram service uses UDP port 138; therefore, answer C is incorrect. Answer A is incorrect because by default the NetBIOS name service doesn't use that port.

Question 7

The correct answers are A and C. A typical IPv4 address looks like this: 123.45.67.222. Answers B and D are incorrect because an IPv4 address cannot contain a value above 255.

Question 8

The correct answers are A, C, D, and F. There are three ways to represent IPv6 addresses as text. The following preferred form consists of hexadecimal values of the address's eight 16-bit pieces:

```
FEDC:BA98:7654:3210:FEDC:BA98:7654:3210
1080:0:0:0:8:800:200C:417A
```

The valid hexadecimal characters are 0 through 9 and A through F. For
example, the following addresses

```
1080:0:0:0:8:800:200C:417A a unicast address
FF01:0:0:0:0:0:0:101 a multicast address
0:0:0:0:0:0:0:1 the loopback address
0:0:0:0:0:0:0:0 the unspecified addresses
```

Can be represented as

```
1080::8:800:200C:417A a unicast address
FF01::101 a multicast address
::1 the loopback address
:: the unspecified addresses
```

This is an IPv6 address in decimal-dot notation:

```
5.40.161.101.255.255.0.0.80.191.119.8.13.201.78.118
```

Using a colon-separated list of 16-bit values, the address looks like this:

```
0528:a165:ff00:50bf:7708:0dc9:4d76
```

In some cases, it's common for addresses to contain long strings of 0 bits.
These addresses are cumbersome to write, however, so a special syntax is
available to compress the zeros. Using :: indicates multiple groups of 16 bits
of zeros. The :: can appear only once in an address. It can also be used to
compress leading and trailing zeros in an address. The following address has
long strings of 0 bits:

```
ff01:8a27:030a:0000:0000:0000:3a1f
```

Using the :: notation to represent all bits set to 0, the address changes to
this:

```
ff01:8a27:030a::3a1f
```

Question 9

The correct answer is C. Given the Class A IPv4 address range of 10.0.0.0 and allowing for no more than 11 subnet bits, you can use a subnet mask of 255.224.0.0 as follows:

```
IP address: 10.0.0.0
Address class: A
Network address: 10.0.0.0
Subnet address: 10.0.0.0
Subnet mask: 255.224.0.0
Subnet bit mask: nnnnnnnn.nnnhhhhh.hhhhhhhh.hhhhhhhh
Subnet bits: 11
Host bits: 21
Possible number of subnets: 8
Hosts per subnet : 2097150
```

Question 10

The correct answer is C. Given the Class B IPv4 address range of 168.10.0.0, you can use a subnet mask of 255.255.248.0 to create at least 32 subnetworks with up to 2,046 hosts per subnet. The subnet mask 255.255.248.0 is valid for the Class B IPv4 address range; therefore, answer A is incorrect. You can create up to 32 subnetworks; therefore, answer B is incorrect. The IPv4 address 168.10.0.0 is a valid Class B address range; therefore, answer D is incorrect.

Question 11

The correct answer is D. Given the Class C IPv4 address range of 192.199.199.0, you can use a subnet mask of 255.255.255.240 and create 16 subnetworks with 14 hosts per subnet. Because the question called for at least 17 subnetworks with at least 13 hosts per subnet, however, the only correct answer is D.

Question 12

The correct answers are B, D, and G. The Internet Assigned Numbers Authority (IANA) has reserved the following three blocks of IP address space for private Internets:

➤ 10.0.0.0–10.255.255.255 with the subnet mask 255.0.0.0

➤ 172.16.0.0–172.31.255.255 with the subnet mask 255.240.0.0

➤ 192.168.0.0–192.168.255.255 with the subnet mask 255.255.0.0

These addresses can be used by anyone setting up internal IP networks, such as a lab or home LAN behind a NAT or proxy server or a router. It is always safe to use them because routers on the Internet never forward packets coming from these addresses. Therefore, answers A, C, E, F, and H are incorrect.

Question 13

The correct answer is B. The buffer setting threshold for inbound packets, called the TCP/IP Receive Window Size, is set to 17,520 bytes on ethernet networks by default. When this threshold is met during a communications session between two clients, the receiving system sends an acknowledgement that data has been received to the sending system and repeats this message every 17,520 bytes until all the data has been transmitted. The TCP/IP Send Window Size is not the setting that needs to be reviewed; therefore, answer A is incorrect. Maximum Transmission Units (MTUs) are based on the type of network that is installed. Therefore, answer C is incorrect. Maximum Segment Size is the largest segment that can be carried in the MTU. Therefore, answer D is incorrect.

Question 14

The correct answer is C. Packet-switching networks are more efficient than circuit-switching systems if some amount of delay is acceptable. Circuit switching is a connection-oriented network in which a dedicated circuit is established for the duration of a transmission; therefore, answer A is incorrect. Packet relays and circuit routing do not match this description; therefore, answers B and D are incorrect.

Question 15

The correct answer is E. Your primary objective is to successfully run scans on all systems in the enterprise for application vulnerability checks against Microsoft Office XP. This objective cannot be met because MBSA cannot scan Windows 98 systems locally or remotely. Therefore, none of the objectives have been met, so answers A, B, C, and D are incorrect.

Question 16

The correct answers are B and F. You can run ICS on your Windows 98 and Windows XP systems. Windows Me and Windows 2000 Professional support ICS, but they are not deployed in your enterprise; therefore, answers D and E are incorrect. Windows NT and 95 do not have ICS; therefore, answers A and C are incorrect.

Question 17

The correct answers are A, B, and D. Also known as thin ethernet, ThinNet, or Cheapernet, 10Base2 uses RG-58 coaxial cable in a bus topology. 10Base5 is the ethernet specification for thick coaxial cable, which transmits signals at 10Mbps with a distance limit of 500 meters per segment without the use of a repeater. Therefore, answer E is incorrect. 10Base2 is the ethernet specification for thin coaxial cable, which transmits signals at 10Mbps with a distance limit of 185 meters per segment without the use of a repeater. Therefore, answer F is incorrect.

Question 18

The correct answer is B. DHCP automatic assignment with reservations is used to "dynamically" assign a DHCP client with the same specific reserved IP address each time the client starts up by using the DHCP service. This allows administrators to automatically assign a static IP address to these systems without actually having to set each system with all the parameters (default gateway, DNS servers, and so on), as is done in manual IP address assignment. In manual IP address assignment, an administrator or similarly delegated person manually enters a static IP address and other subsequent information, such as subnet mask and default gateway, DNS server, WINS server, and so forth. Therefore, answer A is incorrect. DHCP automatic assignment is used to "dynamically" assign any DHCP clients with randomly available IP addresses from available scopes each time they start up by using the DHCP service. This allows administrators to automatically assign clients with IP addresses without actually having to set each system with all the parameters, as is done in manual IP address assignment. Therefore, answer C is incorrect. APIPA does not accomplish the objective; therefore, answer D is incorrect.

Question 19

The correct answer is C. OSPF protocol is a better choice than either version of RIP when the network is designed with redundant paths between locations or when the number of subnets in the overall design is more than 50 routers total. Therefore, answers A and B are incorrect. Border Gateway Protocol (BGP) is a protocol for exchanging routing information between gateway hosts on the Internet; therefore, answer D is incorrect.

Question 20

The correct answers are A and D. Some switches operate at the Data Link layer of the OSI model (Layer 2) and form a border to your collision domains. Bridges also work at Layer 2 and function in the same manner. Layer 3 switches, routers, and hubs are not used for setting up collision domains; therefore, answers B, C, and E are incorrect.

Question 21

The correct answers are B and D. Some switches operate at Layer 2 and form a border to your collision domains. Bridges also work at Layer 2 and function in the same manner. Layer 3 switches, routers, and hubs are not used to segment broadcast domains; therefore, answers A, C, and E are incorrect.

Question 22

The correct answer is B. You should implement Layer 3 switches to create a VLAN. Layer 2 switches, routers, and collision domains do not form a border for broadcast domains; therefore, answers A, C, and D are incorrect.

Question 23

The correct answers are D and E. You cannot connect devices through a hub that feeds back to a switch when the port on the switch is running in Full Duplex mode. Therefore, only answers D and E are correct. None of the other choices explains why user three is having connectivity problems.

Question 24

The correct answer is A. The primary objective of performing the security analysis by checking whether any user accounts are using blank or simple passwords has been met. The secondary objectives have been met by installing MBSA on one system and running scans over the network (which requires the least amount of administrative effort) and determining whether the W3SVC (WWW) and SMTPSVC (SMTP) services are installed and enabled on the systems. Because all the objectives have been met, answers B, C, and D are incorrect.

Question 25

The correct answer is D. Because MBSA cannot perform local scans of Windows NT 4 systems, you cannot meet the primary objective. Installing MBSA on each system doesn't meet the secondary objective of expending the least amount of administrative effort. Although the Check for Unnecessary Services part of the scan can check for the W3SVC (WWW) and SMTPSVC (SMTP) services to determine whether any services listed in the services.txt file are installed, it cannot be run locally on the Windows NT 4 system, so the other secondary objective of scanning all systems for these services has not been met either.

Question 26

The correct answers are B and C. Bridges and Layer 2 switches operate at the Data Link layer (Layer 2 of the OSI model) and automatically forward all broadcast traffic received; therefore, subnets one and two will be part of the same broadcast domain. Although Layer 2 switches can be found at the borders of collision domains, they do not form a border of a broadcast domain. Because Layer 2 switches form the borders of collision domains, subnets one and two will be in different collision domains. Only Layer 3 devices, such as routers or Layer 3 switches, form a border of a broadcast domain. Subnets one and two will not be in different broadcast domains or be part of the same collision domain, so answers A and D are incorrect.

Question 27

The correct answer is D. Because Layer 3 devices, such as routers or Layer 3 switches, form a border of a broadcast domain, the offices will be in different broadcast domains. Layer 3 switches route packets at Layer 3 and forward frames at Layer 2. In most cases, Layer 3 switches are used to connect VLANs or to subdivide larger LANs into smaller broadcast domains; however, with very small branch offices, this solution would work, so answer A is not correct. The offices will be in different collision and broadcast domains, so answers B and C are incorrect.

Question 28

The correct answers are B, C, and F. By installing ISA Server on one server and running it in Integrated mode, you will be able to use the server as a proxy to the Internet for hosts on the network and protect them from the Internet at the same time. Configuring the IP address of the ISA server as the proxy server in Internet Explorer on each client is the only way to get all systems connected to the Internet. Installing ISA Server on one server and running it in Firewall mode protects the systems from a security standpoint, but it doesn't allow clients to connect to the Internet.

Question 29

The correct answer is D. MS-CHAP v1 is the most correct answer for this question; all the other options are either less secure or involve making changes to client systems deployed in the enterprise. The main reason that MS-CHAP v1 must be used instead of the others as the "most secure" is that the network includes Windows 98 and Windows NT 4 systems.

Question 30

The correct answer is A. Because NAT is in use and provides IP address configuration information to clients in the form of an IP address, a subnet mask, a default gateway, and the IP address of a DNS server, the main reason this solution doesn't allow systems to connect to the Internet is because static IP addressing is being used. None of the other choices entirely explains the full reason for failing to connect to the Internet.

Question 31

The correct answer is D. When you set up RRAS and enable NAT, IP addresses and TCP/UDP port numbers of packets will be forwarded between systems on your internal network and the Internet. However, this solution cannot work when systems relocated in different broadcast domains because the clients cannot obtain IP addressing from the NAT server; they end up using APIPA addressing in all locations except the broadcast domain where the NAT server is set up. In that location, this solution will work and is why answer D is the most correct answer for this question. None of the other choices entirely explains the full reason for failing to connect to the Internet.

Question 32

The correct answer is C. When you set up RRAS and enable NAT, IP addresses and TCP/UDP port numbers of packets will be forwarded between systems on your internal network and the Internet. The main problem with this configuration is that the manual DNS entry causes name resolution issues with clients because they try to resolve names via their local DNS server instead of the DNS setting they would normally receive via NAT. This is the reason for answer C being correct. None of the other choices entirely explains the full reason for failing to connect to the Internet.

Question 33

The correct answer is A. By deploying two DHCP servers at each location and using a 50/50 address rule for each scope, you deal with the single-point-of-failure issue for addressing, which happens to be the single point out of each branch office. Your configuration also meets your current business model needs, which require you to choose the least expensive option after ensuring there's no single point of failure. The only option is answer A, which has you deploy two DHCP servers at each location and use a 50/50 address rule for the scope. Deploying three servers, as in answers B and C, does not address your current business model needs. Answer D does not eliminate the single point of failure of a network connection because the relay agents would not be able to assign IP addresses if they cannot forward requests to the two DHCP servers on one site when there is a connectivity issue.

Question 34

The correct answer is E. The main problem with this setup is that the demand-dial router (the Linksys DSL router) will hand out IP addresses at all times, even when the demand connection is not enabled. This setup will cause connectivity issues in the two remote locations, even when the private lease line is enabled. No matter which DHCP solution is implemented, in most cases it will compete with the DSL device for handing out addresses to clients. Because you have been asked to configure a DHCP server solution for your environment that allows all clients to obtain an IP address from DHCP and that does not allow a single point of failure for addressing, the only correct answer for this question is E. None of the other choices entirely or accurately describes what needs to be accomplished in this scenario.

Question 35

The correct answer is E. You should deploy two DHCP servers at the main office and use a 50/50 address rule for the scope. This allows you to deal with the single-point-of-failure issue for IP addressing, which focuses on the DHCP servers. Your configuration also meets your current business model needs, which require you to choose the least expensive option after ensuring no single point of failure. You do not need to configure two other systems to serve as relay agents because the RFC 1542–compliant router can be configured to forward DHCP broadcast messages on its own. You will not be able to use just a single scope because each location needs to have different DNS and default gateway information supplied; this cannot be done via a single scope. None of the other choices entirely or accurately describes what needs to be accomplished in this scenario.

Question 36

The correct answer is B. By deploying two DHCP servers in the area three (the main server area) and using a 50/50 address rule for the scope, you deal with the single-point-of-failure issue for addressing. Your configuration also meets your current business model needs, which require you to choose the least expensive option after ensuring no single point of failure. You do not need to configure two other systems to serve as relay agents because hubs forward DHCP broadcast messages on their own. This makes answer B the best solution for this scenario.

Question 37

The correct answer is C. By deploying two DHCP servers at each location and using a 50/50 address rule for each scope, you deal with the single-point-of-failure issue for addressing. Your configuration also meets your current business model needs, which require you to choose the least expensive option after ensuring no single point of failure; this makes answer C the best choice for this scenario. None of the other choices fully addresses your current business model needs or involves the least amount of administrative effort.

Question 38

The correct answer is D. The best option is to deploy two DHCP servers at the main office, create three different scopes (one for each location), and use a 50/50 address rule for each scope. When you create the necessary client reservations for each scope on both DHCP servers, you ensure that no addresses in the scope are the same as statically assigned ones and that all clients can obtain an IP address from a server hosting DHCP. This design does not allow a single point of failure for addressing because three different scopes (one for each location) are used with the 50/50 address rule for each scope. By using just two DHCP servers at the main office, the solution also addresses your current business model needs, which require you to choose the least expensive option after ensuring no single point of failure. None of the choices fully addresses your current business model needs or makes sure the actions taken involve the least amount of administrative effort.

Question 39

The correct answer is D. By deploying two DHCP servers in the main area and using a 50/50 address rule for the scope, you deal with the single-point-of-failure issue for addressing, which is the DHCP servers. Your configuration also meets your current business model needs, which require you to choose the least expensive option after ensuring no single point of failure. None of the other choices fully addresses your current business model needs or makes sure that actions taken involve the least amount of administrative effort.

Question 40

The correct answer is A. By deploying two DHCP servers at each location and using a 50/50 address rule for each scope, you deal with the single-point-of-failure issue for addressing, which happens to be the single point out of each branch office. Your configuration also meets your current business model needs, which require you to choose the least expensive option after ensuring no single point of failure. The only option is to deploy two DHCP servers at each location and use a 50/50 address rule for the scope.

Question 41

The correct answer is D. By deploying two DHCP servers at each location and using a 50/50 address rule for each scope, you deal with the single-point-of-failure issue for addressing, which happens to be the single point out of each branch office. Your configuration also meets your current business model needs, which require you to choose the least expensive option after ensuring no single point of failure. The best option is to deploy two DHCP servers at the main office. You then need to create three different scopes (one for each location) and use a 50/50 address rule for each scope. Create the necessary client reservations for each scope on both DHCP servers. None of the other choices fully addresses your current business model needs or makes sure that the actions taken involve the least amount of administrative overhead.

Question 42

The correct answer is D. By deploying two DHCP servers in the main area and using a 50/50 address rule for the scope, you deal with the single-point-of-failure issue for addressing, which is the DHCP servers. Your configuration also meets your current business model needs, which require you to choose the least expensive option after ensuring no single point of failure.

Question 43

The correct answer is C. The DHCP service requests access to the authorized server list by IP address within Active Directory when the service starts and once every 60 minutes when the server is authorized (to maintain a check that the server is *still* authorized in the enterprise and that nothing has changed regarding its membership and authorization status). This is one of the main reasons that the DHCP server requires a static IP address: to find its authorization status in the Active Directory by its static IP address assignment. Answer A states that the DHCP servers will be installed and be authorized in the domain, which is not correct. Answer B states that the DHCP servers will be installed, but they will not be authorized in the domain because the DHCPINFORM messages cannot reach the domain controllers. This is not the reason they will not be authorized. Answer D is incorrect because using APIPA addressing does not allow DHCP to operate correctly.

Question 44

The correct answer is B. Windows Server 2003 DHCP servers communicate by using broadcast-based DHCPINFORM messages to access the authorized server list in Active Directory. The DHCP server needs to be able to access the Active Directory DHCPServer object to successfully review the authorized list of IP addresses to determine its own status. Answer A states that the DHCP servers will be installed and be authorized in the domain, which is not correct. Answer C is incorrect because the DHCP server needs a fixed IP address, not a dynamic one. Answer D is incorrect because using APIPA addressing does not allow DHCP to operate correctly.

Question 45

The correct answer is C. Only the members of the Domain Admins group of a domain can authorize DHCP servers in Active Directory; the DHCP Administrators group is found only on the local DHCP server and has no authority at the domain level. You would need Enterprise Administrator rights in a parent domain if you needed to change the authorization level of a DHCP server in a child domain. Answer A states that the DHCP servers will be installed and be authorized in the domain, which is not correct. Answer B states that the DHCP servers will be installed but they will not be authorized in the domain because the DHCPINFORM messages cannot reach the domain controllers. This is not the reason that they will not be authorized. Answer D is incorrect because using APIPA addressing does not allow DHCP to operate correctly.

Question 46

The correct answers are A, B, and C. Some other issues that need to be addressed for this DNS server are the options under answers A, B, and C. The number of DHCP server authorization checks and the number of Global Catalog server references the DNS server needs to address have no direct bearing in this scenario; therefore, answers D and E are incorrect.

Question 47

The correct answer is D. Approximately 4MB of RAM is used when the DNS server is started without any zones; for each zone or resource record added to the server, more RAM should be added to the system. For resource records added to a server zone, 100 bytes is the number used for DNS server memory calculations. For this question, a zone containing a maximum of 250,000 resource records requires 25MB of additional RAM to be installed or considered for DNS service on this server. Therefore, only answer D is correct, as none of the other options specify this amount of RAM.

Question 48

The correct answers are A and B. Situations in which a local DNS server stops responding and traffic is generated during zone transfers affect DNS server placement. The number of DHCP server authorization checks and the number of Global Catalog server references the DNS server needs to address have no direct bearing in this scenario, so answers C and D are incorrect.

Question 49

The correct answers are A, C, E, and G. Because you cannot simply change the subnet mask, you must delete the current scope and then re-create it on any server that holds this scope. Also, you need to re-create any client reservations and IP address exclusions as required. For these reasons, the correct answers are A, C, E, and G. The remaining options do not indicate the steps to make the necessary changes.

Question 50

The correct answer is A. Caching-only DNS servers perform DNS lookups for DNS clients and then cache the results. After the first DNS client has made a request to resolve a name, the caching-only DNS server has this information ready for remaining clients that might also need that name resolution. These types of DNS servers are not configured to be authoritative for a zone, and they do not store Standard Primary or Standard Secondary zones. This has the added benefit of having the most up-to-date information in the cache as the demand for name resolution changes on the network. It also limits the amount of traffic the DNS server creates; because it does not hold any zone information, it does not produce any replication traffic. For this reason, answer A is the best choice.

Question 51

The correct answer is C. A forward-only DNS server stores a cache of lookups and uses this cache to attempt to resolve hostnames. Forwarding-only DNS servers allow you to secure DNS traffic between your network and the Internet by configuring the firewall so that only the forwarding DNS server performs lookups with Internet-based DNS servers. For this reason, answer C the best choice.

Question 52

The correct answers are B, E, F, and G. Low-level security is a DNS configuration that has no security precautions set and is used only when integrity of DNS data isn't a concern. (Normally, this configuration should not be used, considering the untrustworthiness of the open Internet.) A low-level security DNS configuration has UDP and TCP port 53 open on your network firewall for source and destination addresses and exposes the organization's DNS infrastructure to all DNS clients. Standard DNS resolution is performed by all DNS servers in your network, and all the DNS servers are configured with root hints pointing to the root servers for the Internet. All DNS servers are configured to listen on all their IP addresses, and they will permit zone transfers to any server. Dynamic updating is allowed for all DNS zones on DNS servers configured with low-level security. Cache pollution prevention will not be enabled.

Question 53

The correct answers are C, D, and E. Medium-level security is a DNS configuration that has no security precautions set and is used only when integrity of DNS data isn't a concern. Answers C, D, and E demonstrate a medium-level security for the DNS configuration. All the remaining choices reflect options from other levels of DNS security configurations.

Question 54

The correct answers are A and C. High-level security uses the same configuration as medium-level security, and includes the security features found in Active Directory–integrated zones, as all DNS servers will be installed as domain controllers. The DNS infrastructure will also be configured with no Internet communication with internal DNS servers. For these two reasons, answers A and C are correct.

Question 55

The correct answers are A, D, and F. You should use only the characters defined in RFC 1123 in your DNS names, so answer A is correct. You need to register your unique domain name for your DNS namespace that will be exposed to the Internet, as outlined in answer D. In addition, you need to conform to Internet naming standards for your DNS namespace that will be exposed to the Internet, as outlined in answer F. Answer B, which deals with BIND, is not a consideration for this scenario. Internally used DNS namespaces do not necessarily need to be registered when they are not exposed directly to the Internet, so answer C is not correct. Answer E, which deals with conforming to Internet naming standards for your internal DNS namespace, is also incorrect.

Question 56

The correct answers are A, B, and E. The three best tools for troubleshooting efforts centered on client IP address issues are the ones supplied in answers A, B, and E. PING can be used to test your TCP/IP connection by sending a message to the remote node or gateway from a local system. IPCONFIG is used to get the local system's basic IP configuration information from the command line, including the IP address, subnet mask, and default gateway. PATHPING also shows the route taken to reach a remote system and includes more detail and functionality than TRACERT does. NBTSTAT, ROUTE, and HOSTNAME are not the best choices for dealing with client IP address issues; therefore, answers C, D, and F are incorrect.

Question 57

The correct answer is A. PING can be used to test your TCP/IP connection by sending a message to the remote node or gateway from a local system and is by far the simplest tool for testing network connectivity. Although most of the other options allow you to test network connectivity with varying degrees of success, none is simpler than PING.

Question 58

The correct answer is E. Not enough troubleshooting has taken place to determine the most likely cause of this problem, so answer E is your best choice. Routing is not at issue because your counterpart can reach your side of the router, even though you cannot reach the far side of it from your location. This also shows that the default gateway is configured correctly. Name resolution is not an issue because you can PING by workstation name and receive a response. IP address assignment does not appear to be an issue, as clients do respond to PING requests, which denotes that they do have an IP address.

Question 59

The correct answer is C. Although you could log in to the DHCP server to end the client IP addresses for both clients, they would still have to renew their leases on their own. Your best course of action is to run Ipconfig /release and then Ipconfig /renew on each client to ensure that you have successfully released your current IP address and renewed an IP address on the client. Winipcfg is not a viable option because it is the Windows 95 and 98 IP configuration tool.

Question 60

The correct answer is D. APIPA is available for client system use on Windows 98, Windows 2000, Windows XP, and Windows Server 2003 as a self-populating IP addressing solution when no DHCP server is available. In effect, the default gateway assignment from DHCP has not been set correctly, but this is not the best answer. Also, the choice of `Ipconfig /release` and `Ipconfig /renew` was not successful, so it's not the best answer either. The other options, IP routing and WINS proxy not being enabled, are not primary factors in the scenario.

10

Practice Exam 2

Question 1

You are a team member who has been picked to work on setting up and configuring a new DNS deployment. You are working on the design and selection of the required DNS zones.

Your design requirements call for using a certain type of zone. Your remote location is not as secure as it should be, so you need to use a read-only copy of the DNS zone as a precaution. The design requires having an entire copy of the zone data and interoperation of the DNS server and the chosen zone with BIND–based DNS servers.

Which type of zone should be set up at this location?

○ A. Standard Primary zone

○ B. Standard Secondary zone

○ C. Active Directory–integrated zone

○ D. Stub zone

Question 2

You are a team member who has been picked to work on setting up and configuring a new DNS deployment. You are working on the design and selection of the required DNS zones.

Your design requirements call for the use of a zone, where you need to use secure dynamic updates; you must also have interoperation of the DNS server and the chosen zone with BIND–based DNS servers and to have an entire copy of the zone data.

Which type of zone should be set up at this location?

○ A. Standard Primary zone

○ B. Standard Secondary zone

○ C. Active Directory–integrated zone

○ D. Stub zone

Question 3

You are a team member who has been picked to work on setting up and configuring a new DNS deployment. You are working on the design and selection of the required DNS zones.

Your design requirements call for the use of a zone, where you need to configure the clients to use an authoritative DNS server across noncontiguous namespaces.

Which type of zone should be set up at this location?

○ A. Standard Primary zone

○ B. Standard Secondary zone

○ C. Active Directory–integrated zone

○ D. Stub zone

Question 4

You are working as a network administrator for **gunderville.com**. A newly deployed print server named PSERVER1 has network communication problems. A user on the third floor reports that he cannot print to the server and cannot **PING** it from his location. He gives you the following machine information:

```
Physical Address : 02-51-BC-F4-A5-91
DHCP Enabled      Yes
IP address        199.254.15.11
Subnet Mask       255.255.255.0
Default Gateway   199.254.15.1
```

You are in the server area and have verified that all cables are properly attached to PSERVER1. You type **Ipconfig /all** at a command prompt from the print server and get the following printout:

```
Physical Address : 00-50-BA-F8-B5-93
DHCP Enabled      No
IP address        10.67.35.10
Subnet Mask       255.0.0.0
```

You decide to verify whether you can reach the print server, so you **PING** **PSERVER1.gunderville.com** from PSERVER1 and get the expected reply. You then **PING SERVER01**, which is a Windows Server 2003 system on this subnet, from PSERVER1 and receive the expected response. You decide to **PING** **PSERVER1** from SERVER01 and receive the following reply:

```
Pinging PSERVER1 [10.67.35.10] with 32 bytes of data:
Reply from 10.67.35.10: bytes=32 time<10ms TTL=128
Reply from 10.67.35.10: bytes=32 time<10ms TTL=128
Reply from 10.67.35.10: bytes=32 time<10ms TTL=128
Reply from 10.67.35.10: bytes=32 time<10ms TTL=128
Ping statistics for 10.67.35.10:
    Packets: Sent = 4, Received = 4, Lost = 0 (0% loss),
Approximate round trip times in milliseconds:
Minimum = 0ms, Maximum =  0ms, Average =  0ms
```

You then **PING localhost** from PSERVER1 and receive the following reply

```
D:\>ping localhost
Pinging PSERVER1 [127.0.0.1] with 32 bytes of data:
Reply from 127.0.0.1: bytes=32 time<10ms TTL=128
Reply from 127.0.0.1: bytes=32 time<10ms TTL=128
Reply from 127.0.0.1: bytes=32 time<10ms TTL=128
Reply from 127.0.0.1: bytes=32 time<10ms TTL=128
Ping statistics for 127.0.0.1:
    Packets: Sent = 4, Received = 4, Lost = 0 (0% loss),
Approximate round trip times in milliseconds:
    Minimum = 0ms, Maximum =  0ms, Average =  0ms
```

What appears to be the cause of the network communication problem?

- ○ A.   The subnet mask on the user's workstation is incorrect.
- ○ B.   The default gateway on the user's workstation is incorrect.
- ○ C.   PSERVER1 is configured with two IP addresses which is causing inter-mittent failures.
- ○ D.   No default gateway is configured on the printer.

Question 5

You are working as a network administrator for **gunderville.com**. A newly deployed print server named PSERVER1 has network communication problems. A user on the third floor reports that he cannot print to the server and cannot PING it from his location. He gives you the following machine information:

```
Physical Address : 02-51-BC-F4-A5-91
DHCP Enabled      No
IP address        199.254.15.35
Subnet Mask       255.255.255.240
Default Gateway   199.254.15.1
```

You are in the server area and have verified that all cables are properly attached to PSERVER1. You type **Ipconfig /all** at a command prompt from the print server itself and you get the following print out:

```
Physical Address : 00-50-BA-F8-B5-93
DHCP Enabled      No
IP address        10.67.35.10
Subnet Mask       255.0.0.0
Default Gateway   10.33.77.254
```

You decide to verify you can reach the print server, so you PING PSERVER1.**gunderville.com** from PSERVER1 and you get the expected reply. You then PING SERVER01 which is a Windows Server 2003 system on this subnet from PSERVER1 and you receive the expected response. You then PING PSERVER1 from SERVER01 and you receive the following reply:

```
Pinging PSERVER1 [10.67.35.10] with 32 bytes of data:
Reply from 10.67.35.10: bytes=32 time<10ms TTL=128
Reply from 10.67.35.10: bytes=32 time<10ms TTL=128
Reply from 10.67.35.10: bytes=32 time<10ms TTL=128
Reply from 10.67.35.10: bytes=32 time<10ms TTL=128
Ping statistics for 10.67.35.10:
    Packets: Sent = 4, Received = 4, Lost = 0 (0% loss),
Approximate round trip times in milliseconds:
    Minimum = 0ms, Maximum =  0ms, Average =  0ms
```

You then PING localhost from PSERVER1 and you receive the following reply:

```
D:\>ping localhost
Pinging PSERVER1 [127.0.0.1] with 32 bytes of data:
Reply from 127.0.0.1: bytes=32 time<10ms TTL=128
```

```
Reply from 127.0.0.1: bytes=32 time<10ms TTL=128
Reply from 127.0.0.1: bytes=32 time<10ms TTL=128
Reply from 127.0.0.1: bytes=32 time<10ms TTL=128
Ping statistics for 127.0.0.1:
    Packets: Sent = 4, Received = 4, Lost = 0 (0% loss),
Approximate round trip times in milliseconds:
    Minimum = 0ms, Maximum =  0ms, Average =  0ms
```

What appears to be the cause of the network communication problem? (Choose three.)

❑ A. The subnet mask on the user's workstation is incorrect.

❑ B. The default gateway on the user's workstation is incorrect.

❑ C. PSERVER1 is configured with two IP addresses, which is causing intermittent failures.

❑ D. The default gateway on PSERVER1 is incorrect.

❑ E. The IP address on the user's workstation is incorrect.

❑ F. The subnet mask on PSERVER1 is incorrect.

❑ G. The IP address on PSERVER1 is incorrect.

Question 6

You are working as a network administrator for **gunderville.com**. A newly deployed print server named PSERVER1 on the "10" network has network communication problems. Recently, ROUTER1 with an IP address of 10.99.35.1 was not responding and needed to be rebooted. You have verified that it is now online and functioning properly. A user on the third floor with an IP address of 199.254.1546 reports that he cannot print to the server and cannot PING it from his location. He gives you the following machine information:

```
Physical Address : 02-51-BC-F4-A5-91
DHCP Enabled       No
IP address         199.254.15.46
Subnet Mask        255.255.255.240
Default Gateway    199.254.15.32
```

You are in the server area and have verified that all cables are properly attached to PSERVER1. You type **Ipconfig /all** at a command prompt from the print server itself and you get the following printout:

```
Physical Address : 00-50-BA-F8-B5-93
DHCP Enabled       No
IP address         10.67.35.10
Subnet Mask        255.255.255.0
Default Gateway    10.99.35.1
```

You decide to verify you can reach the print server so you PING PSERVER1. **gunderville.com** from PSERVER1 and you get the expected reply. You then PING SERVER01 which is a Windows Server 2003 system on this subnet from PSERVER1 and you receive the expected response. You then PING PSERVER1 from SERVER01 and you receive the following reply:

```
Pinging PSERVER1 [10.67.35.10] with 32 bytes of data:
Reply from 10.67.35.10: bytes=32 time<10ms TTL=128
Reply from 10.67.35.10: bytes=32 time<10ms TTL=128
Reply from 10.67.35.10: bytes=32 time<10ms TTL=128
Reply from 10.67.35.10: bytes=32 time<10ms TTL=128
Ping statistics for 10.67.35.10:
    Packets: Sent = 4, Received = 4, Lost = 0 (0% loss),
Approximate round trip times in milliseconds:
    Minimum = 0ms, Maximum =  0ms, Average =  0ms
```

You then PING localhost from PSERVER1 and you receive the following reply:

```
D:\>ping localhost
Pinging PSERVER1 [127.0.0.1] with 32 bytes of data:
Reply from 127.0.0.1: bytes=32 time<10ms TTL=128
Reply from 127.0.0.1: bytes=32 time<10ms TTL=128
Reply from 127.0.0.1: bytes=32 time<10ms TTL=128
Reply from 127.0.0.1: bytes=32 time<10ms TTL=128
Ping statistics for 127.0.0.1:
    Packets: Sent = 4, Received = 4, Lost = 0 (0% loss),
Approximate round trip times in milliseconds:
    Minimum = 0ms, Maximum =  0ms, Average =  0ms
```

What appears to be the cause of the network communication problem?

○ A. The subnet mask on the user's workstation is incorrect.

○ B. The default gateway on the user's workstation is incorrect.

○ C. PSERVER1 is configured with two IP addresses, which is causing intermittent failures.

○ D. The subnet mask on PSERVER1 is incorrect.

Question 7

You are the domain administrator for **gunderville.com**, which has sites in New York, Boston, Hartford, and Wallingford. Clients in your domain consist of Windows 98, Windows Me, Windows 2000, and Windows XP Professional systems.

You have been asked to secure all IP traffic between the Hartford and Wallingford locations. You must also configure a lower-than-standard level of data encryption because of backward-compatibility issues.

Which of the following options is best suited to meet all the needs for your scenario? (Choose two.)

❑ A. Use Layer Two Tunneling Protocol (L2TP) and IP Security (IPSec).

❑ B. Use Layer Two Tunneling Protocol (L2TP) and Microsoft Point-to-Point Encryption (MPPE).

❑ C. Use Point-to-Point Tunneling Protocol (PPTP) and IP Security (IPSec).

❑ D. Install an RRAS server at the Hartford and Wallingford locations.

❑ E. Install a VPN server at the Hartford and Wallingford locations.

❑ F. Install a VPN server at the Hartford and Wallingford locations.

Question 8

You are the domain administrator for **gunderville.com**, which has small sites in New York, Boston, Hartford, and Wallingford. Clients in your domain consist of Windows 98, Windows Me, Windows 2000, and Windows XP Professional systems.

You have been asked to configure and secure the IP traffic from the Hartford location to the remote office in Wallingford. You need to devise a solution for all clients that supports header encryption and tunnel authentication and provides data encryption.

Your primary objective is to secure the IP traffic that leaves your network traversing an untrusted network and the solution provided must support all the clients in the environment. Your secondary objectives are to carry out these actions with the least amount of administrative effort and to support the necessary header compression, tunnel authentication, and encryption requirements.

What do you need to do to meet all the objectives? (Choose three.)

- ❏ A. The Microsoft L2TP/IPSec VPN client must be installed on systems running Windows 98, Windows 2000, and Windows Me.

- ❏ B. The Microsoft L2TP/IPSec VPN client must be installed on systems running Windows 98 and Windows Me.

- ❏ C. Implement L2TP and IPSec running in Transport mode.

- ❏ D. Configure a local security policy to require security.

- ❏ E. Configure a domain security policy to require security.

- ❏ F. Configure a local security policy to request security.

- ❏ G. Configure a domain security policy to request security.

Question 9

You are the domain administrator for **gunderville.com**, which has sites in New York, Boston, Hartford, and Wallingford. Clients in your domain consist of Windows 98, Windows Me, Windows 2000, and Windows XP Professional systems.

You have been asked to configure and secure the IP traffic from the Hartford location to the remote office in Wallingford and install an RRAS server at each location. You need to devise a solution for all clients that supports header encryption and tunnel authentication and provides data encryption.

Your primary objective is to secure the IP traffic that leaves your network traversing an untrusted network, and the solution must support all clients in the environment. Your secondary objectives are to carry out these actions with the least amount of administrative effort and to support the necessary header compression, tunnel authentication, and encryption requirements.

What do you need to do to meet all the objectives? (Choose two.)

- ○ A. The Microsoft L2TP/IPSec VPN client must be installed on systems running Windows 98 and Windows Me.
- ○ B. Implement L2TP and IPSec running in Tunnel mode.
- ○ C. Configure a local security policy on the clients to require security.
- ○ D. Configure a domain security policy to require security.
- ○ E. Configure a domain security policy to request security.
- ○ F. Configure a local security policy on the RRAS servers to require security.

Question 10

You are the domain administrator for **gunderville.com**, which has sites in New York, Boston, Hartford, and Wallingford. Systems in use consist of Windows 2000 Professional, Windows 2000 Server, Windows Server 2003, and Windows XP Professional.

You have been asked to configure systems in your environment to use Remote Assistance so that local help desk users can log on to the local end users' systems as needed. All Windows XP client systems are running Internet Connection Firewall (ICF).

Your primary objective is to enable Remote Assistance for all client systems in your environment. Your secondary objectives are to meet your goals with the least amount of administrative effort and to not affect (alter) the level of security on the LAN unless you need to.

You open port 3389 on the external firewall for the Remote Assistance traffic and you also open port 3389 on the Windows XP client systems that are running Internet Connection Firewall (ICF).

What is the result of your actions?

- ○ A. The primary objective and both secondary objectives have been met.
- ○ B. The primary objective and one Secondary objective have been met.
- ○ C. The primary objective has not been met. However, both secondary objectives have been met.
- ○ D. Only one secondary objective has been met.
- ○ E. None of the objectives has been met.

Question 11

You are the domain administrator for **gunderville.com**, which has sites in New York, Boston, Hartford, and Wallingford. Systems in use consist of Windows 2000 Professional, Windows 2000 Server, Windows Server 2003, and Windows XP Professional.

The subnet addressing schemes in each location are as follows:

Boston uses 177.25.0.128 with a subnet mask of 255.255.255.192.

Hartford uses 177.25.0.192 with a subnet mask of 255.255.255.192.

New York uses 177.25.1.0 with a subnet mask of 255.255.255.192.

Wallingford uses 177.25.1.64 with a subnet mask of 255.255.255.192.

How many host addresses are available per subnet?

○ A. 30

○ B. 62

○ C. 14

○ D. 126

○ E. 254

Question 12

You are the domain administrator for **gunderville.com**, which has sites in New York, Boston, Hartford, and Wallingford. Systems in use consist of Windows 2000 Professional, Windows 2000 Server, Windows Server 2003, and Windows XP Professional.

The subnet addressing schemes in each location are as follows:

Boston uses 177.25.0.128 with a subnet mask of 255.255.255.192.

Hartford uses 177.25.0.192 with a subnet mask of 255.255.255.192.

New York uses 177.25.1.0 with a subnet mask of 255.255.255.192.

Wallingford uses 177.25.1.64 with a subnet mask of 255.255.255.192.

Which routing protocols are available for your internal Windows Server 2003 network? (Choose two.)

❑ A. RIP version 1 (RIPv1)

❑ B. RIP version 2 (RIPv2)

❑ C. Open Shortest Path First (OSPF)

❑ D. Border Gateway Protocol (BGP)

Question 13

You are the domain administrator for **gunderville.com**, which has sites in New York, Boston, Hartford, and Wallingford. Systems in use consist of Windows 2000 Professional, Windows 2000 Server, Windows Server 2003, and Windows XP Professional.

The subnet addressing schemes in each location is as follows:

Boston uses 177.25.0.128 with a subnet mask of 255.255.255.192. All hosts are internally interconnected by hubs. Their external connection is through an RRAS server.

Hartford uses 177.25.0.192 with a subnet mask of 255.255.255.192. All the hosts are internally interconnected by hubs. Their external connection is through an RRAS server.

New York uses 177.25.1.0 with a subnet mask of 255.255.255.192. All the hosts are internally interconnected by hubs. Their external connection is through an RRAS server.

Wallingford uses 177.25.1.64 with a subnet mask of 255.255.255.192. All the hosts are internally interconnected by hubs. Their external connection is through an RRAS server.

Based on this information, which of the following statements are accurate? (Choose two.)

❑ A. Each location is part of its own broadcast domain.

❑ B. All locations are part of the same broadcast domain.

❑ C. All locations are part of the same collision domain.

❑ D. Each location is part of its own collision domain.

Question 14

You are reviewing some network traces that outline the traffic between a Windows 2000 member server and a Windows Server 2003 domain controller. You need to resolve an in-house application and connectivity inconsistency between the two systems.

You have decided to review the DNS resolution of the application and some subsequent routing information on the subnet, and then prepare a report for management. For the purposes of your report, you need to explain which layer of the TCP/IP architecture you are testing.

At which layer of the TCP/IP architecture will you find the protocol that provides the necessary information for review?

○ A. Application

○ B. Host-to-host transport

○ C. Internet

○ D. Network interface

Question 15

You are reviewing some network traces that outline the traffic between some Windows 2000 client systems in your Windows Server 2003 domain. You are having problems with in-house application and network connectivity inconsistencies, so you have decided to review a cross section of the TCP traffic on the subnet and prepare a report for management. For the purposes of your report, you need to explain which layer of the TCP/IP architecture you are testing.

At which layer of the TCP/IP architecture will you find the protocol that provides the necessary information for review?

○ A. Application

○ B. Host-to-host transport

○ C. Internet

○ D. Network interface

Question 16

You are reviewing some network traces for an issue with in-house application and network connectivity inconsistencies between some Windows XP Professional client systems in your Windows Server 2003 domain. You have decided to review a cross section of the IP traffic on the subnet and create a report for management. For the purposes of your report, you need to explain which layer of the OSI architecture you are testing.

Which layer of the OSI model will you list in your report?

○ A. Application

○ B. Presentation

○ C. Session

○ D. Transport

○ E. Network

Question 17

You are the domain administrator for **gunderville.com**. You have been tasked with reviewing some network access logs for your Windows Server 2003 environment to troubleshoot recent network connectivity inconsistencies between some Windows XP Professional client systems connecting to the network via dial-up connections.

Which of the following logs is the best place to begin your review?

○ A. Windows Authentication logs

○ B. Point-to-Point Protocol logs

○ C. Internet Authentication Service logs

○ D. Audit logs

Question 18

You are the domain administrator for **gunderville.com**. You have been tasked with reviewing network access logs for your Windows Server 2003 environment to troubleshoot recent network connectivity inconsistencies between some Windows XP Professional client systems connecting to the network.

You believe that the problem is with systems connecting to the network with L2TP connections and IPSec encryption because this setup was recently enabled on the network. Which of the following logs is the best place to begin your review?

○ A. Windows Authentication logs

○ B. Point-to-Point Protocol logs

○ C. Internet Authentication Service logs

○ D. Audit logs

Question 19

You are the network administrator for **gunderville.com** and you have been tasked with troubleshooting problems in the domain with users not being able to log on to systems and access resources.

Your investigation into the logon issue for a summer intern has taken you to the security logs on one of the domain controllers, where you are encountering a number of entries showing the event ID 532, indicating failed logon attempts. What is the most likely reason for the failed logon attempts?

- ○ A. A logon attempt was made with an unknown username or a known username with an invalid password.
- ○ B. A logon attempt was made by a user who violated his or her account logon time restriction.
- ○ C. A logon attempt was made using an expired account.
- ○ D. A logon attempt was made using a disabled account.

Question 20

You are a desktop administrator for **gunderville.com** and have been asked to handle a trouble ticket for a new user who just started work today. The user claims that she had a user account and password set up, but she has not been able to log in.

You call HR and find out that the account has been created; however, when you attempt to use the supplied information, the logon fails. Further investigation shows a number of event ID 531 errors in the event logs. What is the most likely reason for the failed logon attempt?

- ○ A. A logon attempt was made with an unknown username or a known username with an invalid password.
- ○ B. A logon attempt was made by a user who violated his or her account logon time restriction.
- ○ C. A logon attempt was made using an expired account.
- ○ D. A logon attempt was made using a disabled account.

Question 21

You are the server administrator for your company's DMZ environment, and you need to delete the persistent static route of 192.168.1.0/24 to your internal sub-net of 111.0.0.0 /8 on the internal NIC only. The server is using an internal IP address of 203.11.4.225 and an external address of 19.10.112.72.

What would you need to enter at the command prompt to remove this current persistent entry?

○ A. **route delete -p 192.168.1.0 mask 255.255.255.0 203.11.4.225**

○ B. **route delete 192.168.1.0 mask 255.255.255.0 203.11.4.225**

○ C. **route delete -p 192.168.1.0/24 203.11.4.225**

○ D. **route delete 192.168.1.0/24 203.11.4.225**

Question 22

You are reviewing some documentation for your new network namespace design. A couple of entries are not clearly defined, and management has asked you to review and update certain sections.

One section in the documentation outlines the definition of a new forest to be deployed. You need to update the currently written section with a better defini-tion of a forest. Which of the following choices is the best definition for this pur-pose?

○ A. A forest is a collection of Active Directory domain trees that are part of a contiguous namespace.

○ B. A forest is a collection of Active Directory domain trees that are never part of a contiguous namespace.

○ C. A forest is a collection of Active Directory domain trees that may or may not be part of a contiguous namespace.

○ D. A forest is a collection of Active Directory domain trees that are never part of a contiguous namespace when the domain functional level is set to Windows 2000 native.

Question 23

You are reviewing some documentation for the new DHCP deployment for your network. You need to define and outline at the highest level the four main planning, design, and implementation steps for upper management. Which of the following outlines includes these steps? (Choose four.)

❏ A. An outline of the proposed DHCP design

❏ B. An outline of the proposed DHCP design and its integration with existing services

❏ C. An outline of the proposed scope configuration for the domain

❏ D. An outline of the proposed implementation of the DHCP solution

❏ E. An outline of the proposed hardware implementation for your DHCP solution

❏ F. An outline of the proposed exclusion ranges for your DHCP scopes

Question 24

You are reviewing some documentation for your new DNS deployment for the **gunderville.com** domain. You need to define and outline at the design level the memory requirements and size calculations to be considered for your design. Under typical design usage, what are the memory requirements for a DNS server? (Choose three.)

❏ A. When a DNS server is started without any zones, 4MB of RAM is the minimum.

❏ B. When a DNS server is started without any zones, 8MB of RAM is the minimum.

❏ C. The DNS server uses additional RAM for each DNS zone added to the server.

❏ D. The DNS server does not use additional RAM for each DNS zone added to the server.

❏ E. For each resource record added to the server's DNS zones, 100 bytes of additional system memory is used.

❏ F. For each resource record added to the server's DNS zones, 1KB of additional system memory is used.

Question 25

You are reviewing some documentation for your new DNS deployment for the **gunderville.com** domain. You need to define and outline the placement of new Windows Server 2003 systems running DNS for remote locations across your enterprise.

You need to provide a DNS solution for your Wallingford office, which has a limited amount of network bandwidth. Although there are plans in the works for increasing the amount of available bandwidth for this location, it will not be in place until the next fiscal year.

The client systems must always be able to resolve DNS queries, and there should be no single point of failure on this site for name resolution.

Which DNS role type is best suited for this location under these conditions?

- ○ A. Two caching-only DNS servers should be in use.
- ○ B. Two non-recursive DNS servers should be in use.
- ○ C. Two forward-only DNS servers should be in use.
- ○ D. Two conditional-forwarder DNS servers should be in use.

Question 26

You are reviewing some documentation for your new DNS deployment for the **gunderville.com** domain. You need to define and outline the placement of new Windows Server 2003 systems running DNS for remote locations across your enterprise.

You need to provide a DNS solution for your Wallingford site to allow those client systems to resolve DNS queries for your domain, but you also need to prevent client systems on the Internet from using your DNS server for name resolution.

The client systems must always be able to resolve their DNS queries for **gunderville.com**, and there should be no single point of failure on this site for name resolution.

Which DNS role type is best suited for this location under these conditions?

- ○ A. Two caching-only DNS servers should be in use.
- ○ B. Two non-recursive DNS servers should be in use.
- ○ C. Two forward-only DNS servers should be in use.
- ○ D. Two conditional-forwarder DNS servers should be in use.

Question 27

You are designing a security configuration for your Windows Server 2003 DNS deployment. Which of the following choices are configuration specifications for a low-level security standard DNS deployment? (Choose three.)

❑ A. All DNS servers permit zone transfers to any server.

❑ B. UDP and TCP/IP port 53 is open on your network firewall for both source and destination addresses.

❑ C. DNS zones are Active Directory integrated.

❑ D. Zone transfers are limited to only the servers listed in the name server (NS) resource records.

❑ E. Dynamic updating is allowed for all DNS zones.

❑ F. Discretionary access control lists (DACL) are in use on the DNS Server service so that only specific accounts can perform administrative tasks on the DNS server.

❑ G. Secure dynamic updates are enabled for DNS zones, except the top-level and root zones.

Question 28

You are designing a security configuration for your Windows Server 2003 DNS deployment. Which of the following choices are configuration specifications for a medium-level security standard DNS deployment? (Choose three.)

❑ A. All DNS servers permit zone transfers to any server.

❑ B. UDP and TCP/IP port 53 is open on your network firewall for both source and destination addresses.

❑ C. DNS zones are Active Directory integrated.

❑ D. Zone transfers are limited to only the servers listed in the name server (NS) resource records.

❑ E. Dynamic updating is allowed for all DNS zones.

❑ F. Cache pollution prevention is enabled.

❑ G. Secure dynamic updates are not enabled for DNS zones.

Question 29

You are designing a security configuration for your Windows Server 2003 DNS deployment for **gunderville.com**, and you need to review naming standards for child domains.

All child domains must be accessible from the Internet, follow standard domain naming conventions for acceptable characters, and be part of the contiguous domain namespace.

Which of the following child domain names is not acceptable? (Choose three.)

- ❑ A. **u.s.a.gunderville.com**
- ❑ B. **usagunderville.com**
- ❑ C. **usa_gunderville.com**
- ❑ D. **usa.internal.gunderville.com**
- ❑ E. **usa.external.gunderville.com**
- ❑ F. **usainternal.gunderville.com**
- ❑ G. **usa-one.gunderville.com**
- ❑ H. **usa#1.gunderville.com**
- ❑ I. **u.s.a-one.gunderville.com**

Question 30

You are designing a security configuration for your Windows Server 2003 DNS deployment for **gunderville.com**, **usa.gunderville.com**, and **connecticut. usa.gunderville.com**. Each domain has two sites. The **connecticut.usa. gunderville.com** has the Wallingford and NH sites; the **usa.gunderville.com** domain has the Connecticut and New England sites; and the **gunderville.com** domain has the HQ and BU sites. Each site has two DNS servers for each DNS namespace.

All DNS servers are configured to use standard DNS zones. How many DNS servers total are deployed in the **gunderville** forest?

- ○ A. 6
- ○ B. 12
- ○ C. 18
- ○ D. 36

Question 31

You are designing a security configuration for your Windows Server 2003 DNS deployment for **gunderville.com**, **usa.gunderville.com**, and **connecticut. usa.gunderville.com**. Each domain has two sites. The **connecticut.usa. gunderville.com** has the Wallingford and NH sites; the **usa.gunderville.com** domain has the Connecticut and New England sites; and the **gunderville.com** domain has the HQ and BU sites. Each site has two DNS servers for each DNS namespace.

All DNS servers are configured to use standard DNS zones. How many Standard Primary zones total are deployed in the **gunderville.com** forest?

○ A. 3

○ B. 6

○ C. 12

○ D. 24

Question 32

You are designing a security configuration for your Windows Server 2003 DNS deployment for **gunderville.com**, **usa.gunderville.com**, and **connecticut.usa. gunderville.com**. Each domain has two sites. The **connecticut.usa. gunderville.com** has the Wallingford and NH sites; the **usa.gunderville.com** domain has the Connecticut and New England sites; and the **gunderville.com** domain has the HQ and BU sites. Each site has two DNS servers for each DNS namespace, and all DNS servers store zone information.

All DNS servers are configured to use standard DNS zones, and all DNS servers for each domain are autonomous for their DNS zones. This means that DNS servers with zone information for **connecticut.usa.gunderville.com** have only those DNS zones (and none of the other domains' DNS zones) as Standard Secondary zones.

How many Standard Secondary zones total are deployed in the **gunderville.com** forest?

○ A. 3

○ B. 6

○ C. 24

○ D. 33

Question 33

You are designing a security configuration for your Windows Server 2003 DNS deployment for **gunderville.com**, **usa.gunderville.com**, and **connecticut. usa.gunderville.com**. Each domain has two sites. The **connecticut.usa. gunderville.com** has the Wallingford and NH sites; the **usa.gunderville.com** domain has the Connecticut and New England sites; and the **gunderville.com** domain has the HQ and BU sites. Each site has two DNS servers for each DNS namespace, and all DNS servers store zone information.

All DNS servers are configured to use standard DNS zones, and all DNS servers for each domain are autonomous for their DNS zones. This means that DNS servers with zone information for **connecticut.usa.gunderville.com** have only those DNS zones (and none of the other domains' DNS zones) as Standard Secondary zones.

How many Standard Secondary zones total are deployed in the **gunderville.com** domain?

○ A. 1

○ B. 2

○ C. 3

○ D. 11

Question 34

You are designing a security configuration for your Windows Server 2003 DNS deployment for **gunderville.com**, **usa.gunderville.com**, and **connecticut. usa.gunderville.com**. Each domain has two sites. The **connecticut.usa. gunderville.com** has the Wallingford and NH sites; the **usa.gunderville.com** domain has the Connecticut and New England sites; and the **gunderville.com** domain has the HQ and BU sites. Each site has two DNS servers for each DNS namespace: a Windows Server 2003 DNS server and a BIND DNS server.

All Windows DNS servers are configured to use Active Directory–integrated DNS zones, and all BIND DNS servers contain Standard Secondary DNS zones for each domain. All domains are autonomous for their DNS zones. This means that DNS servers with zone information for **connecticut.usa.gunderville.com** have only those DNS zones (and none of the other domains' DNS zones) as Standard Secondary zones.

How many Standard Secondary zones total are deployed in the **gunderville.com** forest?

○ A. 6

○ B. 9

○ C. 12

○ D. 18

Question 35

You are designing a security configuration for your Windows Server 2003 DNS deployment for **gunderville.com**, **usa.gunderville.com**, and **connecticut. usa.gunderville.com**. Each domain has two sites. The **connecticut.usa. gunderville.com** has the Wallingford and NH sites; the **usa.gunderville.com** domain has the Connecticut and New England sites; and the **gunderville.com** domain has the HQ and BU sites. Each site has two DNS servers for each DNS namespace: a Windows Server 2003 DNS server and a BIND DNS server.

You are deciding between Active Directory–integrated zones and Standard Primary zones. Which of the following are features of both Standard Primary zones and Active Directory–integrated zones? (Choose three.)

- ❍ A. IETF specifications for domain namespaces
- ❍ B. Stores zone information in Active Directory
- ❍ C. Support for incremental zone transfers
- ❍ D. Allows read/write access to the DNS namespace for all DNS servers
- ❍ E. Allows fault tolerance for DNS updates, regardless of which DNS server fails
- ❍ F. Allows fault tolerance for name resolution, regardless of which DNS server fails

Question 36

You are designing a DNS configuration for your Windows Server 2003 DNS deployment for **gunderville.com**. The DNS design will use Standard Primary and Standard Secondary DNS zones.

A number of different clients are in use in the domain, including Windows 98, Windows NT 4 Workstation, Windows 2000, and Windows XP. There are three workgroup configurations of Windows NT 4 Workstation, Windows 2000 Professional, and Windows XP Professional systems that are not members of the domain.

You are deciding whether to use the DHCP server for dynamic DNS updates or allow clients to do it themselves. What considerations must be made for the different clients in use on the network? (Choose three.)

- ❑ A. Windows 98 clients in the domain cannot update DNS dynamically.
- ❑ B. Windows NT 4 clients in the domain cannot update DNS dynamically.
- ❑ C. Windows NT 4 clients in the workgroup cannot update DNS dynamically.
- ❑ D. Windows 2000 Professional clients in the domain cannot update DNS dynamically.
- ❑ E. Windows 2000 Professional clients in the workgroup cannot update DNS dynamically.
- ❑ F. Windows XP clients in the domain cannot update DNS dynamically.

Question 37

You are designing a DNS configuration for your Windows Server 2003 DNS deployment for **gunderville.com**. The DNS design will use Standard Primary and Standard Secondary DNS zones.

A number of different clients are in use in the domain, including Windows 98, Windows NT 4 Workstation, Windows 2000, and Windows XP. There are three workgroup configurations of Windows NT 4 Workstation, Windows 2000 Professional, and Windows XP Professional systems that are not members of the domain.

You are deciding whether to use the DHCP server for dynamic DNS updates or allow clients to do it themselves. What catalyst is the major breakpoint of this design? (Choose two.)

❑ A. Windows 98 clients can update DNS dynamically.

❑ B. Windows NT 4 clients can update DNS dynamically.

❑ C. Windows NT 4 clients in the workgroup can update DNS dynamically.

❑ D. No clients in the domain can update DNS dynamically because of the zones in use and the security implemented in the DNS design.

❑ E. No clients in the workgroups can update DNS dynamically because of the zones in use and the security implemented in the DNS design.

Question 38

You are designing upgrades to your DNS configuration for **gunderville.com**. The DNS design will use Standard Primary and Standard Secondary DNS zones.

The network has a number of different DNS servers, which include Windows Server 2003 DNS, Windows 2000 Server DNS, Windows NT 4 DNS, BIND DNS version 8.2.1, and BIND DNS version 4.9.7.

How will these different DNS implementations affect your domain's DNS configuration for dynamic updates? (Choose three.)

❑ A. Windows Server 2003 DNS supports dynamic updates.

❑ B. Windows 2000 Server DNS supports dynamic updates.

❑ C. Windows NT 4 DNS supports dynamic updates.

❑ D. BIND DNS version 8.2.1 supports dynamic updates.

❑ E. BIND DNS version 4.9.7 supports dynamic updates.

Question 39

You are designing upgrades to your DNS configuration for **gunderville.com**. The DNS design will use Standard Primary and Standard Secondary DNS zones.

The network has a number of different DNS servers, including Windows Server 2003 DNS, Windows 2000 Server DNS, Windows NT 4 DNS, BIND DNS version 8.2.1, and BIND DNS version 4.9.7.

Which of the following does not affect your domain's DNS configuration for incremental zone transfers?

○ A. Windows Server 2003 DNS supports incremental zone transfers.

○ B. Windows 2000 Server DNS supports incremental zone transfers.

○ C. Windows NT 4 DNS supports incremental zone transfers.

○ D. BIND DNS version 8.2.1 supports incremental zone transfers.

Question 40

You are designing upgrades to your DNS configuration for **gunderville.com**. The DNS design will use Standard Primary and Standard Secondary DNS zones.

The network has a number of different DNS servers, including Windows Server 2003 DNS, Windows 2000 Server DNS, Windows NT 4 DNS, BIND DNS version 8.2.1, and BIND DNS version 4.9.7.

How will these different DNS implementations affect your domain's DNS configuration for WINS and WINS-R lookups? (Choose three.)

❑ A. Windows Server 2003 DNS supports WINS and WINS-R lookups.

❑ B. Windows 2000 Server DNS supports WINS and WINS-R lookups.

❑ C. Windows NT 4 DNS supports WINS and WINS-R lookups.

❑ D. BIND DNS version 8.2.1 supports WINS and WINS-R lookups.

❑ E. BIND DNS version 4.9.7 supports WINS and WINS-R lookups.

Question 41

You are designing upgrades to your DNS configuration for **gunderville.com**. The DNS design will use Standard Primary and Standard Secondary DNS zones.

You need to configure your DNS servers so that they provide DNS resolutions in which the DNS server returns the best possible answer based on its local cache or stored zone data without forwarding the query to another DNS server.

What type of DNS query and lookup request does the DNS server perform when a client is trying to connect to **http://www.gunderville.com**? (Choose two.)

❑ A. Forward DNS lookup

❑ B. Reverse DNS lookup

❑ C. Iterative DNS query

❑ D. Recursive DNS query

❑ E. WINS query

Question 42

You are designing upgrades to your DNS configuration for **gunderville.com**. The DNS design will use Standard Primary and Standard Secondary DNS zones.

You need to configure your DNS servers so that they provide DNS resolutions in which the DNS server assumes the full workload and responsibility for supplying a complete answer to the DNS query.

What type of DNS query and lookup request does the DNS server perform when a client is trying to connect to **http://www.gunderville.com**? (Choose two.)

❑ A. Forward DNS lookup

❑ B. Reverse DNS lookup

❑ C. Iterative DNS query

❑ D. Recursive DNS query

❑ E. WINS query

❑ F. WINS-R query

Question 43

You are designing upgrades to your DNS configuration for **gunderville.com**. The DNS design will use Standard Primary and Standard Secondary DNS zones.

Each domain has six sites, and each site has two DNS servers: a Windows Server 2003 DNS server and a Windows 2000 DNS server. The Windows 2000 Server systems deployed with the DNS service are **DNS1.gunderville.com** through **DNS6.gunderville.com**, and the Windows Server 2003 DNS systems are **DNS7.gunderville.com** through **DNS12.gunderville.com**.

You need to configure your DNS servers so that they provide DNS resolutions in which the DNS server assumes the full workload and responsibility for supplying a complete answer to the DNS query.

You do not want any DNS servers in your enterprise to contain pointer information to root servers on the Internet, except for one designated DNS server. All servers should forward DNS requests for Internet resources to the **DNS1. gunderville.com** DNS server.

Keeping security design and deployment best practices in mind, what steps are required to perform this successfully? (Choose four.)

- ❑ A. Configure all DNS servers, **DNS1.gunderville.com** through **DNS12.gunderville.com**, as forwarders.

- ❑ B. Configure all the Windows 2000 DNS servers, **DNS1.gunderville.com** through **DNS6.gunderville.com**, as forwarders.

- ❑ C. Configure all the Windows Server 2003 DNS servers, **DNS7. gunderville.com** through **DNS12.gunderville.com**, with root hints.

- ❑ D. Configure all the DNS servers, **DNS2.gunderville.com** through **DNS12.gunderville.com**, as forwarders.

- ❑ E. Configure **DNS1.gunderville.com** with the root hints file.

- ❑ F. Configure the firewall rules to allow DNS queries from the internal network to the Internet for resolution.

- ❑ G. Configure the firewall rules to allow **DNS1.gunderville.com** queries from the internal network to the Internet for resolution.

- ❑ H. Remove root hints from **DNS2.gunderville.com** through **DNS12. gunderville.com**.

Question 44

You are designing upgrades to your DNS configuration for **gunderville.com**. The DNS design will use Standard Primary and Standard Secondary DNS zones.

Each domain has six sites, and each site has two DNS servers: a Windows Server 2003 DNS server and a Windows 2000 DNS server. The Windows 2000 Server systems deployed with the DNS service are **DNS1.gunderville.com** through **DNS6.gunderville.com**, and the Windows Server 2003 DNS systems are **DNS7.gunderville.com** through **DNS12.gunderville.com**.

You need to configure your DNS servers so that they are updated more often because the DNS information in your enterprise is very dynamic. Where is the best place to make these changes if you want to adjust the time interval a secondary DNS server waits before querying for updated zone information?

- ○ A. Retry interval on the Start of Authority (SOA) tab of the forward lookup zone
- ○ B. Refresh interval on the Start of Authority (SOA) tab of the forward lookup zone
- ○ C. The TTL (time to live) for this record on the Start of Authority (SOA) tab of the forward lookup zone
- ○ D. Minimum (default) TTL on the Start of Authority (SOA) tab of the forward lookup zone
- ○ E. Expires After settings on the Start of Authority (SOA) tab of the forward lookup zone

Question 45

You are designing upgrades to your DNS configuration for **gunderville.com** and plan to use Standard Primary and Standard Secondary DNS zones.

Each domain has six sites, and each site has two DNS servers: a Windows Server 2003 DNS server and a Windows 2000 DNS server. The Windows 2000 Server systems deployed with the DNS service are **DNS1.gunderville.com** through **DNS6.gunderville.com**, and the Windows Server 2003 DNS systems are **DNS7.gunderville.com** through **DNS12.gunderville.com**.

You need to configure your DNS servers so that they are not providing old or out-of-date name resolution information. Where is the best place to make these changes if you want to shorten the amount of elapsed time before a secondary server stops responding to DNS queries because of failures for zone updates?

- ○ A. Retry interval on the Start of Authority (SOA) tab of the forward lookup zone
- ○ B. Refresh interval on the Start of Authority (SOA) tab of the forward lookup zone
- ○ C. The TTL (time to live) for this record on the Start of Authority (SOA) tab of the forward lookup zone
- ○ D. Minimum (default) TTL on the Start of Authority (SOA) tab of the forward lookup zone
- ○ E. Expires After settings on the Start of Authority (SOA) tab of the forward lookup zone

Question 46

You are designing upgrades to your DNS configuration for **gunderville.com**. The DNS design will use Standard Primary and Standard Secondary DNS zones, and no DNS clients need to resolve DNS names on the Internet.

Each domain has six sites, and each site has two DNS servers: a Windows Server 2003 DNS server and a Windows 2000 DNS server. The Windows 2000 Server systems deployed with the DNS service are **DNS1.gunderville.com** through **DNS6.gunderville.com**, and the Windows Server 2003 DNS systems are **DNS7.gunderville.com** through **DNS12.gunderville.com**.

You need to prevent your DNS servers from communicating with other DNS servers to resolve queries outside your domain. What is the simplest way to do this?

- ○ A. Configure the DNS servers as forwarders.
- ○ B. Disable recursion on the DNS servers.
- ○ C. Update root hints on the DNS servers.
- ○ D. Disable round-robin rotation for multiple-homed names.

Question 47

You are designing a NetBIOS name resolution solution for your small Windows Server 2003 domain that will alleviate the need for resolving names by broadcast. The domain consists of two domain controllers, one of which doubles as a file server and the other is also used as a print server. Both servers are Pentium III 500MHz systems with 192MB of RAM and run the DNS service. An additional Windows 2000 Server is being used as a development system. DHCP is not in use, and all client systems have static IP addresses.

The domain has 14 client systems, all running Windows XP Professional. No business growth is expected this year, and the number of clients and servers is almost always static.

What is the simplest way to deploy a NetBIOS name resolution solution for your small Windows Server 2003 domain? (Choose two.)

❑ A. Configure one domain controller with the additional role of a WINS server.

❑ B. Configure both domain controllers with the additional role of a WINS server.

❑ C. Update the LMHOSTS file and place copies of it on all clients.

❑ D. Update the LMHOSTS file and place copies of it on all servers and domain controllers.

❑ E. Configure the DNS servers to resolve WINS names.

Question 48

You are configuring specific clients on your network to run on a restricted segment, as they are all connected directly to the Internet.

You are performing port filtering on these clients and have disallowed all ports except 25, 53, 67, 68, 80, 443, and 3389.

What traffic and network services will clients be able to use, assuming that no default ports have been changed? (Choose three.)

❑ A. FTP

❑ B. SMTP

❑ C. DNS

❑ D. LDAP

❑ E. Terminal Services

Question 49

You are an enterprise administrator for **gunderville.com**. Client systems in use are Windows 2000 Professional and Windows XP Professional. You have been tasked with enabling a password policy for the **sales.gunderville.com** child domain and have set the Password Must Meet Complexity Requirements policy at the domain level. You have also set the minimum password length to five characters.

Some users have called the help desk complaining that they cannot set passwords for their user accounts according to the instructions they were issued, which stated that passwords must be at least five characters.

The help desk has traced the problem to five-character passwords. All passwords longer than five characters work, but those that are exactly five characters are not accepted.

What is the main reason this problem is occurring?

○ A. Having the Password Must Meet Complexity Requirements policy enabled is causing the problem with the minimum password length.

○ B. The minimum password length is set to five characters, which means passwords need to be longer than five characters.

○ C. Both policies are linked at the domain level and are conflicting with each other.

○ D. Computer policies are conflicting with user policies.

Question 50

You are configuring clients on your Windows Server 2003 network to use a NetBIOS name server as their only means of resolving NetBIOS names. These systems are said to be configured in which mode?

○ A. P-node (peer-to-peer) configured clients

○ B. B-node (broadcast) configured clients

○ C. M-node (mixed) configured clients

○ D. H-node (hybrid) configured clients

Question 51

Your network is set up in two remote locations, each containing a Windows 2000 Server and a mix of 50 Windows 2000 Professional and Windows XP Professional systems. The two servers are set up as software routers, but the two routers are not directly connected to each other; they are connected by a third hardware router.

Users in both locations want to provide multicast-based virtual meetings to the other site instead of having staff travel from one site to the other. You add Internet Group Management Protocol (IGMP) to both servers. The hardware router does not support multicast forwarding or routing.

How should you configure the network to allow IP multicast traffic between the two locations? (Choose three.)

- ❑ A. Create an IP-in-IP interface between the servers.
- ❑ B. Assign the interface to the IGMP routing protocol.
- ❑ C. Run the interface in IGMP proxy mode.
- ❑ D. Run the interface in IGMP point-to-point mode.
- ❑ E. Run the interface in IGMP router mode.
- ❑ F. Run the interface in IGMP proxy mode.

Question 52

You are the network administrator for your Windows 2003 domain. Systems in use in your domain include Windows 2000 Professional and Windows XP Professional. Two systems are configured as Windows Server 2003 domain controllers; four servers in the server room are running WINS, DHCP, and DNS; and one system has been configured as a Web server.

You want to configure the Internet Information Services (IIS) ports on your Windows 2000 server as follows:

Open port 80 on the IIS server.

Block port 119 on the IIS server.

Block port 110 on the IIS server.

Open port 25 on the IIS server.

Open port 443 on the IIS server.

What are the results of these actions if no default ports have been changed? (Choose three.)

❑ A. The IIS service is configured correctly, so all clients can use HTTP.

❑ B. The IIS service is configured correctly, so all clients can use POP3.

❑ C. The IIS service is configured correctly, so all clients can use FTP.

❑ D. The IIS service is configured correctly, so all clients can use SMTP.

❑ E. The IIS service is configured correctly, so all clients can use HTTPS.

❑ F. The IIS service is configured correctly, so all clients can use NetBIOS communications.

Question 53

You are the network administrator for your Windows 2003 domain. Systems in use in your domain include Windows 2000 Professional and Windows XP Professional. Two systems are configured as Windows Server 2003 domain controllers; four servers in the server room are running WINS, DHCP, and DNS; and one system has been configured as a Web server.

You want to create an outline for management describing the similarities and differences between L2TP and PPTP. What are some key differences between these protocols? (Choose three.)

❏ A. PPTP can be used only in a IP-based network. L2TP requires only that the tunnel media provide packet-oriented, point-to-point connectivity.

❏ B. L2TP can be used only in a IP-based network. PPTP requires only that the tunnel media provide packet-oriented, point-to-point connectivity.

❏ C. PPTP supports header compression; L2TP does not.

❏ D. L2TP supports header compression; PPTP does not.

❏ E. PPTP uses PPP encryption. L2TP requires IPSec for encryption

❏ F. PPTP uses IPSec encryption. L2TP requires PPP for encryption

Question 54

You are the domain administrator for **gunderville.com**. Your enterprise has 15 Windows Server 2003 systems, 5 of which are installed as domain controllers.

Clients in your domain consist of 22 Windows 95 systems, 177 Windows 98 systems, 314 Windows NT 4 workstations, 829 Windows 2000 Professional systems, 89 Windows 2000 Server systems, and 279 Windows XP Professional systems.

You have been asked to analyze as many desktop systems in your environment as possible with Microsoft Baseline Security Analyzer (MBSA) and report which systems could not be scanned.

You are performing all scans remotely from a single console. What is the total number of desktop systems that can be scanned successfully across the network?

○ A. 1,422

○ B. 1,437

○ C. 1,459

○ D. 1,638

Question 55

You are the domain administrator for **gunderville.com**. Your enterprise has 15 Windows Server 2003 systems, 5 of which are installed as domain controllers.

Clients in your domain consist of 22 Windows 95 systems, 177 Windows 98 systems, 314 Windows NT 4 workstations, 829 Windows 2000 Professional systems, 89 Windows 2000 Server systems, and 279 Windows XP Professional systems.

For application compatibility reasons, File and Print Sharing is not enabled on any desktop systems, except the Windows NT 4 workstations. All member servers and domain controllers have File and Print Sharing disabled.

All systems connect to the Internet via an Internet Security and Acceleration (ISA) server at the company's headquarters. You have been asked to perform a security analysis of systems in your environment.

You need to be able to run application vulnerability checks on Microsoft Office 2000 and Windows XP for all systems in your enterprise. You also need to scan all systems remotely with the least amount of administrative effort and without altering the current network configuration or client setup.

You install MBSA version 1.1.1, which supports local and remote scanning on a Windows Server 2003 server in your domain. On which operating systems will you not be able to perform these actions with the current system configuration? (Choose four.)

- ❏ A. Windows 95
- ❏ B. Windows 98
- ❏ C. Windows NT 4
- ❏ D. Windows 2000 Professional
- ❏ E. Windows 2000 Server
- ❏ F. Windows XP Professional
- ❏ G. Windows Server 2003

Question 56

You are the domain administrator for **gunderville.com**. Your enterprise has 15 Windows Server 2003 systems, 5 of which are installed as domain controllers.

Clients in your domain consist of 22 Windows 95 systems, 177 Windows 98 systems, 314 Windows NT 4 workstations, 829 Windows 2000 Professional systems, 89 Windows 2000 Server systems, and 279 Windows XP Professional systems.

You have been asked to develop a single software update solution for all systems in the enterprise for security updates. This solution must allow administrative approval of all updates before they are deployed to any systems and support scheduling the installation of downloaded content.

You decide to deploy automated updates via the Windows Update site, using the Automatic Update client. Update scheduling will be configured via GPOs linked at the domain level and at the Domain Controllers OU.

What is the result of your actions? (Choose three.)

❏ A. The solution allows administrative approval of all updates before they are deployed to any systems.

❏ B. The solution does not allow administrative approval of all updates before they are deployed to any systems.

❏ C. The solution supports scheduling the installation of downloaded content.

❏ D. The solution does not support scheduling the installation of downloaded content.

❏ E. The solution allows you to configure a software update solution for all clients in your environment.

❏ F. The solution does not allow you to configure a software update solution for all clients in your environment.

Question 57

You are the domain administrator for **gunderville.com**. Your enterprise has 15 Windows Server 2003 systems, 5 of which are installed as domain controllers.

Clients in your domain consist of 22 Windows 95 systems, 177 Windows 98 systems, 314 Windows NT 4 workstations, 829 Windows 2000 Professional systems, 89 Windows 2000 Server systems, and 279 Windows XP Professional systems.

You have been asked to configure a software update solution for your environment that allows all security updates and fixes to be installed for all systems in your enterprise and that provides downloads of the latest Windows operating system and IE service packs.

All downloads are required to have administrative approval before they are deployed to any systems. You decide to deploy automated updates via the Windows Update site, using the Automatic Update client. Update scheduling will be configured via GPOs linked at the domain level and at the Domain Controllers OU.

What is the result of your actions? (Choose four.)

- ❏ A. The solution allows administrative approval of all updates before they are deployed to any systems.

- ❏ B. The solution does not allow administrative approval of all updates before they are deployed to any systems.

- ❏ C. The solution supports scheduling the installation of downloaded content.

- ❏ D. The solution does not support scheduling the installation of downloaded content.

- ❏ E. The solution allows you to configure a software update solution for all the clients in your environment.

- ❏ F. The solution does not allow you to configure a software update solution for all the clients in your environment.

- ❏ G. The solution allows you to provide downloads of the latest Windows operating system and IE service packs.

- ❏ H. The solution does not allow you to provide downloads of the latest Windows operating system and IE service packs.

Question 58

You are the domain administrator for **gunderville.com**. Clients in your domain consist of Windows 98, Windows Me, Windows 2000, and Windows XP Professional systems.

You have been asked to configure and secure the IP traffic traveling from your headquarters to remote offices over an untrusted network. Your solution must be able to be used on an IP network, be available to all clients in use, support header encryption and tunnel authentication, and provide encryption.

You need to secure IP traffic traversing an untrusted network in a manner that supports all clients in the environment. You decide to implement a strategy using L2TP and IPSec running in Tunnel mode between the RRAS server at headquarters and the server installed at the remote office in New York. You will enforce this security setting via the local security policies of those two servers. For legacy client systems to use this security solution, you will install the Microsoft L2TP/IPSec VPN client on the Windows 98, Me, and NT 4 systems.

What is the result of your actions? (Choose four.)

❑ A. All IP traffic traveling from your network over an untrusted network will be secured.

❑ B. All IP traffic traveling from your network over an untrusted network will not be secured.

❑ C. All clients in the environment will be supported under this solution.

❑ D. All clients in the environment will not be supported under this solution.

❑ E. The Microsoft L2TP/IPSec VPN client does not need to be installed on legacy systems.

❑ F. The Microsoft L2TP/IPSec VPN client does need to be installed on legacy systems.

❑ G. Header encryption and tunnel authentication are provided in this solution.

❑ H. Header encryption and tunnel authentication are not provided in this solution.

Question 59

You are the domain administrator for **gunderville.com**. You have decided to use public key certificates as the authentication method to be used with your IPSec policy.

What are the main characteristics of an environment that normally needs to use public key certificates? (Choose four.)

❑ A. Systems need to be manually configured.

❑ B. All subject systems are members of the same Active Directory domain.

❑ C. Legacy clients before Windows 2000 are used.

❑ D. Client systems are authenticating over the Internet.

❑ E. Client systems are not members of your domain.

❑ F. Client systems are connecting to your network via an extranet.

Question 60

You are the domain administrator for **gunderville.com**. The systems in use at your main office and branch offices are as follows:

Branch one has four Windows XP Professional workstations, two Windows 2000 Professional workstations, and one Windows Server 2003 system connected locally by one Windows Server 2003 system running RRAS. All clients use manually assigned IP addresses.

Branch two has five Windows 2000 Professional workstations, six Windows XP Professional workstations, and one Windows 2000 server. These systems are also connected locally by one Windows Server 2003 system running RRAS. All clients use manually assigned IP addresses.

Branch three has four Windows 2000 Professional workstations, three Windows XP Professional workstations, two Windows 2000 servers, one Windows Server 2003 system, and two Windows NT 4 Servers running SP6a. These systems are also connected locally by one Windows Server 2003 system running RRAS. All clients use manually assigned IP addresses.

The main office has six Windows 2000 Professional workstations, six Windows XP Professional workstations, two Windows 2000 servers, and three Windows Server 2003 systems. These systems are also connected locally by one Windows Server 2003 system running RRAS. All clients use manually assigned IP addresses.

You need to provide the most secure connection possible for all systems between your main office and your branch offices. This connection must always be available and work on all clients in all locations with the least amount of administrative effort.

You have decided to use L2TP and IPSec encryption in its default mode to provide the necessary security for your environment. All communications will be set to "require" security.

What are the results of your efforts? (Choose three.)

❑ A. Your solution provides a secure connection for all systems between your main office and your branch offices.

❑ B. Your solution does not provide a secure connection for all systems between your main office and your branch offices.

❑ C. Communications are set to "require" security, but it's not the most secure setting; "request" security should be used.

❑ D. Your solution works for all operating systems in use on the network.

❑ E. Communications are set to "require" security because it is the most secure setting.

11

Answers to
Practice Exam 2

1. B	**31.** A
2. C	**32.** D
3. D	**33.** D
4. D	**34.** D
5. A, B, E	**35.** A, C, F
6. D	**36.** A, B, C
7. A, D	**37.** D, E
8. B, C, E	**38.** A, B, D
9. B, F	**39.** C
10. E	**40.** A, B, C
11. B	**41.** A, C
12. B, C	**42.** A, D
13. A, D	**43.** D, E, G, H
14. A	**44.** B
15. B	**45.** E
16. E	**46.** B
17. B	**47.** C, D
18. D	**48.** B, C, E
19. C	**49.** A
20. D	**50.** A
21. B	**51.** A, B, C
22. C	**52.** A, D, E
23. A, B, C, D	**53.** A, D, E
24. A, C, E	**54.** A
25. A	**55.** A, B, D, F
26. D	**56.** B, C, F
27. A, B, E	**57.** B, C, F, G
28. D, F, G	**58.** A, C, E, G
29. B, C, H	**59.** C, D, E, F
30. D	**60.** B, D, E

Question 1

The correct answer is B. Standard Primary and Standard Secondary DNS zones are sometimes referred to as traditional DNS zone files. Both types are stored as text files on the DNS server's hard drive. Active Directory–integrated zones and Standard Primary DNS zones are both read/write copies of the DNS zone; therefore, answers A and C are incorrect. Stub zones are read-only copies of a DNS zone that contain a subset of the records associated with that zone, but the scenario called for an entire copy of the zone data and interoperation of the DNS server and the zone with BIND–based DNS servers; therefore, answer C is incorrect.

Question 2

The correct answer is C. An Active Directory–integrated zone is a type of DNS zone that allows for secure dynamic updates. Standard Primary and Standard Secondary DNS zones are sometimes referred to as traditional DNS zone files. Both types are stored as text files on the DNS server's hard drive. These zone types do not allow for secure dynamic updates; therefore, answers A and B are incorrect. Stub zones are read-only copies of a DNS zone that contain a subset of the records associated with that zone. These zone types do not allow for secure dynamic updates; therefore, answer D is incorrect.

Question 3

The correct answer is D. A DNS server configured with a stub zone is not authoritative for that zone, but it identifies the DNS servers that are authoritative for the zone.

Question 4

The correct answer is D. The actual issue here is that no default gateway is configured for PSERVER1, so it has no way to communicate outside its own subnet, which makes answer D the best choice. The PING `localhost` should return the result of 127.0.0.1. The subnet mask on the user's workstation is fine, so this eliminates answer A, and answer B states that the default gateway on the user's workstation is incorrect, when it's actually missing, so this answer is not correct.

Question 5

The correct answers are A, B, and E. There is no way a workstation with an IP address of 199.254.15.35 can use a subnet mask of 255.255.255.240 and default gateway of 199.254.15.1. There is nothing wrong with the settings on PSERVER, so none of these selections is the correct answer; therefore, answers C, D, F, and G are incorrect.

Question 6

The correct answer is D. The question stated that PSERVER1 is on the 10 network; that means its hostname should be 67.35.10 (with an IP address of 10.67.35.10). The question also mentioned that ROUTER1 has an IP address of 10.99.35.1. For these two systems to be on the same subnet, they both need to use the same subnet mask of 255.0.0.0. Although it might seem odd, the IP address of 10.67.35.10 using a subnet mask of 255.0.0.0 and a default gateway of 10.99.35.1 for PSERVER1 is fine. There are no incorrect settings on the workstation, and none of the other settings on PSERVER is incorrect; therefore, answers A, B, and C are incorrect.

Question 7

The correct answers are A and D. Unless another mechanism is already installed to facilitate the connection, an RRAS server needs to be installed at the Hartford and Wallingford locations to secure the connection between the two locations. L2TP and IPSec are the only suitable protocols; therefore, answers B and C are incorrect. Installing VPN servers does not secure all IP traffic between the Hartford and Wallingford locations; therefore, answers E and F are incorrect.

Question 8

The correct answers are B, C, and E. The Microsoft L2TP/IPSec VPN client must be installed on systems running Windows 98, Windows Me, or Windows NT Workstation 4.0 because those legacy operating systems cannot support this client on their own. Windows 2000 supports these protocols; therefore, answer A is incorrect. Implementing an L2TP and IPSec strategy running in Transport mode is necessary to set up secure traffic. The best way to implement it is by configuring a domain security policy, so answers C and E are also applicable. You do not need to configure a local security policy; therefore, answers D and F are incorrect. You want to set up required security, not requested; therefore, answer G is incorrect.

Question 9

The correct answers are B and F. The easiest way to configure and secure the IP traffic from the Hartford location to the remote office in Wallingford is to use the installed RRAS server and configure a local security policy to require security for all communications between them. Answer A is incorrect because you do not need to install the Microsoft L2TP/IPSec VPN client—the security association is made between the two RRAS servers, as this is the least amount of administrative effort. None of the other options completely addresses all the scenario's needs and requirements better than these two choices; therefore, answers A, C, D, and E are incorrect.

Question 10

The correct answer is E. None of the primary or secondary objectives has been met. Remote Assistance will not be enabled for all client systems in your environment because the Windows 2000 systems cannot be administered. Additionally, security will be changed by opening port 3389 on the firewall when it isn't necessary.

Question 11

The correct answer is B. Using the Classless Inter-Domain Routing setup of 177.25.0.128/26 allows 6 bits of host addressing, which means 62 host addresses are available per subnet, so answer B the only correct choice.

Question 12

The correct answers are B and C. RIPv2 can use CIDR and VLSM. OSPF is a link-state protocol based on an algorithm that determines the shortest path between source and destination nodes on a routed network. OSPF is a better choice than either version of RIP when you are considering routing 17 hops between the farthest segments of a network. RIPv1 is difficult to deploy in larger environments because it supports the main classes of IP addresses only and cannot use CIDR or VLSM (; therefore, answer A is incorrect. BGP uses TCP to send detected routing changes and updated router table information between gateway hosts on autonomous systems, such as gateway hosts on the Internet. The routing table contains a list of known routers, the IP addresses they can reach, and any cost metric associated with the routes; therefore, answer D is incorrect.

Question 13

The correct answers are A and D. Bridges and switches operate at the Data Link layer (Layer 2 of the OSI model) and automatically forward all broadcast traffic received; therefore, Subnets 1 and 2 will be part of the same broadcast domain, making answer A correct. Although Layer 2 switches can be found at the borders of collision domains, they do not form a border of a broadcast domain. Because Layer 2 switches do form the borders of collision domains, Subnets 1 and 2 will be in different collision domains, making answer D correct. Because answers B and C state the opposite, they are incorrect.

Question 14

The correct answer is A. The Application layer hosts the Telnet, FTP, DNS, SMTP, RIP, and SNMP protocols. The host-to-host transport layer of the TCP/IP architecture hosts both TCP and UDP; therefore, answer B is incorrect. The Internet layer hosts the IP, ARP, ICMP, and IGMP protocols; therefore, answer C is incorrect. The network interface layer hosts standards such as frame relay, ATM, ethernet, and token ring; therefore, answer D is incorrect.

Question 15

The correct answer is B. The host-to-host transport layer of the TCP/IP architecture hosts both TCP and UDP. The Application layer of the TCP/IP architecture hosts the Telnet, FTP, DNS, SMTP, RIP, and SNMP protocols; therefore, answer A is incorrect. The Internet layer hosts the IP, ARP, ICMP, and IGMP protocols; therefore, answer C is incorrect. The network interface layer hosts standards such as frame relay, ATM, ethernet, and token ring; therefore, answer D is incorrect.

Question 16

The correct answer is E. Protocols normally found at the Network layer of the OSI model are IP, ARP, RARP, ICMP, RIP, OSFP, IGMP, IPX, NWLink, NetBEUI, OSI, DDP, and DECnet. Because IP traffic is what you need to report on, answer E is correct. The protocols normally found at the Application layer are DNS, FTP, TFTP, BOOTP, SNMP, RLOGIN, SMTP, MIME, NFS, FINGER, TELNET, NCP, APPC, AFP, and SMB; therefore, answer A is incorrect. The Presentation layer translates from application to network format and vice versa; therefore, answer B is incorrect. The protocols normally found at the Session layer are NetBIOS, Named Pipes, Mail Slots, and RPC; therefore, answer C is incorrect. The protocols normally found at the Transport layer are TCP, SPX, NWLink, NetBIOS, NetBEUI, and ATP; therefore, answer D is incorrect.

Question 17

The correct answer is B. PPP logs provide control and error messages for a PPP connection and are one of the best resources available for troubleshooting PPP connectivity issues. When systems on your network are configured with RRAS enabled for network access by clients, you can use Windows Authentication or Windows Accounting to log authentication and accounting information for network access connections. This level of logging is in addition to any events recorded in the System log, but it does not give you the required information, so answer A is incorrect. The RRAS service supports logging authentication events and information for remote connections via the Remote Authentication Dial-In User Service (RADIUS) server when RADIUS authentication and accounting are enabled through the Internet Authentication Service. However, this does not give you the required information, so answer C is incorrect. You can use audit logging in Windows Server 2003 to monitor IPSec events to troubleshoot unsuccessful L2TP connections and IPSec encryption; therefore, answer D is incorrect.

Question 18

The correct answer is D. You can use audit logging in Windows Server 2003 to monitor IPSec events to troubleshoot unsuccessful L2TP connections and IPSec encryption. When systems on your network are configured with RRAS enabled for network access by clients, you can use Windows

Authentication or Windows Accounting to log authentication and account-ing information for network access connections, but it does not give you the required information, so answer A is incorrect. PPP logs provide control and error messages for a PPP connection and are one of the best resources avail-able for troubleshooting PPP connectivity issues, but they do not give you the required information, so answer B is incorrect. The RRAS service sup-ports logging authentication events and information for remote connections via the RADIUS server when RADIUS authentication and accounting are enabled through the Internet Authentication Service, but it does not give you the information necessary, so answer C is incorrect.

Question 19

The correct answer is C. Event 532 means that a logon attempt was made using an expired account. Event ID 529 indicates that a logon attempt was made with an unknown username or a known username with an invalid pass-word; therefore, answer A is incorrect. Event ID 530 indicates that a logon attempt was made by a user who violated account logon time restrictions; therefore, answer B is incorrect. Event ID 531 indicates that a logon attempt was made using a disabled account; therefore, answer D is incorrect.

Question 20

The correct answer is D. Event ID 531 indicates that a logon attempt was made using a disabled account. Answer A is incorrect because event ID 529 indicates that a logon attempt was made with an unknown username or a known username with an invalid password. Answer B is incorrect because event ID 530 indicates that a logon attempt was made by a user who violat-ed account logon time restrictions. Answer C is incorrect because event ID 532 indicates that a logon attempt was made using an expired account.

Question 21

The correct answer is B. The only correct choice is `route delete 192.168.1.0 mask 255.255.255.0 203.11.4.225`. Entering `route delete -p 192.168.1.0 mask 255.255.255.0 203.11.4.225` throws an error; therefore, answer A is incorrect. Likewise, entering `route delete -p 192.168.1.0/24 203.11.4.225` causes an error; therefore, answer C is incorrect. Entering `route` `delete` `192.168.1.0/24` `203.11.4.225` deletes the persistent route from the external connection; therefore, answer D is incorrect.

Question 22

The correct answer is C. A forest is a collection of Active Directory domain trees that may or may not be a part of a contiguous namespace, which makes answer C the only possible correct answer. None of the other answers correctly defines a forest; therefore, answers A, B, and D are incorrect.

Question 23

The correct answers are A, B, C, and D. When you need to define and outline at the highest level the four main planning, design, and implementation steps for upper management, you need to include information about the proposed DHCP design for your environment, an outline of integrating the DHCP design with existing services, an outline of the proposed scope configuration for the domain, and an outline of the proposed implementation of the DHCP solution. Answer E implies that an outline of the proposed hardware implementation for your DHCP solution is required, but you don't need this information until you go into a deep design plan during the outline of the overall proposed DHCP design; therefore, answer E is incorrect. Answer F implies that an outline of the proposed exclusion ranges for your DHCP scopes is required, but this information is normally part of the deeper outline of the proposed scope configuration for the domain; therefore, answer F is incorrect.

Question 24

The correct answers are A, C, and E. When you are designing your DNS deployment for your enterprise, you need to scale the system for memory requirements and size calculations. Under typical design usage, 4MB of RAM is the minimum requirement when a DNS server is started without any zones and uses additional RAM for each DNS zone added to the server. Note that an additional 100 bytes of RAM is used for each resource record added to the server's DNS zones. The remaining answers do not supply the required values; therefore, answers B, D, and F are incorrect.

Question 25

The correct answer is A. When your solution needs to allow client systems to resolve DNS queries as often as possible on a network with limited bandwidth and to make sure there is no single point of failure on this site for name resolution, your only option is installing two caching-only DNS servers locally. Forward-only DNS servers do not function if the external link to other DNS servers goes down. This is also true for non-recursive DNS servers and conditional-forwarder DNS servers; therefore, answers B, C, and D are incorrect.

Question 26

The correct answer is D. A conditional-forwarder DNS server forwards specific DNS queries according to the DNS domain name in the query. Because the question specified that client systems must always be able to resolve DNS queries for gunderville.com and have no single point of failure for name resolution, the best answer to this question is D. None of the other answers supplies the correct solution; therefore, answers A, B, and C are incorrect.

Question 27

The correct answers are A, B, and E. Low-level security DNS deployments have little to no security configurations. They can be found in designs and deployments where an enterprise's DNS infrastructure is fully exposed to the Internet and name resolution is performed by all DNS servers in the network. Often these DNS servers are configured with root hints pointing to root servers for the Internet, and all DNS servers have cache pollution prevention disabled. The DNS servers in a low-level security configuration have dynamic updating enabled on all DNS zones, and UDP and TCP port 53 traffic are allowed to pass at the network firewall. Only answers A, B, and E outline the parameters of a low-level security DNS deployment. All other options are for medium-level and high-level DNS security designs; therefore, answers C, D, F, and G are incorrect.

Question 28

The correct answers are D, F, and G. A medium-level security configuration is usually deployed with security features that are available to the DNS service when servers are configured with Standard Primary DNS zones on member servers. This type of DNS configuration might have limited direct exposure to the Internet, so zone transfers are limited to only the servers listed in the name server (NS) resource records. The DNS servers can use other DNS servers as forwarders when they cannot resolve names locally, and proxy servers and gateways are used for name resolution for Internet systems. Dynamic updating is not configured for any DNS zones, and cache pollution prevention is enabled. Only answers D, F, and G outline the parameters of a medium-level security DNS deployment. All other options are for low-level and high-level DNS security designs; therefore, answers A, B, C, and E are incorrect.

Question 29

The correct answers are B, C, and H. The usagunderville.com domain is not a child of gunderville.com because it is not part of the contiguous namespace. The usa_gunderville.com name uses a non-compliant underscore (_) character. The usa#1.gunderville.com name uses a # symbol, which is not RFC 1123 compliant. As defined in RFC 1123, you can use all uppercase letters (A–Z), lowercase letters (a–z), numbers (0–9), and the hyphen (-) for DNS namespaces on the Internet. The name u.s.a.gunderville.com is an acceptable child domain to gunderville.com; u would be a child of the s domain, which is a child of the a domain; therefore, answer A is incorrect. The names usa.internal.gunderville.com, usa.external.gunderville.com, usainternal. gunderville.com, u.s.a-one.gunderville.com, and usa-one.gunderville.com all use RFC 1123–compliant characters and are part of the contiguous namespace, so they are not incorrect.

Question 30

The correct answer is D. Each site has two DNS servers for each DNS namespace. So the Wallingford site has two DNS servers for gunderville.com, two DNS servers for usa.gunderville.com, and two DNS servers for connecticut.usa.gunderville.com—a total of six DNS servers in that site. Because there are six sites, there are 36 DNS servers total, making answers A, B, and C incorrect.

Question 31

The correct answer is A. Each site has two DNS servers for each DNS namespace. So the Wallingford site has two DNS servers for gunderville.com, two DNS servers for usa.gunderville.com, and two DNS servers for connecticut.usa.gunderville.com—a total of six DNS servers in that site. Because there are six sites, there are 36 DNS servers total. There can be only one Standard Primary zone for any DNS name space; there are three domain namespaces total, so answer A is the only correct answer.

Question 32

The correct answer is D. Each site has two DNS servers for each DNS namespace. So the Wallingford site has two DNS servers for gunderville.com, two DNS servers for usa.gunderville.com, and two DNS servers for connecticut.usa.gunderville.com—a total of six DNS servers in that site. Because there are six sites, there are 36 DNS servers total. There can be only one Standard Primary zone for any DNS name space; there are three domain namespaces total, so there are three Standard Primary zones. That means the remaining 33 DNS servers have a total of 33 Standard Secondary DNS zones.

Question 33

The correct answer is D. Each site has two DNS servers for each DNS namespace. So the Wallingford site has two DNS servers for gunderville.com, two DNS servers for usa.gunderville.com, and two DNS servers for connecticut.usa.gunderville.com—a total of six DNS servers in that site. Because there are six sites, there are 36 DNS servers total.

There can be only one Standard Primary zone for any DNS name space; there are three domain namespaces total, so there are three Standard Primary zones. That means the remaining 33 DNS servers have a total of 33 Standard Secondary DNS zones. All DNS servers store zone information. For gunderville.com, that means the Wallingford site has two DNS servers, the NH site has two DNS servers, the Connecticut site has two DNS servers, and the New England site has two DNS servers. The HQ site and the BU site for gunderville.com also have two DNS servers. Therefore, 12 DNS servers store zone information for gunderville.com, and one server is a

Standard primary DNS zone. That means 11 DNS servers are deployed across the sites with Standard Secondary DNS zones, so only answer D is correct.

Question 34

The correct answer is D. Each site has two DNS servers for each DNS namespace. So the Wallingford site has two DNS servers for gunderville.com—a Windows Server 2003 DNS server and a BIND DNS server with a Standard Secondary zone. There are two DNS servers for usa.gunderville.com—a Windows Server 2003 DNS server and a BIND DNS server with a Standard Secondary zone. The connecticut.usa.gunderville.com domain has two DNS servers—a Windows Server 2003 DNS server and a BIND DNS server with a Standard Secondary zone. Therefore, this site has six DNS servers, three of which are Windows Server 2003 DNS servers with Active Directory–integrated zones and three BIND DNS servers with Standard Secondary zones. With six sites total, that means 18 DNS servers are running BIND and hosting Standard Secondary zones. Therefore, only answer D is correct.

Question 35

The correct answers are A, C, and F. Both Standard Primary zones and Active Directory–integrated zones support standards outlined in the IETF specifications for domain namespaces. They also support incremental zone transfers and allow fault tolerance for name resolution, regardless of which DNS server fails, because Standard Secondary zones still resolve current DNS names if the Standard Primary DNS zone fails.

Only Active Directory–integrated DNS zones store zone information in Active Directory and allow read/write access to the DNS namespace for all DNS servers in a domain. Also, only Active Directory–integrated DNS zones allow fault tolerance for DNS updates, regardless of which DNS server fails, because these zones are multimaster copies of the zone information and can be updated on any DNS server. Answers B, D, and E are not examples of these features of Standard Primary zones and Active Directory–integrated zones.

Question 36

The correct answers are A, B, and C. Standard dynamic updates of DNS consider only the client operating system and its innate ability to update DNS, not the client membership or lack thereof in the domain. Windows 98 and NT 4 systems cannot update DNS; the DHCP service needs to be enabled to perform this action. Windows 2000 Professional clients in the domain and the workgroup can update DNS dynamically, so answers D and E are incorrect. The same can be said for Windows XP clients, so answer F is incorrect.

Question 37

The correct answers are D and E. Secure dynamic updates require that the DNS zone be Active Directory integrated, and this DNS zone is not. Regardless of whether clients are in a workgroup or a domain, none of the clients can update DNS dynamically because of the zones in use and the security implemented in the DNS design. Windows 98 and NT 4 systems cannot update DNS in this scenario, even if the zone is Active Directory integrated, and the operating systems cannot perform this action. The DHCP service needs to perform this task on behalf of clients.

Question 38

The correct answers are A, B, and D. Dynamic updates require that DNS servers support that type of update. This support can be found in Windows Server 2003 DNS, Windows 2000 Server DNS, and BIND DNS version 8.2.1. Windows NT 4 DNS and BIND DNS version 4.9.7 servers do not support dynamic updates, so answers C and E are incorrect.

Question 39

The correct answer is C. Windows NT 4 DNS and BIND DNS version 4.9.7 do not support incremental zone transfers. Incremental zone transfers require that the DNS servers support this type of transfer. This support can be found in Windows Server 2003 DNS, Windows 2000 Server DNS, and BIND DNS version 8.2.1, at a minimum. Newer versions of BIND 8.2.1 also support this feature.

Question 40

The correct answers are A, B, and C. DNS in Windows Server 2003, 2000, and NT 4 can use the WINS service to look up names not found in DNS by checking for the NetBIOS name in WINS. This type of lookup often resolves name resolution issues in environments with hosts that do not use WINS for name registration or lookups, such as you might find with Unix hosts or when the client's primary registration is with WINS, as with Windows NT 4 or 9x clients. These configuration options are available only on Windows Server 2003 DNS, 2000 DNS, and NT 4 DNS configurations. None of the BIND DNS versions supports WINS and WINS-R lookups; therefore, answers D and E are incorrect.

Question 41

The correct answers are A and C. An iterative query is a DNS resolution query made from a client to a DNS server, in which the server returns the best answer possible based on its local cache or stored zone data. If the server performing the iterative query does not have an exact match for the name request, it returns an error message saying that the requested name cannot be found, or it supplies a pointer to an authoritative server in another level of the domain namespace or to the Internet to query an ISP DNS name server or the root DNS servers on the Internet. A recursive query is a DNS resolution query made from a client to a DNS server, in which the server assumes the full workload and responsibility for providing a complete answer to the query. The DNS server returns a name resolution to the client system, or returns a "name not found" error if the DNS server cannot locate the DNS server that is authoritative for the requested domain name or if a lookup timeout condition is met. Answers B, D, and E describe different types of name resolution lookups.

Question 42

The correct answers are A and D. A DNS name server can resolve a query only for a zone for which it has authority. When DNS servers receive a resolution request, they attempt to locate the requested information in their own database. An iterative query is a DNS resolution query made from a client to a DNS server, in which the server returns the best answer possible based on its local cache or stored zone data. If the server performing the iterative query does not have an exact match for the name request, it returns an error message saying that the requested name cannot be found, or it supplies a pointer to an authoritative server in another level of the domain namespace or to the Internet to query an ISP DNS name server or the root DNS servers on the Internet. A recursive query is a DNS resolution query made from a client to a DNS server, in which the server assumes the full workload and responsibility for providing a complete answer to the query. The DNS server returns a name resolution to the client system, or returns a "name not found" error if the DNS server cannot locate the DNS server that is authoritative for the requested domain name or if a lookup timeout condition is met. Answers B, C, E, and F describe different types of name resolution lookups.

Question 43

The correct answers are D, E, G, and H. To successfully configure your DNS servers so that they provide DNS resolutions and assume the full workload and responsibility for supplying complete answers to DNS queries, you must set up your DNS servers so that they perform recursive DNS lookups on behalf of DNS clients. You do not want any DNS servers in your enterprise (except for one designated DNS server, DNS1.gunderville.com) to contain any pointer information to root servers on the Internet, so you will need to remove root hints from DNS2.gunderville.com through DNS12.gunderville.com. Because all servers should forward DNS requests for Internet resources to the DNS1.gunderville.com DNS server, you must configure all DNS servers, DNS2.gunderville.com through DNS12.gunderville.com, as forwarders and configure them to forward to DNS1.gunderville.com. You must also allow only DNS1.gunderville.com to perform DNS queries from the internal network through the firewall to the Internet for DNS resolution. This configuration prevents client systems manually configured with IP addresses of other DNS servers on the Internet—for example, DNS servers that belong to an ISP— from being able to make DNS resolution requests to those Internet systems. Answers A, B, C, and F do not produce the results the scenario requires.

Question 44

The correct answer is B. The zone transfer refresh interval on the Start of Authority (SOA) tab of the forward lookup zone is the best place to make changes if you want to adjust the time interval a secondary DNS server waits before querying for updated zone information. The default setting for the refresh interval is 15 minutes (900 seconds). When this threshold is met, the secondary DNS server requests a copy of the current SOA record and compares the serial number of the source server's SOA record with the serial number in its own local SOA record. If they are different, the secondary DNS server requests a zone transfer from the primary DNS server to update its information. If the default setting is not sufficient, lower the value to initiate requests more often so that updates occur more frequently. The DNS information in this scenario is very dynamic, so you need to lower the refresh interval so that your DNS servers are updated more often. None of the other options offers a better solution.

Question 45

The correct answer is E. The zone transfer expire interval is the best place to make changes if you want to adjust the amount of elapsed time that must occur before a secondary server stops responding to DNS queries because of failures for zone updates. After this threshold time has been exceeded, data in this replica of DNS information is assumed to be out of date because it has not been updated. The default value is 24 hours (86,400 seconds) and can be adjusted as necessary. If your environment is more sensitive to DNS changes and has a highly dynamic DNS configuration, you might need to shorten the expire interval so that these servers go "offline" sooner than 24 hours.

Question 46

The correct answer is B. When you need to configure your DNS servers from communicating with other DNS servers to resolve queries outside your domain, you need to disable recursion on DNS servers. Configuring DNS servers as forwarders actually tells them which other DNS servers to communicate with. Updating root hints has the same result. Round-robin rotation has nothing to do with allowing or preventing the DNS server from communicating with other DNS servers to resolve queries outside the domain. Caching-only DNS server are normally used to intentionally cache DNS lookup results gathered from other DNS servers.

Question 47

The correct answers are C and D. In such a small environment, the best solution is to use LMHOSTS files and place them on all systems. Configuring DNS servers to resolve the WINS names does not work in this scenario because there is no NetBIOS (WINS) name resolution in place. You could configure one or both domain controllers with the additional role of a WINS server, but this method is not the simplest way to deploy a NetBIOS name resolution solution for your small Windows Server 2003 domain. Also, you need to consider the hardware of current domain controllers; they are already overloaded when you take their hardware configuration into account. In addition, no business growth is expected this year, and the number of clients and servers is almost always static.

Question 48

The correct answers are B, C, and E. FTP runs on port 20 and 21. Because neither port is listed, clients will not be able to use this service or use LDAP, which runs on port 389. The other listed services would be allowed, as port filtering does not close out their default ports. DHCP on ports 67 and 68 would be permitted, as would HTTP and HTTPS traffic.

Question 49

The correct answer is A. When the Password Must Meet Complexity Requirements policy is enabled, passwords must meet the minimum complexity requirements, such as being at least six characters long. Answer B is incorrect because when the minimum password length is set, the password needs to be *at least* the indicated number, not more than the indicated number. Answer C is incorrect because both policies can be linked at the domain level and not conflict with each other. Answer D is incorrect because computer policies do not conflict with user policies in this scenario.

Question 50

The correct answer is A. P-node (peer-to-peer) configured clients use a NetBIOS/WINS server to resolve NetBIOS names. B-node (broadcast) configured clients use broadcasts for name registration and resolution; therefore, answer B is incorrect. M-node (mixed) configured clients use both B-node and P-node name resolution. B-node is used by default, and if the name is not resolved by broadcast, M-node clients try to resolve the name via the WINS server (P-node); therefore, answer C is incorrect. H-node (hybrid) configured clients use both P-node and B-node name resolution; therefore, answer D is incorrect.

Question 51

The correct answers are A, B, and C. To configure the network to allow IP multicast traffic between the two locations, you need to create an IP-in-IP interface between the servers, assign the interface to the IGMP routing protocol, and run the interface in IGMP proxy mode. Multicasting is useful for point-to-multipoint delivery of information on a network. Multicast traffic "hits" only nodes that are specifically listening for it. IP multicast addresses are reserved and assigned from within the Class D address range of 224.0.0.0 through 239.255.255.255. IGMP is used to exchange membership status information between IP routers that support multicasting and members of multicast groups. IP-in-IP tunnels are often used for forwarding IP multicast traffic from one area of the intranet to another, across a portion of the intranet that does not support multicast forwarding or routing. IGMP router mode keeps track of multicast hosts on the network. IGMP proxy-mode interfaces are designed to work with IGMP router mode interfaces. The purpose of proxy mode is to connect the multicast router to a private network or the Internet.

Question 52

The correct answers are A, D, and E. You open port 80 on the IIS server to allow HTTP traffic. You block port 119 on the IIS server, which denies newsgroup server traffic. You block port 110 on the IIS server, which denies POP3 traffic. You open port 25 on the IIS server to allow use of SMTP. You open port 443 on the IIS server, which allows secure HTTP connections. For this scenario, only answers A, D, and E describe the results of the actions taken if no default ports have been changed.

Question 53

The correct answers are A, D, and E. PPTP can be used only on a IP-based network. L2TP requires only that the tunnel media provide packet-oriented, point-to-point connectivity. L2TP can use UD, frame relay permanent virtual circuits (PVCs), X.25 VCs, or Asynchronous Transfer Mode (ATM) VCs to operate over an IP network. L2TP supports header compression; PPTP does not. When header compression is enabled, L2TP operates with 4 bytes of overhead, compared with 6 bytes for PPTP. L2TP supports tunnel authentication; PPTP does not. When PPTP or L2TP is used with IPSec, IPSec provides tunnel authentication so that L2TP tunnel authentication isn't necessary. PPTP uses PPP encryption. L2TP requires IPSec for encryption. Answer B is incorrect because L2TP is not limited to IP based networks. Answer C is incorrect because PPTP does not support header compression. Answer F is incorrect because PPTP uses MPPE, not IPSec.

Question 54

The correct answer is A. The question called for you to scan as many desktop systems across the network as possible with the MSBA tool. This includes all desktop systems running Windows NT 4.0 SP4 and later. (Although MBSA can remotely scan systems running Windows NT 4.0 SP4 and later, it cannot be installed locally on the system and run locally.) It also includes all desktop operating systems running Windows 2000 and Windows XP, for a total of 1,422: 314 Windows NT 4 workstations, 829 Windows 2000 Professional systems, and 279 Windows XP Professional systems. None of the other options is the correct number of desktop systems that can be scanned successfully across the network.

Question 55

The correct answers are A, B, D, and F. You cannot scan the Windows 95 and 98 systems simply because those platforms are not supported. You can scan the Windows NT 4 systems, as over-the-network scans are the only way that MBSA can scan NT 4 systems. This is why answer C is not correct. You can also scan all Windows Server 2003 and Windows 2000 Server systems because they have File and Print Sharing enabled. Because File and Print Sharing is not enabled on any desktop systems, except the Windows NT 4 workstations, you cannot scan the Windows 2000 Professional or Windows XP Professional systems. You can successfully scan the Windows 2000 Server and Windows Server 2003 systems because these servers have no File and Print Sharing restriction, so answers E and G are incorrect.

Question 56

The correct answers are B, C, and F. Because you have decided to deploy automated updates via the Windows Update site, using the Automatic Update client, the solution does not allow administrative approval of all updates before they are deployed to systems because clients simply download all available updates posted to the public Microsoft Web site. Although this solution allows you to schedule the installation of downloaded content, it cannot be used on all clients in your environment. For these reasons, answers A, D, and E are not correct.

Question 57

The correct answers are B, C, F, and G. Because you have decided to deploy automated updates via the Windows Update site, using the Automatic Update client, the solution does not allow administrative approval of all updates before they are deployed to systems because clients simply download all available updates posted to the public Microsoft Web site. Although this solution does allow you to schedule the installation of downloaded content, it cannot be used on all clients in your environment. The clients allow downloading of the latest Windows operating system and IE service packs via the Windows Update site. For these reasons, answers A, D, E, and H are not correct.

Question 58

The correct answers are A, C, E, and G. When your setup uses Tunnel mode, the two RRAS servers negotiate all security for the traffic, so the Microsoft L2TP/IPSec VPN client does not need to be installed on legacy systems. All IP traffic traveling from your network over an untrusted network will be secured and support all clients in the environment. Addressing requirements for header encryption, tunnel authentication, and encryption are met by using L2TP and IPSec, as L2TP can be used on IP, frame relay, X.25, or ATM-based networks.

Question 59

The correct answers are C, D, E, and F. Usually when systems need to be manually configured, a shared secret is being used. Kerberos is usually the authentication method when all subject systems are members of the same Active Directory domain. A public key certificate is often used in Internet settings, such as e-commerce, or when computer systems are not members of the local domain. Public key certificates are also used with legacy systems that cannot use Kerberos or when you have customers using an extranet, as these systems are not normally domain members and have no way to use Kerberos.

Question 60

The correct answers are B, D, and E. IPSec Transport mode authenticates and encrypts data flowing between any two computers running Windows 2000 Server or Windows Server 2003. It provides security for the network and can potentially support a secure connection with multiple computers at a time. Transport mode is the default IPSec mode.

Using IPSec in Tunnel mode authenticates and encrypts data flowing within an IP tunnel created between two routers. Windows 2000 Server and Window Server 2003 require RRAS to implement Tunnel mode for IPSec. You enable Tunnel mode in the IPSec Management console and configure Tunnel mode settings by supplying an IP address for each end of the tunnel. This encrypts all data sent between systems from one location to another via the two RRAS servers.

You need to provide a secure connection for all systems between your main office and your branch offices. This requirement has not been met because IPSec Transport mode does not cover all traffic from all systems. The solution also needs to be "always" available for all systems, but the NT 4 systems cannot use this solution.

Forcing all communications to "require" security encrypts all data transferred between all hosts. With this deployment, the NT 4 systems cannot communicate with other systems. "Request" security is less secure than "require" security because "request" security still allows unsecured network connections between systems. For those NT 4 systems to be able to use L2TP/IPSec, the Microsoft L2TP/IPSec VPN client needs to be installed.

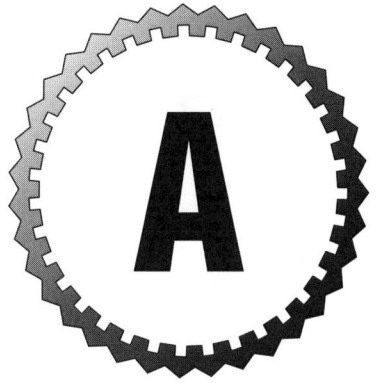

Windows Server 2003 Resources

Whether you are planning to sit down to reference a particular topic or you are preparing to study for an entire certification exam, you need to outline what it is you want to study or what you feel you need a refresher on. Only through an honest self-assessment can you ascertain whether you are ready to take on any certification exam, Microsoft or otherwise.

You can use a number of resources to extend your knowledge on the exam material, but I liken this section of the book to the "where can you go to learn more about the product" section of a product Web site.

First, I recommend the Microsoft Web site. Although many of the links there tend to move from time to time, there is no better free source of information. If a link on the Microsoft Web site is ever broken, try linking to http://www.microsoft.com/windows and performing a search from there.

Make sure you check the new TechNet site for Windows Server 2003 at http://www.microsoft.com/technet/prodtechnol/windowsserver2003/default.asp. This page offers a host of technical resources, tools, security guides, and other information designed to help IT professionals deploy, maintain, and support Windows Server 2003. Although many areas of reference are available, I recommend concentrating on the following section to prepare for this particular exam:

➤ *Terminal Server*—http://www.microsoft.com/technet/prodtechnol/windowsserver2003/serverroles/terminalserver/default.asp

➤ *Remote Access*—http://www.microsoft.com/technet/prodtechnol/windowsserver2003/serverroles/remoteaccessserver/default.asp

➤ *Domain Controller*—http://www.microsoft.com/technet/prodtechnol/ windowsserver2003/serverroles/domaincontroller/default.asp

➤ *DNS Server*—http://www.microsoft.com/technet/prodtechnol/ windowsserver2003/serverroles/dnsserver/default.asp

➤ *DHCP Server*—http://www.microsoft.com/technet/prodtechnol/ windowsserver2003/serverroles/dhcpserver/default.asp

➤ *WINS Server*—http://www.microsoft.com/technet/prodtechnol/ windowsserver2003/serverroles/winsserver/default.asp

For additional information on different versions of the Windows Server 2003 family, you can also review the online help files and the files for IIS6:

➤ *Standard Edition Help*—http://www.microsoft.com/technet/prodtechnol/ windowsserver2003/proddocs/standard/default.asp

➤ *Enterprise Edition Help*—http://www.microsoft.com/technet/prodtechnol/ windowsserver2003/proddocs/entserver/default.asp

➤ *Datacenter Edition Help*—http://www.microsoft.com/technet/prodtechnol/ windowsserver2003/proddocs/datacenter/default.asp

➤ *Internet Information Services 6.0 Help*—http://www.microsoft.com/technet/ prodtechnol/windowsserver2003/proddocs/standard/iiswelcome.asp

It's not critical to know every nuance of the different operating system versions, but recognizing a few major ones is important, such as which versions support clustering, which systems can be installed as domain controllers, and so forth.

The Microsoft Windows Server 2003 Deployment Kit provides administrators with strategies and recommendations for designing and deploying Windows Server 2003 in their enterprises and includes the following books, all available online:

➤ *Planning, Testing, and Piloting Deployment Projects*—http://www. microsoft.com/technet/prodtechnol/windowsserver2003/proddocs/deployguide/ dpgPDP_overview.asp

➤ *Deploying Network Services*—http://www.microsoft.com/technet/ prodtechnol/windowsserver2003/proddocs/deployguide/dpgDNS_overview.asp

➤ *Designing and Deploying Directory and Security Services*—http://www. microsoft.com/technet/prodtechnol/windowsserver2003/proddocs/deployguide/ dpgDSS_overview.asp

➤ *Planning Server Deployments*—http://www.microsoft.com/technet/ prodtechnol/windowsserver2003/proddocs/deployguide/dpgSDC_overview.asp

➤ *Automating and Customizing Installations*—http://www.microsoft.com/ technet/prodtechnol/windowsserver2003/proddocs/deployguide/ dpgACI_overview.asp

➤ *Designing a Managed Environment*—http://www.microsoft.com/technet/ prodtechnol/windowsserver2003/proddocs/deployguide/dpgDME_overview.asp

If you have any doubt as to whether you fully understand a concept, you can find the answers in the Microsoft Windows Server 2003 Deployment Kit. The kit also includes a Registry Reference for Windows Server 2003 at http://www.microsoft.com/technet/prodtechnol/windowsserver2003/proddocs/ deployguide/regentry_overview.asp, which is not critical for the exam, but is a valuable reference tool.

The following are excellent resources for managing the various features of Windows Server 2003:

➤ *Performance Counters Reference for Windows Server 2003 section of the Microsoft Windows Server 2003 Deployment Kit* (http://www.microsoft.com/ technet/prodtechnol/windowsserver2003/proddocs/deployguide/counters_ overview.asp)—A reference guide for the available performance counters used by the System Monitor and Performance Logs and Alerts.

➤ *Microsoft Windows Server 2003 Resource Kit Tools* (http://go.microsoft.com/ fwlink/?linkid=4544)—Available as a separate download, these tools are used primarily by administrators to assist with management and troubleshooting tasks in their environments.

➤ *Deploying Internet Information Services (IIS) 6.0 guide* (http://www. microsoft.com/technet/prodtechnol/windowsserver2003/proddocs/deployguide/ iisDG60_overview.asp)—A solid reference for administrators to secure their Web server deployments of IIS 6.

➤ *Web and Application Services in Windows Server 2003 Web site* (http://www. microsoft.com/technet/prodtechnol/windowsserver2003/technologies/webapp/ default.asp)—Additional information on IIS 6.

For the most part, the information supplied in the Windows Server 2003 Resource Kit Tools and the Deploying Internet Information Services (IIS) 6.0 guide is not going to be in high demand as a reference for the 70-293 exam. You can find some pertinent information, but in most cases, the information goes into more depth than what the exam covers. I have listed the additional information here as material for a point of reference and further study.

Microsoft Windows Server 2003, Enterprise Edition, and Windows Server 2003, Datacenter Edition, provide the Windows Clustering technologies by default. You can find a wealth of information on the Cluster Service on the Microsoft Web site at http://www.microsoft.com/technet/prodtechnol/windowsserver2003/technologies/clustering/default.asp.

Additional reference information on Terminal Services in Microsoft Windows Server 2003 can be found at http://www.microsoft.com/technet/prodtechnol/windowsserver2003/technologies/terminal/default.asp.

Although security information is increasingly needed in many enterprises, there is only a moderate need to know this material for the exam. Still, with the increase of demand for information, it would not hurt to review the material at http://www.microsoft.com/technet/prodtechnol/windowsserver2003/technologies/security/default.asp because certain sections of the site do reference Windows Update, Automatic Updates, Software Update Services (SUS), and Systems Management Server (SMS), which are detailed in the 70-293 exam.

The management services in Windows Server 2003 pertain mainly to information about using the Group Policy Microsoft Management Console (MMC). Some sections are relevant to overviews of Windows Server 2003 Management Services as a whole; for a review, go to http://www.microsoft.com/technet/prodtechnol/windowsserver2003/management/default.asp.

There are truly no single points of reference for any certification topic or area of concentration for any technology. Even your day-to-day routine might not encompass enough of a cross section of responsibilities to enable you to touch on all needed areas of study. The links and references I have supplied in this appendix are my best suggestions as starting points for further information and research.

What's on the CD-ROM

This appendix provides a brief summary of what you'll find on the CD-ROM that accompanies this book. For a more detailed description of the PrepLogic Practice Exams, Preview Edition exam simulation software, see Appendix C, "Using the PrepLogic Practice Exams, Preview Edition Software." In addition to the PrepLogic Practice Exams, Preview Edition software, the CD-ROM includes an electronic version of the book in Portable Document Format (PDF) and the source code used in the book.

The PrepLogic Practice Exams, Preview Edition Software

PrepLogic is a leading provider of certification training tools. Trusted by certification students worldwide, PrepLogic is the best practice exam software available. In addition to providing a means of evaluating your knowledge of this book's material, PrepLogic Practice Exams, Preview Edition features several innovations that help you improve your mastery of the subject matter.

For example, the practice tests enable you to check your score by exam area or domain to determine which topics you need to study further. Another feature gives you immediate feedback on your responses in the form of explanations for correct and incorrect answers.

PrepLogic Practice Tests, Preview Edition exhibits all the full-test simulation functionality of the Premium Edition but offers only a fraction of the total questions. To get the complete set of practice questions, visit `http://www.preplogic.com` and order the Premium Edition for this and other challenging exam training guides.

For a more detailed description of the features of the PrepLogic Practice Exams, Preview Edition software, see Appendix C.

An Exclusive Electronic Version of the Text

As mentioned previously, the CD-ROM that accompanies this book also contains an electronic PDF version of this book. This electronic version comes complete with all figures as they appear in the book. You can use Acrobat's handy search capability for study and review purposes.

C

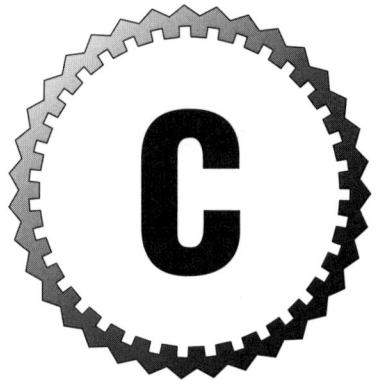

Using the PrepLogic Practice Exams, Preview Edition Software

This book includes a special version of the PrepLogic Practice Exams software, a revolutionary test engine designed to give you the best in certification exam preparation. PrepLogic offers sample and practice exams for many of today's most in-demand and challenging technical certifications. A special Preview Edition of the PrepLogic Practice Exams software is included with this book as a tool for assessing your knowledge of the training guide material and to give you the experience of taking an electronic exam.

This appendix describes in detail what PrepLogic Practice Exams, Preview Edition is, how it works, and what it can do to help you prepare for the exam. Note that although the Preview Edition includes all the test simulation functions of the complete retail version, it contains only a single practice test. The Premium Edition, available at http://www.preplogic.com, contains a complete set of challenging practice exams designed to optimize your learning experience.

The Exam Simulation

One of the main functions of PrepLogic Practice Exams, Preview Edition is exam simulation. To prepare you to take the actual vendor certification exam, PrepLogic is designed to offer the most effective exam simulation available.

Question Quality

The questions provided in PrepLogic Practice Exams, Preview Edition are written to the highest standards of technical accuracy. The questions tap the content of this book's chapters and help you review and assess your knowledge before you take the actual exam.

The Interface Design

The PrepLogic Practice Exams, Preview Edition exam simulation interface gives you the experience of taking an electronic exam. This interface enables you to effectively prepare to take the actual exam by making the test experience familiar. Using this test simulation can help eliminate the sense of surprise or anxiety you might experience in the testing center because you will already be acquainted with computerized testing.

The Effective Learning Environment

The PrepLogic Practice Exams, Preview Edition interface provides a learning environment that not only tests you through the computer, but also teaches the material you need to know to pass the certification exam. Each question includes a detailed explanation of the correct answer, and most of these explanations provide reasons for the other answers being incorrect. This information helps reinforce the knowledge you already have and provides practical information you can use on the job.

Software Requirements

PrepLogic Practice Exams requires a computer with the following:

➤ Microsoft Windows 98, Windows Me, Windows NT 4.0, Windows 2000, or Windows XP

➤ A 166MHz or faster processor

➤ A minimum of 32MB of RAM

➤ 10MB of hard drive space

> **NOTE**
>
> **Performance** As with any Windows application, the more memory, the better the performance.

Installing PrepLogic Practice Exams, Preview Edition

You install PrepLogic Practice Exams, Preview Edition by following these steps:

1. Insert the CD that accompanies this book into your CD-ROM drive. The Autorun feature of Windows should launch the software. If you have Autorun disabled, select Start, Run. Go to the root directory of the CD and select setup.exe. Click Open, and then click OK.

2. The Installation Wizard copies the PrepLogic Practice Exams, Preview Edition files to your hard drive. It then adds PrepLogic Practice Exams, Preview Edition to your desktop and the Programs menu. Finally, it installs test engine components to the appropriate system folders.

Removing PrepLogic Practice Exams, Preview Edition from Your Computer

If you elect to remove PrepLogic Practice Exams, Preview Edition, you can use the included uninstallation process to ensure that it is removed from your system safely and completely. Follow these instructions to remove PrepLogic Practice Exams, Preview Edition from your computer:

1. Select Start, Settings, Control Panel.

2. Double-click the Add/Remove Programs icon to display a list of software installed on your computer.

3. Select the PrepLogic Practice Exams, Preview Edition title you want to remove. Click the Add/Remove button to remove the software from your computer.

How to Use the Software

PrepLogic is designed to be user friendly and easy to learn. Because the software has a smooth learning curve, your time is maximized because you can start practicing with it almost immediately. PrepLogic Practice Exams, Preview Edition has two major modes of study: Practice Exam and Flash Review.

In Practice Exam mode, you can develop your test-taking abilities and knowledge by using the Show Answer option. While you are taking the test, you can display the answers along with detailed explanations of why answers are right or wrong. This feature helps you better understand the material.

Flash Review mode is designed to reinforce exam topics rather than quiz you. In this mode, you are shown a series of questions but no answer choices. You can click a button that reveals the correct answer to each question and a full explanation for that answer.

Starting a Practice Exam Mode Session

Practice Exam mode enables you to control the exam experience in ways that actual certification exams do not allow. To begin studying in Practice Exam mode, click the Practice Exam radio button in the main exam customization window to enable the following options:

➤ *The Enable Show Answer button*—Clicking this button activates the Show Answer button, which enables you to view the correct answers and a full explanation for each question during the exam. When this option is not enabled, you must wait until after your exam has been graded to view the correct answers and explanation for each question.

➤ *The Enable Item Review button*—Clicking this button activates the Item Review button, which enables you to view your answer choices. This option also facilitates navigation between questions.

➤ *The Randomize Choices option*—You can randomize answer choices from one exam session to the next. This makes memorizing question choices more difficult, thereby keeping questions fresh and challenging longer.

On the left side of the main exam customization window is the option of selecting the preconfigured practice test or creating your own custom test. The preconfigured test has a fixed time limit and number of questions. With custom tests, you can configure the time limit and number of questions in your exam.

The Preview Edition on this book's CD-ROM includes a single preconfigured practice test. You can get the compete set of challenging PrepLogic Practice Exams at www.preplogic.com to make certain you're ready for the big exam.

You click the Begin Exam button to begin your exam.

Starting a Flash Review Mode Session

Using Flash Review mode is an easy way to reinforce topics covered in the practice questions. To begin studying in Flash Review mode, click the Flash Review radio button in the main exam customization window. Then you select the preconfigured practice test or create your own custom test.

You click the Begin Exam button to begin a Flash Review mode session.

Standard PrepLogic Practice Exams, Preview Edition Options

The following list describes the function of each button you see across the bottom of the window:

NOTE

Button status Depending on the options, some buttons are grayed out and inaccessible—or they might be missing completely. Buttons that are relevant to the mode you're in are active.

➤ *Exhibit*—This button is visible if an exhibit is available to support the question. An *exhibit* is an image that provides supplemental information that is necessary to answer a question.

➤ *Item Review*—This button leaves the question window and opens the Item Review window, from which you can see all questions, your answers, and your marked items. You can also see correct answers listed here, when appropriate.

➤ *Show Answer*—This option displays the correct answer, with an explanation of why it is correct. If you select this option, the current question is not scored.

➤ *Mark Item*—You can select this check box to flag a question you need to review further. You can view and navigate your marked items by clicking the Item Review button (if it is enabled). When your exam is being graded, you are notified if you have any marked items remaining.

➤ *Previous Item*—You can use this option to view the previous question.

➤ *Next Item*—You can use this option to view the next question.

➤ *Grade Exam*—When you have completed your exam, you can click Grade Exam to end your exam and view your detailed score report. If you have unanswered or marked items remaining, you are asked if you would like to continue taking your exam or view the exam report.

Seeing Time Remaining

If your practice test is timed, the time remaining is displayed in the upper-right corner of the application window. It counts down the minutes and seconds remaining to complete the test. If you run out of time, you are asked if you want to continue taking the test or if you want to end your exam.

Getting Your Examination Score Report

The Examination Score Report window appears when the Practice Exam mode ends—as a result of time expiration, completion of all questions, or your decision to end the exam early.

This window provides a graphical display of your test score, with a breakdown of scores by topic domain. The graphical display at the top compares your overall score with the PrepLogic Exam Competency Score, which reflects the level of subject competency required to pass the particular vendor's exam. Although this score does not directly translate to a passing score, consistently matching or exceeding this score does suggest that you have the knowledge needed to pass the actual vendor exam.

Reviewing Your Exam

From the Your Score Report window, you can review the exam you just completed by clicking the View Items button. You can navigate through the items and view the questions, your answers, the correct answers, and the explanations for those questions. You can return to your score report by clicking the View Items button.

Contacting PrepLogic

If you would like to contact PrepLogic for any reason, including to get information about its extensive line of certification practice tests, you can do so online at www.preplogic.com.

Customer Service

If you have a damaged product and need to contact customer service, please call 800-858-7674.

Product Suggestions and Comments

PrepLogic values your input! Please email your suggestions and comments to feedback@preplogic.com.

License Agreement

YOU MUST AGREE TO THE TERMS AND CONDITIONS OUTLINED IN THE END USER LICENSE AGREEMENT ("EULA") PRESENTED DURING THE INSTALLATION PROCESS. IF YOU DO NOT AGREE TO THESE TERMS, DO NOT INSTALL THE SOFTWARE.

Glossary

3DES (Triple DES)

Uses the same algorithm as standard DES, but increases the key space by encrypting, decrypting, and then encrypting the data again, using different keys in an effort to prevent a brute-force attack. 3DES leverages all the security of DES while effectively lengthening the key. See also DES.

10Base2

The ethernet specification for thin coaxial cable, which transmits signals at 10Mbps (megabits per second), with a distance limit of 185 meters per segment without using a repeater. The *10* in the media type designation refers to the transmission speed in Mbps. The *Base* refers to baseband signaling. The last number varies for different media types. A *T*, for examples, means "twisted-pair cable," and *F* stands for "fiber-optic cable."

Numbers such as 2, 5, and 36 represent coaxial cable segment lengths. The 185-meter length in 10Base2 has been rounded up to *2* for 200, but it's actually only 185 meters. 10Base2 is also known as thin ethernet, ThinNet, or Cheapernet; it uses RG-58 coaxial cable in a bus topology.

10Base5

The ethernet specification for thick coaxial cable, which transmits signals at 10Mbps, with a distance limit of 500 meters per segment without using a repeater. Also known as thick ethernet or ThickNet, 10Base5 uses RG-8 coaxial cable in a bus topology.

10BaseF

The ethernet specification for fiber-optic cable, which transmits signals at 10Mbps, with a distance limit of 1,000 meters per segment without using a repeater.

100BaseT

The ethernet specification for Fast Ethernet. There are three types of physical wiring that can carry signals: 100BaseT4 (four pairs of telephone twisted-pair wire), 100BaseTX (two pairs of data-grade twisted-pair wire), and 100BaseFX (a two-strand fiber-optic cable).

100BaseT4

This 100Mbps Fast Ethernet physical layer specification uses Category 3 unshielded twisted-pair (UTP) cable in a star topology. (For the most part, Category 5 UTP cable is now used as part of the 100BaseTX specification.) 100BaseT4 has a maximum segment length of 100 meters, without using repeaters.

100BaseTX

This 100Mbps Fast Ethernet physical layer specification uses Category 5 or better UTP cable in a star topology, with a maximum segment length of 100 meters without using repeaters. 100BaseTX uses only two pairs of wires in the cable because the specification insists on high-quality Category 5 cable.

access

The interfacing between a user, program, service, or another computer system and an object, usually a computer, a network resource, or a device attached to the computer, that results in the transfer of data.

access permissions

Permissions such as Read and Write that can be set to allow or deny for users and groups. Access permissions, sometimes referred to as "access rights," can be set for files, folders, system and domain objects, and network resources.

access token

Contains security information for a logon session for a user or a service. Access tokens are created when a user logs on to identify the user, the user's groups, and the user's privileges, and every process that takes place on a network on behalf of the user has a copy of the token. Network resources use the access token to control access rights of users, groups, or services. Access tokens also refer to smart cards; a user enters a password first and then the token displays a constantly changing ID code (set to a specific timeframe, such as every 240 seconds) that can be used to log in to a network at that particular time.

accounting

Tracking user activity, such as the length of the session, the services that were used, and the amount of data transferred during the session for trend analysis, audit comparisons, capacity planning, and other similar uses.

accountability

The principle of tracing specific actions to a specific user or users by using identification and authorization techniques to track, monitor, and log user actions on a system or within an environment.

ACE (access control entry)

An entry in an Access Control List (ACL) that designates the access rights that are allowed or denied for Discretionary ACLs or that are audited for System ACLs.

ACL (Access Control List)

A list of security settings configured by the user or group. An ACL is set by ACEs that can be applied to folders, files, objects, or anything else having a security descriptor. There are two main types of ACLs: Discretionary ACLs and System ACLs.

Active Directory distribution group

Used to gather a specific set of users for nonsecurity-related functions. Sending email messages to a distribution group is a primary example. You cannot use distribution groups to assign rights and permissions.

Active Directory security group

Used to gather a specific set of users to assign access rights and permissions via the group, instead of individually to each user object. You can also use security groups as email distribution lists.

Administrator

The default account name for the main system management account in Windows NT, 2000, and 2003

operating systems. The ROOT account is the default account name for the main system management account in Unix systems.

anycast

Anycast communications are designed to facilitate sending data and information from a single sender to the nearest of several target hosts under IPv6. Anycast communication is most often used when a single system is used to update information for many other systems. For example, a single router might be used to communicate routing updates to other routers.

APIPA (Automatic Private IP Addressing)

APIPA is available on Windows 98, Windows Me, Windows 2000, Windows XP, and the Windows Server 2003. If a DHCP client doesn't receive any responses to its DHCPDISCOVER broadcast, it continues to make attempts to lease an address by retransmitting the message at varying intervals. If there is still no response, APIPA-aware clients can automatically configure IP addresses and subnet masks by using a selected address from the Microsoft-reserved Class B network, 169.254.0.0, with the subnet mask 255.255.0.0.

application filtering

Network traffic is filtered in and out of a network based on application-level parameters at the router, gateway, or firewall. Network filtering increases network security and limits the type of traffic allowed to pass in either direction.

Application layer (OSI Layer 7)

This layer, used by applications written to run over the network, allows access to network services that support those applications. Protocols normally found at this level are HTTP, S-HTTP or HTTPS, FTP, TFTP, SMTP, POP3, IMAP4, Network Time Protocol (NTP), DHCP, and SNMP.

ARP (Address Resolution Protocol)

This is the TCP/IP protocol that resolves IP addresses of computers on a LAN to MAC addresses. ARP is also a command-line utility used to display the IP-to-physical (MAC) address translation tables that the ARP protocol uses. You can also use ARP to set manual and static entries in the table.

authentication

In this process, credentials are presented and challenged when users or systems need to provide something, such as a smart card or a password, to prove that they are who they claim to be in the identification process. The main means of user authentication are access passwords (something the user knows), access tokens (something the user owns, such as a keycard), and biometrics (something that is part of the user, such as a fingerprint or voice print). Any combination of these three means can be required for authentication, depending on the rules of the local network and the system.

authorization

Authorization is the level of access granted to users or systems and specifies what they are allowed to do with that access. Authorization is limited via file and data owners, the principle of least privilege, and the separation of duties and responsibilities. File and data owners are people responsible for managing and sustaining applicable rights and permissions for network resources. Authorization occurs after a user's or system's identification has been acknowledged and verified through authentication.

availability

The process of making certain that systems and data are available to permitted personnel in a timely manner.

backup

The process of duplicating data for storage, archival, and restoration. For Windows systems and in NTBackup, there are five different types of backups: normal, copy, daily, incremental, and differential.

bastion host

A networked system on the public side of the DMZ that is not protected by a firewall or filtering router. Firewalls and routers can be considered bastion hosts, as can mail servers, DNS servers, Web servers, and FTP servers, for example. These systems are sometimes configured as a honeypot to deliberately provide hackers a target to hit and can be used to track and monitor attempted break-ins.

BOOTP (Bootstrap Protocol)

An Internet protocol that enables a diskless workstation to discover its own IP address, the IP address of a BOOTP server on the network, and a file to be loaded into memory to boot the machine. This is how workstations without a hard drive usually start up.

bridge

An OSI Layer 2 (Data Link) network device that is deployed to connect two LANs of similar topologies. Bridges and other Layer 2 devices, such as Layer 2 switches, form the boundaries of collision domains. All network devices that are interconnected by bridges are part of the same broadcast domain. Bridges simply forward packets without analyzing and rerouting messages, so they are protocol independent.

broadcast

A type of general traffic, usually limited to a subnet. A client system sends out special broadcast frames to all available hosts at the same time. The frames are designed so that every host in the subnet receives the announcement, as no one client is specifically designated to receive the message. Broadcast messages are often used to advertise a network service, for name resolution, and other similar uses.

broadcast domains

Network segments in which all devices on those segments can hear broadcast and multicast messages. Broadcast and multicast frames are found at Layer 3 of the OSI model, so devices such as Layer 2 switches and bridges simply pass these packets along. To create borders for broadcast domains so that you can segment which network devices hear broadcast messages, you need to use a Layer 3 switch or a router that operates at the Network layer.

brouter

A network device that functions as a router and a bridge. Brouters understand how to route specific types of packets, such as TCP/IP packets. Any other packets they receive are simply forwarded to other networks connected to the device.

brute-force attack

A type of attack in which every possible key or username/password combination is attempted until the key or username/password combination is guessed.

buffer overflow

In this attack on the buffer (a predetermined area of memory that holds data for processing), the data sent to the buffer is too large for it to handle. Depending on the error-handling routine of the program where the buffer overflow is occurring, the extra data could result in an output error (the correct response to this type of action, intentional or not) or the system becoming unstable and crashing. The excess data might also overwrite legitimate data in the adjacent space and allow the data sent to the buffer to overwrite and change the return address of a function call; this could even allow the attacker to run malicious code.

CA (Certificate Authority)

A trusted organization (often a third-party body) that issues digital certificates used to create digital signatures and public-private key pairs. A CA guarantees that the party granted the unique certificate is, in fact, who it claims to be. Certificates are the digitally signed documents that match public key pairs and guarantee that the public key belongs to the party that presents it.

CHAP (Challenge Handshake Authentication Protocol)

A challenge-response authentication protocol that uses the MD5 one-way encryption scheme to encrypt the response. Remote access servers return a challenge to potential clients in the form of a session identifier and an arbitrary challenge string. The remote access client then sends a response containing the username and a one-way encryption of the challenge string, the session identifier, and the password. The remote access server checks the response and allows the connection if all the information supplied is valid.

CIDR (Classless Inter-Domain Routing)

CIDR was once referred to as "supernetting," but today CIDR (pronounced "cider") is the common term for a way to allocate and specify Internet addresses that client systems use, outside the standard IP address class ranges. An example of a CIDR IP address is 201.77.181.0/20; the 201.77.181.0 is the network address and the 20 means that the first 20 bits of the entire address are the network portion. CIDR allows using the last 12 bits for host addressing. Although CIDR is supported by the Border Gateway Protocol, Exterior Gateway Protocol, and Routing Information Protocol do not support CIDR.

Cipher

This command-line utility displays or alters the encryption state of data on NTFS partitions. Cipher is used with EFS.

circuit-level filtering

Enables inspection of networked sessions between systems, instead of inspecting the connections or the transmitted packets. Circuit-level filtering increases network security and limits the type of traffic allowed to pass in either direction.

collision domain

A network segment in which all devices on the segment can "hear" when a collision happens. If a network design includes a switch at one end and a bridge at the other, for example, all hosts between those two network devices are considered part of a single collision domain. Devices beyond the Layer 2 switch and bridge typically belong to a different collision domain.

copy backup

This backup option backs up all selected files and folders that do not rely on the archive bit. This process is similar to normal or full backups—it simply backs up everything selected. The difference is that the copy backup does *not* reset the archive bit during the backup process, as in a normal backup. If you need to back up files and folders and do not want to affect other backup types by resetting the archive bit, a copy backup is the best option.

cryptography

Protecting information by encrypting it into an unreadable format (ciphertext), so that only specific key holders can decipher (decrypt) the message into a readable text format.

CSMA/CA (Carrier Sense Multiple Access/Collision Avoidance)

This access, defined in the IEEE 802.11 standard, minimizes collisions caused by simultaneous transmissions on the network.

CSMA/CD (Carrier Sense Multiple Access with Collision Detection)

This protocol, part of the IEEE 802.3 standard, is used by network devices for carrier transmission access on ethernet networks. Each device uses CSMA/CD to sense whether the line is available for use or whether traffic is present. When nodes believe the line is available, they begin their transmissions. If another node tries to send at the same time, a collision occurs, and data frames from both nodes are discarded. Each node then waits a random amount of time and retries until it's successful.

CSU/DSU (Channel Service Unit/Data Service Unit)

A hardware device that converts digital data frames from the communications technology used on a LAN into frames appropriate for a WAN, and vice versa.

DAC (Discretionary Access Controls)

This set of controls allow the data or resource owner to specify who can access certain resources; access is restricted via a permission structure set for users. The most common implementation of DAC is Access Control Lists (ACLs).

daily backup

This backup option does not rely on or reset the archive bit. It is used to back up all selected files and folders that have changed during that day.

Data Link layer (OSI Layer 2)

This layer handles moving data across a physical link in a network. It contains two sublayers, Media Access Control (MAC) and Logical Link Control (LLC), that are described in the IEEE-802 LAN standards.

DES (Data Encryption Standard)

A 64-bit block cipher using a 56-bit key (originally used a 128-bit key). Developed by IBM, DES was formally selected as the U.S. government's standard encryption algorithm and quickly became the most widely used symmetric encryption algorithm by the National Security Agency (NSA). DES is no longer secure enough to use on sensitive data, however, so 3DES is recommended. Although the DES algorithm hasn't been cracked, the increased computing power available to hackers means that keys could be found by brute-force attacks within a matter of hours and at a lower cost than before. See also 3DES.

DHCP (Dynamic Host Configuration Protocol)

This protocol is used to dynamically assign IP addresses to clients from a pool of addresses called a "scope." There are three different types of IP addressing: manual addressing, dynamic addressing, and Automatic Private IP Addressing (APIPA).

DHCPACK

DHCP message type used by servers to acknowledge a client's acceptance of an offered IP address.

DHCPDECLINE

DHCP message type used by clients to reject an offered IP address.

DHCPDISCOVER

DHCP message type used by clients to request configuration parameters from a DHCP server.

DHCPINFORM

DHCP message type used by clients to obtain additional TCP/IP configuration parameters from a server.

DHCPNAK

DHCP message type used by servers to reject a client's acceptance of an offered IP address.

DHCPOFFER

DHCP message type used by servers to offer IP addresses to requesting clients.

DHCP Relay Agent

Relays DHCP and BOOTP messages between clients and servers on different subnets. The DHCP leasing process uses broadcast transmissions, which are limited to the subnet where they originated.

When a router running a DHCP relay agent receives broadcasts from DHCP clients, it relays them to DHCP servers on other networks.

DHCPRELEASE
DHCP message type used by clients to terminate an IP address lease.

DHCPREQUEST
DHCP message type used by clients to accept or renew an IP address assignment.

DHCP reservation
If a client on the network requires the same IP address at all times, a DHCP reservation can be configured to ensure that it always leases the same IP address from the DHCP server.

differential backup
This backup option is normally used on a daily basis, between normal backups. It backs up only selected files and folders that have an archive bit set. During a differential backup, the archive bit is *not* reset (in other words, it is not turned off).

digital signature
This security mechanism ensures a message's authenticity and integrity. A digital signature is generated by using a hash value, or message digest, of a document so that if the message is altered in any way, it no longer produces the same hash value from the same hash algorithm.

DMZ (demilitarized zone)
Used for company resources available to the Internet, such as Web servers and FTP servers, to separate that environment from the private, internal network. The DMZ is normally established between the Internet and an internal network's line of defense of firewalls, gateways, and proxy servers.

DNS spoofing
An attack in which a DNS server accepts and uses incorrect information from a host that has no authority to give that information. These spoofing attacks can cause security issues for DNS servers that are vulnerable to such attacks, and users who might be misdirected to other Web sites because of bogus zone data updates. Email servers could be affected, because their SRV and MX records used for email delivery could force email to be routed to nonauthorized mail servers, where attackers could collect it.

domain
The core unit of the logical structure in Active Directory that can span one or more physical locations. All network objects exist within a domain, and each domain stores information only about the objects it contains. A Windows 2000 or 2003 domain is an administrator-defined logical grouping of computer systems, servers, and other networked resources that share a common directory database.

domain tree

A grouping of domains that have a contiguous hierarchical namespace, connected by the default two-way transitive trust. The tree shares a common schema, configuration, and Global Catalog. Any child domains that are created have names that are combined with the name of the parent domain to form its DNS name.

DoS (denial-of-service) attack

This attack is generically defined as an attack against an organization in an effort to deny legitimate users access to that organization's resources. One example is an attack against a public Web site, in which an intentional flood of bogus connection requests (or any other type of traffic flooding) makes the service unavailable for legitimate users when they attempt to contact the site. A number of different types of attacks can be used as a DoS attack, such as buffer overflow attacks, SYN attacks, and viruses.

dual-homed gateway

A simple firewall consisting of a host system with two NICs installed. The system is configured so that it does not route packets between the two connected networks. When a dual-homed gateway is used with a packet-filtering router placed at the Internet connection for additional security, it helps create a screened subnet that functions as a complete block to IP traffic between the Internet and an enterprise's intranet.

EAP (Extensible Authentication Protocol)

Supports additional authentication methods in PPP, such as tokens, one-time passwords, public key authentication using smart cards, certificates, and others.

Event Viewer

Administrators use this utility to view system events, errors, service conditions, and other notable occurrences that are marked in a series of logs and kept on the local system. By default, three main logs are available for viewing in Event Viewer: System, Security, and Application. Five primary event types are logged in the Event Viewer: error, warning, information, success audit, and failure audit.

extranet

A segment of a company's intranet that has been intentionally made available to certain external entities in an effort to share and exchange data without making the entire intranet available.

FDDI (Fiber Distributed Data Interface)

A high-speed networking topology that runs at a rate of 100Mbps or faster. It is normally set up as a dual ring for redundancy, with the primary ring generally used for traffic and the secondary ring for backup. If the primary ring breaks down, the secondary ring reconfigures itself and flows in the opposite direction.

firewall

Hardware and software security implementations (sometimes a combination of both) designed to prevent unauthorized access to or from a private network. Firewalls are designed to limit the activity of allowed network traffic, such as firewalls that protect a DMZ or an intranet. There are several types of firewall techniques, including packet filters, application gateways, circuit-level gateways, and proxy servers.

forest

A collection of one or more Active-Directory–based domains that share a common schema, configuration, and Global Catalog. If there is a single domain tree in the forest, it has a common domain namespace. Because there can be more than one domain tree in a forest, different domain trees have their own contiguous namespaces, but they still share a common schema, configuration, and Global Catalog.

forward DNS lookup request

A name resolution–to–IP address request that's used to locate a server's IP address so that when you enter `http://www.examcram.com`, for example, the name is resolved to its IP address. Forward lookup zones are required to be configured on DNS servers that are authoritative for a zone.

FTP (File Transfer Protocol)

This protocol is used to transfer files from system to system.

Full Duplex mode

In this data transmission configuration, two hosts on the same transmission medium can communicate at the same time when sending or receiving data. This configuration is much like the telephone: Both parties can speak and hear at the same time. See also Half Duplex mode.

gateway

A gateway (sometimes called a "default gateway") is simply the default route from one subnet to other network locations on the LAN, WAN, or the Internet. Proxy servers and firewall servers that fully segment internal hosts on a network from the Internet are considered gateway devices.

Global Catalog

A central repository of information for all objects in the domain. The Global Catalog contains a partial replica consisting of some information for all object attributes contained in the directory for every domain in the forest. The attributes most frequently used in queries are stored in the Global Catalog by default to ensure that it contains the information needed to determine the location of any object in the directory. For the local domain in which a Global Catalog server resides, the Global Catalog contains information for all objects in that domain.

hacking

An attempt to circumvent the security controls of a network or network host.

Half Duplex mode

In this data transmission configuration, hosts on the same transmission medium can communicate only one at a time. This configuration is much like a walkie-talkie: Only one person at a time can speak while others on the same frequency listen. Whoever has the "speak and send" action at a certain point is the only one who can be heard on other walkie-talkies set to that frequency. See also Full Duplex mode.

hardening

The process of optimizing a system's security configuration by "locking down" the underlying operating system by removing unneeded services and closing unused ports, for example.

host

Any system or network resource found on a network.

HOSTS file

A manually updated text file on a local system used to map fully qualified domain names (FQDNs) to their IP addresses.

hotfix

A code update (sometimes called a patch or a security update) that is normally released to correct a bug in a software product or to deploy a needed code upgrade to ensure system stability. Although hotfixes are normally associated with operating systems, the term is not exclusive to operating system patches and updates. Hotfixes are leased for browsers, for example, but Microsoft blurs the line between the operating system and the Internet Explorer browser.

hub

An OSI Layer 1 (Physical layer) device used as a simple interconnect for a network's physical topology.

ICF (Internet Connection Firewall)

Used on a system-by-system basis to restrict the information communicated between the Internet and your system.

ICMP (Internet Control Message Protocol)

A message control and error-reporting protocol defined by RFC 792 that can be used between different hosts or between a host and a gateway or router. ICMP is used by utilities such as PING and TRACERT.

ICS (Internet Connection Sharing)

Used to connect one or more systems on a small network to the Internet through the NIC configured with ICS on one system. This allows the one system to have a direct connection to the Internet, and all the other systems can access the Internet via this one system.

IEEE 802.2

The IEEE standard Logical Link Control provides Data Link layer support for NetBIOS when frames are being carried "on the wire" instead of being encapsulated in another protocol. When NetBIOS is used on token ring topologies, NetBIOS frames are mapped directly to the 802.2 frames, and the NetBIOS frame is contained in the information field of the 802.2 frame.

IEEE 802.3

The IEEE standard Carrier Sense Multiple Access with Collision Detection (CSMA/CD) Access Method and Physical Layer Specifications is a set of rules for determining how network devices respond when two devices have caused a collision by trying to use a single data channel at the same time. After a collision on the line has been detected, an IEEE 802.3 compatible device waits a random amount of time and then attempts to retransmit the message. If the node detects a collision again, it waits twice as long before trying to transmit the message again.

IEEE 802.4

The IEEE standard Token-Passing Bus Access Method specifies an implementation of the Physical layer and the MAC sublayer of the Data Link layer. Token passing, based on the token bus LAN architecture, is used instead of a bus topology.

IEEE 802.5

The IEEE standard Token Ring Access Method and Physical Layer Specifications. Token ring networks are widely used on a LAN (second only to ethernet); all computers are connected in a ring topology and use a token-passing scheme to prevent data collisions between nodes. The IEEE 802.5 token ring technology provides for data transfer rates of 4Mbps or 16Mbps. The token is an empty frame that continuously circulates on the ring until a node has a message to send. The node then inserts a token and the data and destination information in the empty frame. The frame is checked at each node. If a node sees that it is not the intended recipient, it simply ignores the data. If a node sees that it is the destination for the message, it copies the message from the frame and changes the token back to 0 to show that it has been accessed. When the frame gets back to the originating node, it sees that the token has been changed to 0 and the message has been copied and received. The originating node then removes the message from the frame.

IEEE 802.11

The IEEE standard Wireless LAN Medium Access (MAC) and Physical Layer (PHY) Specifications details the standard method of wireless networked communications using the 2.4GHz microwave band designated for low-power unlicensed use by the FCC. Under the current specification, there are two different and incompatible methods of encoding: FHSS (Frequency Hopping Spread Spectrum) and DSSS (Direct Sequence Spread Spectrum), which allows Wired Equivalent Privacy encryption at the MAC (Media Access Control) layer. FHSS spreads the conversation across 75 1MHz subchannels, continually skipping between them. DSSS breaks the band into 14 overlapping 22MHz channels and uses one at a time.

IETF (Internet Engineering Task Force)

IETF is a large, open, international community of network architects, operators, vendors, and researchers concerned with the architecture, evolution, and smooth operation of the global Internet. The IETF provides a forum for these working groups to coordinate technical development and selection of the Internet protocol suite (a collection of de facto standards). It was originally organized in 1986 as a forum for technical coordination by U.S. Department of Defense (DoD) contractors working on ARPANET and related DoD networks.

IGMP (Internet Group Management Protocol)

An Internet protocol that allows computers to report their multicast group membership status to local routers.

incremental backup

This backup option is normally used to back up only selected files and folders with an archive bit set; only the data that has changed is backed up. During an incremental backup, the archive bit is reset (turned off). When data is edited or changed after being backed up, the archive bit is turned on. This backup option makes nightly backups of incrementally changed data from the previous day faster, but it does data restores slightly longer.

Internet

All computer systems and servers interconnected on the public network infrastructure. Originally part of the U.S. government network of interconnected systems called Advanced Research Projects Agency Network (ARPANET), the original intention was to create a network of linked computer systems that could allow different research facilities to use available resources. The original design of the network still in place today was configured so that it could continue to operate (at a potentially reduced capacity) if parts of it were inaccessible because of a military attack or natural disaster.

intranet

A private network of LANs and WANs within an enterprise that is almost identical in nature and design to the public Internet, except that it's intended only for internal organizational use.

IP (Internet Protocol)

Defines the format of packets (datagrams) and how they are moved from one system to another. It also handles packet addressing so that data is sent to the correct host. IP is a connectionless protocol, responsible only for delivering data. A higher level protocol, such as TCP, is responsible for the connection between two systems and for reassembling the data on the receiving system in the correct order. IP functions at Layer 3 (Network layer) of the OSI model.

IPCONFIG

Command-line utility used to get the local system's basic IP configuration information, including the IP address, subnet mask, and default gateway. The IPCONFIG/all switch produces a detailed configuration report for all interfaces, including any configured remote access adapters.

IPSec (Internet Protocol Security)

A set of protocols that supports secure exchange of packets at the IP layer. IPSec in Transport mode ensures end-to-end security by authenticating and encrypting data flowing between two computers to enforce IPSec policies for traffic between systems. Transport mode, which is the default IPSec mode, can potentially support a secure connection with more than one other computer. Using IPSec in Tunnel mode authenticates and encrypts data flowing within an IP tunnel created between two routers. IPSec requires an IP address for each end of the tunnel, but this allows all traffic flowing through the tunnel to be encrypted, regardless of where it originated.

IPX (Internetwork Packet Exchange)

Connectionless networking protocol that functions at the Network layer of the OSI stack and relies on SPX for packet acknowledgment. IPX confirms that all packets have been received and requests retransmission when they haven't.

iterative DNS query

A DNS client query made to DNS servers. The server returns the best answer it can provide based on its cache or zone data. If that DNS server does not have an exact match for the client request, it provides a pointer to an authoritative server in another level of the domain namespace that can assist in answering the query.

Kerberos

The default authentication protocol on Windows operating systems (Windows 2000 runs on TCP port 88 and uses secret keys for encryption and authentication) used to authenticate requests for network resources. Kerberos verifies the user's identity and the integrity of the session data. The Kerberos service is installed on each domain controller, and a Kerberos client is installed on all computers running Windows 2000.

L2TP (Layer 2 Tunneling Protocol)

A network protocol that encapsulates PPP frames to be sent over IP, X.25, frame relay, or Asynchronous Transfer Mode (ATM) networks. L2TP can function as a tunneling protocol over the Internet when using IP, or it can be used in private LAN-to-LAN networking.

LAN (local area network)

A local network of host systems and other network nodes that share a common local network communications line or other private network, such as a wireless setup. LANs are usually limited to privately owned network structures, such as locally owned ethernet or fiber networks, and can encompass many floors of a building or a number of buildings at a site.

LDAP (Lightweight Directory Access Protocol)

An Internet standard protocol that identifies Directory Information Tree objects based on the X.500 naming convention. This convention uses the object class and the object's actual name.

linear bus topology

A single-cable network design that terminates at both ends. A linear bus topology requires less cable than most other network topology deployments, and connecting devices is easy with this design.

LMHOSTS file

A manually updated text file on a local system used to map NetBIOS names to their IP addresses.

MAC (Media Access Control)

A unique hardware-level network address that each network device has on its network card. A MAC address is also referred to as a Data Link Control (DLC) address.

MD5 (Message Digest 5)

A security hashing algorithm, in which a 128-bit key is used to encrypt passwords.

mesh topology

In this network design, devices are connected with multiple redundant interconnections between network nodes. In full mesh topologies, every node is connected to every other node in the network. In partial mesh topologies, some nodes are deployed as full mesh, but others are connected to only one or two other nodes in the network.

metric

The term "metric" has many different uses. In network routing, it's a measure of cost used to calculate the next best route for packet delivery.

MIME (Multipurpose Internet Mail Extension)

IETF standards RFC 1521 and 1522 spell out how an electronic message is organized.

MPPE (Microsoft Point-to-Point Encryption)

Encrypts data in PPP and PPTP dial-up connections VPN connections.

MS-CHAP (Microsoft Challenge Handshake Authentication Protocol)

Sometimes referred to as MS-CHAP version 1, MS-CHAP is a one-way, encrypted password authentication protocol. Servers using MS-CHAP as the authentication protocol can use MPPE to encrypt data to the client or server. MS-CHAP is enabled by default on Windows 2000 remote access servers.

MS-CHAP v2 (Microsoft Challenge Handshake Authentication Protocol version 2)

Uses stronger initial data encryption keys and different encryption keys for sending and receiving. Windows 2000 dial-up and VPN connections can use MS-CHAP v2. Systems running Windows NT 4.0 and Windows 98 can use MS-CHAP v2 authentication for VPN connections only.

MSAU (multistation access unit)

A special type of hub used in token ring networks that physically connects network nodes in a star topology, while retaining the logical ring structure required on a token ring network. One of the major problems with token ring topologies is that any single point of failure on the network can break the entire ring. The MSAU solves this problem because it can short out nonoperating nodes and maintain the ring structure.

multicast

Multicast communications are designed to facilitate sending data and information between a single host to any number of recipients on a specified network. Multicast traffic is often used for online virtual meetings, where content is streamed from one server to a number of connected host systems requesting the data.

NAT (Network Address Translation)

The process of mapping external public IP addresses to internal private IP addresses. This mapping preserves the limited pool of publicly available IP addresses and protects the internal IP address scheme from public view.

NBTSTAT

NetBT Statistics (NBTSTAT.exe) is a command-line utility for troubleshooting network NetBIOS names over TCP/IP (NetBT) resolution problems from the command line. It displays protocol statistics and current TCP/IP connections that are using NetBT.

NCP (Netware Core Protocol)

Used to access Novell NetWare file and print service functions via the underlying IPX or IP transport protocol.

NETSTAT

NETSTAT.exe is a command-line utility used to display TCP/IP statistics and active connections to and from your computer. It includes an option to display the number of bytes sent and received and the number of network packets dropped (if any).

Network Layer (Layer 3 of the OSI model)

Responsible for a packet's complete journey from the system that created it to its final destination. This layer translates logical network addresses and names to their physical addresses. It is responsible for addressing, determining routes for sending, and managing network problems, such as packet switching, data congestion, and routing. If a router can't send data frames as large as the source node sends, the Network layer compensates by dividing the data into smaller units

on the outgoing system. The Network layer on the receiving node reassembles the data. Protocols normally found at the Network layer are IP, ARP, RARP, ICMP, RIP, OSFP, IGMP, IPX, NWLink, NetBEUI, OSI, DDP, and DECnet.

nonrepudiation

The process by which the sender of data is given proof of delivery, and the receiver is assured of the sender's identity. Neither party can deny sending or receiving the data in question. Using digital signatures is one process that aims to ensure a message's authenticity and integrity and to provide nonrepudiation for that message.

normal backup

Sometimes referred to as full backups, normal backups back up all selected files and folders. This backup type does not rely on the archive bit to determine which files to back up. It simply backs up everything selected, regardless of the archive setting. A normal backup clears any existing archive bits it finds and marks all backed up files as having been backed up. Normal backups are most efficient during the restoration process because the backed up files are the most current, and you do not need to restore multiple backup jobs. Their main drawback is the time it takes to perform the initial backup.

. . . .

OSI (Open System Interconnection)

An ISO worldwide standard for communications that outlines a networking framework in seven layers. Sometimes referred to as the OSI Reference Model, the seven layers are listed in this order: Layer 1 is the Physical layer, Layer 2 is the Data Link layer, Layer 3 is the Network layer, Layer 4 is the Transport layer, Layer 5 is the Session layer, Layer 6 is the Presentation layer, and Layer 7 is the Application layer.

OSPF (Open Shortest Path First)

This link-state protocol is based on an algorithm that computes the shortest path between one host and the other hosts. OSPF is typically used in networks with more than 50 routers and multiple redundant paths and in networks where destinations might be farther than 14 hops away. When an OSPF router receives changes to known routes, it multicasts the updated information only to other hosts in the network so that all have the same routing table information. OSPF sends only updated routing information and communicates to other routers only when a change has taken place.

OU (Organizational Unit)

This container object is used in Active Directory to organize objects within a domain. An OU can contain objects such as user accounts, groups, computers, printers, applications, file shares, and other OUs from the same domain. The OU hierarchy within a domain is independent of the OU hierarchy structure of other domains. The OU is also the smallest unit in Active Directory to which permissions can be assigned.

packet

A segment of data, broken down from a larger segment of data so that it can be successfully handled on a switched network and delivered properly. Sometimes referred to as a "datagram."

packet filtering

Enables inspection of all packets passed between systems in and out of a network at the router, gateway, or firewall. This filtering increases network security and limits the type of traffic allowed to pass in either direction. Packet-filtering firewalls are the easiest way to make use of this network security enhancement in most environments. These firewalls are installed at the gateway to the external network (normally the Internet). Network administrators can configure packet-filtering rules in the firewall so that protocols and IP addresses you want to keep out of the network can be filtered.

PAP (Password Authentication Protocol)

Uses clear-text passwords and provides almost no protection against unauthorized access. If the passwords match, the server grants access to the remote access client. This protocol, the least secure authentication protocol, is often used only when clients and servers cannot negotiate a more secure confirmation.

password attack

An attempt to obtain or crack the password key of a user account to compromise a system. This attack often uses password dictionaries, cracking programs, and password sniffers.

password-sniffing attack

Uses a sniffer to capture passwords as they pass across a network. The type of network makes no difference—it can be a LAN, a WAN, or the Internet itself. The sniffer could be a hardware device or a software package intentionally deployed or installed onto a LAN via a Trojan horse program.

PATHPING

This command-line utility can be used to show the route taken to reach a remote system. TRACERT can be used for the same purpose, but PATHPING offers more detail and functionality.

Performance Console

This MMC console has two preinstalled snap-ins: System Monitor, which collects real-time data about memory, disk, processor, network, and other activity in graph, histogram, or report form, and Performance Logs and Alerts, which collects performance data from local or remote systems. Administrators can configure these logs to record performance data and set system alerts to notify them when a specific counter indicates a value above or below a configurable threshold.

PING (Packet Internet or Inter-Network Groper)

This command-line tool can be used to test your TCP/IP connection by sending a message to the remote node or gateway from a local system. (It can also be used to test the loopback locally to see whether it is working correctly.) If the remote node or gateway receives the message, it responds with a reply message. The reply consists of the remote node or gateway's IP address, the number of bytes in the message, how long it took to reply (given in milliseconds), and the length of Time To Live (TTL) in seconds. The reply also shows any packet loss in terms of percentages.

PKI (Public Key Infrastructure)

A system of digital certificates, normally assigned by Certificate Authorities (CAs), that verify and authenticate the validity of each party involved in an Internet transaction. The best example is Internet commerce. When you buy from Company.com on its Internet site, the certificate assigned by a CA (normally a third party) is what verifies that the company is who it claims to be.

poison-reverse processing

Used with split-horizon processing in an effort to improve RIP convergence by advertising all network IDs.

PPTP (Point-to-Point Tunneling Protocol)

An extension of PPP that encapsulates PPP frames into IP datagrams for transmission over an IP internetwork, such as the Internet. PPTP uses a TCP connection for tunnel maintenance and encapsulated PPP frames for tunneled data that can be encrypted and compressed.

principle of least privilege

This principle means that users are given *only* the minimum level of access to network resources they need to perform their jobs.

protocol

A specification for transmitting data between two devices that defines error checking for the data and the type of compression to be used, if any. Protocols in use between two hosts also define the termination of an established connection after all the data has been sent.

protocol filtering

Enables inspection of all protocols passed between systems in and out of a network at the router, gateway, or firewall. This inspection increases network security and limits the type of traffic allowed to pass in either direction.

RADIUS (Remote Authentication Dial-In User Service)

This authentication service checks whether the supplied information (such as a username and password) is correct. After this information is verified, RADIUS normally allows access to the network.

RAID (redundant array of independent [or inexpensive] disks)

A drive configuration of three or more drives in which data is written to all drives in equal amounts to spread the workload. For fault tolerance, parity information is added to the written data to allow for drive failure recovery. There are two different types of RAID: software and hardware. Hardware RAID is deployed on a computer system and controlled at a hardware level; it can be a controller card or other device that is independent of the operating system. With a software-based RAID solution, the operating system creates and stores the logical structure of drives in the array.

RAS (Remote Access Service)

A service primarily associated with enabling users to log in to a LAN from a WAN or the Internet.

RCP

This command-line utility can be used to copy files to and from computers running the Remote Shell Daemon (RSHD) service. RCP uses TCP for connected, reliable delivery of data between the client and the host. It can be scripted in a batch file and does not require a password. The remote host must be running the RSHD service, and the user's username must be configured in the remote host's .rhosts file. RCP is one of the r-commands available on all Unix systems.

recursive DNS query

A DNS client makes a recursive DNS query to a DNS server, and the DNS server assumes the full workload and responsibility for providing a complete answer to the query. The server performs separate iterative queries to other servers (on behalf of the client) to assist in answering the recursive query.

reverse DNS lookup request

An IP address resolution to a name request that is used when you want to find the domain name associated with an IP address. Reverse DNS lookup zones are not required to be configured on DNS servers that are authoritative for a zone.

REXEC

This command-line utility is used to issue commands on remote hosts running the REXEC service. It authenticates the username on the remote host before carrying out the specified command.

ring topology

A LAN topology in which all network nodes are connected to each other. Each device is connected directly to two other devices, until a closed loop is formed. Ring topology networks are commonly used in token ring environments.

RIP (Routing Information Protocol)

Network routers use this protocol exchange routing information on IP or IPX networks. RIP routers maintain routing tables by using a distance vector routing algorithm to dynamically calculate the cost (metric) of each possible path and send that information in the form of announcements to other RIP routers. RIP version 1 uses IP broadcast packets for its announcement; RIP version 2 uses IP multicast packets for its announcements. In both versions, routers using RIP send all their current routing information, not just changes to the routes.

ROUTE

This command-line utility is used to define and configure network routing tables. Routes are specific paths that packets can use to travel from source to destination in an effort to establish communications on LANs and WANs.

RSH

This TCP/IP utility that runs from the command line enables clients to issue commands directly on remote hosts running the RSH service without having to log on to the remote host. RSH is one of the Unix r-commands available on all Unix systems.

SAP (Service Advertisement Protocol)

An IPX protocol that network resources, such as file servers and print servers, use to advertise their addresses and the services they provide. Advertisements are sent via SAP every 60 seconds. Services are identified by a hexadecimal number, which is called a SAP identifier.

screened host

A host with a direct connection between a border router and the intranet. Screened hosts are often more flexible than a dual-homed gateway firewall.

separation of duties and responsibilities

A system of checks and balances in a security structure that ensures no one user can have sole control of anything in the system. For example, responsibilities can be divided so that one person orders equipment and another person authorizes purchases.

Session layer (Layer 5 of the OSI model)

Data translation between the computer and the network format takes place at the Session layer, which establishes, maintains, and ends sessions across the network and manages who can transmit data at a certain time and for how long. Protocols found at the Session layer include NetBIOS, named pipes, mail slots, and RPC.

SHA (Secure Hash Algorithm)

A high-security hashing algorithm, in which a 160-bit key is used to encrypt passwords.

S-HTTP or HTTPS (Secure Hypertext Transfer Protocol)

A security protocol that works with HTTP to provide secure user authentication and data encryption services to Web client/server transactions.

site

One or more highly available, well-connected IP subnets created for replication traffic optimization and to make it easier for users to connect to a local domain controller for network connection, logon, and authentication functions, whenever possible.

S/MIME (Secure Multi-Purpose Internet Mail Extensions)

Secure method of sending email that uses the Rivest-Shamir-Adleman encryption system.

SNMP (Simple Network Management Protocol)

A network management protocol used to gather information about network components with remote programs (agents) and Management Information Bases (MIBs). The resulting information is transmitted to a central network management console. SNMP operates by default on TCP port 161. (SNMP TRAP messages operate on TCP port 162.)

spam

Unsolicited email or messages sent via the Internet.

SPAP (Shiva Password Authentication Protocol)

An older, hardware-based, proprietary, two-way reversible encryption mechanism originally designed by Shiva Corporation (acquired by Intel in February 1999). SPAP encrypts the password data sent between the client and server.

split-horizon processing

This route-advertising method prevents advertising routes in the same direction in which they were learned, which prevents routing loop situations.

SSH (Secure Socket Shell)

A Unix-based command interface and protocol for securely accessing a remote computer. SSH is actually a suite of three utilities—slogin, ssh, and scp—that are secure versions of the earlier Unix utilities rlogin, rsh, and rcp. SSH commands are encrypted at both ends

of the client/server connection. They are authenticated by using a digital certificate, and passwords are protected by being encrypted.

SSL (Secure Sockets Layer)

This protocol controls the security of a message transmission on an untrusted network, such as the Internet. TLS is the successor to the SSL, and although TLS and SSL do not work with each other, clients that support SSL can handle data sent with TLS.

star topology

In this physical network topology, data is passed through a hub or other routing device (such as a switch or router) before continuing to its intended destination. Each device is connected directly to the networked hardware device, not directly to one another on the cable. Star topologies are most common with twisted-pair cabling, but they can also be found in coaxial cable and fiber-optic cable networks. Token ring networks sometimes use a similar topology, called a "star-wired ring."

subnet mask

A numerical designation used to differentiate the network address portion of an IP address from the host portion. A standard Class C IP address is 200.111.35.7, and it uses a subnet mask of 255.255.255.0. The section of the subnet-masked information, designated by turning the bits "on" for the mask, is designed to hide the address portion that belongs to the network name. In this example, 255.255.255 is hiding 200.111.35; that means the host designation from the IP address is 7 and the network designation is 200.111.35.

switch

Switches are found at two layers of the OSI model, depending on their make. Layer 2 switches work at the Data Link layer, that form the borders of a collision domain. Layer 3 switches work at the Network layer, which forms the borders of a broadcast domain. Generically, a switch is a network device that directly forwards incoming data to a specific output port that takes the data to its intended destination.

Task Manager

This system tool displays current summary information about programs currently running on the local system and some real-time performance information. It can also indicate the current status of programs that appear to have stopped responding to the system so that you can end those programs if needed.

TCP (Transmission Control Protocol)

This connection-oriented protocol is responsible for establishing network connections between hosts and for guaranteeing the delivery of data packets in the correct order. TCP, found at Layer 4 (Transport layer) of the OSI model, is responsible for breaking data down on the sending system so that it can be sent to a recipient system. On the receiving system, TCP is responsible for reassembling the data into the correct order.

TCP/IP (Transmission Control Protocol/Internet Protocol)

TCP/IP is the communication protocol of the Internet and is the most often used communications protocol on private networks. It's primarily a point-to-point, client/server model of communication. Protocols related to TCP/IP include ICMP, Interior Gateway Protocol (IGP), Exterior Gateway Protocol (EGP), Border Gateway Protocol (BGP), HTTP, FTP, Telnet, and SMTP.

TCP/IP version 4 (IPv4) classful address

Made of up four 8-bit fields (octets), this address is 32 bits total. There are five IPv4 address types: A, B, C, D, and E. Class A ranges from 1 to 126 (127 is reserved for loopback testing and interprocess communication on the local computer; it is not a valid network address). Class B ranges from 128 to 191 (169.254.0.0 to 169.254.255.255 is reserved for APIPA). Class C ranges from 192 to 223. Class D ranges from 224 to 239. Class D addresses are used for multicast purposes and should not be assigned to hosts on a network. Class E ranges from 240 to 255. Class E addresses are reserved for special use and should not be assigned to hosts on a network.

Telnet

Telnet is a terminal emulation program that enables user to perform commands on a remote computer from a command window.

TFTP (Trivial File Transfer Protocol)

A low-overhead version of FTP that can be used to transfer files between TCP/IP systems across a network.

tickets

Used in some authentication protocols (most commonly, Kerberos) that allow using cryptography with a secret key for client/server applications.

TLS (Transport Layer Security)

This protocol ensures privacy between systems over an untrusted network, such as the Internet. TLS ensures that no third party can eavesdrop, tamper with, or intercept data in transit. TLS is the successor to the SSL, and although TLS and SSL do not work with each other, clients that support SSL can handle data sent with TLS.

tokens

These devices store information about a user's level of access. Users then supply a password (something the user knows) along with the tokens to grant them their defined level of access.

TRACERT

This command-line diagnostic utility determines the route taken to a specific destination IP address by using ICMP Echo Request and Echo Reply messages. By using varying Time To Live (TTL) values in the IP header, packets time out at each successive router on the way to the destination. TRACERT uses the timeout error messages to display a list of the routers forming the path to the destination address.

Transport layer (Layer 4 of the OSI model)

This layer is responsible for packet handling as well as error and flow control. It helps manage the flow control of data between network nodes by dividing data into packets on the outgoing system. The Transport layer of the receiving node reassembles the message from packets and provides error checking to guarantee error-free data delivery and acknowledge successful transmissions. Protocols normally found at the Transport layer include TCP, SPX, NWLink, NetBIOS, NetBEUI, and ATP.

tree

See domain tree.

UDP (User Datagram Protocol)

A connectionless communications protocol used to send data from one host to another. Unlike TCP, UDP does not divide the message into packets and reassemble them at the other end, and it doesn't provide packet sequencing.

UTP (unshielded twisted-pair) cable

A type of cable that consists of two unshielded wires twisted around each other. Because it's a very affordable cable type, UTP cabling is used extensively for networking.

VLAN (virtual local area network)

VLANs are logical segmentations of LANs that allow network administrators to section off parts of networks without having to physically rewire them. This is most often done with networking equipment, such as ethernet switches that support VLAN technologies. Network administrators use the switches to create virtual network segments with a logical topology that's totally independent of the physical network topology.

VLSM (Variable Length Subnet Mask)

A VLSM allows you to use different subnet address lengths so that a single IP address class can be divided outside the "normal" subnet mask range. The standard subnet mask for a Class C address is 255.255.255.0; however, you can also use 255.255.255.248 to create 32 subnets with 6 hosts per subnet.

VPN (virtual private network)

VPNs are an extension of a private internal network over a public network, such as the Internet. The public network is used as the connection route, and data in transit is secured by using a tunneling protocol and encryption. Two common examples of tunneling protocols used with encryption are L2TP using IPSec encryption and PPTP using built-in MPPE encryption.

WAN (wide area network)

WANs are used to connect geographically dispersed LANs by way of public networks, such as leased lines (although these lines might be wholly owned by a company).

WAP (Wireless Application Protocol)

This specification for a set of communication protocols standardizes the way that wireless devices can be used for different levels of access to the Internet. The different WAP layers are Wireless Application Environment (WAE), Wireless Session Layer (WSL), Wireless Transport Layer Security (WTLS), and Wireless Transport Layer (WTP).

well-known ports

Previously assigned by Internet Assigned Numbers Authority (IANA) in the range of 0 to 1023. This task is now handled by Internet Corporation for Assigned Names and Numbers (ICANN). Well-known ports are those from 0 through 1023. Registered ports are those from 1024 through 49151. Dynamic and/or private ports are those from 49152 through 65535.

WML (Wireless Markup Language)

Used to create pages that can be delivered using WAP, in the same manner that HTML is used to create pages that can be delivered to your Web browser. Sometimes called Handheld Devices Markup Languages (HDML), WML allows the text portions of Web pages to be displayed on cell phones and personal digital assistants (PDAs) via wireless access.

WTLS (Wireless Transport Layer Security)

This security layer for WAP was developed to address security issues for mobile network devices and wireless devices to provide authentication, data integrity, and privacy protection mechanisms.

Index

D

E-F

G-H

I

M

M-node (mixed) WINS clients, 135
Mail Exchanger (MX) resource records, 125
mail server role, 57-59
majority node set server clusters, 196-197
Maximum Segment Size (MSS) setting, 99
MBSA (Microsoft Baseline Security Analyzer), 253-257
    IIS vulnerabilities check, 256
    installing, 254
    local scans, 254
    multiple-system scans, 255-257
    operating systems supported, 253
    remote scans, 254-255
    security updates check, 256-257
    SQL vulnerabilities check, 256
    starting, 254
    weak passwords check, 256
    Windows vulnerabilities check, 256
MD5 message-digest algorithm, 166
Mean Time Between Failure (MTBF), 182
Microsoft Application Center 2000, 182-183
Microsoft Baseline Security Analyzer. *See* MBSA
Microsoft certification exams. *See* certification exams
Microsoft ISA Server, 161-162
Microsoft Point-to-Point Encryption (MPPE), 164
Microsoft Training and Certification Web site, 24
mil domain, 129
mixed (M-node) WINS clients, 135
mixed networks, 198
Most Significant Bit (MSB), 91
MPPE (Microsoft Point-to-Point Encryption), 164
MS-CHAP, 165-167
MS-CHAP v2, 165-167
MSB (Most Significant Bit), 91
MSS (Maximum Segment Size), 99
Mssecure.xml database, 257
MTBF (Mean Time Between Failure), 182
multicast announcements, 152
MX (Mail Exchanger) resource records, 125

N

Name Server (NS) resource records, 125
NAT. *See* Network Address Translation (NAT) protocol
NAT-Traversal extensions for IPSec, 160
NBTSTAT command, 103-104
Negotiate Security filter, 222
net domain, 129
NetBIOS name resolution, 103-104
    LMHOSTS file, 135
    WINS. *See* WINS
NetBIOS over TCP/IP (NetBT), 103-104
Netdiag command, 229
netsh command, 228-229
NETSTAT command, 104
Network Address Translation (NAT) protocol
    configuring for RRAS, 160-161
    GET calls, 159
    Internet Connection Sharing and, 160
    Internet connectivity, 159-160
    IPSec support of, 160
network collisions, 156-157
Network Interface layer, TCP/IP protocol suite, 89
Network layer, OSI model, 88
Network Load Balancing (NLB), 182-185
    32-bit ethernet configurations, 185
    64-bit ethernet configurations, 185
    adding hosts, 184
    configuring, 184
    connecting to existing clusters, 184
    deleting clusters, 184
    dropping nodes, 184
    implementing, 183-184
    network compatibility, 185
    TCP/IP setup, 184
    Windows NT Load Balancing Service, 182
Network Load Balancing Manager, 183-184
Network Monitor, 162-163
Network Name resource, 200
New Scope Wizard, 64-65
NLB. *See* Network Load Balancing
NLBMGR command, 183-184
normal backups, 189
NS (Name Server) resource records, 125
NTBACKUP utility
    Automated System Recovery backups, 191-192
    command-line switches, 187-189

How can we make this index more useful? Email us at indexes@quepublishing.com

X-Y-Z